Mastering Agricultural Extension Education

NIPA® GENX ELECTRONIC RESOURCES & SOLUTIONS P. LTD.
New Delhi-110 034

Other Books by Same Author

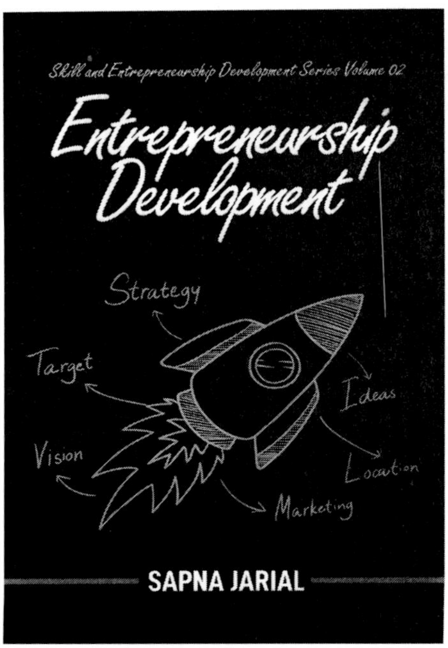

ISBN: 9789395319249

ISBN: 9788119103218

Mastering Agricultural Extension Education A Comprehensive MCQ Guide

Sapna Jarial
Associate Professor
Agricultural Extension
School of Agriculture
Lovely Professional University

NIPA® GENX ELECTRONIC RESOURCES & SOLUTIONS P. LTD.
New Delhi-110 034

NIPA® GENX ELECTRONIC RESOURCES & SOLUTIONS P. LTD.

101,103, Vikas Surya Plaza, CU Block
L.S.C. Market, Pitam Pura, New Delhi-110 034
Ph : +91 11 27341616, 27341717, 27341718
E-mail:newindiapublishingagency@gmail.com
www: www.nipabooks.com

For customer assistance, please contact
Phone: + 91-11-27 34 17 17
Fax: + 91-11- 27 34 16 16
E-Mail: feedbacks@nipabooks.com

ISBN: 978-93-58871-28-9

Composed and Designed by NIPA.

Preface

In the quest for excellence in agricultural extension education, both students and researchers often look for resources that not only give them a lot of information but also give them tools they can use to evaluate and prepare. "Mastering Agricultural Extension Education: A Comprehensive MCQ Guide" is a pioneering effort in this direction.

Purposefully curated for aspirants of junior research fellowship, senior research fellowship, and agricultural recruitment services examination, this book serves as a reservoir of multiple-choice questions aimed at enhancing their knowledge. A standout feature is its strategic use of one-liners. These succinct pointers act as a clarifying tool, making it straightforward for readers to discern and understand the subtle differences between interrelated concepts.

The twenty-two-chapter book offers a comprehensive exploration of the multifaceted world of extension education discipline. While each chapter's subject matter is diverse, they all strive to bring clarity, knowledge, and practise.

In essence, this book is not only a study guide, but also a quick reference for those who wish to thrive in agricultural extension education. It promises intensive preparation, an in-depth comprehension, and, most significantly, the self-assurance to face any academic or professional challenge.

Contents

1

Comparative Views on Agricultural Extension: India and the World

1. The shift from hunting-gathering to cultivation led to the foundation of human civilization by:
   a) Providing stable food sources
   b) Developing advanced technologies
   c) Establishing trade routes
   d) Creating social hierarchies

2. The discipline of agricultural extension justifies its existence by providing advisory on:
   a) Cultural practices in agriculture
   b) Natural calamities and problems in agriculture
   c) Economic policies affecting agriculture
   d) Technological advancements in agriculture

3 Earliest evidence of agricultural extension can be found in which ancient civilization?
   a) Mesopotamia b) Egypt
   c) Greece d) Rome

4. In China, the minor official post of 'master farmers' known as '**nongsh**i' were appointed for:
   a) Managing agricultural fairs and exhibitions
   b) Supervising water management in rice cultivation
   c) Selling farm products in local markets
   d) Establishing agricultural research centers

5. The first modern agricultural extension service was established in the middle of the 19th century in:
   a) Germany b) United States
   c) Ireland d) France

Bold Means Correct Answer

6. The Morrill Act in the United States established Land Grant Colleges for the dissemination of agricultural information to:
   a) Government officials
   b) Scientists and researchers
   c) Farmers
   d) International organizations

7. The system of itinerant agricultural teachers known as 'Wanderlehrer' was first adopted in:
   a) Denmark **b) Germany**
   c) France d) Japan

8. In Japan, the development of agricultural societies was formalized by legislation in:
   a) 1868 b) 1879
   c) 1881 **d) 1899**

9. The experimental and demonstration botanical gardens were opened in 1821 at:
   a) Peradeniya, Sri Lanka b) Kyoto, Japan
   c) Rome, Italy d) Cairo, Egypt

10. What was the outcome of the shift from hunting-gathering to cultivation in ancient civilizations?
   a) Decreased human population
   b) Establishment of stable food sources
   c) Disruption of social hierarchies
   d) Introduction of advanced technologies

11. The discipline of agricultural extension primarily deals with:
   a) Cultural practices in agriculture
   b) Natural disasters affecting agriculture
   c) Economic policies in agriculture
   d) Technological advancements in agriculture

12. The earliest evidence of agricultural extension can be traced back to:
   a) Rome b) Egypt
   c) Mesopotamia d) Greece

13. In ancient China, **'Rice Men'** were appointed for the supervision of:
    a) Crop planting and water management
    b) Agricultural fairs and exhibitions
    c) Farm product marketing
    d) Livestock management

14. The term "extension" in the context of education originated in which country during the second half of the nineteenth century?
    a) Germany
    b) United States
    c) England
    d) France

15. Who is known as the "Father of University Extension"?
    a) Seaman A. Knapp
    b) James Stuart
    c) Prof. Holden
    d) Father of Trinity College

16. In which year was the University Extension system accepted by the University of Cambridge?
    a) 1850
    b) 1867
    c) 1873
    d) 1890

17. Which subject initially dominated the lectures in the University Extension movement?
    a) Agricultural subjects
    b) Social topics
    c) Literature
    d) Science and technology

18. The University Extension movement, which began in England, had a significant influence on the development of similar activities in which country?
    a) France
    b) Germany
    c) United States
    d) China

19. Who is referred to as the "Father of Extension Work" in the United States?
    a) Seaman A. Knapp
    b) James Stuart
    c) Prof. Holden
    d) Father of Trinity College

20. The Seed Corn Trains were organized in which state of the United States to promote better corn seeds?
    a) Iowa
    b) California
    c) Texas
    d) New York

21. The agricultural economy of ancient India was based on:
    a) Trade and commerce
    b) Industry and manufacturing
    c) Agriculture
    d) Fishing and hunting

22. During which period in ancient India were fields cultivated collectively with irrigation channels laid by the community?
    a) Vedic period
    b) Buddhist period
    c) Mauryan period
    d) Gupta period

23. Which ancient text mentions the practice of general principles of plant nutrition by farmers in ancient India?
    a) Kautilya Arthasastra
    b) Manu Smriti
    c) Amarakosha
    d) Krisi-Samgraha

24. The British East India Company's arrival in India resulted in the breakdown of which economy?
    a) Industrial economy
    b) Service-based economy
    c) Agricultural economy
    d) Trade-based economy

25. The establishment of the Imperial Agricultural Research Institute at Pusa marked the beginning of:
    a) Organized agricultural research
    b) Formal education in agriculture
    c) Government control over agriculture
    d) Export of agricultural products

26. The Indian Council of Agricultural Research (ICAR) was established in which year?
    a) 1866
    b) 1881
    c) 1901
    d) 1929

27. The first State Agricultural University (SAU) in India was established in which year?
    a) 1866
    b) 1881
    c) 1901
    d) 1960

28. Organized extension services in India started with which program in 1952?
    a) National Extension Service (NES)
    b) Community Development Programme (CDP)
    c) Agricultural Extension Scheme (AES)
    d) Rural Development Initiative (RDI)

29. The University Extension system originated in which country?

a) United States b) France

c) England d) Germany

30. When did ICAR launch the four Transfer of Technology (ToT) projects?

a) After independence

b) During the British colonial period

c) In the 19th century

d) In 1971

31. Which section was established at ICAR's headquarters in 1971 and later renamed as Division of Agricultural Extension?

a) Division of Agricultural Research

b) Section of Extension Education

c) Department of Technology Transfer

d) Division of Rural Development

32. The concept of Frontline extension was initiated in which agricultural research system?

a) SAUS

b) State Department of Agriculture

c) ICAR

d) Ford Foundation

33. The All India Coordinated Research Project on National Demonstration focused on the transfer of technology related to which type of crops?

a) Horticultural crops

b) Pulses

c) Major food crops (mainly cereals)

d) Cash crops

34. What was the main objective of the Operational Research Project (ORP)?

a) Conducting research on operational techniques in agriculture

b) Demonstrating the impact of new technologies on a large scale

c) Improving administrative efficiency in agriculture

d) Studying the feasibility of agricultural projects

35. The first Krishi Vigyan Kendra (KVK) was established in which year?

a) 1950 b) 1964

c) 1971 **d) 1974**

36. What are the three fundamental principles of the Krishi Vigyan Kendra (KVK) programme?

a) Agricultural production, market development, and infrastructure improvement

b) Work-experience, need-based training, and priority to weaker sections

c) Sustainable agriculture, environmental protection, and community development

d) Research and development, capacity building, and technology transfer

37. The Lab to Land Programme (LLP) was launched by ICAR in 1979 as part of its Golden Jubilee celebration to:

a) Transfer agricultural land to farmers

b) Promote research in agriculture

c) Improve the economic condition of small and marginal farmers

d) Develop new agricultural technologies

38. When did the teaching of extension education at the undergraduate level start at the College of Agriculture, Calcutta University?

a) 1920 b) 1947

c) 1950 d) 1964

39. Which country's extension system has significantly influenced the Indian extension system and derives many features from the Cooperative Extension Service and Land Grant College System?

a) United Kingdom

b) United States of America (USA)

c) Japan

d) China

40. The United States Department of Agriculture was established in which year?

a) 1862 b) 1875

c) 1887 d) 1914

41. In Japan, agricultural discussion societies (Nodan-Kai) were established in which decade?

a) 1860s b) 1870s

c) 1880s d) 1890s

42. Which country has the world's largest public extension system with one extension staff per 283 farm households?

a) United States of America (USA) b) India

c) China d) Japan

43. The Public Agricultural Technology Extension (ATE) system is a Government organization under which ministry in China?

a) Ministry of Education

b) Ministry of Finance

c) Ministry of Agriculture

d) Ministry of Rural Development

44. The Extension Information Network (El-net) is a notable innovation of which country's extension system?

a) India

b) United States of America (USA)

c) Japan

d) China

45. Which act in the United States provided generous financial assistance to states for the establishment of Cooperative Extension Service in 1914?

a) The Hatch Act

b) The Morrill Act

c) The Smith Lever Act

d) The Cooperative Extension Act

46 In India, the teaching of extension education at the postgraduate level was launched in which agricultural college?

a) College of Agriculture, Calcutta University

b) Bihar Agricultural College, Sabour

c) College of Agriculture, Nagpur

d) Indian Agricultural Research Institute, New Delhi

47. The Lab to Land Programme (LLP) was launched in which year as part of ICAR's Golden Jubilee celebration?

    a) 1955
    b) 1964
    c) 1979
    d) 1992

48. The Krishi Vigyan Kendra (KVK) concept was designed to provide vocational training to:

    a) Students pursuing degrees in agriculture
    b) Urban youth interested in farming
    c) Practicing farmers, in-service field level extension workers, and those seeking self-employment
    d) Government agricultural officers

49. The Lab to Land Programme (LLP) was launched by ICAR with the objective of improving the economic condition of which group of farmers and agricultural laborers?

    a) Large-scale farmers
    b) Urban farmers
    c) Small and marginal farmers and landless agricultural laborers, particularly scheduled castes and scheduled tribes
    d) Large commercial farmers

50. The main objective of the All India Coordinated Research Project on National Demonstration was to:

    a) Conduct research on major food crops
    b) Transfer technology from one state to another
    c) Demonstrate new technologies to farmers' fields
    d) Promote international collaborations

51. What was the conceptual framework of the Operational Research Project (ORP)?

    a) To conduct research on operational techniques in agriculture
    b) To develop new agricultural technologies
    c) To demonstrate the impact of new technologies on a large scale involving a whole village or a cluster of villages at a time
    d) To study the feasibility of agricultural projects

52. The Krishi Vigyan Kendra (KVK) concept focuses on influencing the productivity to achieve social justice for which sections of society?

a) Urban population

b) Wealthy farmers

c) Tribal farmers, small and marginal farmers, agricultural laborers, drought and flood-affected farmers, and others in need

d) Large commercial farmers

53. The Public Agricultural Technology Extension (ATE) system is managed by which organization in China?

a) Information Centre

b) Ministry of Agriculture

c) Ministry of Rural Development

d) Ministry of Finance

54. Which agricultural research system initiated the concept of Frontline extension?

a) SAUS

b) State Department of Agriculture

c) ICAR

d) Ford Foundation

55. The All India Coordinated Research Project on National Demonstration focused on transferring technology related to:

a) Horticultural crops

b) Pulses

c) Major food crops (mainly cereals)

d) Cash crops

56. The Operational Research Project (ORP) aimed to disseminate proven technology in a discipline/area among farmers on a watershed basis and concurrently study:

a) Agricultural marketing

b) Constraints to the rapid spread of improved technical know-how

c) Administrative efficiency

d) Technological advancements

57. The Krishi Vigyan Kendra (KVK) concept was designed to impart need-based and skill-oriented vocational training to practicing farmers, in-service field level extension workers, and those seeking:

a) Higher education in agriculture
b) Urban employment
c) Self-employment
d) Government jobs

58. Which act in the United States provided generous financial assistance to states for the establishment of Cooperative Extension Service in 1914?

a) The Hatch Act
b) The Morrill Act
c) The Smith Lever Act
d) The Cooperative Extension Act

59. The Krishi Vigyan Kendra (KVK) concept focuses on influencing the productivity to achieve social justice for which sections of society?

a) Urban population
b) Wealthy farmers
c) Tribal farmers, small and marginal farmers, agricultural laborers, drought and flood-affected farmers, and others in need
d) Large commercial farmers

60. What percentage of the total national farmer households in China participated in at least one cooperative?

a) 15%
b) 28.5%
c) 40%
d) 50%

61. Which innovative extension strategy in China aims to promote traceability and increase farmers' income by eliminating intermediaries?

a) The Dragon Head Companies Programme
b) Direct Farm Programme
c) China agriculture extension special task force (AESTF)
d) Syngenta/CropLife partnership

62. The Dragon Head Companies Programme in China promotes agricultural industrialization through contract arrangements between which entities?

a) Large agribusinesses and government agencies
b) Large agribusinesses and rural banks
c) Large agribusinesses and small-scale farmers organized in economic cooperatives
d) Large agribusinesses and foreign companies

63 What special benefits are granted to Dragon Head Companies in China?

a) Tax exemptions and access to loans

b) Exemption from cooperative regulations

c) Exclusive access to government grants

d) Priority in land acquisition

64. The National Agro-tech Extension and Service Center (NATESC) in China provides training on what aspect of agriculture?

a) Distribution of agricultural machinery

b) Crop planting techniques

c) Adequate management and use of distributed pesticides

d) Irrigation and water management

65. In the Philippines, what percentage of the population is employed in the agriculture sector?

a) 10% **b) 29%**

c) 40% d) 50%

66. What type of schools were established by Spanish missionaries in the Philippines from 1521 to 1854?

a) Agricultural universities

b) Demonstration farms

c) Model farms Granjas Modelos

d) Fisheries training centers

67. In the Philippines, which government agency was responsible for extension activities and created in 1952?

a) Bureau of Agriculture

b) Bureau of Plant Industry

c) Bureau of Animal Industry

d) Bureau of Agricultural Extension (BAEx)

68 What happened to the Ministry of Agriculture in the Philippines in 1984?

a) It was renamed as the Ministry of Agriculture and Food (MAF).

b) It was dissolved and replaced by regional agricultural directors.

c) It was merged with the Bureau of Agriculture.

d) It was downsized to focus on fisheries and livestock.

69. Which organization was established in 1987 and serves as the apex agency for agricultural and fisheries extension services in the Philippines?

    a) Department of Trade and Investment

    b) International Fund for Agricultural Development (IFAD)

    c) Agricultural Training Institute (ATI)

    d) Rural Microenterprise Promotion Program (RuMEPP)

70. What programs does the Agricultural Training Institute (ATI) offer for extension services?

    a) Shared Services Facility Program and High Value Crops Development Program

    b) e-Extension program and Farmers' Contact Center

    c) Traditional training at Farmers' Field Schools and Farmers Information and Technology Services (FITS) Centers

    d) Farmers' Contact Center and Open Academy for Philippine Agriculture (OPAPA)

71 Which department in the Philippines plays a significant role in identifying investment priorities and promoting investment in high-value crops and downstream processing of agricultural products?

    a) Ministry of Agriculture and Food

    b) Department of Science and Technology (DOST)

    c) International Fund for Agricultural Development (IFAD)

    d) Department of Trade and Investment

72. What projects financed by the International Fund for Agricultural Development (IFAD are running in the Philippines?

    a) Rural Microenterprise Promotion Program (RuMEPP) and Cordillera Highland Agricultural Resource Management Project (CHARMP)

    b) Shared Services Facility Program and Farmers Information and Technology Services (FITS) Centers

    c) e-Extension Program and Open Academy for Philippine Agriculture (OPAPA)

    d) Farmers' Text Center and School on Air (SOA)

73. Which level of government in the Philippines is involved in both planning and implementation of national projects related to agriculture and fisheries extension?

a) International level institutions

b) Non-governmental organizations

c) Local Government Units (LGUs)

d) Department of Agriculture and Food

74. Which institutions in the Philippines provide education, training, extension, and communication in agriculture, making information more accessible to those who need it?

a) Agricultural cooperatives

b) Farmers' Contact Center (FCC)

c) Open Academy for Philippine Agriculture (OPAPA)

d) Non-public institutions

75. What is the primary objective of the Shared Services Facility Program in the Philippines?

a) To promote investment in commercial production of high-value crops

b) To provide processing machinery for micro and small enterprises

c) To establish training centers for farmers and fishermen

d) To support rural community development in agricultural aspects

76. Which program in the Philippines aims to support the development of modern value chains in 20 high-value agricultural crops?

a) Farmers Information and Technology Services (FITS) Centers

b) Farmer Scientist Bureau (FSB)

c) High Value Crops Development Program

d) Mobile Internet Bus

77. Which institution in the Philippines serves as the focal ICT training center?

a) Agricultural Training Institute (ATI)

b) Department of Science and Technology (DOST)

c) Philippine Council for Agriculture, Aquatic and Natural Resources Research and Development (PCAARRD)

d) Rural Microenterprise Promotion Program (RuMEPP)

78. What was launched on December 11, 2007, with the introduction of the e-Extension Portal and inauguration of the first component e-Learning?
   a) Farmers' Contact Center (FCC)
   b) Farmers Information and Technology Services (FITS) Centers
   c) e-Extension Program
   d) School on Air (SOA)

79. What is the name of the web portal for Philippine extension and agricultural training?
   a) Farmers' Text Center
   b) Farmers Information and Technology Services (FITS) Centers
   c) e-Extension Program
   d) ATI Interactive

80. Which facility in the Philippines allows farmers to access ICT-based information and services in support of farming and marketing?
   a) Farmers' Contact Center (FCC)
   b) Farmers Information and Technology Services (FITS) Centers
   c) School on Air (SOA)
   d) Mobile Internet Bus

81. What is the Farmer Scientist Bureau (FSB) in the Philippines composed of?
   a) Government officials and agricultural experts
   b) Outstanding farmers who have applied scientific and indigenous technologies successfully
   c) Farmers involved in rural community development projects
   d) Private sector representatives and agribusiness companies

82. What is the purpose of the Mobile Internet Bus in the Philippines?
   a) To provide training on modern value chains for high-value crops
   b) To offer business advisory services to farmers
   c) To make information more accessible to those who need it in rural areas
   d) To support rural microenterprises in agricultural processing

83. What is the primary focus of the Farmers' Text Center (Smart Farmer Call Center) in the Philippines?

a) Providing centralized coordination for agricultural extension activities

b) Facilitating communication between farmers and subject-matter specialists

c) Providing ICT-based services for farming and marketing

d) Offering training courses in agriculture

84. What is the School on Air (SOA) program in the Philippines based on?

a) The use of radio and text messaging to disseminate information on rice technologies

b) The provision of processing machinery for micro and small enterprises

c) Providing central direction, leadership, and coordination of all scientific and technological activities

d) Web-based information system of agricultural projects

85. What does the Rural and Development Information System (RDMIS) in the Philippines monitor?

a) Agricultural cooperatives and their functions

b) Ongoing and completed agricultural projects

c) Business advisory services for micro and small enterprises

d) Investment priorities for high-value crops

85. Which organization in the Philippines offers several training courses in agriculture?

a) Shared Services Facility Program

b) Open Academy for Philippine Agriculture (OPAPA)

c) Rural Microenterprise Promotion Program (RuMEPP)

d) The Mindanao Baptist Rural Life Center

87. What is the primary objective of the Department of Science and Technology (DOST) in the Philippines?

a) Providing education and training in agricultural disciplines

b) Identifying investment priorities for high-value crops

c) Coordinating agricultural extension activities at the national level

d) Providing central direction for scientific and technological activities

88. What is the role of agricultural cooperatives in the Philippines?
    a) Providing business advisory services to farmers
    b) Offering training and education in agricultural disciplines
    c) Promoting investment in commercial production of agricultural products
    d) Covering various agri-business functions, including input supply and marketing

89. What is the purpose of the Research Information Storage and Retrieval System (RETRES) in Vietnam?
    a) To promote agricultural technology adoption among farmers
    b) To provide credit support for agricultural export
    c) To store completed research projects and relevant literature
    d) To establish farmers' training centers

90. Which database in Vietnam is meant for enhancement of inter-connectivity for sustained e-based agriculture, forestry, and natural resources?
    a) Commodity Information Network (CIN)
    b) Agriculture and Natural Resources Information Network (AGRINET)
    c) Micro Small Medium Scale Enterprise IS (MSMSE)
    d) Research Information Storage and Retrieval System (RETRES)

91. What are the key activities of the National Agricultural Extension Center (NAEC) in Vietnam?
    a) Building up demonstration models and selling farm inputs
    b) Information dissemination and propaganda/advocacy
    c) Providing credit policy for purchasing agricultural inputs
    d) Implementing extension communication and training activities for districts

92. In Vietnam, which organization is the focal agency for countrywide extension covering agriculture, livestock, forestry, fishery, and rural industry?
    a) Vietnamese Academy of Agricultural Sciences (VAAS)
    b) National Agricultural Extension Center (NAEC)
    c) Rural Microenterprise Promotion Program (RuMEPP)
    d) Department of Agriculture (DOA)

93 What is the primary focus of the Techno Gabay Program in Vietnam?

a) **Technical assistance program for farmers involving public institutions and private sector**

b) Establishing farmers' training centers

c) Providing credit support for agricultural export

d) Implementing mass media content and creating websites for farmers

94. What is the main objective of the National Nutrition Strategy for 2011-2020 in Vietnam?

a) **To reduce malnutrition among children**

b) To enhance agricultural technology for smallholder farmers

c) To strengthen the competitiveness of farmers in project provinces

d) To develop a modern land information system for online government services

95. What is the target set by Vietnam to lift the income for farming communities by the year 2020?

a) **VND45 million ($2,020) per year**

b) VND2 million ($90) per year

c) VND100 million ($4,500) per year

d) VND1 million ($45) per year

96. What is the focus of the Agriculture Competitiveness Project initiated for Vietnam?

a) **Strengthening the competitiveness of smallholder farmers in project provinces**

b) Providing credit policy for investment in machinery and equipment

c) Enhancing agricultural technology for farmers

d) Implementing a modern land information system

97. What is the purpose of the Vietnam Land Administration Project (VLAP) initiated in 2008?

a) Providing online government services to the public

b) Establishing farmers' training centers

c) Enhancing agricultural technology for farmers

d) **Developing a modern land information system**

98. Which program in Vietnam aims at delivering online government services to the public related to land administration?
    a) Research Information Storage and Retrieval System (RETRES)
    b) Mass media content and website creation
    c) Vietnam Land Administration Project (VLAP)
    d) Management Information System for the Forestry Sector (FORMIS)

99. What is the focus of the Management Information System for the Forestry Sector (FORMIS) in Vietnam?
    a) Providing credit support for agricultural export
    b) Enhancing agricultural technology for smallholder farmers
    c) Technological solutions for information integration
    d) Promoting the growth of the food and beverage processing sectors

100. Which organization controls the mass media content and the creation of websites in Vietnam?
    a) Ministry of Agriculture and Rural Development (MOARD)
    b) Vietnamese Academy of Agricultural Sciences (VAAS)
    c) Ministry of Information and Culture
    d) National Agricultural Extension Center (NAEC)

101. What is the primary role of the government Vietnam Television (VTV) in Vietnam?
    a) Implementing mass media content and creating websites for farmers
    b) Building up demonstration models for farmers
    c) **Operating five channels focusing on educational content for farmers and the rural population**
    d) Providing credit policy for purchasing agricultural inputs

102. What is the primary focus of the Farmers' Training Centers in Vietnam?
    a) Enhancing agricultural technology for smallholder farmers
    b) Providing credit policy for investment in machinery and equipment
    c) Building up demonstration models for farmers
    d) Implementing mass media content and creating websites for farmers

103. Which policy in Vietnam aims to reduce the burden on agricultural production and increase competitiveness for the industry?

a) Credit policy for purchasing input of agricultural production

b) Tax and fee policy for agricultural export

c) National Nutrition Strategy for 2011-2020

d) Techno Gabay Program for farmers

104. What is the primary purpose of the Commodity Information Network (CIN) in Vietnam?

a) Providing credit support for agricultural export

b) Enhancing agricultural technology for smallholder farmers

c) Creating separate information networks for major commodities

d) Building up demonstration models for farmers

105. What are the components of the Extension Program of the Agricultural Training Center in Vietnam?

a) Credit policy, tax and fee policy, and e-Extension program

b) E-Learning, E-Farming, and E-Trading

c) Research Information Storage and Retrieval System (RETRES), Micro Small Medium Scale Enterprise IS (MSMSE), and Agriculture and Natural Resources Information Network (AGRINET)

d) Techno Gabay Program, Farmers' training centers, and Farmers Information and Technology Services (FITS) Centers

106. What is the primary objective of the Credit Policy for purchasing input of agricultural production in Vietnam?

a) To promote agricultural technology adoption among farmers

b) To provide credit support for agricultural export

c) To enhance agricultural technology for smallholder farmers

d) To reduce the burden on agricultural production

107. What is the primary purpose of the Farmers' Contact Center in Vietnam?

a) To facilitate online trading and provide marketing information

b) To strengthen the competitiveness of smallholder farmers

c) To provide technical assistance to farmers

d) To store completed research projects and relevant literature

108. What is the primary role of the Vietnamese Academy of Agricultural Sciences (VAAS) in Vietnam?
    a) Operating five channels focusing on educational content for farmers and the rural population
    b) Providing credit support for agricultural export
    c) Enhancing agricultural technology for smallholder farmers
    d) Establishing farmers' training centers

109. What is the primary objective of the Farmers Information and Technology Services (FITS) Centers in Vietnam?
    a) Providing credit support for agricultural export
    b) Enhancing agricultural technology for smallholder farmers
    c) Building up demonstration models for farmers
    d) Implementing mass media content and creating websites for farmers

110. Which organization is the national level extension organization in Vietnam, covering agriculture, livestock, forestry, fishery, and rural industry?
    a) Vietnamese Academy of Agricultural Sciences (VAAS)
    b) Rural Microenterprise Promotion Program (RuMEPP)
    c) National Agricultural Extension Center (NAEC)
    d) Department of Agriculture (DOA)

111. What is the primary objective of the National Agricultural Extension Center (NAEC) in Vietnam?
    a) To store completed research projects and relevant literature
    b) To provide credit policy for purchasing agricultural inputs
    c) To enhance agricultural technology for smallholder farmers
    d) To implement extension communication and training activities for districts

112. What is the purpose of the Agriculture and Natural Resources Information Network (AGRINET) in Vietnam?
    a) To promote agricultural technology adoption among farmers
    b) To provide credit support for agricultural export
    c) To store completed research projects and relevant literature
    d) To enhance inter-connectivity for e-based agriculture, forestry, and natural resources

113. What is the share of agriculture in Thailand's GDP?

a) 20% b) 15%

c) 10% d) 5%

114. Which commodity is the top foreign exchange earner among farm commodities in Thailand?

a) Rice b) Cassava starch

c) Rubber d) Canned pineapple

115. What is Thailand's ranking as a rice exporter in the world?

a) First b) Second

c) Third d) Fourth

116. Which organization is the main public organization responsible for providing extension services to farmers in Thailand?

a) Department of Community Development

b) Department of Fisheries

c) Department of Agriculture and Cooperatives (DOAE)

d) Royal Forestry Department

117. What are the key activities of the Sky Irrigation Scheme in Thailand?

a) Providing technical assistance to farmers

b) Managing Village Water Management Committees

c) Promoting and protecting organic trade

d) Implementing low interest loans for farmers

118. Which association in Thailand is responsible for promoting and protecting organic trade?

a) Thai Farmers Association

b) Thai Poultry Farmers Association

c) Thai Tapioca Trade Association

d) Thai Rice Exporters Association

119. What is the main objective of the Community Based Integrated Rural Development (CBIRD) program in Thailand?

a) To promote and protect organic trade

b) To facilitate self-help development procedures and group cooperation

c) To enhance agricultural technology for smallholder farmers

d) To provide employment opportunities for rural residents

120. Which initiative in Brazil involves large purchases of agricultural production from small farmers at a stable price?
   a) State food purchases from farmers
   b) Food Acquisition Program
   c) Bahia Sustainable Rural Development Project
   d) Brazilian Agricultural Extension Program

121. What is the main objective of the Food Acquisition Program in Brazil?
   a) To address issues of rural poverty, hunger, and food insecurity
   b) To increase market integration and net revenue
   c) To promote and protect organic trade
   d) To enhance agricultural technology for smallholder farmers

122. Which country is one of the major export markets for Brazil's agricultural products, contributing to the high growth rate in export markets?
   a) China
   b) Russia
   c) India
   d) USA

123. In which year was the Agricultural Information Network initiated in Thailand?
   a) 2002 b) 1987
   c) 1977 d) 1999

124. What is the primary focus of the Thai Business in Rural Development (TBIRD) program?
   a) Enhancing agricultural technology for smallholder farmers
   b) Providing employment opportunities for rural residents
   c) Promoting support from private businesses in rural areas
   d) Establishing cooperatives for farmers

125. What is the main objective of the Bahia Sustainable Rural Development Project in Brazil?
   a) To increase market integration and net revenue
   b) To address issues of rural poverty, hunger, and food insecurity
   c) To enhance agricultural technology for smallholder farmers
   d) To improve access to water supply and sanitation services

126. How many companies are responsible for the significant progress in Brazil's food and beverage industry, contributing to a 10% share in the country's GDP?

a) 10 thousand companies
b) 33 thousand companies
c) 20 thousand companies
d) 50 thousand companies

127. Which UN development agencies are cooperating with Thailand for education, research, and institutional development?

a) UN Economic and Social Commission for Asia and the Pacific (ESCAP) and World Bank

b) Food and Agriculture Organization (FAO) and World Bank

c) UN Economic and Social Commission for Asia and the Pacific (ESCAP) and Asian Development Bank (ADB)

d) Food and Agriculture Organization (FAO) and Asian Development Bank (ADB)

128. What is the focus of the present approaches to extension in India?

a) Production and productivity improvement

b) Income and marketing efficiency

c) Resource exploitation

d) Centralized funding

129. What is the primary purpose of the Bank for Agriculture and Agricultural Cooperatives (BAAC) in Thailand?

a) Running radio and television programs to link farmers

b) Providing credit support for agricultural export

c) Enhancing agricultural technology for smallholder farmers

d) Establishing farmers' training centers

130. Which initiative in Thailand provides training in areas such as management, negotiation, and funding to facilitate self-help development procedures and group cooperation?

a) Sky Irrigation Scheme

b) Thai Business in Rural Development (TBIRD)

c) **Community Based Integrated Rural Development (CBIRD)**

d) Farmers' associations

131. Which initiative in Brazil involves large purchases of agricultural production by a State Company from small farmers at an agreed price?
   a) Bahia Sustainable Rural Development Project
   b) Food Acquisition Program
   c) State food purchases from farmers
   d) Brazilian Agricultural Extension Program

132. What is the main objective of the State food purchases from farmers initiative in Brazil?
   a) To promote and protect organic trade
   b) To address issues of rural poverty, hunger, and food insecurity
   c) To increase market integration and net revenue
   d) To enhance agricultural technology for smallholder farmers

133. What is a farming system?
   a) A single crop farming practice
   b) An integrated set of activities performed by farmers to maximize productivity and income
   c) A system of livestock management only
   d) A government-led agricultural program

134. What are the components considered in a farming system?
   a) Soil, water, crops, and labor only
   b) Soil, water, crops, livestock, labor, capital, and energy
   c) Crops, livestock, and labor only
   d) Soil, water, crops, and capital only

135. What is the central focus in the interaction of farming system components?
   a) The government's control and choice
   b) The farmers' exercise of control and choice
   c) The input suppliers' control and choice
   d) The livestock management control and choice

136. Why is a judicious mix of enterprises recommended for small and marginal farms?
   a) To reduce competition between enterprises
   b) To maximize competition between enterprises
   c) To avoid complementarity between enterprises
   d) To minimize complementarity between enterprises

137. What is the purpose of the Farming System Approach (FSA)?
   a) To promote competition among farmers
   b) To develop diversified models for different types of farmers
   c) To provide top-down extension services
   d) To introduce new technologies from outside the country

138. What is the main advantage of the Farmer Field School (FFS) approach?
   a) It automatically assumes alternative practices are superior to conventional practices.
   b) It provides a risk-free setting for farmers to experiment with new agricultural management ideas.
   c) It promotes top-down extension methods of the Green Revolution.
   d) It focuses solely on seed-to-seed approaches.

139. What is the primary focus of market-led extension?
   a) Maximizing seed availability
   b) Ensuring remunerative prices to primary producers
   c) Promoting agricultural cooperatives
   d) Improving soil fertility

140. What are the components that facilitate market-led extension?
   a) Market information, market intelligence, and market news
   b) Crop management, irrigation, and pest control
   c) Seed quality, fertilizer application, and harvesting techniques
   d) Market reform, agronomic practices, and market promotion

141. What is the primary purpose of Farmer Producer Organizations (FPOs)?
   a) To provide a bargaining edge to farmers
   b) To focus on crop management techniques
   c) To ensure remunerative prices for consumers
   d) To reduce the cost of cultivation for large farmers

142. What does PTD stand for in the context of extension approaches?
   a) Private Technology Development
   b) Progressive Technology Development
   c) Participatory Technology Development
   d) Public Technology Development

143. What is the purpose of pluralistic extension in agriculture?
   a) To provide quality and timely services to the farming community
   b) To focus solely on public sector extension
   c) To introduce new technologies without farmer involvement
   d) To eliminate public-private partnerships

144. What does FSA stand for in the context of agricultural extension?
   a) Farmer Support Approach
   b) Farming System Approach
   c) Farmer Sustainability Approach
   d) Farming Support Agency

145. What is the main role of a farmer in the Farmer Field School (FFS) approach?
   a) The farmer decides which conventional practices to use.
   b) The farmer is guided by a trained facilitator in the field.
   c) The farmer is responsible for training extension agents.
   d) The farmer acts as a government representative.

146. Why is farmer-led extension important?
   a) It focuses on introducing new technologies from outside the country.
   b) It helps farmers address complex and counter-intuitive problems in their fields.
   c) It promotes top-down extension methods.
   d) It eliminates the need for farmer participation.

147. What is the primary objective of the Farm School concept?
   a) To promote marketing efficiency for farmers
   b) To identify potential farmers for awards
   c) To provide technical training to farmers in the field
   d) To establish large-scale agricultural cooperatives

148. What is the primary focus of the Market Led Extension approach?
   a) Focusing solely on seed-to-seed approaches
   b) Enhancing farmer participation in decision-making
   c) Linking farmers with the market for better prices
   d) Promoting top-down extension methods

149. What is the main objective of the Farmer Field School (FFS) approach?

a) To provide a risk-free setting for farmers to experiment with new agricultural management ideas

b) To introduce conventional practices to farmers

c) To eliminate the use of toxic pesticides in farming

d) To ensure remunerative prices for farmers

150. What is the focus of Participatory Technology Development (PTD)?

a) Introducing new technologies from elsewhere

b) Improving local technologies through experimentation

c) Promoting private technology companies

d) Eliminating farmer involvement in technology innovation

151. What is the central focus in the interaction of farming system components?

a) The farmers' exercise of control and choice

b) The input suppliers' control and choice

c) The government's control and choice

d) The livestock management control and choice

152. Why is a judicious mix of enterprises recommended for small and marginal farms?

a) To minimize competition between enterprises

b) To maximize competition between enterprises

c) To reduce competition between enterprises

d) To avoid complementarity between enterprises

153. What is the primary focus of market-led extension?

a) Maximizing seed availability

b) Ensuring remunerative prices to primary producers

c) Promoting agricultural cooperatives

d) Improving soil fertility

154. What is the purpose of the National Agriculture Market (eNAM)?

a) To create a unified national market for agricultural commodities

b) To eliminate all APMC mandis and promote direct sales to consumers

c) To increase transaction costs and information asymmetry

d) To reduce the number of small and marginal farmers

155. How are Grameen Agricultural Markets (GrAMs) linked to eNAM?

a) GrAMs are exempted from regulations of APMCs.

b) GrAMs focus solely on direct sales to consumers.

c) GrAMs are connected to large agribusinesses.

d) GrAMs eliminate the need for eNAM.

156. What is the main objective of the Farmer Interest Group (FIG) approach?

a) To promote large-scale agricultural cooperatives

b) To establish a participatory extension mechanism for farmers

c) To encourage direct sales to bulk purchasers

d) To eliminate the need for farmer participation

157. What is the purpose of para professional extension agents?

a) To increase the cost of extension services

b) To reduce cost and support trained manpower

c) To eliminate the need for training in a particular subject

d) To channelize resources away from farming communities

158. What is the objective of the Diploma in Agricultural Extension Services for Input Dealers (DAESI) program?

a) To build technical competency in agriculture for farmers

b) To provide formal agricultural education to input dealers

c) To train para-extension professionals among input dealers

d) To provide farmers with information about agricultural inputs

159. What is the role of Go Mitra in agriculture?

a) They are private AI workers providing door step service and preventive vaccinations.

b) They serve as para-extension professionals for farmers.

c) They provide formal agricultural education to farmers.

d) They are involved in the management of agricultural markets.

160. How are Pranibandhus selected for their role in agriculture?

a) They are self-employed mobile private workers selected from the inhabitants of the concerned Gram Panchayat.

b) They are trained veterinarians assigned to each Gram Panchayat.

c) They are large-scale agribusiness owners

d) They are randomly selected from the population.

161. What is the primary function of eNAM?
   a) To replace all physical APMC mandis with online markets
   b) To provide door step service for AI to farmers
   c) To connect existing APMC mandis and create a unified national market
   d) To train para-extension professionals in agriculture

162. What is the main advantage of GrAMs linked to eNAM?
   a) They eliminate the need for APMC mandis
   b) They provide direct sales to consumers only
   c) They reduce transaction costs and information asymmetry
   d) They focus solely on large-scale farmers

163. How do para professional extension agents contribute to agriculture?
   a) They increase the cost of extension services
   b) They reduce cost and support trained manpower
   c) They eliminate the need for training in a particular subject
   d) They channelize resources away from farming communities

164. What is the main goal of the Diploma in Agricultural Extension Services for Input Dealers (DAESI) program?
   a) To build technical competency in agriculture for farmers
   b) To provide formal agricultural education to input dealers
   c) To train para-extension professionals among input dealers
   d) To provide farmers with information about agricultural inputs

165. What is the role of Go Mitra in agriculture?
   a) They are private AI workers providing door step service and preventive vaccinations.
   b) They serve as para-extension professionals for farmers.
   c) They provide formal agricultural education to farmers.
   d) They are involved in the management of agricultural markets.

166. What is the significance of ICT in agriculture?
   a) To reduce the use of digital tools and technologies
   b) To address the increasing resource base in agriculture
   c) To promote youth leaving agriculture
   d) To support and complement the extension system

167. Which of the following is an example of an ICT-based initiative in agriculture?
   a) Crop residue management
   b) Climate resilience through innovations
   c) Mulching and incorporation of crop residues
   d) Mobile application-based agro-advisory services

168. What is the purpose of the Farmers' portal developed by the Ministry of Agriculture?
   a) To provide weather forecasts to farmers
   b) To promote large-scale agricultural cooperatives
   c) To deliver timely information and services to farmers
   d) To offer insurance and credit facilities to farmers

169. Which initiative integrates more than 100 agriculture-related Apps developed by ICAR institutes?
   a) VKC
   b) AGMARKNET
   c) KISAN
   d) Kisan Call Centers

170. How many Climate Resilient Villages (CRVs) were developed under the National Innovations on Climate Resilient Agriculture (NICRA) program?
   a) 50
   b) 100
   c) 151
   d) 200

171. What is the role of Village Climate Risk Management Committee (VCRMC) in NICRA villages?
   a) To operate custom hiring centers for farm implements
   b) To implement resilient practices in the entire village
   c) To manage the distribution of farm inputs to farmers
   d) To conduct training programs for smallholder farmers

172. Which states are considered as the heartlands of the Green Revolution in India?
   a) Kerala and Tamil Nadu
   b) Maharashtra and Karnataka
   c) Punjab, Haryana, and western Uttar Pradesh
   d) Assam and West Bengal

173. What is the main problem caused by crop residue burning in the rice-wheat system?

a) Increase in soil fertility

b) Reduction in environmental pollution

c) Shortage of labor in the fields

d) Phenomenal environmental pollution

174. What is the suggested method for in situ straw management to tackle crop residue burning?

a) Use of Happy Seeder

b) Mulching the crop residues

c) Incorporating crop residues into the soil

d) Burning the crop residues in a controlled manner

175. Which ICT-based initiative aims to deliver agro-advisory services to farmers through mobile applications?

a) Kisan Call Centers
b) VKC
c) AGMARKNET
d) mKisan

176. What is the role of ICT in addressing the challenges faced by Indian agriculture?

a) It increases resource base in agriculture

b) It encourages more youth to stay in agriculture

c) It mitigates the harmful impact of climate change on agriculture

d) It promotes traditional farming practices

177. Which platform provides a single interface for multiple Indian language-based agricultural apps?

a) AGMARKNET
b) VKC
c) KISAN
d) NICRA

178. How are community radios utilized in reaching out to farmers?

a) To provide market price information to farmers

b) To produce need-based agricultural programs in local languages

c) To promote large-scale agricultural cooperatives

d) To distribute farm inputs to farmers

179. How does the SMS Portal for Farmers empower government organizations and institutes in agriculture?
   a) It helps them to deliver advisory to farmers through SMS
   b) It facilitates bulk hiring of farm machinery
   c) It provides weather forecasts to farmers
   d) It promotes large-scale agricultural cooperatives

180. Which initiative promotes climate resilience through technological, institutional, and community-led innovations?
   a) VKC
   b) AGMARKNET
   c) NICRA
   d) Kisan Call Centers

181. What percentage of the total net sown area in India is rainfed?
   a) 40%
   b) 60%
   c) 70%
   d) 80%

182. Which crops are predominantly grown under rainfed farming in India?
   a) Wheat and rice
   b) Rice and cotton
   c) Coarse cereals and pulses
   d) Oilseeds and cotton

183. Which project is conducting site-specific research programs in arid, semiarid, and sub-humid agro-ecologies for developing contingency crop planning in India?
   a) ASCI
   b) VATICA
   c) NARI
   d) All India Coordinated Research Project for Dryland Agriculture (ICAR)

184. What is the main focus of the Nutri-sensitive Agricultural Research and Innovations (NARI) program?
   a) Promoting nutrition-sensitive agriculture practices
   b) Increasing overall food production
   c) Improving irrigation techniques
   d) Providing credit to farmers

185. Which state became the third in the country to provide a wholesome meal to the poor at an affordable price through the Deendayal Thali initiative?
   a) Rajasthan
   b) Tamil Nadu
   c) Madhya Pradesh
   d) Karnataka

186. What is the aim of the Nutri Smart Villages initiative in Madhya Pradesh?

a) To develop smart villages with advanced technology

b) To control malnutrition by fulfilling villagers' needs with local harvest

c) To promote tourism in rural areas

d) To increase the number of animal husbandry and fisheries activities

187. What is the main objective of the Knowledge System for Homestead Agricultural Management in Tribal Areas (KSHAMATA) program?

a) To promote indigenous technical knowledge in tribal areas

b) To provide technology support to tribal farmers

c) To facilitate capacity building of farmers in tribal areas

d) To increase the area of homestead agricultural land in tribal regions

188. What is the concept behind the Value Addition and Technology Incubation Centre in Agriculture (VATICA)?

a) To provide skill development training to rural youth in agriculture

b) To create a facility for incubation training in processing and value addition

c) To establish model units for technology management

d) To provide financial support to agricultural startups

189. Which approach ensures the sustainability of an extension system by involving stakeholders in designing programs and policies?

a) Indigenous Technical Knowledge (ITK)

b) Cost-based extension

c) Demand-driven extension

d) Nutri-sensitive Agricultural Research and Innovations (NARI)

190. What is the main aim of documenting and registering Indigenous Technical Knowledge (ITK) in agriculture?

a) To promote modern knowledge and technology system

b) To preserve and promote traditional knowledge and technologies

c) To increase the income of farmers

d) To facilitate the export of agricultural products

191. Which organization was established to build the capacity of farmers, agricultural laborers, and entrepreneurs in the agriculture sector?
   a) **ASCI** (Agriculture Sector Skill Council of India)
   b) NARI
   c) CAR
   d) NSDC

192. How does the Agriculture Sector Skill Council of India (ASCI) plan to improve the skills of farmers and laborers?
   a) By establishing public-private partnership mode training programs
   b) By organizing awareness campaigns for farmers
   c) By providing financial assistance to farmers for skill development
   d) By promoting urban agriculture initiatives

193. What is the focus of the skill training program for rural youth in agriculture and allied sectors?
   a) Training in specific vocational areas
   b) Establishment of agro-processing units
   c) Promotion of urban agriculture
   d) Training in crop production and irrigation techniques

194. What services are offered by the private extension system in India to supplement the public extension efforts?
   a) Paid extension services for affordable farmers
   b) Self-help groups of farmers
   c) Information support through media organizations
   d) All of the above

195. Which approach involves direct charging for individual services that produce a direct return in the form of improved income?
   a) Public financing by taxpayers
   b) Cost sharing by farmers' groups
   c) Cost-based and cost-saving extension
   d) Contracting services to small groups

196. What is the main objective of the VATICA initiative?
   a) To promote technology incubation in rural areas
   b) To provide financial support to agricultural startups
   c) To develop model units for technology management
   d) To provide skill development training to rural youth

197. Which approach involves direct charging for individual services that produce a direct return in the form of improved income?

a) Public financing by taxpayers

b) Cost sharing by farmers' groups

c) Cost-based and cost-saving extension

d) Contracting services to small groups

198. What is the objective of the National Agricultural Higher Education Project (NAHEP)?

a) To support research and development in agricultural universities

b) To improve the quality of education in agricultural universities

c) To promote collaboration between agricultural universities and private industry

d) To raise funds for infrastructure development in agricultural universities

199. Which institutions are targeted under the National Agricultural Higher Education Project (NAHEP)?

a) State Agricultural Universities and ICAR Deemed-to-be Universities

b) All public and private universities in India

c) Central Universities with Agricultural faculty

d) Private agricultural colleges

200. How is the collaboration between research and extension institutions institutionalized at the national level in India?

a) Through joint meetings of senior officers from ICAR and DAC

b) Through seasonal workshops at the zonal level

c) Through regional committees comprising researchers and extension officers

d) Through contractual agreements with private sector entities

201. What is the key to a successful education program in agriculture?

a) High investment in infrastructure

b) Attracting talented students to agriculture

c) Quality of faculty and career-oriented curricula

d) Providing subsidies to students

202. How can research-extension linkages be strengthened at the regional level?
   a) By organizing joint meetings of senior officers from ICAR and DAC
   b) By forming regional committees to review research and development status
   c) By promoting public-private partnerships
   d) By providing financial assistance to farmers

203. What is the primary focus of the farming systems approach?
   a) Maximizing farm inputs
   b) Increasing crop yield
   c) Enhancing farmers' income and standard of living
   d) Minimizing environmental degradation

204. What is the aim of involving a wide range of service providers and farmer organizations in stakeholder processes?
   a) To increase the demand for extension services
   b) To create a more competitive extension system
   c) To improve the quality of services
   d) To promote research and development

205. What is the main goal of privatization of extension services?
   a) To eliminate public extension services entirely
   b) To increase the involvement of private sector organizations
   c) To reduce the number of extension service providers
   d) To restrict extension services to the corporate sector only

206. What is the purpose of a public-private partnership in agricultural extension?
   a) To share skills and assets between public and private sectors
   b) To replace public extension services with private ones
   c) To privatize the entire agricultural sector
   d) To promote corporate farming

207. How can the private extension system complement the public sector extension service?
   a) By providing free services to farmers
   b) By offering specialized and competitive services
   c) By replacing public extension services entirely
   d) By reducing the number of extension service providers

208. What is the significance of mainstreaming women farmers in agriculture?
   a) To reduce the cost of farm inputs
   b) To address environmental degradation
   c) To increase the diversity of farm activities
   d) To take full advantage of agricultural opportunities

209. Which courses can be introduced in the extension education curricula to address current challenges and priorities?
   a) Governance, Livelihoods, and Resources
   b) Persuasion and Social Influence
   c) Market Trade and Analysis
   d) Environment, Science, and Health

210. What is the primary limitation of the degree of Agricultural Extension in addressing specific sector-related issues?
   a) Lack of practical training in agricultural practices
   b) Lack of awareness about agricultural opportunities
   c) Focus on social sciences rather than biological sciences
   d) Inadequate infrastructure in agricultural universities

211. How can the extension system be strengthened to make the extension efforts sustainable?
   a) By increasing the number of public extension officers
   b) By introducing new technology to extension services
   c) By involving private sector organizations in extension activities
   d) By adopting a dynamic approach comprising research, education, and field service

212. What is the overall objective of the National Agricultural Higher Education Project (NAHEP)?
   a) To increase the number of agricultural universities in India
   b) To attract talented students to non-conventional agricultural courses
   c) To improve the quality of higher education in agricultural universities
   d) To establish partnerships with private industry for research and development

213. How are research-extension linkages institutionalized at the regional level in India?

a) Through joint meetings of senior officers from ICAR and DAC

b) Through seasonal workshops at the zonal level

c) Through regional committees comprising researchers and extension officers

d) Through contractual agreements with private sector entities

214. What is the primary focus of the farming systems approach?

a) Maximizing farm inputs

b) Increasing crop yield

c) Enhancing farmers' income and standard of living

d) Minimizing environmental degradation

215. What is the main goal of privatization of extension services?

a) To eliminate public extension services entirely

b) To increase the involvement of private sector organizations

c) To reduce the number of extension service providers

d) To restrict extension services to the corporate sector only

2

Methodologies of Agricultural Extension in India

1 An approach in the context of a system refers to:

a) The resources and linkages of the system

b) The leadership pattern of the system

c) The philosophy and style of action within the system

d) All of the above

2 What does an extension approach in the agricultural sector entail?

a) Setting the pace for all activities within the system

b) Organizing the structure and leadership position of the extension system

c) Planning and implementing programs with specific objectives

d) All of the above

3 Which extension approach was followed in India during the late 1990s?

a) Philanthropic approach

b) Community development approach

c) Linear transfer of technology (ToT) approach

d) Market-driven and privatized extension approach

4. What was the outcome of the reform initiatives in agricultural extension in India?

a) Even coverage and access to extension services for all farmers

b) Limited access to information on modern technology for farmers

c) Successful implementation of the Training and Visit (T&V) approach

d) Increased reliance on the public sector extension system

Bold Means Correct Answer

5. What is the purpose of analyzing agricultural extension approaches in India?
   a) To determine the nature of the information gap
   b) To suggest extension approaches for specific circumstances
   c) To reach maximum farmers in a cost-effective manner
   d) All of the above

6. How many prevalent extension approaches are there across the world, based on problem seven dimensions?
   a) 7 **b) 8**
   c) 9 d) 10

7. Which extension approach is considered the most classical and common?
   a) Commodity-based extension approach
   b) T&V system of extension
   c) Public extension approach
   d) Participatory extension approach

8. The public extension approach is synonymous with:
   a) NGO-based extension approach
   b) Private extension
   c) Farmer First approach
   d) General extension approach

9. What does the public extension approach assume?
   a) Local farmers have access to appropriate technology and knowledge
   b) Farming communities are not using available technologies effectively
   c) Extension programs should focus on community development
   d) Farmers need financial support for agricultural practices

10. How is the success of the public extension approach measured?
   a) Increase in adoption rate of recommended technologies
   b) Increase in national production and productivity
   c) Farmer satisfaction with extension services
   d) Increase in government funding for agricultural programs

11. Which extension system in India is an example of the general extension approach?
    a) Ministry-based extension programs
    b) T&V system of extension
    c) Farmer First approach
    d) State agricultural department extension system

12. What is a major advantage of the general extension approach?
    a) Two-way flow of information between farmers and extension agents
    b) Low cost and efficient implementation
    c) High level of accountability of field staff to farmers' needs
    d) Extensive extension network and outreach even at the village level

13. Which of the following is a limitation of the general extension approach?
    a) Ineffective message delivery to farming communities
    b) Low impact of technology adoption among farmers
    c) Easy controlling and monitoring of extension programs
    d) Efficient and cost-effective extension services

14. The commodity-based extension approach focuses on:
    a) Export crops and commercially important cash crops
    b) Staple food crops
    c) Livestock farming
    d) Organic farming

15. What is the main assumption of the commodity-based extension approach?
    a) Better production and productivity can be achieved through vertical integration of functions related to a specific commodity
    b) Farmers need access to a wide range of extension services
    c) Farmers are capable of making their own decisions regarding crop selection
    d) The government should control all aspects of commodity production and marketing

16. How is extension planning and implementation controlled in the commodity-based extension approach?
    a) By private sector firms
    b) By specialized public bodies
    c) By individual farmers
    d) By government agencies

17. How is the success of the commodity-based extension approach measured?
    a) Increase in farmers' income
    b) Increase in crop diversity
    c) Increase in total production of the specific commodity
    d) Increase in farmers' knowledge and skills

18. What is a major characteristic of the commodity-based extension approach?
    a) Focuses on small-scale farmers
    b) Provides a wide range of services beyond extension
    c) Emphasizes environmental sustainability
    d) Extension personnel are highly skilled

19. What are the strong points of the commodity-based extension approach?
    a) Strong coordination with input suppliers and marketing agents
    b) Focus on environmental factors and sustainability
    c) Inclusion of all farmers in the value chain
    d) Adoption rate of technology is low

20. What is a limitation of the commodity-based extension approach?
    a) Conflict may arise if farmers want to switch to other commodities
    b) Extension objectives are determined by farmers' needs and priorities
    c) All farmers have equal access to extension services
    d) Input usage is strictly monitored by government agencies

21. What is the main objective of the Training and Visit (T&V) system of extension?
    a) Strengthen the extension management system
    b) Improve the extension agent-farmer ratio
    c) Enhance communication between extension staff and farmers
    d) All of the above

22. What assumption does the T&V system of extension make about extension staff?
    a) They are poorly trained and not up to date
    b) They visit farmers' fields regularly
    c) They have adequate management and supervision
    d) They are responsible for non-extension work

23. What is a characteristic of the T&V system of extension?

a) Multiple lines of administrative command

b) Emphasis on non-agricultural activities

c) Regular contact with farmers on a predefined schedule

d) Lack of linkage with research institutions

24. How is the T&V system of extension linked to research?

a) Extension agents solve all research problems in the field

b) Researchers transfer unresolved problems to field extension agents

c) Extension agents conduct research studies alongside their extension work

d) There is no linkage between the T&V system and research

25. What advantage does the T&V system of extension provide?

a) Creation of new agricultural technologies

b) Cost-effective implementation

c) Closer technical supervision and monitoring of field staff

d) Flexibility to change programs based on farmers' needs

26. What limitation is associated with the T&V system of extension?

a) Lack of two-way communication with farmers

b) Low production without complementary development packages

c) Selection of contact farmers based on political pressure

d) Supply-driven extension approach

27. What is the basic assumption of the participatory extension approach?

a) Farmers have little knowledge about farming practices in their own land

b) Effective extension requires active participation of farmers and research services

c) Farmers should rely solely on indigenous knowledge for agricultural improvement

d) Programme planning should be centrally controlled by government agencies

28. Who exercises greater control over extension priorities and activities in the participatory extension approach?

a) Government agencies

b) Research institutions

c) Local farmers' groups or associations

d) International organizations

29. What is a characteristic of the participatory extension approach?
   a) Heavy reliance on external resources
   b) Centralized decision-making
   c) Limited relevance of messages to farmers
   d) Involvement of local stakeholders in program planning

30. What are the major advantages of the participatory extension approach?
   a) High control from central authorities
   b) Low relevance of messages to farmers
   c) Mutual support among participants
   d) Dependency mentality among farmers

31 What is a setback of the participatory extension approach?
   a) Lack of long-term commitment from bureaucracies
   b) Strong community autonomy and cohesion
   c) Client-centered programs rather than subject-centered programs
   d) Absence of village politics in program implementation

32. According to the PEOPLE model, what should the extension program encourage?
   a) Dependence on extension agents
   b) Responsibility, initiative, and decision making
   c) Centralized planning at the national level
   d) Reliance on external resources

33. What is the first step in the PEOPLE model?
   a) Environmental planning
   b) Organizational action
   c) Performance evaluation
   d) Promotional analysis

34. What does environmental planning in the PEOPLE model refer to?
   a) Assessment of activities and output
   b) Identification of limitations in achieving goals
   c) Decentralized planning at the local level
   d) Assistance from extension agents

35. What does organizational action in the PEOPLE model involve?
   a) Thorough analysis of participants, social system, and situation
   b) Assessment of activities and output
   c) Implementation of the program by the people with assistance from extension agents
   d) Identification of limitations and remedial measures

36. What is the purpose of performance evaluation in the PEOPLE model?

a) Thorough analysis of participants, social system, and situation

b) Decentralized planning at the local level

c) Assessment of activities and output

d) Identification of limitations and remedial measures

37. What is the final step in the PEOPLE model?

a) Encouragement for sustainability

b) Limitation analysis

c) Performance evaluation

d) Organizational action

38. The integrated development model emphasizes the importance of:

a) Technology and education only

b) Physical inputs and markets only

c) Combination of factors including technology, education, physical inputs, markets, and fair prices

d) Government subsidies and credit programs

39. Which program in India exemplifies the integrated development model?

a) National Rural Employment Guarantee Scheme (NREGS)

b) Integrated Rural Development Programme (IRDP)

c) Swachh Bharat Abhiyan (Clean India Mission)

d) Pradhan Mantri Kisan Samman Nidhi (PM-KISAN)

40. What is the objective of the integrated development model?

a) Cross the poverty line

b) Provide education to farmers

c) Increase agricultural productivity

d) Implement subsidy programs

41 What does the integrated development model recognize as essential for agriculture to prosper?

a) Technology and education only

b) Access to physical inputs and markets

c) Fair prices and government subsidies

d) All of the above

42. Which approach is NOT emphasized in the integrated development model?
    a) Fair prices for agricultural products
    b) Government support through credit and subsidies
    c) Access to physical inputs and markets
    d) Sole reliance on technology for agricultural development

43. What is the main objective of community development?
    a) To solve people's problems through joint study and discussion
    b) To provide educational opportunities to all community members
    c) To promote economic improvements in the community
    d) To bring people from different walks of life together

44. How is community development considered an educational process?
    a) It focuses on imparting academic knowledge to community members
    b) It aims to change attitudes and behaviors that hinder social and economic progress
    c) It provides vocational training to community members
    d) It encourages community members to pursue higher education

45. What does community development aim to promote?
    a) Government intervention in solving community problems
    b) Individual achievements and goals
    c) Dependency on external assistance
    d) People's ability and capacity to help themselves

46. What is the process involved in community development?
    a) Joint study, discussion, decision making, and action
    b) Economic planning and implementation
    c) Centralized decision making by community leaders
    d) Training and skill development programs

47. What is the role of community members in community development?
    a) To rely on external organizations for solutions to their problems
    b) To participate actively in problem-solving and decision-making processes
    c) To solely depend on government initiatives for community development
    d) To provide financial resources for community projects

48. What is the primary focus of the self-help model?
    a) Transformation of rural infrastructure
    b) Implementation of government programs
    c) Transformation of attitude and behavior of the people
    d) Economic development through external assistance

49. Which country is known for the Gramin Bank model, an example of the self-help approach?
    a) Indi
    b) Bangladesh
    c) Nigeri
    d) Brazil

50. Which model in India exemplifies the self-help approach?
    a) National Rural Employment Guarantee Scheme (NREGS)
    b) Self-help group model
    c) Swachh Bharat Abhiyan (Clean India Mission)
    d) Pradhan Mantri Kisan Samman Nidhi (PM-KISAN)

51. What is the main principle of the self-help model?
    a) Dependency on external assistance for development
    b) Transformation of rural infrastructure
    c) Transformation of the attitude and behavior of the people themselves
    d) Implementation of government policies and programs

52. Which cooperative model in India is considered an example of the self-help model?
    a) Amul cooperative model
    b) Farmer producer organizations (FPOs)
    c) National Rural Livelihood Mission (NRLM)
    d) Integrated Child Development Services (ICDS)

53. What is the primary purpose of the government-aided participatory model?
    a) To encourage villagers to rely solely on government support
    b) To empower villagers to take ownership of their development efforts
    c) To discourage independent efforts of villagers
    d) To limit the role of government in rural development initiatives

54. What is the role of villagers in the government-aided participatory model?
    a) To rely solely on government support for their development efforts
    b) To take ownership and actively participate in their own development initiatives
    c) To depend on external organizations for support
    d) To resist any government intervention in rural development

55. What is a characteristic of the government-aided participatory model?
    a) Government taking complete control of rural development initiatives
    b) Villagers relying on external organizations for support
    c) Villagers' efforts being independent of government support
    d) Government providing technical and financial assistance to villagers' efforts

56. What is the primary objective of the project approach in agricultural extension?
    a) To achieve quick results within a specific time period
    b) To provide long-term support to farmers
    c) To focus on sustainable development
    d) To promote social equality in rural areas

57. What is a key assumption of the project approach?
    a) The current extension system has been successful in making a significant impact
    b) Outside resources are not necessary for project success
    c) High impact activities can continue even without financial support
    d) Project-based extension is not effective for agricultural development

58. Which of the following is an example of a project-based extension approach?
    a) National Rural Employment Guarantee Scheme (NREGS)
    b) Intensive Agricultural District Programme
    c) Swachh Bharat Abhiyan (Clean India Mission)
    d) Pradhan Mantri Kisan Samman Nidhi (PM-KISAN)

59. What is a major strength of the project approach?
    a) Long-term support for farmers
    b) Cost-effectiveness in achieving desired outcomes
    c) Quick results and easy evaluation of effectiveness
    d) Promotion of social equality among beneficiaries

60. What is a limitation of the project approach?
   a) Continuous support and resources after project completion
   b) Social divide between project personnel and non-beneficiaries
   c) Cost-effectiveness compared to other approaches
   d) Long-term sustainability of project activities

61. Which programmes are project based?
   a) Intensive Agricultural District Programme (1960)
   b) Operational Research project (1974)
   c) Lab to land programme (1979)
   d) IARI-Post office linkage extension model (2009)
   e) All of the above

62. What was the main drawback of the conventional research and extension system?
   a) Lack of funding for research projects
   b) Incompatibility with farmers' value system
   c) Insufficient training of extension personnel
   d) Limited accessibility to research findings

63. What was the purpose of introducing the Farming System Research and Extension (FSR&E) approach?
   a) To promote the use of modern technology in farming
   b) To involve farmers in the development process
   c) To prioritize profitability and stability in farming systems
   d) To reduce the cost of extension services

64. What is the primary characteristic of FSR&E approach?
   a) Sole control by agricultural researchers
   b) Reliance on external expertise for technology transfer
   c) Emphasis on productivity, profitability, stability, and sustainability
   d) Exclusive focus on cropping systems

65. How is the success of FSR&E measured?
   a) Number of research papers published
   b) Adoption and continued use of recommended technologies by farmers
   c) Increase in government funding for agricultural research
   d) Collaboration between research scientists and extension specialists

66. What is a benefit of the FSR&E approach?
   a) Emphasis on top-down planning and decision-making
   b) Limited consideration of farmers' needs and desires
   c) Facilitation of faster adoption of recommended technology
   d) Exclusively targeting resource-rich farming families

67. Which of the following is NOT a successful example of the Farming System Research and Extension (FSR&E) model?
   a) Rural demonstration and training centre in Padhri Kalan, Amritsar Punjab, India
   b) Bio-resource complex at the University of Agricultural Science Bengaluru, India
   c) Roopa farm of Mohinder Singh Grewal, Punjab, India
   d) Agro-resource center in Mumbai, Maharashtra, India

68. What is the purpose of the 'Rural demonstration and training centre' in Padhri Kalan, Amritsar, Punjab, India?
   a) Conducting agricultural research experiments
   b) Providing agricultural training to farmers
   c) Promoting tourism in rural areas
   d) Showcasing modern farming technologies

69. Which institution is associated with the 'Bio-resource complex'?
   a) University of Agricultural Science, Bengaluru, India
   b) Indian Council of Agricultural Research (ICAR)
   c) Indian Agricultural Research Institute (IARI)
   d) Punjab Agricultural University, Ludhiana, India

70. Who is the owner of the Roopa farm in Punjab, India?
   a) Mohinder Singh Grewal
   b) Rohit Sharma
   c) Ramesh Gupt
   d) Rajesh Kumar

71. What is the primary assumption of the cost sharing approach in agricultural extension?
   a) Extension personnel are unlikely to serve farming communities without local payment
   b) Farm people are financially capable of paying the entire cost of extension services
   c) The central and state government should bear the full cost of extension services
   d) Farm people are too poor to pay the whole cost, but can contribute a portion of it

72. What is the purpose of the cost sharing approach in agricultural extension?

a) To make extension services more affordable for the central government

b) To encourage farm people to take full responsibility for extension services

c) To ensure the relevance of program content and methods to farming communities

d) To reduce the adoption rate of technology among farmers

73. hat is an advantage of the cost sharing approach?

a) Reduction of financial burden on local communities

b) Increased complexity and difficulty in administrative aspects

c) Lack of confidence from rural people due to local personnel selection

d) Higher adoption rate of technology due to cost-sharing responsibility

74. What is a limitation of the cost sharing approach?

a) Governments' reluctance to share any cost for providing extension services

b) Marginal farming categories being overlooked in the cost-sharing process

c) Easy management and financial reporting of extension services

d) Farm people behaving like owners and taking full responsibility for extension services

75. What is a challenge associated with the cost sharing approach?

a) Limited interest and participation from farming communities

b) High financial burden on the central government

c) Lack of confidence in local personnel selected for extension services

d) Low adoption rate of technology among farmers

76. What is the primary mandate of agricultural universities and colleges regarding extension activities?

a) Providing agricultural education and research

b) Offering practical training to farmers

c) Improving the practical utility of teaching and research functions

d) Implementing extension programs in rural areas

77. What is the purpose of incorporating extension as part of the academic curriculum in agricultural universities and colleges?
    - **a) To focus on practical utility and quality of teaching and research**
    - b) To ensure efficient use of human resources in extension activities
    - c) To compete with ministry of agriculture in providing extension services
    - d) To establish a presence at the grassroots level for extension work

78. Which approach assumes that faculties or colleges of agriculture have relevant technical knowledge for farmers?
    - a) Government-aided participatory approach
    - b) Commodity-based extension approach
    - **c) Educational institution-based extension approach**
    - d) Project approach

79. What are the advantages of the educational institution-based extension approach?
    - a) Practical and useful lectures from the farmers' perspective
    - **b) Improved working relationship between scientists and field extension personnel**
    - c) Increased competition between extension staff of different institutions
    - d) Presence at the grassroots level for wide-scale implementation

80. What is a limitation of the educational institution-based extension approach?
    - **a) Highly academic-oriented programs**
    - b) Mental divide between subject matter specialists and field personnel
    - c) Extensive operation in rural areas with wide coverage
    - d) Financial burden on national government for providing extension services

81. What is the dominant extension system across the world?
    - a) Private sector extension
    - **b) Public sector extension**
    - c) Non-governmental organization extension
    - d) University-based extension

82. What percentage of agricultural extension personnel worldwide are engaged in public extension systems?
    - a) 50%
    - b) 75%
    - **c) 95%**
    - d) 100%

83. Which of the following is synonymous with the public sector agricultural extension approach?

a) **Ministry-based extension**
b) Commodity-based extension
c) Participatory extension
d) Self-help model

84. What is the primary focus of public sector extension?

a) **Transfer of technology**
b) Financial assistance to farmers
c) Marketing and price support
d) Capacity building of extension workers

85. What is one of the reasons for the strong role of public sector extension?

a) Promotion of private sector involvement in agriculture
b) **Insurance against agricultural risks**
c) Maximizing profits for farmers
d) Encouraging adoption of non-profitable technologies

86. What is a criticism of public sector extension?

a) **Relevance of services for all farmers**
b) Efficient use of public funds
c) Low manpower recruitment at the field level
d) Effective communication from ministry level to rural people

87. What is the current extension worker to farmer ratio in India?

a) 1:100
b) 1:1,000
c) **1:5,000**
d) 1:10,000

88. What is one of the major limitations of public extension?

a) High motivation of staff
b) Adequate training in extension methods
c) Low cost and high impact of extension programs
d) **Growing conflicts between farmers' interest and policy goals**

89. What is the current name of the section of agricultural extension and education within ICAR?

a) **Division of Agricultural Extension**
b) Agricultural Technology Application Research Institute (ATARI)
c) Krishi Vigyan Kendra (KVK)
d) Farmers FIRST programme

90. What are the primary methods used by ICAR to disseminate modern farm technologies and advisory services?
    a) Research institutes and universities
    b) Operational research projects
    c) Krishi Vigyan Kendras (KVKs)
    d) Farmers FIRST programme

91. In which year was the Farmers FIRST programme initiated by ICAR?
    a) 1964 b) 1971
    c) 1979 **d) 2016**

92. What is the role of the Directorate of Extension of State Agricultural Universities (SAUs)?
    a) Research and development of new agricultural technologies
    b) Planning, organizing, and coordinating regional or zonal extension activities
    c) Providing advisory services to farmers
    d) Implementation of government agricultural programs

93. What are the major extension activities carried out by university-based extension?
    a) Research and development of new agricultural technologies
    b) Training, advisory service, and input supply
    c) Policy formulation and implementation
    d) Marketing and distribution of agricultural products

94. What are the units through which university-based extension is implemented?
    a) Research institutes and laboratories
    b) Krishi Vigyan Kendras (KVKs) or Agricultural Technology Information Centre (ATICs) or Farmer Training Centre (FTCs)
    c) Government agricultural departments
    d) Agricultural cooperatives and societies

95. Apart from training and advisory services, what other activities are organized by university-based extension?
    a) Agricultural research projects
    b) Crop cultivation and production
    c) Farmers' fair or krishi mela, exhibition demonstration program
    d) Government policy formulation workshops

96 Which institution is primarily responsible for university-based extension activities?

a) Indian Council of Agricultural Research (ICAR)

b) Ministry of Agriculture and Farmers Welfare

c) State Agricultural Universities (SAUs)

d) Krishi Vigyan Kendras (KVKs)

97. Which of the following is a major public extension service provider in India?

a) State line department

b) Private agricultural companies

c) Non-profit organizations

d) International agricultural research institutes

98. Which ministry in India is the main source of public extension services?

a) Ministry of Finance

b) Ministry of Agriculture and Farmers Welfare

c) Ministry of Commerce

d) Ministry of Rural Development

99. Which organization in India is responsible for disseminating modern farm technologies and advisory services through its network of research institutes and universities?

a) Indian Council of Agricultural Research (ICAR)

b) Food Corporation of India (FCI)

c) National Bank for Agriculture and Rural Development (NABARD

d) Central Institute for Cotton Research (CICR)

100. What is the role of State Agricultural Universities (SAUs) in extension services?

a) Planning and coordinating regional extension activities

b) Implementing government marketing programs

c) Providing financial assistance to farmers

d) Conducting research on new farming technologies

101. Which organizations under the Ministry of Commerce provide extension services for specific commodities?

a) State line department

b) Indian Council of Agricultural Research (ICAR)

c) Commodity boards

d) Marketing boards

102. Which type of organization is responsible for providing advisory services on marketing information to help farmers make informed decisions about selling their produce?
   a) State line department
   b) Indian Council of Agricultural Research (ICAR)
   c) Commodity boards
   d) Marketing boards

103. What is the main characteristic of private extension approach?
   a) Funding and delivery of extension services by private individuals or organizations
   b) Centralized control by the Ministry of Agriculture
   c) Free dissemination of information through various media channels
   d) Focus on public good and insurance against agricultural risks

104. Why is private extension becoming popular in some countries?
   a) To restrict the flow of information to paid members only
   b) To increase the economic burden on governments
   c) To provide free extension services to small and marginal farmers
   d) To reduce the burden on budget-starved public extension systems

105. What is one criticism of private extension services?
   a) Lack of relevance and effectiveness for farmers
   b) High involvement of input companies in technology transfer
   c) Limited availability in remote and difficult areas
   d) Overreliance on government funding

106. What are the reasons for the implementation of private extension services in India?
   a) Increasing involvement of NGOs in rural development programs
   b) Declining trend in government expenditure for extension services
   c) Focus on delivering sustainable agricultural practices
   d) Changing cropping pattern and emergence of contract farming

107. What is the main objective of private extension services?
   a) Maximizing profit for clients through advisory services
   b) Providing free and accessible services to all farmers
   c) Enhancing the role of government in extension activities
   d) Focusing on public goods and environmental sustainability

108. Which funding sources are commonly used in private extension?

a) Government grants and subsidies

b) Farmers' contributions and development agencies

c) Public-private partnerships and tax revenues

d) International aid and donations

109. What is a major advantage of NGO-based extension systems?

a) They provide free extension services to all farmers.

b) They have a strong network at the grassroots level.

c) They receive significant financial support from the government.

d) They have a hierarchical and centralized management structure.

110. Which characteristic is associated with NGO/VO-based extension systems?

a) Limited operation within a specific geographic area

b) Hierarchical and top-down decision-making approach

c) Focus on providing general extension services

d) Strong coordination with government extension agents

111. What role do NGOs play as field testers in agricultural extension?

a) They assist in the formation of local groups.

b) They innovate new technologies and methods.

c) They interact and network with other NGOs.

d) They conduct crop trials and research activities.

112. How do NGOs contribute to advocacy in agricultural development?

a) They provide financial support to marginalized farmers.

b) They focus on generating and supplying large-scale technologies.

c) They critically analyze government policies affecting the poor.

d) They partner with government organizations for joint projects.

113. What is the role of NGOs in empowerment?

a) They implement top-down development initiatives.

b) They work with marginalized groups to build capacity and control over livelihoods.

c) They focus on profitability and profit maximization for farmers.

d) They provide free extension services to resource-poor farmers.

114. What is the main objective of the Farmer Field School (FFS) extension approach?
    a) To reduce the dependency of farmers on pesticide usage
    b) To provide formal education to farmers
    c) To promote large-scale commercial farming practices
    d) To establish government-controlled learning centers for farmers

115. What is the typical duration of a Farmer Field School (FFS)?
    a) One day
    b) One month
    c) One crop growing season (typically 14 weeks)
    d) One year

116. Which of the following is a major advantage of the FFS based extension approach?
    a) High adoption rate and quick results
    b) Low program and travel costs
    c) Limited need for field extension personnel
    d) Encouragement of pesticide usage for crop protection

117. What is the primary role of extension workers in the FFS approach?
    a) To deliver lectures and teach farmers
    b) To act as facilitators and not as teachers
    c) To provide financial support to farmers
    d) To promote the use of pesticides in farming

118. What is the main characteristic of FFS educational methods?
    a) Experiential, participatory, and learner-centered
    b) Lecture-based and teacher-directed
    c) Technology-driven and top-down approach
    d) Hierarchical and centralized decision-making

119. What is the main objective of organizing farmers into specific producer groups or cooperatives?
    a) To provide agricultural inputs to farmers
    b) To promote collective production and marketing
    c) To regulate commodity prices in the market
    d) To enforce government regulations on farmers

120. Which type of farmer organization focuses on a specific commodity or activity, such as fruits, vegetables, or water management?

a) **Grower Associations**
b) User Associations
c) Farmer Interest Groups (FIGs)
d) Farmers' Clubs

121. Which organization is known for its role in marketing cooperatives for agricultural produce in India?

a) Indian Farmers Association
b) **National Agricultural Cooperative Marketing Federation of India (NAFED)**
c) Indian Farmers Fertilizer Cooperative Limited (IFFCO)
d) Agriculture Technology Management Agency (ATMA)

122. What is the main purpose of forming farmers' clubs?

a) To provide financial assistance to farmers for agricultural activities
b) **To promote awareness and mutual benefit among village farming communities**
c) To regulate banking services in rural areas
d) To facilitate government policies for farmers

123. What is the key characteristic of a farmer cooperative?

a) It is owned and controlled by government authorities.
b) It operates for entrepreneur profit and is not owned by farmers.
c) It provides economic services on a substantially unequal basis.
d) **It is owned and controlled on an equal basis by those for whom the service is rendered.**

124. What does PPP stand for in the context of extension services?

a) **Public-Private Partnership**
b) Producer-Producer Partnership
c) Public-Private Program
d) Partnership for Progressive Extension

125. What is the main objective of a PPP in extension services?

a) Maximizing profits for the private sector
b) Reducing the role of the public sector
c) **Enhancing the effectiveness and efficiency of extension services**
d) Excluding small-scale farmers from accessing services

126. Who are the primary partners involved in a PPP?
   a) Only the government and NGOs
   b) Only the private sector companies
   c) Both the public and private sectors
   d) Only the agricultural research institutes

127. What are some benefits of PPP in extension services?
   a) Increased accountability and transparency
   b) Improved access to resources and expertise
   c) Enhanced service delivery and innovation
   d) All of the above

128. Which model of funding and delivery under PPP involves private delivery and public finance?
   a) Public delivery and public finance
   b) Public delivery and private finance
   c) Private delivery and private finance
   d) Private delivery and public finance

129. What role does the private sector typically play in a PPP?
   a) Providing financial support to the public sector
   b) Implementing and delivering extension services
   c) Setting policy and strategic direction
   d) Conducting research and development activities

130. What is a potential challenge or disadvantage of PPP in extension services?
   a) Limited control over service delivery by the public sector
   b) Increased costs due to profit margins of private sector partners
   c) Exclusion of small-scale farmers from accessing services
   d) All of the above

131. What is the main characteristic of a pluralistic extension approach?
   a) It relies solely on public sector funding and delivery.
   b) It excludes NGOs and farmer's organizations.
   c) It combines both public and private actors in funding and delivery.
   d) It focuses exclusively on commercial production and marketing firms.

132. Which sector is NOT considered an actor in the pluralistic extension system?

a) Public sector
b) Private non-profit sector
c) Private for-profit sector
d) Academic institutions

133. What is the purpose of partnering in a pluralistic extension system?

a) To compete with other actors in the agricultural industry.
b) To establish a monopoly in the extension services market.
c) To promote collaboration and effectiveness among actors.
d) To reduce the influence of the public sector.

134. What is the principle of convergence in a pluralistic extension system?

a) It emphasizes the importance of location-specific approaches.
b) It advocates for a centralized decision-making process.
c) It encourages competition among different actors.
d) It focuses on maximizing profits for commercial firms.

135. Why has pluralistic extension become popular in some countries?

a) Due to the dominance of public extension organizations.
b) Because of the lack of resources and management constraints in public extension.
c) To exclude private for-profit sectors from the agricultural industry.
d) To eliminate the need for NGOs and farmer's organizations.

136. What is the main focus of a pluralistic extension approach?

a) Maximizing profits for commercial firms
b) Increasing the influence of the public sector
c) Improving cost reduction and labor productivity
d) Excluding NGOs and farmer's organizations

137. What is the main characteristic of corporate extension?

a) It is solely funded and delivered by public sector organizations.
b) It involves private corporate bodies in providing extension services.
c) It focuses exclusively on input firms.
d) It excludes consultancy firms and contracting firms.

138. Which of the following is NOT a category of private groups involved in corporate extension?

a) Input firms
b) Consultancy firms
c) Contracting firms
d) Public sector organizations

139. What is the role of input firms in corporate extension?
   a) They provide consultancy services to farmers.
   b) They contract with farmers to deliver extension services.
   c) They supply agricultural inputs to farmers.
   d) They fund and manage extension programs.

140. What is the main focus of consultancy firms in corporate extension?
   a) Providing agricultural inputs to farmers.
   b) Contracting with farmers for extension services.
   c) Offering specialized advisory services to farmers.
   d) Managing corporate farming operations.

141. What do contracting firms do in corporate extension?
   a) Provide input supplies to farmers.
   b) Deliver extension services directly to farmers.
   c) Consult with farmers on business strategies.
   d) Manage the operations of consultancy firms.

142. Which sector is primarily responsible for funding and managing corporate extension programs?
   a) Public sector organizations
   b) Input firms
   c) Consultancy firms
   d) Contracting firms

143. What is the key difference between corporate extension and other extension approaches?
   a) Corporate extension focuses solely on profit-making activities.
   b) It excludes the involvement of private sector organizations.
   c) Corporate extension is primarily funded by farmers themselves.
   d) It involves private corporate bodies in delivering extension services.

144. What does ATMA stand for?
   a) Agricultural Technology Management Agency
   b) Agricultural Training and Management Association
   c) Agricultural Technology and Extension Agency
   d) Agricultural Training and Extension Management

145. What is the main role of ATMA?
   a) Conducting research in agricultural technologies
   b) Managing agricultural training institutes
   c) Disseminating agricultural technologies at the district level
   d) Providing consultancy services to farmers

146. Which organization was responsible for training ATMA directors and extension staff during the initial phase of the project?
   a) SAMETI
   b) MANAGE
   c) KVKs
   d) NATP

147. What is the role of SAMETI in the ATMA model?
   a) Providing on-farm research services
   b) Conducting need-based training programs for extension staff
   c) Managing the operational funds of ATMA
   d) Promoting agricultural value-added technologies

148. What is the main function of KVKs in relation to ATMA?
   a) Providing consultancy services to ATMA
   b) Managing the day-to-day operations of ATMA
   c) Conducting on-farm research for ATMA projects
   d) Providing technical and research services to ATMA

149. Which organization acted as an apex training institute for capacity building of extension staff in each state?
   a) SAMETI
   b) MANAGE
   c) KVKs
   d) NATP

150. What is the objective of ATMA in terms of agricultural development?
   a) Conducting research on sustainable agricultural practices
   b) Integrating research and extension activities at the district level
   c) Providing consultancy services to farmers for project planning
   d) Establishing training institutes for agricultural extension staff

151. Which committee is responsible for the overall management of ATMA at the district level?
   a) Governing Board (GB)
   b) Farmer Advisory Committee (FAC)
   c) Block Technology Team (BTT)
   d) Farmer Interest Groups (FIGS)

152. Which committee is responsible for providing advisory support and feedback to ATMA at the district level?
   a) Governing Board (GB)
   b) Farmer Advisory Committee (FAC)
   c) Block Technology Team (BTT)
   d) Farmer Interest Groups (FIGS)

153. Which committee is responsible for coordinating and implementing technology-related activities at the block level?
   a) Governing Board (GB)
   b) Farmer Advisory Committee (FAC)
   c) Block Technology Team (BTT)
   d) Farmer Interest Groups (FIGS)

154. Which committee is responsible for representing the interests and needs of farmers at the village level?
   a) Governing Board (GB)
   b) Farmer Advisory Committee (FAC)
   c) Block Technology Team (BTT)
   d) Farmer Interest Groups (FIGS)

155. Which committee is responsible for setting program priorities, policies, and procedures of operation of ATMA at the district level?
   a) ATMA Management Committee (AMC)
   b) Farmer Advisory Committee (FAC)
   c) Governing Board (GB)
   d) Block Technology Team (BTT)

156. Who is the chairman of the ATMA Governing Board?
   a) Project Director (PD of ATMA)
   b) District Collector/Magistrate
   c) Head of Research Institutes
   d) Farmer Representatives

157. Which committee is responsible for planning and reviewing day-to-day activities of ATMA?
   a) ATMA Management Committee (AMC)
   b) Farmer Advisory Committee (FAC)
   c) Governing Board (GB)
   d) Block Technology Team (BTT)

158. Which committee is responsible for coordinating the execution of annual work plans among various line departments, KVKS, NGOs, and FIGS?

   a) ATMA Management Committee (AMC)

   b) Farmer Advisory Committee (FAC)

   c) Governing Board (GB)

   d) Block Technology Team (BTT)

159. What is the role of the Farm Information and Advisory Centre (FIAC) in ATMA?

   a) Prepare Block Action Plans (BAPs)

   b) Implement the Strategic Research and Extension Plan (SREP)

   c) Coordinate extension activities at the block level

   d) Provide feedback to the Farmer Advisory Committee (FAC)

160. Which committee advises the Block Technology Team (BTT) on extension priorities and reviews and approves the Block Action Plan (BAP)?

   a) ATMA Management Committee (AMC)

   b) Farmer Advisory Committee (FAC)

   c) Governing Board (GB)

   d) Block Technology Team (BTT)

161. What is the purpose of the Strategic Research and Extension Plan (SREP) in ATMA?

   a) Allocate annual funds to carry out research and extension activities

   b) Identify problems and constraints faced by farmers

   c) Set program priorities and extension strategies for the district

   d) Provide technical support to farmers' organizations

162. Which component of ATMA reforms emphasizes the importance of research entities from ICAR and SAUS in contributing to research priorities?

   a) Research system reforms

   b) Policy reform

   c) Organizational and structural refinements

   d) Communications strategy reform

163. What is the purpose of moving from decentralization to devolution in ATMA?

a) **To involve Panchayati Raj institutions in monitoring extension services**

b) To centralize decision-making in extension activities

c) To increase the involvement of private bodies in extension services

d) To improve research-extension linkages

164. Which reform in ATMA focuses on improving convergence at both the district and state levels?

a) Moving from decentralization to devolution

b) Improving implementation flexibility and innovation

c) **Allowing implementation flexibility and innovation to reach the unreached**

d) Improving accountability for better research-extension linkages

165. What is the basis for choosing the lead department in ATMA at the district level?

a) **Agro-ecology of the district**

b) Contribution of various commodities to the district economy

c) Availability of human resources

d) Research priorities of SAUS and ICAR institutions

166. Which reform in ATMA emphasizes the importance of public-private partnerships in extension advice and delivery?

a) Reform in human resource development policy

b) **Emphasis on public-private partnerships**

c) Communications strategy reform

d) Financial sustainability

167. What is the focus of the communications strategy reform in ATMA?

a) **Use of ICT in reaching farmers**

b) Long-term financing strategy

c) Monitoring and evaluation framework

d) Human resource development policy

168. What is the shift in focus in the monitoring and evaluation framework reform in ATMA?

a) From research-extension linkages to policy reforms

b) From decentralization to devolution

c) From activity monitoring to evaluating outcomes

d) From public to private sector involvement

169. What does AKIS stand for in the context of agriculture?

a) Agricultural Knowledge and Innovation System

b) Agricultural Knowledge and Information System

c) Agricultural Knowledge and Integration System

d) Agricultural Knowledge and Implementation System

170. What is the basic premise of AKIS?

a) Research and extension should be seen as separate institutions

b) Farmers should be excluded from the knowledge generation process

c) Scientists and extension agents should work together in a single system

d) Knowledge and information processes are not essential for farming

171. Which of the following is NOT a component of AKIS?

a) Farmers

b) Agricultural educators

c) Researchers

d) Financial institutions

172. What is the importance of information input from external sources in AKIS?

a) It enhances the capacity of the system to generate knowledge

b) It hinders the development of small-scale farmers

c) It eliminates the need for social organization among farmers

d) It creates barriers to agricultural development

173. What is a linkage mechanism in the context of AKIS?

a) A device that operationalizes the interface between components

b) A concrete procedure for generating knowledge

c) A specialized software used for knowledge storage

d) An arrangement for financial transactions within the system

174. What are MOOCs in the context of AKIS?
    a) Methods of Overcoming Obstacles in Crop farming
    b) Modules for Optimizing Organic Crop Systems
    c) Massive Open Online Courses
    d) Models for Organizing Online Collaborations

175. What is the purpose of an information kiosk in AKIS?
    a) To provide public internet access
    b) To facilitate visitor check-in processes
    c) To offer financial services to customers
    d) To improve knowledge and information sharing

176. Indigenous Technical Knowledge (ITK) refers to:
    a) Knowledge generated by universities and research institutions
    b) The local knowledge unique to a given culture or society
    c) Intellectual Property Rights (IPR) managed by indigenous communities
    d) Knowledge that is limited to traditional practices only

177. Indigenous agricultural practices (IAPs) are:
    a) Written records of traditional farming methods
    b) Modern technologies used by indigenous communities
    c) Codified knowledge shared among indigenous populations
    d) An unwritten body of knowledge based on tradition and experience

178. Indigenous knowledge systems are dynamic and influenced by:
    a) Internal creativity and experimentation
    b) International trade agreements
    c) Technological advancements
    d) Universities and research institutions

179. Indigenous Technical Knowledge (ITK) is concerned with:
    a) Developing modern agricultural technologies
    b) Theories and perceptions of nature and culture
    c) Actual application of local people's thinking in agriculture and allied areas
    d) Record-keeping and formal documentation of indigenous practices

180. What makes Indigenous Technical Knowledge (ITK) hard to formalize and communicate?
   a) It is deeply rooted in its environment
   b) It is recorded in written documents
   c) It is similar to scientific knowledge
   d) It is exclusive to indigenous communities

181. Intellectual Property Management (IPM) aims to:
   a) Reduce international trade and tariffs
   b) Protect traditional knowledge from external influences
   c) Ensure financial security and stability
   d) Manage and protect intellectual property rights

182. GATT (General Agreement on Trade and Tariffs) was initiated in:
   a) 1947 b) 1995
   c) 2000 d) 2010

183. The WTO (World Trade Organization) has its headquarters in:
   a) Washington D.C., USA b) New York, USA
   c) Geneva, Switzerland d) London, UK

184. Under WTO obligations, each member country must provide a minimum level of protection to:
   a) Indigenous Technical Knowledge (ITK)
   b) Traditional cultural practices
   c) Intellectual Property Rights (IPRs)
   d) Foreign trade and investments

185. The TRIPS (Trade-Related Aspects of Intellectual Property Rights) agreement covers the minimum standards for the protection of:
   a) Plant varieties and agricultural practices
   b) Traditional knowledge and indigenous practices
   c) Copyrights, trademarks, geographical indications, industrial designs, and patents
   d) Intellectual property rights for pharmaceuticals only

186. Copyrights and related rights are required to be protected for a minimum term of:
   a) 10 years b) 20 years
   c) 50 years d) 100 years

187. Geographical Indication (GI) protection aims to prevent the use of any means that suggests a good originates from a specific:

a) Country
b) City
c) Village
d) Geographical area

188. The Geographical Indication of Goods (Registration & Protection) Act, 1999 was enacted in India to provide better protection to:

a) Copyrights
b) Trademarks
c) Industrial designs
d) Geographical indications

189. Indian patent laws currently provide for protection of:

a) Both product and process patents
b) Only product patents
c) Only process patents
d) Neither product nor process patents

190. Under WTO obligations, inventions in all fields of technology shall be patentable if they meet the tests of being:

a) Novel, involving an inventive step, and having industrial application
b) Novel, involving a creative idea, and benefiting society
c) Unique, non-obvious, and marketable
d) Advanced, feasible, and commercially viable

191. The protection of independently created new or original industrial designs is required under WTO obligations, excluding designs dictated by:

a) Aesthetic considerations
b) Technical or functional considerations
c) Traditional practices
d) Government regulations

192. Layout designs of integrated circuits are granted protection for a term of:

a) 5 years
b) 10 years
c) 20 years
d) 50 years

193. Indigenous Technical Knowledge (ITK) contrasts with scientific knowledge systems on:

a) Contextual grounds
b) Methodological and epistemological grounds
c) Substantive grounds
d) All of the above

194. ITK is characterized as explicit or codified knowledge that is:
   a) Exclusive to indigenous communities
   b) Personal and content-specific
   c) Transmittable in formal, systematic language
   d) Rooted in modern technologies

195. Which of the following refers to a cognitive structure in which theories and perceptions of nature and culture are conceptualized?
   a) Indigenous Knowledge (IK)
   b) Indigenous Technical Knowledge (ITK)
   c) Intellectual Property Management (IPM)
   d) Indigenous Knowledge System (IKS)

196. ITK represents the information base for a society and facilitates:
   a) Financial stability and growth
   b) Communication and decision making
   c) International trade agreements
   d) Collaboration with research institutions

197. The ITK that can be expressed in words and numbers represents:
   a) The entirety of the indigenous people's knowledge
   b) The minimum standards required by WTO obligations
   c) Only a small portion of the entire body of knowledge possessed by the indigenous people
   d) The knowledge shared between indigenous communities

198. Under WTO obligations, each member country must provide a minimum level of protection to which of the following?
   a) Traditional cultural practices
   b) Intellectual Property Rights (IPRs)
   c) Environmental sustainability practices
   d) Health and safety regulations

199. Under Indian patent laws, currently, which type of patents are not provided for?
   a) Product patents
   b) Process patents
   c) Both product and process patents
   d) Neither product nor process patents

200. What does FAO define gender as in relation to men and women?

a) The physical differences between men and women

b) The roles and responsibilities of men and women in society

c) The perceptual and material relationship between men and women

d) The division of labor between men and women in farming

201. What is the term used to describe the significantly high and growing population of female-headed households in agriculture?

a) Gender budgeting

b) Feminization of agriculture

c) Gender analysis

d) Access to resources

202. How many hours, on average, do women in agriculture spend on agriculture and allied activities each day?

a) 5-6 hours

b) 8-9 hours

c) 12-13 hours

d) 15-16 hours

203. Lack of access to land, credit, training, extension, and marketing facilities are common constraints faced by:

a) Men farmers

b) Wealthy farmers

c) Rural women

d) Government institutions

204. What is a major obstacle for women to increase their contributions and benefits in agriculture?

a) Lack of access to credit

b) Lack of support services

c) Lack of adequate training

d) Lack of access to land or insecure tenure

205. What does gender analysis examine?

a) The overall economic situation of men and women

b) The specific activities and conditions of men in agriculture

c) The specific activities, conditions, needs, and access to resources of men and women

d) The access to development benefits and decision-making of men and women

206. Biotechnology in farming has been critical for enhancing:
   a) Traditional farming practices
   b) Crop and livestock production
   c) Manual labor in agriculture
   d) Gender equality in farming

207. Which technology is recognized for increasing cotton yield in farming?
   a) Green Revolution technology
   b) Bio-fortification technology
   c) Mycorrhia technology
   d) BT cotton technology

208. What is the role of bio-fortification technology in nutrition management?
   a) Enhancing crop protection
   b) Increasing crop yield
   c) Combating malnutrition through food and fodder
   d) Improving soil fertility

209. Which of the following technologies promotes increased yield of a crop called Samba Mashuri?
   a) Bovine rhinotracheitis (IBR) vaccine
   b) Mycorrhia technology
   c) BLB resistant Samba Mashuri (RP-Bio 22)
   d) Rhizobium technologies

210. What is the main focus of gender budgeting in agriculture?
   a) Enhancing crop yield and productivity
   b) Promoting gender equality through restructuring revenues and expenditure
   c) Providing financial support to farmers
   d) Improving access to land and resources for women

211. Which of the following is NOT a common constraint faced by rural women in agriculture?
   a) Lack of access to land
   b) Lack of access to credit and financial institutions
   c) Lack of support services like child care and maternity care
   d) Lack of access to social services for consumption

212. Which technology in agriculture is used for nutrition management to combat malnutrition?
   a) Bio-fortification technology
   b) Mycorrhia technology
   c) Rhizobium technologies
   d) BT cotton technology

213. Which of the following livestock species is traditionally owned by women in many societies?
   a) Cattle
   b) Poultry
   c) Goats
   d) Buffalo

214. The responsibility for animals kept at the homestead is typically the domain of:
   a) Men
   b) Women
   c) Children
   d) Elderly people

215. Which technology is used for increasing cattle yield in farming?
   a) Green Revolution technology
   b) BT cotton technology
   c) Mycorrhia technology
   d) Bovine rhinotracheitis (IBR) vaccine

216. What is one of the major issues associated with the use of rDNA technology in agriculture?
   a) Breakdown of natural species boundaries
   b) Violating environmental ethics
   c) Disturbing religious and cultural beliefs
   d) Increasing social divide

217. Which of the following is NOT a potential environmental risk posed by transgenic crops?
   a) Herbicide resistance in weeds
   b) Production of environmental toxins
   c) Development of beneficial insect populations
   d) Unintentional gene transfer to other plants

218. What is the term used for the development of weed resistance due to the repeated use of a single herbicide on a crop?
   a) Herbicide immunity
   b) Pest adaptation
   c) Resistance accumulation
   d) Herbicide resistance

219. Which of the following was NOT a concern related to GM food and human health?
   a) Development of allergenic properties in soybeans
   b) Toxic effects of glyphosate on non-target beneficial species
   c) Risk of cancer in humans from using glyphosate
   d) Accumulation of environmental toxins in fruits and tubers

220. Which role of extension agents is critical for coordinating various actors within the rural sector to address climate change issues?
   a) Technology demonstrations
   b) Capacity development
   c) Coordination
   d) Investment in research and extension

221. What is one way in which extension can help farmers adapt to climate change?
   a) Promoting monoculture farming
   b) Introducing high-risk technologies
   c) Developing new crop varieties
   d) Using more chemical inputs

222. Extension agents can help in changing farmers' attitudes and values towards climate change by providing:
   a) Financial incentives
   b) Government regulations
   c) Climate education and information
   d) Punishments for non-compliance

223. One of the issues related to public investment in extension is:
   a) Lack of funding for agricultural research
   b) Low investment in environmental education
   c) Disparity in allocation of resources by region
   d) Overuse of external inputs in agriculture

224. The average rate of return from investment in extension was approximately:
   a) 14% b) 48%
   c) 56% **d) 75%**

225. What is one potential environmental consequence of the indiscriminate use of inputs in agriculture?
    a) Increased crop yields
    b) Enhanced soil fertility
    c) Threat to natural resources and pest resistance
    d) Reduced need for extension services

226. The development of transgenic crops may violate ethical boundaries related to:
    a) Cultural diversity
    b) Species boundaries and natural kinds
    c) Food safety regulations
    d) Emotional reactions to biotech products

227. Which of the following is NOT a potential issue related to the use of terminator technology?
    a) Destruction of the gene-pool
    b) Dependence on outside sources for seed
    c) Decreased social divide among farmers
    d) Loss of farmer-saved seed

228. What is the main concern regarding the use of bromoxynil pesticide in Bt crops?
    a) It causes birth defects in laboratory animals
    b) It has toxic effects on non-target beneficial species
    c) It alters soil biology and reduces nitrogen fixation
    d) It poses hazards to farmers and farm workers

229. In India, which movement is famous for forest conservation, particularly the protection of trees?
    a) Narmada Bachao Andolan
    b) Chipko movement
    c) Green Revolution movement
    d) Anti-GM crop movement

230. The investment in agricultural research and extension should ideally be what percentage of Ag GDP in a developing country?
    a) 0.09%
    b) 0.14%
    c) 0.22%
    d) 1%

231. Which model of environmental education warrants action-based method of ecological learning?

a) Cognitive model
b) Ecopedagogy
c) Cognitive-experimental model
d) Emotive model

232. What is one potential consequence of the overuse of external inputs like fertilizers and plant protection chemicals in agriculture?

a) Increased productivity and yield
b) Enhanced biodiversity in the ecosystem
c) Threat to natural resources and pest resistances
d) Decreased need for eco-friendly production technologies

233. Which model of environmental education criticizes the socio-economic system?

a) Cognitive-experimental model
b) Cognitive model
c) Emotive model
d) Ecopedagogy

3

Foundational Ideas and Values of Agricultural Extension Education

1. Extension Education is an interdisciplinary applied social science that primarily focuses on:
   a) Engineering practices
   b) Medical advancements
   c) Vocational training
   d) Political science
2. Which countries have the greatest relevance for Extension Education?
   a) Developed and industrialized countries
   b) African countries
   c) European countries
   d) Developing and underdeveloped countries
3. When was the Community Development Programme launched in India?
   a) 2 October 1947
   b) 2 October 1952
   c) 15 August 1947
   d) 15 August 1952
4. What was the name given to the extension program extended to the entire country in India?
   a) National Agricultural Program
   b) Agricultural Development Scheme
   c) National Extension Service
   d) Community Improvement Program
5. The main motto of Extension Education is to improve:
   a) Political participation
   b) Academic achievements
   c) Socio-economic well-being and living standards
   d) Environmental conservation

Bold Means Correct Answer

6. Extension Education aims to bring about planned behavioral changes that encompass:
   a) Knowledge, skill, and attitude
   b) Physical strength and agility
   c) Religious beliefs and practices
   d) Artistic creativity and expression

7. Objectives in Extension Education are categorized into:
   a) Basic objectives and specific objectives
   b) Fundamental objectives and general objectives
   c) Broad objectives and specific objectives
   d) Primary objectives and secondary objectives

8. The basic objective of Extension Education for any nation is to:
   a) Achieve self-sufficiency in food production
   b) Attain global dominance in agricultural exports
   c) Improve literacy rates among farmers
   d) Establish a strong political presence in the international community

9. Specific objectives in Extension Education:
   a) Refer to specific components of a broad objective
   b) Focus only on the agricultural sector
   c) Are unrelated to the overall objectives
   d) Are determined by international organizations

10. Which of the following is an example of a broad objective in Extension Education?
   a) Promoting drip/sprinkler irrigation
   b) Establishing food processing centers
   c) Achieving self-sufficiency in food production
   d) Developing new varieties under major food crops

11. Under the broad objective of achieving self-sufficiency in food production, a specific objective could be:
   a) Enhancing environmental conservation efforts
   b) Expanding urban infrastructure
   c) Strengthening subsidy for fertilizer usage
   d) Encouraging tourism in rural areas

12. Specific objectives in Extension Education address:
    a) Overall objectives of unrelated fields
    b) Environmental concerns only
    c) Components/items of broad objectives
    d) Political challenges in the agricultural sector

13. The principle of need and interest in Extension Education emphasizes:
    a) Addressing immediate necessities of people
    b) Focusing on un-felt needs of individuals
    c) Ignoring the interests of the target audience
    d) Considering cultural diversity in extension programs

14. Extension Education adopts a whole family approach to:
    a) Exclude certain family members based on age or gender
    b) Promote gender equality in agricultural practices
    c) Involve all family members in the family profession or enterprise
    d) Provide special benefits to elderly family members

15. The principle of continuous education process in Extension Education emphasizes that:
    a) Extension activities should be time-bound and have fixed deadlines
    b) Resources and demands in the agricultural sector are static
    c) Extension education should adapt to dynamic problems and solutions
    d) Extension workers should only focus on short-term goals

16. The principle of flexibility in Extension Education is necessary because:
    a) Nature and agriculture are constantly changing
    b) Extension activities should be rigidly planned and structured
    c) Human elements demand strict adherence to schedules
    d) Extension workers should avoid accommodating unforeseen circumstances

17. The principle of cultural difference in Extension Education emphasizes:
    a) Promoting cultural assimilation among diverse communities
    b) Discouraging indigenous practices in favor of modern techniques
    c) Respecting and maintaining cultural diversity of individuals
    d) Ignoring cultural beliefs and traditions in extension programs

18. The principle of grassroots approach in Extension Education means that:
    a) Extension work should start at the national level and trickle down to individuals
    b) Extension activities should be exclusively based on urban communities
    c) Programs should be developed based on local people's preferences
    d) Extension workers should prioritize high-level stakeholders over local communities

19. The principle of indigenous technical knowledge in Extension Education emphasizes:
    a) Discarding traditional practices in favor of new technology
    b) Promoting the use of modern technology without considering local knowledge
    c) Encouraging the preservation and utilization of local knowledge
    d) Belittling the value of indigenous practices in agriculture

20. The principle of learning by doing in Extension Education suggests that:
    a) Extension workers should rely solely on theoretical knowledge
    b) People should be convinced through result demonstrations
    c) Extension activities should be conducted in a lecture-based format
    d) Individuals should be discouraged from practical involvement

21. The principle of voluntary participation in Extension Education means that:
    a) Extension programs should be mandatory for the target audience
    b) People should be forced to participate in extension activities
    c) Extension workers should motivate people to participate willingly
    d) Individuals should be rewarded for participating in extension programs

22. The principle of leadership in Extension Education focuses on:
    a) Discouraging the development of leadership qualities among individuals
    b) Promoting the involvement of opinion leaders in agricultural technologies
    c) Ensuring top-down decision-making in extension activities
    d) Excluding leaders from the extension education process

23. The principle of co-operation in Extension Education emphasizes:

a) Encouraging individuals to work in isolation

b) Promoting competition among farmers

c) Developing mutual support and shared ideas among people

d) Ignoring the need for collaboration with stakeholders

24. The principle of adaptability in Extension Education suggests that:

a) Extension workers should rigidly adhere to standard recommendations

b) Extension programs should be resistant to change

c) Recommendations should be adaptable to local situations and needs

d) Local situations should be disregarded in extension activities

25. The principle of integrated farming system and sustainability in Extension Education emphasizes:

a) Focusing solely on crop production for sustainability

b) Promoting specialization in a single farming enterprise

c) Integrating multiple aspects of farming for sustainable livelihoods

d) Ignoring the importance of sustainability in agricultural practices

26. The principle of ICT promotion and usage in Extension Education highlights the importance of:

a) Minimizing the use of technology in extension activities

b) Restricting access to Information and Communication Technology (ICT)

c) Utilizing ICT to provide professional messages for farmers

d) Discouraging the use of modern technology in agriculture

27. The principle of self-help groups in Extension Education focuses on:

a) Excluding community participation in extension programs

b) Restricting the role of local communities in decision-making

c) Strengthening and expanding self-help groups for wider impact

d) Eliminating the need for collective action and support

28. The principle of satisfaction in Extension Education emphasizes that:
    a) The ultimate goal is financial profit for farmers
    b) Extension workers should prioritize their own satisfaction
    c) Continued participation and involvement are ensured through satisfaction
    d) Extension programs should solely focus on meeting basic needs

29. The principle of evaluation in Extension Education is important for:
    a) Setting objectives in extension programs
    b) Monitoring progress and making improvements
    c) Eliminating the need for future planning
    d) Ignoring the impact of extension activities

30. The philosophy of Extension Education is primarily focused on:
    a) Providing financial support to farmers
    b) Imparting theoretical knowledge to individuals
    c) Helping people to help themselves
    d) Promoting dependency on extension workers

31. The philosophy of Extension Education aims to teach people:
    a) What to think and how to think
    b) What to believe and what not to believe
    c) How to think and not what to think
    d) How to follow specific guidelines and instructions

32. The success of Extension Education philosophy is reflected in:
    a) Proverbs and sayings about the importance of farmers
    b) Financial prosperity of extension workers
    c) Government policies on agricultural development
    d) Technological advancements in the agricultural sector

33. Extension education aims to build a strong bond among:
    a) Farmers and extension workers only
    b) Farmers and government officials
    c) All stakeholders in agricultural development
    d) Local communities and international organizations

34. The knowledge generated by extension workers contributes to:
   a) Personal growth and development of extension professionals
   b) Academic research and publications
   c) Strengthening the philosophy of extension education
   d) Implementation of government policies

35. In a democratic setup, the philosophy of extension education emphasizes:
   a) Fulfilling the desires of individuals without planning
   b) Ignoring the needs of people in the decision-making process
   c) Considering people's needs and fulfilling them in a planned manner
   d) Imposing regulations and restrictions on agricultural practices

36. According to the Chinese proverb mentioned, the philosophy of extension education focuses on:
   a) Providing direct assistance to individuals in need
   b) Encouraging self-sufficiency and independence
   c) Promoting reliance on government support
   d) Discouraging individuals from learning new skills

37. The philosophy of extension education has produced great leaders in the country who:
   a) Follow strict guidelines and instructions
   b) Rely on external assistance for their success
   c) Embrace the principles of self-help and empowerment
   d) Reject the importance of agricultural development

38. What is teaching?
   a) A process of self-activity
   b) A process of guided interaction
   c) A process of acquiring knowledge
   d) A process of behavioral change

39. Learning is defined as:
   a) A process of self-activity
   b) A process of guided interaction
   c) A process of acquiring knowledge
   d) A process of behavioral change

40. According to the teaching-learning process, effective teaching requires coordination between:

a) The teacher and the learner only

b) The teacher and the subject matter only

c) The teacher, the learner, and the subject matter

d) The learner and the subject matter only

41. What qualities should an instructor have for effective teaching?

a) Knowledge, enthusiasm, and good communication skills

b) Patience, discipline, and strictness

c) Authority, dominance, and control

d) Introversion, passivity, and lack of enthusiasm

42. What qualities should learners possess in the teaching-learning process?

a) Eagerness to acquire knowledge and interest

b) Passive listening and disinterest

c) Dependence on the instructor for all information

d) Lack of motivation and capability to learn

43. What should the subject matter in teaching be like?

a) Irrelevant and outdated

b) Well-organized and presented clearly

c) Complex and confusing

d) Isolated from the overall objectives

44. What should be the characteristics of physical facilities for effective teaching?

a) Outside distractions and uncomfortable temperature

b) Poor lighting and seating discomfort

c) Good air circulation and comfortable temperature

d) Limited space and inadequate equipment

45. What should be the characteristics of teaching equipment?

a) Availability and skillful handling

b) Inaccessibility and limited usage

c) Outdated and irrelevant

d) Expensive and complex

46. Which type of education is highly institutionalized and follows a hierarchical structure?

a) **Formal education**
b) Informal education
c) Nonformal education
d) Lifelong education

47. Which type of education is acquired through daily experiences and exposure to the environment?

a) Formal education
b) **Informal education**
c) Nonformal education
d) Lifelong education

48. Which type of education is organized outside of the formal education system and targets specific subgroups?

a) Formal education
b) Informal education
c) **Nonformal education**
d) Lifelong education

49. What are the key elements involved in a non-formal education situation?

a) Learner, physical facilities, instructor, subject matter, and teaching equipment
b) **Learner, facilitator, physical facilities, instructor, and subject matter**
c) Learner, teacher, books, curriculum, and examinations
d) Learner, technology, laboratories, research, and projects

50. What is the role of flexibility in non-formal education?

a) **Flexibility allows for personalized learning experiences**
b) Flexibility restricts the learning process
c) Flexibility eliminates the need for planning
d) Flexibility is not relevant in non-formal education

51. In a non-formal education situation, who acts as a catalyst and organizes educational activities?

a) Learner
b) Instructor
c) **Facilitator**
d) Administrator

52. Which type of education includes vocational training and adult education?

a) Formal education
b) Informal education
c) **Nonformal education**
d) Lifelong education

53. Which type of education encompasses learning throughout one's life?
    a) Formal education
    b) Informal education
    c) Nonformal education
    d) Lifelong education

54. The scope of extension education includes:
    a) Achieving self-sufficiency in food production
    b) Promoting entrepreneurship development
    c) Improving marketing strategies
    d) All of the above

55. Extension education can play a vital role in:
    a) Educating rural masses on community resources
    b) Enhancing standard of living among rural masses
    c) Achieving sustainability of farming systems
    d) All of the above

56. The scope of communication in extension education is to:
    a) Achieve self-sufficiency in food production
    b) Educate rural masses on community resources
    c) Communicate technologies for primary and secondary agriculture
    d) Promote entrepreneurship development

57. Primary agriculture refers to:
    a) Cultivation of crop plants for crop production
    b) Value addition and processing of food products
    c) Achieving sustainability of farming systems
    d) Promoting climate and environment-related technologies

58. Secondary agriculture refers to:
    a) Achieving self-sufficiency in food production
    b) Promoting entrepreneurship development
    c) Value addition and processing of food products
    d) Educating rural masses on community resources

59. Extension education plays a role in:
    a) Achieving sustainability of farming systems
    b) Improving marketing strategies
    c) Educating rural masses on community resources
    d) All of the above

60. The scope of extension education is important in achieving progress in:

a) USA b) India

c) African continent **d) All of the above**

61. What is the role of agricultural extension in technological upgradation?

a) Providing advisory services to farmers

b) Ensuring timely input supply

c) Implementing supportive and welfare programs

d) Maintaining natural resource base

62. Which component of agricultural development involves strengthening co-operatives and establishing linkages with financial institutions?

a) Technological upgradation

b) Infrastructure development

c) Promoting mechanization

d) Extending market and processing facilities

63. In the context of contingent planning, what does "gambling with monsoon" refer to?

a) Predicting rainfall accurately

b) Relying on rainfall for agricultural production

c) Developing crop insurance policies

d) Implementing drought management strategies

64. What is the role of agricultural extension in maintaining the natural resource base?

a) Educating rural masses to conserve resources

b) Providing timely input supply to farmers

c) Promoting interests of small and marginal farmers

d) Ensuring ecological balance

65. How does agricultural extension contribute to the maintenance of ecological balance?

a) By promoting interests of small and marginal farmers

b) By providing advisory services to farmers

c) By supporting technology upgradation

d) By focusing on climate change issues

66. What is the role of agricultural extension in rural development?
    a) Providing urban amenities to rural areas
    b) Promoting mechanization in agriculture
    c) Upgrading technological competence of farmers
    d) Implementing supportive and welfare programs

67. Which program aims to attract and retain youth in agriculture?
    a) PURA
    b) ARYA
    c) Smith Lever Act
    d) Attracting Rural Youth

68. What is the objective of the PURA program?
    a) Increasing income of farm youth
    b) Providing urban amenities to rural areas
    c) Resolving rural population issues effectively
    d) Implementing programs through Krishi Vigyan Kendras

69. Which of the following is a general function of agricultural extension education?
    a) Identifying farmers' needs and interests
    b) Providing feedback to researchers
    c) Prompt supply of agricultural inputs
    d) Attending operations on time

70. What is one of the specific functions of extension workers?
    a) Creating social awareness among members of society
    b) Deciding the needs of farmers in consultation with them
    c) Attending to their works on time
    d) Enhancing knowledge level of farming community

71. What is one of the educational functions of extension education?
    a) Identifying problems in agriculture
    b) Ensuring prompt supply of agricultural inputs
    c) Spreading importance of value education
    d) Implementing welfare programs

72. Which function of extension education involves addressing social, political, cultural, and spiritual aspects?
    a) General functions
    b) Specific functions
    c) Educational functions
    d) Contingent planning

73. What is the aim of the educational function of extension education?

a) To enhance knowledge level of farming community

b) To create social awareness among members of society

c) To provide feedback to researchers

d) To address problems related to law and order

74. Which function of extension education involves maintaining a data base on different crop/livestock/subsidiary enterprises?

a) General functions

b) Specific functions

c) Educational functions

d) Contingent planning

75. What is one of the specific functions of extension workers related to agricultural inputs?

a) Building rapport among the clientele group

b) Sharing market information with farming community

c) Ensuring stocking and prompt supply of agricultural inputs

d) Standing for what they commit

76. Which function of extension education involves implementing welfare programs?

a) General functions **b) Specific functions**

c) Educational functions d) Contingent planning

77. What is the difference between extension education and agricultural extension?

a) Extension education is a non-formal system of education, while agricultural extension focuses specifically on farmers.

b) Extension education provides information and skills for various vocations, while agricultural extension focuses solely on agriculture.

c) Extension education is organized and has a flexible curriculum, while agricultural extension has a fixed syllabus.

d) Extension education is focused on improving living standards, while agricultural extension aims to improve productivity and production.

78. What is the difference between transfer of technology and extension service?

a) **Transfer of technology involves transferring technologies from research institutions, while extension service refers to services provided by extension agencies.**

b) Transfer of technology focuses on reaching end users (farmers), while extension service focuses on providing advisory and consultancy services.

c) Transfer of technology is carried out by development departments, while extension service is provided by universities and research institutions.

d) Transfer of technology ensures the availability of seeds, fertilizers, and plant protection chemicals, while extension service focuses on market and credit guidance.

79. What is the difference between rural development and community development?

a) **Rural development focuses on infrastructure and institution development, while community development focuses on addressing common problems.**

b) Rural development refers to changes in socio-economic conditions, while community development refers to tackling problems at different levels.

c) Rural development involves growth combined with qualitative changes, while community development involves working together in a social system.

d) Rural development addresses problems at the village level, while community development addresses problems at the national level.

80. What is the difference between rural extension and urban extension?

a) Rural extension focuses on crop cultivation and livestock, while urban extension focuses on scientific cultivation and waste management.

b) Rural extension addresses problems related to farms, while urban extension addresses problems related to household gardens.

c) **Rural extension is carried out in rural areas, while urban extension is carried out in urban areas.**

d) Rural extension covers micro enterprise development, while urban extension covers hi-tech agriculture and allied sectors.

81. What is the difference between farm extension and agro-eco tourism extension (AETE)?

a) **Farm extension focuses on problems related to crops and livestock, while AETE focuses on promoting planned visits to rural areas.**

b) Farm extension provides information and solutions for farming enterprises, while AETE promotes interest in agriculture among urban people.

c) Farm extension is carried out in rural areas, while AETE is gaining momentum in urban areas.

d) Farm extension addresses the needs of full-time farmers, while AETE addresses the needs of part-time farmers.

82. What is the first step in the Extension Education process?

a) Setting objectives based on felt needs

b) Gathering facts and analyzing the situation

c) Teaching and dissemination of information

d) Evaluation of the educational process

83. What should the objectives in Extension Education be based on?

a) General knowledge and information

b) Long-term goals of the extension worker

c) Felt needs of the people

d) Available resources and materials

84. What is the focus of the teaching step in Extension Education?

a) Evaluating the outcomes and results

b) Setting SMART objectives

c) Gathering facts and analyzing the situation

d) Providing appropriate teaching methods and content

85. What is the purpose of evaluation in the Extension Education process?

a) Gathering facts and analyzing the situation

b) Setting objectives based on felt needs

c) Determining the extent of achievement of set objectives

d) Reconsidering the outcome and making future plans

86. What is the final step in the Extension Education process?

a) Gathering facts and analyzing the situation

b) Setting objectives based on felt needs

c) Teaching and dissemination of information

d) Reconsidering the outcome and making future plans

87. What is the relationship between teaching and learning?

a) Teaching and learning are unrelated processes

b) Teaching is the process of learning

c) Learning is the process of teaching

d) Teaching and learning are interconnected processes

88. How is learning defined?

a) The process of informing people

b) The intentional purposeful process of transforming individuals

c) The progressive behavior adaptation through individual efforts

d) The arrangement of situations to bring about desired changes

89. What is the role of teaching in the teaching-learning process?

a) To inform individuals about important things

b) To transform individuals and bring about desired changes

c) To develop interest and desire in learners

d) To adapt behavior through experiences

90. What is the purpose of the teaching-learning process?

a) To promote action in learners

b) To inform individuals about important things

c) To develop learners' interest and desire

d) To arrange situations for behavior adaptation

91. How are teaching and learning related?

a) Teaching is the process of learning

b) Learning is the process of teaching

c) Teaching and learning are unrelated processes

d) Teaching and learning are interconnected processes

92. Which principle of learning states that individuals learn best when they are physically, mentally, and emotionally ready?

a) Principle of readiness
b) Principle of exercise
c) Principle of effect
d) Principle of primacy

93. According to the principle of exercise, what leads to improvement in learning?

a) Meaningful practice and review
b) Positive feedback
c) Repetition of response
d) All of the above

94. The principle of effect suggests that learning is strengthened when it is:

a) Desirable
b) Enjoyable
c) Pleasant
d) All of the above

95. Which principle of learning states that things learned first create a strong impression in the mind?

a) Principle of primacy
b) Principle of recency
c) Principle of intensity
d) Principle of freedom

96. The principle of recency states that:

a) Things most recently learned are best remembered
b) Learning is effective when learners participate actively
c) Learners must have freedom of choice and action
d) Learning is more effective when the material is taught intensively

97. According to the principle of intensity, learners are likely to gain greater understanding of tasks by:

a) Reading about them
b) Listening to lectures
c) Observing others perform the tasks
d) Performing the tasks themselves

98. Which principle of learning emphasizes the importance of freedom for learners?

a) Principle of readiness
b) Principle of recency
c) Principle of freedom
d) Principle of requirement

99. The principle of requirement states that learners must have:

a) Freedom of choice and action
b) Something to obtain or do something
c) Meaningful practice and review
d) Positive feedback

100. According to research, which sense contributes the most to the learning process?

a) Taste | b) Touch
c) Smell | **d) Sight**

101. How much of what is read can learners retain?

a) 10% | b) 20%
c) 30% | d) 50%

102. According to Dale's Cone of Experience, the experiences at the bottom of the cone are:

a) More abstract | **b) More concrete**
c) More difficult | d) More challenging

103. What does Dale's Cone of Experience emphasize in terms of participant involvement?

a) Level of difficulty | b) Level of abstraction
c) Number of senses involved | d) Level of engagement

104. How much of what is done can learners retain?

a) 30% | b) 50%
c) 70% | **d) 90%**

105. Which stage in Dale's Cone of Experience is closer to the peak and involves more abstract experiences?

a) Bottom stage | b) Middle stage
c) Top stage | d) All stages are equally abstract

106. According to research, which sense contributes the least to the learning process?

a) Hearing | b) Smell
c) Taste | d) Touch

107. What is the purpose of Dale's Cone of Experience?

a) To determine the level of difficulty in learning activities
b) To illustrate the hierarchy of learning objectives
c) To emphasize the importance of abstract thinking in learning
d) To show the relationship between learning activities and participant involvement

108. Effective learning requires clear and defined teaching objectives that are:

a) Purposeful and useful to the learners

b) Broad and flexible for adaptation

c) Challenging and complex

d) Strictly adhered to without any deviations

109. Which of the following is not an essential element of a suitable learning situation?

a) Teacher/instructor

b) Learners

c) Subject matter

d) Teaching materials and physical facilities

110. Effective communication in the teaching-learning process involves all the following elements except:

a) Communicator
b) Message

c) Channel
d) Feedback

111. Learning should involve appropriate activity by the learners that engages:

a) A maximum number of senses

b) Only the sense of sight

c) The sense of hearing and touch

d) No sensory involvement

112. What is an essential criterion for motivating people to learn?

a) A strict and rigid teaching approach

b) Learning that is easy and straightforward

c) Challenging and satisfying learning experiences

d) Providing extrinsic rewards for learning

113. Effective learning should result in desirable changes in which of the following aspects?

a) Knowledge, attitude, skill, and action

b) Knowledge and skill only

c) Attitude and action only

d) Action and skill only

114. The teaching-learning process requires evaluation to determine:
   a) The extent or level of desirable changes in learners
   b) The strict adherence to teaching objectives
   c) The number of teaching hours completed
   d) The accuracy of the subject matter delivery

115. According to the principles of teaching, the teacher should create a friendly and informal climate to:
   a) Establish authority over the learners
   b) Maintain a strict learning environment
   c) Encourage learners to ask questions and seek clarification
   d) Discourage learner participation

116. The principles of teaching emphasize the importance of involving learners in the teaching-learning process because it:
   a) Reduces the workload for the teacher
   b) Keeps learners occupied and busy
   c) Increases learner responsibility and participation
   d) Allows the teacher to maintain control over the class

117. A teacher's enthusiasm about teaching is important because it:
   a) Keeps the learners entertained and engaged
   b) Helps maintain discipline in the classroom
   c) Creates a positive and motivating learning environment
   d) Demonstrates the teacher's expertise in the subject matter

118. According to the principles of teaching, a teacher should vary and use appropriate methods of instruction because:
   a) It keeps the learners entertained
   b) It demonstrates the teacher's flexibility
   c) It caters to different learning styles and preferences
   d) It helps the teacher cover more content in less time

119. The principle of teaching suggests that a teacher should continuously update their teaching contents and subject matter because:
   a) It impresses the learners with the teacher's knowledge
   b) It allows the teacher to experiment with new ideas
   c) It ensures the relevance and accuracy of the information taught
   d) It prevents the learners from getting bored with repetitive content

120. According to the stages of teaching, which stage involves creating a desire for information in learners?

a) Attention

b) Interest

c) Desire

d) Conviction

121. In the teaching-learning process, the stage of action is crucial because it:

a) Evaluates the effectiveness of the teaching effort

b) Measures the satisfaction of the learners

c) Converts conviction into tangible results

d) Determines the learner's level of interest

122. The ultimate goal of the extension teaching effort is:

a) Conviction

b) Action

c) Satisfaction

d) Interest

123. What is the primary distinction between andragogy and pedagogy?

a) Andragogy focuses on adult learners, while pedagogy focuses on child learners.

b) Andragogy emphasizes self-directed learning, while pedagogy emphasizes teacher-directed learning.

c) Andragogy is based on theory, while pedagogy is based on practice.

d) Andragogy is a modern concept, while pedagogy has been used for centuries.

124. According to the principles of andragogy, why is it important for adults to have a strong inner motivation to learn?

a) It ensures that adults are free to direct their own learning.

b) It helps adults develop new skills and acquire knowledge.

c) It makes learning more effective and enjoyable for adults.

d) It allows adults to choose their learning objectives.

125. Which principle of adult learning emphasizes the importance of active participation and practice?

a) Adults will learn only what they feel they need to learn.

b) Adults learn by doing.

c) Adult learning focuses on problem solving.

d) Experience affects adult learning.

126. How does experience affect adult learning?

   a) Experience can interfere with the integration of new information.

   b) Experience is not relevant to adult learning.

   c) Experience helps adults solve problems and make connections.

   d) Experience hampers the learning process for adults.

127. What type of learning environment do adults prefer according to the principles of andragogy?

   a) Informal learning environment

   b) Formal learning environment

   c) Structured learning environment

   d) Competitive learning environment

128. What role does the teacher play in the adult learning process according to the principles of andragogy?

   a) The teacher is responsible for imparting knowledge and directing the learning.

   b) The teacher acts as a facilitator and guide.

   c) The teacher is not involved in the learning process.

   d) The teacher controls and dictates the learning objectives.

129. Which condition is necessary for effective adult learning?

   a) Variety of teaching methods

   b) Challenging and satisfying learning opportunities

   c) Effective communication and cooperation

   d) All of the above

130. What is a key characteristic of adult learning according to the principles of andragogy?

   a) Learning is a lifelong process.

   b) Learning is based on comprehension, organization, and synthesis of knowledge.

   c) Learning is self-directed and autonomous.

   d) All of the above

131. Why is it important to apply principles of adult learning in the training of farm youth?

a) The skills learned by farm youth during their early years become obsolete as they grow older.

b) Farm youth are more self-directed and benefit from experiential learning.

c) Training should be problem-centered and need-based for effective learning.

d) All of the above.

132. What is a key characteristic of adult learners like farm youth?

a) They have a long attention span when listening to lectures.

b) They rely heavily on others for guidance and direction.

c) They learn best when they have control over the learning process.

d) They prefer subject-centered learning over problem-centered learning.

133. Why do farm youth have a short attention span when sitting and listening to someone?

a) They are easily bored and prefer active learning methods.

b) They lack interest in the training topics.

c) They have limited cognitive abilities.

d) They prefer self-directed learning rather than listening to others.

134. What is the role of the trainer in the training of farm youth?

a) The trainer has full control over the learning outcome.

b) The trainer's role is mainly facilitative and not as important to learning.

c) The trainer should provide lectures and direct instruction.

d) The trainer should assess the learners' progress and performance.

135. How should the contents of training for farm youth be designed?

a) They should be subject-centered and theory-based.

b) They should be based on the trainer's expertise and interests.

c) They should be problem-centered and need-based.

d) They should be standardized for all farm youth regardless of their individual needs.

136. What type of assessment is emphasized in the training of farm youth?
   a) Trainer-led assessment
   b) Self-assessment by the learners
   c) Formal written exams
   d) Peer assessment by other trainees

137. What is the motivation to learn like for farm youth?
   a) It is externally driven by rewards and punishments.
   b) It is internally driven by their own interests and goals.
   c) It is not a significant factor in their learning process.
   d) It is influenced by the trainer's control over the learning environment.

138. What is the main focus of pedagogy?
   a) Teaching strategies and decisions
   b) The development of human potential
   c) Imparting specific skills
   d) Connecting school and the community

139. What is the goal of problem posing in pedagogy?
   a) Encouraging students to question assumed knowledge
   b) Teaching specific vocational skills
   c) Establishing a social and intellectual environment
   d) Furthering liberal education

140. How do child learners in pedagogy typically approach learning?
   a) They actively relate previous experiences to new learning.
   b) They critically analyze and question what they are told.
   c) They passively listen to the teacher and accept information uncritically.
   d) They have control over the learning environment.

141. According to Paulo Freire, how should pedagogy treat learners?
   a) As empty vessels to be filled with knowledge
   b) As independent co-creators of knowledge
   c) As passive recipients of information
   d) As individuals with limited life experience

142. What is the concept of conscientization in pedagogy?
  a) Focusing on achieving in-depth understanding of the world
  b) Taking action against oppressive elements in one's life
  c) Making connections between school and the community
  d) Listening to and including students' knowledge and perspectives

143. How does critical consciousness relate to pedagogy?
  a) It emphasizes the importance of vocational education.
  b) It encourages passive listening and acceptance of information.
  c) It focuses on exposing social and political contradictions.
  d) It supports the traditional banking model of education.

144. Experiential learning is a process of learning from:
  a) Lectures and case studies **b) Reflection and analysis**
  c) Abstract conceptualization d) Active experimentation

145. The Experiential Learning Cycle involves the following phases, except:
  a) Experience phase b) Process phase
  c) Generalization phase **d) Application phase**

146. In the Experiential Learning Cycle, the process phase involves:
  a) Active involvement in doing something
  b) Drawing conclusions and generalizations
  c) Recalling and sharing the experience
  d) Incorporating learning into day-to-day behavior

147. The Experiential Learning Cycle emphasizes the importance of:
  a) Lectures and simulations
  b) Abstract conceptualization
  c) Technical information before experience phase
  d) Creative thinking and skill practice

148. Experiential learning is learner-centered and allows learners to:
  a) Passively listen to the teacher
  b) Rely on others for knowledge
  c) Manage and share responsibilities for their learning
  d) Focus on abstract conceptualization

149. Experiential learning involves the transformation of experience through:
   a) Grasping and transforming experience
   b) Abstract conceptualization and active experimentation
   c) Concrete experience and reflective observation
   d) Lecture-based teaching and teacher-centered approach

150. What is an extension programme?
   a) A list of events and activities
   b) A proclamation of objectives and solutions
   c) A course of action prepared in advance
   d) All of the above

151. What is the purpose of extension programme planning?
   a) To provide a blueprint for action
   b) To address the situation, objectives, problems, and solutions
   c) To achieve long-term and short-term programme objectives
   d) All of the above

152. What is the end-product of extension programme planning?
   a) Extension teaching plans
   b) Programme objectives
   c) A written statement of situation, objectives, problems, and solutions
   d) A set of clearly defined goals and aims

153. Which element of an extension programme specifies the work to be done?
   a) Situation
   b) Problem and solution
   c) Goal, aims, and objectives
   d) Project

154. What does a plan of work in an extension programme outline?
   a) Activities to be done and procedures to be followed
   b) Chronological arrangement of work
   c) Time schedule of work
   d) All of the above

155. What is a calendar of work in an extension programme?
   a) A blueprint for action
   b) A time schedule of work
   c) An outline of activities
   d) A plan of work arranged chronologically

156. Extension programme planning should be based on:
   a) Future needs only
   b) Present situation only
   c) Past experiences, present situation, and future needs
   d) Local people's consent only

157. Extension programme planning selects problems based on:
   a) Program objectives
   b) People's interest and needs
   c) Available resources
   d) Government guidelines

158. A sound extension programme has:
   a) Permanence with flexibility
   b) Constant changes
   c) Strict guidelines
   d) No room for adjustments

159. Extension programme planning should ensure:
   a) Emphasis on one specific area
   b) Comprehensive coverage of all interests
   c) Quick completion of objectives
   d) Exclusion of certain groups

160. Programme planning is a continuous process because:
   a) The situation never changes
   b) The programme is perfect from the beginning
   c) Tomorrow's problems will be different from today's
   d) Extension work is not required in the future

161. Extension programme planning is a teaching process because:
   a) It involves educating local people
   b) It requires the involvement of teachers
   c) It includes conducting workshops and training sessions
   d) It teaches people to think, make decisions, and act through participation

162. Programme building is a coordinating process because it:
   a) Involves various leaders and groups
   b) Determines the most important problems
   c) Coordinates the efforts of agencies and resources
   d) All of the above

163. Extension programme planning involves:
   a) Only external experts
   b) Local people and their institutions
   c) Government officials
   d) International organizations

164. Extension programme planning provides opportunity for:
   a) Continuous evaluation
   b) Immediate implementation
   c) Program revision
   d) Equitable distribution of benefits

165. Extension programme planning should ensure:
   a) Focus on affluent sections of society
   b) Exclusion of resource-poor sections
   c) Equitable distribution of benefits
   d) Benefit to a few selected individuals

166. The first step in extension programme planning is:
   a) Analysis of the situation
   b) Identification of problems
   c) Collection of facts
   d) Determination of objectives

167. After collecting facts, the next step in extension programme planning is:
   a) Analysis of the situation
   b) Identification of problems
   c) Determination of objectives
   d) Developing a plan of work

168. The step-in extension programme planning that involves categorizing problems and prioritizing them is:
   a) Collection of facts
   b) Analysis of the situation
   c) Identification of problems
   d) Determination of objectives

169. Determination of objectives in extension programme planning should be done:
   a) By the extension worker alone
   b) Without consulting local people
   c) In consultation with local people
   d) Based on personal preferences

170. Developing a plan of work and calendar of operations is the step that involves:
   a) Setting clear objectives
   b) Identifying problems
   c) Collecting facts
   d) Listing activities and assigning responsibilities

171. The step-in extension programme planning that emphasizes proper implementation of activities is:
   a) Developing a plan of work and calendar of operations
   b) Follow through plan of work and calendar of operations
   c) Evaluation of the programme
   d) Reconsideration and revision of the programme

172. Evaluation of the programme in extension programme planning is important to:
   a) Determine objectives
   b) Collect facts
   c) Monitor progress and gather feedback
   d) Identify problems

173. The final step in extension programme planning involves:
   a) Collecting facts
   b) Developing a plan of work
   c) Reconsideration and revision of the programme
   d) Determination of objectives

174. Which organization was responsible for formulating Five Year Plans for the economic development of India?
   a) National Planning Committee   **b) Planning Commission**
   c) NITI Aayog   d) Union Cabinet

175. When was the Planning Commission set up in India?
   a) 1934   b) 1938
   c) 1950   d) 2015

176. Why was NITI Aayog formed?
   a) To replace the Planning Commission
   b) To focus on growth and social justice
   c) To foster Cooperative Federalism
   d) All of the above

177. What is the role of NITI Aayog?
   a) To provide policy inputs to the Government of India
   b) To engage states with the Central government
   c) To promote research and innovation
   d) All of the above

178. What are the two key tasks of NITI Aayog?
   a) Team India Hub and Knowledge and Innovation Hub
   b) Designing strategic policies and providing technical advice
   c) Formulating Five Year Plans and fostering Cooperative Federalism
   d) Union Cabinet and Planning Commission

179. What is the role of NITI Aayog as a State-of-the-Art Resource Centre?
   a) To act with speed and provide strategic policy vision
   b) To promote research and innovation
   c) To deal with contingent issues
   d) All of the above

180. When was NITI Aayog formed?
   a) 1934
   b) 1933
   c) 1950
   d) 2015

181. Which approach is widely used in development programs and activities?
   a) Participatory approach
   b) Top-down approach
   c) Authoritarian approach
   d) Centralized approach

182. What is the role of participatory planning in identifying problems?
   a) Mobilizing self-help
   b) Choosing intervention options
   c) Delegating authority
   d) Facilitating expression of demands

183. What are the key elements of participation?
   a) Empowerment, organization, and contribution
   b) Mobilization, delegation, and decision-making
   c) Self-help, self-management, and planning
   d) Expression of demands, monitoring, and evaluation

184. Which mode of participation is initiated by external agencies like NGOs?
   a) Initiated participation
   b) Facilitated participation
   c) Co-opted participation
   d) Induced participation

185. What is the characteristic of co-opted participation?
   a) Originates within the people
   b) Initiated by external agencies
   c) Persuasion through incentives
   d) Undertaken by government departments

186. How is induced participation encouraged?
   a) Through self-motivation of participating groups
   b) By creating awareness and motivation through campaigns
   c) By mobilizing local resources
   d) Through delegation of authority

187. Which mode of participation involves decision-making based on consensus?
   a) Initiated participation
   b) Facilitated participation
   c) Co-opted participation
   d) Induced participation

188. Which tools can be used for situation analysis and problem identification in participatory planning?
   a) Matrix ranking and decision analysis
   b) Social and resource map and transact walk
   c) Visioning and wealth ranking
   d) Gender analysis and problem-cause diagram

189. Which mode of participation is initiated by NGOs and involves creating awareness and motivation?
   a) Initiated participation
   b) Facilitated participation
   c) Co-opted participation
   d) Induced participation

190. What are the indicators used to measure participation?
   a) Number of members in the group and attendance in group meetings
   b) Presence of representatives in local governing bodies
   c) Participation in decision-making process
   d) All of the above

191. Which constitutional amendment brought significant changes to the Panchayati Raj System?
   a) 73rd Constitutional Amendment
   b) 74th Constitutional Amendment
   c) 71st Constitutional Amendment
   d) 72nd Constitutional Amendment

192. What is the distribution of powers between the State legislature and the Panchayats called?
   a) 9th Schedule
   b) 11th Schedule
   c) 10th Schedule
   d) 12th Schedule

193. What is the provision for reservation of seats for women in Panchayats?
   a) One-third of the total seats
   b) One-fourth of the total seats
   c) One-half of the total seats
   d) One-fifth of the total seats

194. What is the shelf of works maintained by Gram Panchayats under the MGNREGA Act?
   a) Development plan
   b) Evaluation plan
   c) Implementation plan
   d) Monitoring plan

195. During which period were rural development programmes mostly undertaken by philanthropists and nationalists?
   a) Pre-independence era
   b) Post-independence era
   c) Colonial era
   d) Modern era

196. Which campaign was launched by the interim Government just before independence?
   a) Grow More Food Campaign
   b) Community Development Project
   c) Etawah Pilot Project
   d) Indian Village Service

197. What was the objective of the Grow More Food Campaign in post-independence India?
   a) Attainment of self-sufficiency in food grains by 1952
   b) Achieving rural electrification in all villages
   c) Promoting small-scale industries in rural areas
   d) Improving healthcare services in rural communities

198. Which committee was appointed in 1952 to examine the working of the Grow More Food Campaign?
   a) Etawah Pilot Project Committee
   b) Daniel Hamilton's Scheme Committee
   c) Rabindranath Tagore's Committee
   d) Committee on Agricultural Production

199. What was the major breakthrough in the development block program?
   a) Formation of rural cooperatives
   b) Introduction of multipurpose village level worker
   c) Implementation of land reforms
   d) Establishment of rural healthcare centers

200. The Etawah Pilot Project launched by Albert Mayer was a forerunner of which project?
   a) Grow More Food Campaign
   b) Community Development Project
   c) Sevagram Approach
   d) Indian Village Service

201. When were the Community Development Pilot Projects started?
   a) 1947 **b) 1952**
   c) 1958 d) 1963

202. How many villages were included in each development block under the Community Development Programme?
   a) 50 villages **b) 100 villages**
   c) 200 villages d) 500 villages

203. What was the aim of the Community Development Programme?
   a) Achieving overall socio-economic transformation of rural people
   b) Providing financial assistance to rural entrepreneurs
   c) Promoting agricultural exports from rural areas
   d) Improving infrastructure in rural communities

204. When was the National Extension Service (NES) started?
   a) 1947 b) 1952
   c) 1953 d) 1958

205. How many stages were there in the modified pattern of the Community Development Programme?

a) 2 stages
b) 3 stages
c) 4 stages
d) 5 stages

206. Which committee recommended the implementation of the Panchayat Raj System?

a) Balwant Rai Mehta Committee
b) Ford Foundation Committee
c) Community Development Enquiry Committee
d) National Extension Service Committee

207. In which state was the Panchayati Raj System first implemented on a trial basis?

a) Andhra Pradesh
b) Rajasthan
c) Maharashtra
d) Uttar Pradesh

208. When was the Panchayati Raj System formally inaugurated in Nagore district of Rajasthan?

a) 1947
b) 1952
c) 1959
d) 1963

209. When was the Intensive Agricultural District Programme (IADP) launched in India?

a) 1950
b) 1960
c) 1970
d) 1980

210. How many districts were initially selected for the IADP?

a) 3 districts
b) 5 districts
c) 7 districts
d) 10 districts

211. What was the central idea behind the IADP?

a) Poverty alleviation
b) Industrial development
c) Increased agricultural productivity
d) Infrastructure improvement

212. What was the approach to agricultural development under the IADP?

a) Extensive development in all districts
b) Sectoral development focusing on livestock
c) Intensive development in selected areas
d) Organic farming promotion

213. What was the role of the Project Officer in the IADP?
    a) Head of the program at the national level
    b) Head of the program at the district level
    c) Head of the program at the block level
    d) Head of the program at the village level

214. What was the objective of the Intensive Agricultural Area Programme (IAAP)?
    a) To reduce the cost of agricultural inputs
    b) To provide credit facilities to farmers
    c) To extend the benefits of improved technology in agriculture nationwide
    d) To promote organic farming practices

215. How did the IADP impact the farming community?
    a) It resulted in reduced crop yields
    b) It created new job opportunities in urban areas
    c) It led to increased agricultural productivity
    d) It caused a decline in agricultural production

216. What was the purpose of the Subject Matter Specialists (SMS) in the IADP?
    a) To provide financial assistance to farmers
    b) To assist the Project Officer at the district level
    c) To promote cooperative farming practices
    d) To manage the implementation of credit programs

217. When was the High Yielding Varieties Programme (HYVP) launched?
    a) 1950 **b) 1965**
    c) 1970 d) 1980

218. What was the objective of the HYVP?
    a) To promote organic farming practices
    b) To achieve self-sufficiency in foodgrains
    c) To improve livestock production
    d) To develop drought-prone areas

219. What factors contributed to the success of the Green Revolution in India?

   a) Balanced fertilizer application, irrigation, and improved implements

   b) Organic farming practices and traditional seeds

   c) Reduction in fertilizer usage and reliance on natural rainfall

   d) Introduction of hybrid seeds and chemical pesticides

220. When were Farmers Training Institutes (FTI) established in India?

   a) 1950 **b) 1960**

   c) 1970 d) 1980

221. What role did the Farmers Training Institutes play in agriculture?

   a) Promotion of organic farming practices

   b) Providing subsidies to small farmers

   c) Improving agricultural productivity through training and knowledge transfer

   d) Implementing irrigation projects in drought-prone areas

222. When was the Small Farmers' Development Agency (SFDA) established?

   a) 1950 b) 1960

   c) 1970 d) 1980

223. What was the aim of the SFDA?

   a) To improve agricultural productivity in drought-prone areas

   b) To provide credit and inputs to small farmers

   c) To promote horticulture and dairying practices

   d) To address the needs of agricultural laborers

224. What was the purpose of the Drought Prone Area Programme (DPAP)?

   a) To develop irrigation projects in drought-prone areas

   b) To promote organic farming practices in arid regions

   c) To restore ecological balance and stabilize the income of people in drought-prone areas

   d) To provide subsidies to farmers affected by drought

225. When was the Training and Visit System (T&V System) introduced in India?

   a) 1954 b) 1965

   c) 1974 d) 1982

226. Who developed the Training and Visit System (T&V System)?

a) Daniel Benor b) Mohan Sinha Mehta

c) Albert Mayer d) Balwant Rai Mehta

227. What is the main objective of the Training and Visit System (T&V System)?

a) To promote organic farming practices

b) To coordinate research, training, and extension activities effectively

c) To establish Krishi Vigyan Kendras (KVKs) in every district

d) To provide subsidies to small farmers

228. How many farmers are usually assigned to one Agricultural Assistant (AA) in the Training and Visit System?

a) 200-400 **b) 800-1000**

c) 1500-2000 d) 3000-4000

229. What is the main method of imparting training in Krishi Vigyan Kendras (KVKs)?

a) Classroom lectures **b) Field demonstrations**

c) Online courses d) Hands-on workshops

230. What is the main goal of the Krishi Vigyan Kendras (KVKs)?

a) Promotion of organic farming practices

b) Imparting technical literacy to extension agents

c) Agricultural production breakthrough

d) Conducting on-farm research for technology refinement

231. What is the funding institution for Krishi Vigyan Kendras (KVKs)?

a) ICAR b) FAO

c) SAU d) NGO

232. What are the major mandates of Krishi Vigyan Kendras (KVKs)?

a) Conducting training programs, frontline demonstrations, and on-farm testing

b) Providing subsidies to small farmers

c) Imparting technical literacy to farmers and fishermen

d) Conducting research on agricultural technology

233. When was the Desert Development Programme (DDP) launched?
a) 1960-61
b) 1977-78
c) 1994
d) 1999

234. Which of the following areas were covered under the Desert Development Programme (DDP)?
a) Coastal areas
b) Arid desert areas
c) Hill regions
d) Urban centers

235. What were the objectives of the Desert Development Programme (DDP)?
a) Promotion of organic farming practices
b) Rehabilitation of wildlife sanctuaries
c) Construction of dams and canals
d) Afforestation, groundwater development, and agriculture development

236. When was the Small Farmers' Agribusiness Consortium (SFAC) established?
a) 1977
b) 1985
c) 1994
d) 1999

237. What is the main objective of the Small Farmers' Agribusiness Consortium (SFAC)?
a) Promoting organic farming practices
b) Linking small farmers to agricultural value chains
c) Providing subsidies to small farmers
d) Conducting research on agribusiness models

238. When was the Institute Village Linkage Programme (IVLP) initiated?
a) 1960
b) 1977
c) 1994
d) 1999

239. What is the concept behind the Institute Village Linkage Programme (IVLP)?
a) Top-down approach in technology transfer
b) Farmer-scientist linkages in a participatory mode
c) Exclusive focus on large-scale farming systems
d) Collaboration between international research institutes

240. When was the Agricultural Technology Information Centre (ATIC) established?

a) 1960 b) 1977

c) 1994 d) 1999

241. What is the main purpose of the Agricultural Technology Information Centre (ATIC)?

a) Research and development of new agricultural technologies

b) Providing diagnostic services to farmers

c) Offering training programs for farmers

d) Providing a single window system for agricultural products and services

242. When was the National Agricultural Technology Project (NATP) launched?

a) 1960 b) 1977

c) 1994 **d) 1999**

243. What is the objective of the Innovations in Technology Dissemination component under the National Agricultural Technology Project (NATP)?

a) Developing a demand-driven transfer of technology system

b) Enhancing agricultural research funding

c) Promoting sustainable farming practices

d) Establishing more agricultural research institutes

244. When was the Agricultural Technology Management Agency (ATMA) established?

a) 1960 b) 1994

c) 1999 **d) 2005**

245. What is the main responsibility of ATMA?

a) Research and development of agricultural technologies

b) Coordination of technology dissemination activities at the district level

c) Implementation of rural development programs

d) Promotion of organic farming practices

246. When was the National Horticulture Mission (NHM) launched?

a) 1999-2000 **b) 2005-06**

c) 2010-11 d) 2014-15

247. What is the objective of the National Horticulture Mission (NHM)?
   a) Promoting organic farming practices
   b) Development of horticulture sector through regionally differentiated strategies
   c) Enhancing agricultural productivity and profitability
   d) Supporting poverty alleviation and income generation

248. When was the National Agricultural Innovation Project (NAIP) launched?
   a) 1994
   b) 2005
   c) 2006
   d) 2010

249. What is the main objective of the National Agricultural Innovation Project (NAIP)?
   a) Promoting research in agricultural sciences
   b) Building capacity of the Indian Council of Agricultural Research (ICAR)
   c) Enhancing agricultural productivity and profitability
   d) Facilitating technology-led innovative systems in rural areas

250. When was the Rashtriya Krishi Vikash Yojana (RKVY) launched?
   a) 1994
   b) 2005
   c) 2007-08
   d) 2014-15

251. What is the objective of the Rashtriya Krishi Vikash Yojana (RKVY)?
   a) Promoting organic farming practices
   b) Achieving 4% growth rate in agriculture and allied sectors
   c) Enhancing market infrastructure for agriculture products
   d) Supporting research institutions in agriculture

252. When was the National Food Security Mission (NFSM) launched?
   a) 1994
   b) 2005
   c) 2007
   d) 2010

253. What is the major objective of the National Food Security Mission (NFSM)?
   a) Increasing production and productivity of wheat, rice, and pulses
   b) Ensuring sustainable agriculture practices
   c) Promoting organic farming practices
   d) Enhancing market infrastructure for food grains

254. What is the main objective of the Watershed Development Programme (WDP)?
   a) Increasing water use efficiency in agriculture
   b) Promoting sustainable agriculture practices
   c) Harnessing and conserving degraded natural resources
   d) Enhancing market access for agricultural products

255. When were Integrated Wasteland Development Programme (IWDP), Drought Prone Area Programme (DPAP), and Desert Development Programme (DDP) brought under the comprehensive Integrated Watershed Management Programme (IWMP)?
   a) 1998 **b) 2008**
   c) 2015 d) 2020

256. Which mission derives its mandate from the Sustainable Agriculture Mission outlined under the National Action Plan on Climate Change (NAPCC)?
   a) National Food Security Mission (NFSM)
   b) Watershed Development Programme (WDP)
   c) National Mission for Sustainable Agriculture (NMSA)
   d) Pradhan Mantri Krishi Sinchay Yojana (PMKSY)

257. What are the key dimensions encompassed by the National Mission for Sustainable Agriculture (NMSA)?
   a) Improved crop seeds, livestock and fish cultures, and pest management
   b) oil health management, water use efficiency, and access to information
   c) Nutrient management, agricultural insurance, and credit support markets
   d) Improved farm practices, access to information, and livelihood diversification

258. What are the three major components of the National Mission for Sustainable Agriculture (NMSA)?
   a) Rainfed Area Development (RAD), Pest Management (PM), and Climate Change Adaptation (CCA)
   b) Soil Health Management (SHM), Water Use Efficiency (WUE), and Livelihood Diversification (LD)
   c) Rainfed Area Development (RAD, Soil Health Management (SHM), and Climate Change and Sustainable Agriculture (CCSA)
   d) Pest Management (PM), Livelihood Diversification (LD), and Climate Change Adaptation (CCA)

259. When was the pilot programme for promoting Farmer Producer Organizations (FPOs) launched?

a) 2005-06
b) 2011-12
c) 2013-14
d) 2016-17

260. What is the primary objective of mobilizing farmers into member owned FPOs?

a) Enhancing production, productivity, and profitability of agriculturists
b) Providing access to modern technology for farmers
c) Strengthening market tie-ups for agricultural products
d) Promoting cooperative spirit among farmers

261. What is the hybrid nature of a producer company?

a) It combines the features of a cooperative society and a public limited company.
b) It combines the features of a private limited company and a cooperative society.
c) It combines the features of a partnership firm and a public limited company.
d) It combines the features of a cooperative society and a partnership firm.

262. How many directors must a producer company have?

a) At least 3 and not more than 10 directors
b) At least 5 and not more than 15 directors
c) At least 2 and not more than 5 directors
d) At least 10 and not more than 20 directors

263. Which crop insurance scheme replaced the National Agricultural Insurance Scheme (NAIS) and Modified NAIS?

a) Pradhan Mantri Fasal Bima Yojana (PMFBY)
b) Rashtriya Krishi Vikas Yojana (RKVY)
c) National Food Security Mission (NFSM)
d) Watershed Development Programme (WDP)

264. What is the uniform premium rate for kharif crops under PMFBY?

a) 1%
b) 2%
c) 3%
d) 5%

265. What types of risks are covered under PMFBY?

a) Preventable risks such as pests and diseases

b) Risks due to fire, flood, and drought

c) Risks related to market fluctuations

d) Risks associated with post-harvest losses

266. When was Pradhan Mantri Krishi Sinchayee Yojana (PMKSY) formulated?

a) 2015 **b) 2016**

c) 2017 d) 2018

267. What is the vision of PMKSY?

a) Extending the coverage of irrigation to every field

b) Improving water use efficiency in agriculture

c) Focusing on end-to-end solutions for water management

d) All of the above

268. Which schemes were amalgamated to form PMKSY?

a) Accelerated Irrigation Benefit Programme (AIBP)

b) Integrated Watershed Management Programme (IWMP)

c) On-Farm Water Management (OFWM)

d) All of the above

269. What is the total outlay for PMKSY over a period of five years?

a) 10,000 crore b) 25,000 crore

c) 50,000 crore d) 100,000 crore

270. When was Pradhan Mantri Kaushal Vikas Yojana (PMKVY) launched?

a) 2013 b) 2014

c) 2015 d) 2016

271. What is the objective of PMKVY?

a) To provide industry-relevant skill training to Indian youth

b) To enhance the livelihood opportunities for individuals

c) To assess and certify prior learning experience or skills

d) All of the above

272. Which agency is responsible for coordinating and driving PMKVY?
   a) Ministry of Skill Development and Entrepreneurship (MSDE)
   b) National Skill Development Corporation (NSDC)
   c) Agriculture Skill Council of India (ASCI)
   d) Sector Skill Councils (SSC)

273. The Integrated Child Development Services (ICDS) scheme aims to improve the nutritional and health status of children below the age of _____.
   a) 5 years
   b) 6 years
   c) 7 years
   d) 8 years

274. The Integrated Rural Development Programme (IRDP) was launched in _____ by the Government of India.
   a) 1965
   b) 1975
   c) 1980
   d) 1990

275. The Development of Women and Children in Rural Areas (DWCRA) program was initiated as a sub-scheme of _____.
   a) ICDS
   b) IRDP
   c) Swayamsiddha
   d) Mahila Samridhi Yojana

276. A Self-Help Group (SHG) is a small voluntary association of poor people that promotes:
   a) Women empowerment
   b) Financial literacy among children
   c) Healthcare services for rural areas
   d) Environmental conservation practices

277. Which program was launched to provide economic security to rural women and encourage the saving habit among them?
   a) Mahila Samridhi Yojana (MSY)
   b) Indira Mahila Yojana (IMY)
   c) Swayamsiddha
   d) Rashtriya Mahila Kosh

278. The Mid-Day Meal Scheme aims to improve the nutritional status of:
   a) Pregnant women
   b) School-age children
   c) Elderly population
   d) Orphaned children

279. Which act guarantees 100 days of wage employment in a year to every rural household in India?

a) ICDS
b) IRDP
c) MGNREGA
d) NRLM

280. National Rural Livelihood Mission (NRLM) was replaced by:

a) Integrated Child Development Services (ICDS)
b) Mahatma Gandhi National Rural Employment Guarantee Act (MGNREGA)
c) Deen Dayal Antyodaya Yojana (DAY)
d) Swashakti Project (SP)

281. Which project is a joint effort by the World Bank and the International Fund for Agricultural Development (IFAD) to empower rural women?

a) ICDS
b) IRDP
c) Mahatma Gandhi National Rural Employment Guarantee Act (MGNREGA)
d) Swashakti Project (SP)

282. Rashtriya Mahila Kosh provides credit for facilitating production and economic activities primarily to:

a) Self-Help Groups (SHGs)
b) District Rural Development Agencies (DRDAs)
c) Integrated Child Development Services (ICDS)
d) Mahatma Gandhi National Rural Employment Guarantee Act (MGNREGA)

283. The Mid-Day Meal Scheme is funded by the central and state governments in the ratio of:

a) 70:30
b) 60:40
c) 50:50
d) 80:20

284. Mahatma Gandhi National Rural Employment Guarantee Act (MGN-REGA) guarantees days of wage employment in a year.

a) 50
b) 75
c) 90
d) 100

285. The main objective of the National Rural Livelihood Mission (NRLM) is to:
   a) Provide free education to children in rural areas
   b) Improve the health status of women and children
   c) Enhance the economic security of rural households
   d) Promote sustainable agriculture practices

286. Which program focuses on creating awareness among women and providing income sources to them?
   a) Indira Mahila Yojana (IMY)
   b) Swashakti Project (SP)
   c) Mahila Samridhi Yojana (MSY)
   d) Development of Women and Children in Rural Areas (DWCRA)

287. The Mahatma Gandhi National Rural Employment Guarantee Act (MNREGA) guarantees wage employment to:
   a) All adults in rural areas
   b) Women and children in rural areas
   c) Landless laborers in urban areas
   d) Rural households below the poverty line

288. The primary focus of the Swayamsiddha program is to empower women by:
   a) Enhancing their skills and awareness
   b) Providing financial support for education
   c) Improving healthcare services in rural areas
   d) Promoting environmental conservation

289. Rashtriya Mahila Kosh provides financial assistance primarily to:
   a) Urban women entrepreneurs
   b) Self-Help Groups (SHGs)
   c) Children in rural areas
   d) Women above 60 years of age

290. The Mid-Day Meal Scheme provides meals to school-age children in India up to which grade?
   a) Grade 8
   b) Grade 10
   c) Grade 12
   d) Grade 6

291. Mahila Samridhi Yojana (MSY) encourages rural women to open savings accounts at:
   a) Public sector banks
   b) Cooperative banks
   c) Rural post offices
   d) Private banks

292. The National Rural Livelihood Mission (NRLM) aims to provide livelihood opportunities primarily to:
   a) Rural women
   b) Urban youth
   c) Tribal communities
   d) Elderly population

293. Which program was launched to empower rural women and reduce drudgery through the reduction of time-consuming tasks?
   a) Development of Women and Children in Rural Areas (DWCRA)
   b) Swashakti Project (SP)
   c) Mahila Samridhi Yojana (MSY)
   d) Mahatma Gandhi National Rural Employment Guarantee Act (MGNREGA)

294. The main objective of the Rashtriya Mahila Kosh is to provide financial assistance for the:
   a) Education of rural women
   b) Entrepreneurial activities of rural women
   c) Health services for women and children
   d) Skill development of rural women

295. The Mid-Day Meal Scheme is implemented for school-age children on _____ days.
   a) Weekdays
   b) Weekends
   c) School holidays
   d) All days of the week

296. Mahatma Gandhi National Rural Employment Guarantee Act (MGNREGA was launched to provide employment to agricultural hands during the _____ season.
   a) Harvesting
   b) Monsoon
   c) Sowing
   d) Lean

297. The National Rural Livelihood Mission (NRLM) was replaced by:
   a) Integrated Rural Development Programme (IRDP)
   b) Mahatma Gandhi National Rural Employment Guarantee Act (MGNREGA)
   c) Deen Dayal Antyodaya Yojana (DAY)
   d) Development of Women and Children in Rural Areas (DWCRA)

298. The primary focus of the Mahila Samridhi Yojana (MSY) is to provide economic security to:
   - a) Urban women above 30 years of age
   - **b) Rural women below the poverty line**
   - c) Adolescent girls in rural areas
   - d) Widows and single mothers

299. The Indira Mahila Yojana (IMY) aims to create awareness among women and provide income sources through:
   - **a) Skill development programs**
   - b) Healthcare services
   - c) Educational scholarships
   - d) Infrastructure development

300. The Swayamsiddha program aims to create self-renewing behavior among women through:
   - **a) Skill development programs**
   - b) Financial literacy training
   - c) Health and sanitation campaigns
   - d) Environmental conservation projects

301. The Mahatma Gandhi National Rural Employment Guarantee Act (MGNREGA) guarantees _____ days of wage employment to rural households.
   - a) 50
   - b) 75
   - c) 90
   - **d) 100**

302. The National Rural Livelihood Mission (NRLM) primarily focuses on enhancing the economic security of:
   - a) Urban households
   - **b) Rural households below the poverty line**
   - c) Tribal communities
   - d) Elderly population

4

Overseeing the Agricultural Extension Institutions

1. Management is defined as:
   a) **The art of getting things done through others and with formally organized groups.**
   b) The ability to forecast and plan activities of others.
   c) The process of controlling physical resources in an organization.
   d) The art of knowing what one wants to do and then seeing that one does it in the best and the cheapest manner.

2. What activities are included in the scope of management in extension organizations?
   a) Setting broad objectives and policies.
   b) Identifying and classifying activities in the organization.
   c) Training and technological interventions.
   d) All of the above.

3. The function of management responsible for influencing, motivating, and leading employees is:
   a) Planning b) Organizing
   c) Staffing **d) Directing**

4. Which management skill is particularly important for top-level administrators?
   a) Technical skills b) Conceptual skills
   c) Human skills d) **Leadership skills**

5. Administration and management differ in terms of:
   a) Their focus on people and work.
   b) **Their role in decision making and policy formulation.**
   c) Their authority level within the organization.
   d) Their applicability to business and non-business organizations.

Bold Means Correct Answer

6. The role of administration is to:
   a) Handle the business aspects of the organization, such as finance.
   b) Carry out the decisions and policies set by management.
   c) Manage and motivate employees.
   d) **Formulate broad objectives, goals, and policies of the organization.**

7. Henri Fayol defined management as the ability to:
   a) Forecast and plan activities of others.
   b) Control and coordinate activities in an organization.
   c) Command and lead people in an organization.
   d) **Forecast, plan, organize, command, coordinate, and control activities of others.**

8. The process by which human resources, physical resources, job tasks, and technology are effectively combined to achieve organizational goals is called:
   a) Decision making
   b) **Organizing**
   c) Forecasting
   d) Coordinating

9. The primary purpose of staffing in extension organizations is to:
   a) Allocate financial resources effectively.
   b) Identify and classify activities in the organization.
   c) **Recruit and assign capable individuals for extension work.**
   d) Formulate broad objectives and goals.

10. Which function of management involves unifying and harmonizing activities of extension personnel from different work groups?
   a) Controlling
   b) **Coordinating**
   c) Directing
   d) Staffing

11. Management in an organization involves activities such as:
   a) Forecasting, planning, and directing.
   b) Organizing, staffing, and reporting.
   c) Budgeting, human resource development, and decision making.
   d) **All of the above**

12. The skill required for lower and middle-level managers to understand and work well with others is known as:
    a) Conceptual skills
    b) **Human skills**
    c) Technical skills
    d) Leadership skills

13. Extension organizations aim to:
    a) Control activities of others.
    b) Transfer technology to other organizations.
    c) **Improve performance and efficiency**.
    d) Forecast and plan for the future.

14. The major task of management is to:
    a) Formulate broad objectives and policies.
    b) **Manage people, motivate them, and lead them to achieve organizational goals**.
    c) Control and coordinate all activities in the organization.
    d) Forecast and plan for future activities.

15. The focus of management is on:
    a) Setting broad objectives and goals for the organization.
    b) **Managing people in the organization and their work.**
    c) Coordinating and harmonizing activities of extension personnel.
    d) Formulating policies and decision making.

16. Which of the following is NOT part of the scope of management in extension organizations?
    a) Planning for extension programs and objectives.
    b) Identification and communication of roles and responsibilities.
    c) Setting broad objectives and policies for the organization.
    d) **Measurement and correction of activities by establishing standards**.

17. What is the main difference between management and administration?
    a) Management involves planning and organizing, while administration involves staffing and directing.
    b) **Management is focused on people and their work, while administration is concerned with policy formulation and decision making**.
    c) Management deals with non-business organizations, while administration deals with profit organizations.
    d) Administration involves human skills, while management involves technical skills.

18. The ability to forecast and plan activities of others is attributed to:
    a) Henri Fayol
    b) FW Taylor
    c) Harold Koontz
    d) **All of the above**

19. The primary goal of management in extension organizations is to:
    a) Improve performance and efficiency.
    b) Handle the business aspects of the organization.
    c) Set broad objectives and policies.
    d) **Achieve organizational goals and objectives.**

20. The process of controlling and coordinating activities in an organization is called:
    a) Directing
    b) Coordinating
    c) Organizing
    d) **Management**

21. What activities are NOT included in the scope of management in extension organizations?
    a) Staffing and recruitment of capable individuals for extension work.
    b) Planning for extension programs, objectives, and goals.
    c) Identification and classification of activities in the organization.
    d) **Setting broad objectives, goals, and policies of the organization.**

22. Which theory of management emphasized strict control of workers, predictability of behavior, and unidirectional downward influence?
    a) Theory of Bureaucracy
    b) **Theory of Scientific Management**
    c) Administrative Theory
    d) Neo-classical Theory

23. Who is often referred to as the "Father of Scientific Management"?
    a) Max Weber
    b) **Frederick Taylor**
    c) Henri Fayol
    d) Hugo Munsterberg

24. The theory of scientific management aims at:
    a) Maximizing worker capacity and profits.
    b) Promoting harmony and individualism in the workplace.
    c) Encouraging strict adherence to rules of thumb.
    d) **Focusing on the psychological aspects of workers.**

25. Which of the following is NOT one of the four principles of scientific management?
    a) Replace working by rule of thumb with scientific methods.
    b) Match workers to jobs based on capability and motivation.
    c) Eliminate supervision and instructions for workers.
    d) **Monitor worker performance and provide supervision.**

26. Who developed the administrative theory and outlined the fourteen principles of management?
    a) Max Weber
    b) Frederick Taylor
    c) Hugo Munsterberg
    d) **Henri Fayol**

27. The administrative theory focuses on:
    a) Analyzing individual tasks and job requirements.
    b) Utilizing scientific methods to increase worker productivity.
    c) **The rational legal authority of managers**.
    d) Improving worker motivation through financial incentives.

28. What are the five functions of management according to Gulick and Urwick's POSDCORB?
    a) **Planning, Organizing, Staffing, Directing, Coordinating**
    b) Hierarchy, Rules, Professional Qualities, Training, Free Selection
    c) Planning, Order, Stabilization, Equity, Maximization
    d) Division of Work, Authority, Discipline, Unity of Command, Remuneration

29. The Neo-classical theories of management are also known as:
    a) **Human Relation Movement** (HRM)
    b) Theory X and Y
    c) Theory of Bureaucracy
    d) Quantitative or Mathematical Approach

30. Which major experiment conducted at the Hawthorne plant influenced the development of Neo-classical theories?
    a) Maslow's Hierarchy of Needs
    b) **The Hawthorne Effect**
    c) Theory X and Y
    d) The Theory of Z

31. The Neo-classical theories of management emphasized the importance of:
    a) Strict rules and regulations in the workplace.
    b) **Informal organization and emotions of workers.**
    c) Quantitative analysis for decision making.
    d) Administrative principles and hierarchy in organizations.

32. Which management approach viewed organization as a structured process with interacting individuals?
    a) Quantitative or Mathematical Approach
    b) **Systems Approach**
    c) Contingency Approach
    d) Classical Approach

33. The Contingency Approach to management suggests that managerial policies and practices should be:
    a) Universally applicable and unchanging.
    b) **Adapted to changes in the environment.**
    c) Based on individual worker motivations.
    d) Focused on strict control and supervision.

34. The modern theories of management are characterized by:
    a) Strict adherence to classical principles.
    b) Emphasis on informal organization and emotions of workers.
    c) **A multi-level, multidisciplinary, and adaptive approach.**
    d) Exclusively quantitative analysis for decision making.

35. The Theory of Bureaucracy was proposed by:
    a) Frederick Taylor
    b) Henri Fayol
    c) Max Weber
    d) Hugo Munsterberg

36. The primary focus of the Theory of Bureaucracy is on:
    a) Informal communication and emotions of workers.
    b) **Rational legal authority and organizational structure.**
    c) Motivation and satisfaction of employees.
    d) Quantitative analysis for decision making.

37. Which approach in management uses mathematical and statistical models for decision making?

    a) **Quantitative or Mathematical Approach**

    b) Systems Approach

    c) Contingency Approach

    d) Administrative Approach

38. According to the system approach to management, an organization is composed of interacting and interdependent:

    a) Employees
    b) **Subsystems**
    c) Departments
    d) Tasks

39. Which major experiment conducted at the Hawthorne plant influenced the development of Neo-classical theories?

    a) Maslow's Hierarchy of Needs
    b) **The Hawthorne Effect**
    c) Theory X and Y
    d) The Theory of Z

40. The Neo-classical theories of management emphasized the importance of:

    a) Strict rules and regulations in the workplace.

    b) **Informal organization and emotions of workers.**

    c) Quantitative analysis for decision making.

    d) Administrative principles and hierarchy in organizations.

41. Which management approach viewed organization as a structured process with interacting individuals?

    a) Quantitative or Mathematical Approach

    b) Systems Approach

    c) Contingency Approach

    d) Classical Approach

42. The Contingency Approach to management suggests that managerial policies and practices should be:

    a) Universally applicable and unchanging.

    b) **Adapted to changes in the environment**.

    c) Based on individual worker motivations.

    d) Focused on strict control and supervision.

43. The system approach to management emphasizes:
    a) Contingency and adaptation to environmental changes.
    b) **Interrelated and interdependent parts of the organization.**
    c) Predictability and stability in the workplace.
    d) Strict rules and regulations for worker behavior.

44. The Theory of Bureaucracy was proposed by:
    a) Frederick Taylor
    b) Henri Fayol
    c) **Max Weber**
    d) Hugo Munsterberg

45. The primary focus of the Theory of Bureaucracy is on:
    a) Informal communication and emotions of workers.
    b) **Rational legal authority and organizational structure.**
    c) Motivation and satisfaction of employees.
    d) Quantitative analysis for decision making.

46. Which approach in management uses mathematical and statistical models for decision making?
    a) **Quantitative or Mathematical Approach**
    b) Systems Approach
    c) Contingency Approach
    d) Administrative Approach

47. Which of the following is NOT one of the four principles of scientific management?
    a) Replace working by rule of thumb with scientific methods.
    b) Match workers to jobs based on capability and motivation.
    c) Eliminate supervision and instructions for workers.
    d) Monitor worker performance and provide supervision.

48. Who developed the administrative theory and outlined the fourteen principles of management?
    a) Max Weber
    b) Frederick Taylor
    c) Hugo Munsterberg
    d) Henri Fayol

49. The administrative theory focuses on:
    a) Analyzing individual tasks and job requirements.
    b) Utilizing scientific methods to increase worker productivity.
    c) The rational legal authority of managers.
    d) Improving worker motivation through financial incentives.

50. Which of the following is NOT one of the five functions of managers?

a) Staffing b) Coordinating
c) Delegating d) **Commanding**

51. The term 'POSDCORB' describes functions of managers. What does it stand for?

a) **Planning, Organizing, Staffing, Directing, Coordinating, Reporting, and Budgeting**
b) Planning, Organizing, Staffing, Delegating, Coordinating, Reviewing, and Budgeting
c) Planning, Organizing, Staffing, Directing, Coordinating, Communicating, and Budgeting
d) Planning, Organizing, Staffing, Delegating, Coordinating, Reporting, and Controlling

52. Which function of managers involves assigning roles and responsibilities and developing productive relationships among resources?

a) Planning b) **Organizing**
c) Staffing d) Controlling

53. The function of managers that deals with identifying the right person for the right job is called:

a) Planning b) Organizing
c) **Staffing** d) Directing

54. What does MBO stand for in management?

a) Management by Operations b) Management by Organization
c) Management by Observation d) **Management by Objectives**

55. What is the primary purpose of planning in management?

a) To review past achievements
b) To assign roles and responsibilities
c) **To achieve organizational goals**
d) To maintain employee motivation

56. Which principle of planning suggests that planning should be done at all levels of management?

a) Principle of contribution to objective
b) Principle of navigational change
c) Principle of limiting factors
d) **Principle of pervasiveness of planning**

57. What type of plan involves short-range planning to support strategic and tactical plans?
    a) Vision plans
    b) Strategic plans
    c) **Tactical plans**
    d) Operational plans

58. What are the essential characteristics of a good plan?
    a) Vagueness and uncertainty
    b) Rigid and inflexible
    c) **Based on clearly-defined objectives**
    d) Independent of organizational goals

59. What are the general steps involved in the planning process?
    a) Establishing verifiable goals, Evaluation of alternatives, Implementation and monitoring of the decision
    b) Deciding the planning period, Finding alternative courses of action, Monitoring and measuring progress
    c) Establishing planning premises, Measuring and controlling progress, Setting verifiable goals
    d) **Establishing verifiable goals, Deciding the planning period, Finding alternative courses of action.**

60. What type of objectives are those that can be measured and quantified?
    a) Non-verifiable objectives
    b) Ambiguous objectives
    c) **Verifiable objectives**
    d) Non-quantifiable objectives

61. What is the main aim of Management by Objectives (MBO)?
    a) To involve only top-level managers in goal setting
    b) **To improve performance by defining clear objectives**
    c) To emphasize inputs rather than accomplishments
    d) To eliminate the participative decision-making process

62. What is the potential drawback of using participative decision-making in organizations?
    a) Decreased accountability of employees
    b) Limited employee engagement
    c) **Time-consuming process**
    d) Inability to generate creative ideas

63. What stage in the decision-making process involves identifying and diagnosing the problem?
    a) **Investigation of the situation**
    b) Development of alternatives
    c) Evaluation of alternatives and selection
    d) Implementation and monitoring

64. Which group decision-making technique involves generating as many ideas as possible without any verbal exchange among members?
    a) Brainstorming
    b) Delphi technique
    c) Synectics
    d) **Nominal Group Technique**

65. The Nominal Group Technique (NGT) involves which of the following steps?
    a) Generation of ideas in a silent manner by writing
    b) Sharing of ideas in a round-robin fashion, recording each idea on a flip-chart or blackboard
    c) Group interaction around ideas for clarification and evaluation
    d) **All of the above**

66. Which type of plan involves long-term objectives, formulation of vision and strategies, and allocation of resources to pursue organizational goals?
    a) Operational plans
    b) **Strategic plans**
    c) Tactical plans
    d) Vision plans

67 What type of plan focuses on developing specific action steps to support strategic and tactical plans?
    a) Strategic plans
    b) Vision plans
    c) Tactical plans
    d) **Operational plans**

68. Which function of managers deals with setting standards and measuring employee performance?
    a) Planning
    b) Organizing
    c) **Controlling**
    d) Directing

69. Which function of managers involves increasing work efficiency, providing better leadership, and using effective communication methods in the organization?
    a) Planning
    b) Coordinating
    c) **Directing**
    d) Controlling

70. Which principle of planning suggests that plans should use all available resources and opportunities before creating new authorities and resources?
   a) Principle of contribution to objective
   b) Principle of navigational change
   c) **Principle of limiting factors**
   d) Principle of flexibility

71. What are the characteristics of verifiable objectives?
   a) Cannot be measured or quantified
   b) **Measurable, concrete, and involve a time element**
   c) Based on vague assumptions
   d) Not related to organizational goals

72. What is the purpose of the "mission" in an organization?
   a) To outline specific action steps to achieve goals
   b) **To define the fundamental purpose of the organization**
   c) To set short-term objectives for employees
   d) To provide guidelines for individual performance evaluation

73. What is the last step in the Five-step MBO process?
   a) Evaluating performance
   b) Reviewing performance
   c) Monitoring
   d) **Cascading objectives to employees**

74. What is the potential drawback of using participative decision-making in organizations?
   a) Decreased accountability of employees
   b) Limited employee engagement
   c) **Time-consuming process**
   d) Inability to generate creative ideas

75. Which stage in the decision-making process involves identifying and diagnosing the problem?
   a) **Investigation of the situation**
   b) Development of alternatives
   c) Evaluation of alternatives and selection
   d) Implementation and monitoring

76. What does "Synectics" mean in Greek?
   a) The fitting together of diverse elements
   b) Creative thinking
   c) **Novel and bizarre alternatives**
   d) Problem-solving technique

77. What is the primary aim of Synectics?
   a) To stimulate group discussions
   b) To analyze problems thoroughly
   c) **To involve the preconscious mind in decision-making**
   d) To select members based on background and training

78. How does Synectics stimulate creative thinking?
   a) By limiting the ideas to familiar concepts
   b) By focusing only on relevant ideas
   c) **By combining distinct and apparently irrelevant ideas**
   d) By avoiding thought-provoking exercises

79 What is the main purpose of involving the preconscious mind in Synectics?
   a) To limit the scope of ideas generated
   b) To encourage logical thinking
   c) To promote role-playing and group discussions
   d) **To access unique and imaginative solutions**

80 Which type of problems is Synectics particularly useful for?
   a) Simple and straightforward problems
   b) Emotional and personal problems
   c) **Complex and technical problems**
   d) Short-term and immediate problems

81 What is the definition of an organization?
   a) A group of individuals with similar interests
   b) **A formal structure of roles and positions**
   c) A gathering of people for social activities
   d) A team working towards individual goals

82. Which type of organization is characterized by a fixed set of rules and hierarchy?

a) Bureaucracy
b) Informal organization
c) Line organization
d) **Formal organization**

83. What is the primary function of line authority in an organization?

a) To investigate and research
b) To provide advisory support
c) **To achieve organizational objectives**
d) To support the line function

84. What is the key difference between authority and power?

a) Power is derived from legitimacy, while authority is derived from influence.
b) Authority is broader and more encompassing than power.
c) **Power is the ability to induce or influence others, while authority refers to the right to exercise power.**
d) Authority is given by subordinates, while power is given by superiors.

85. What does delegation of authority in an organization mean?

a) **Division of authority and power to subordinates**
b) Transfer of power to the top management
c) Centralization of decision-making
d) The establishment of informal relationships

86. Which term describes the shared assumptions, values, and beliefs that govern behavior in an organization?

a) Line and staff
b) Authority and power
c) **Organizational culture**
d) Delegation of authority

87. What does organizational change refer to?

a) The stability of an organization over time
b) The resistance to change within an organization
c) The process of achieving organizational objectives
d) **A difference in form, quality, or state over time in an organizational entity**

88. What is the purpose of refreezing in the context of organizational change?
    a) To create chaos and confusion
    b) **To establish a new equilibrium state**
    c) To resist any form of change
    d) To increase resistance to future change

89. Why is effective management of change necessary in organizations?
    a) To prevent any form of change from occurring
    b) To reduce motivation among employees
    c) **To implement planned strategies and prevent loss in benefits**
    d) To eliminate the need for future changes

90. Which of the following is a cause of organizational change?
    a) Maintaining the status quo
    b) Decreasing global competition
    c) **Privatization and downsizing**
    d) Reducing outsourcing activities

91. What are the two approaches for change management?
    a) Incremental change and visionary change
    b) Persuasion and coercive methods
    c) Fundamental change and forced participation
    d) **Incremental change and fundamental change**

92. John P. Kotter's eight steps to successful change management include all of the following EXCEPT:
    a) Increase urgency
    b) Communicate for buy-in
    c) Ignore resistance to change
    d) **Create short-term wins**

93. Organizational development (OD seeks to improve effectiveness and employee well-being through:
    a) Dictatorial methods
    b) **Humanistic-democratic values**
    c) Centralized decision-making
    d) Bureaucratic structures

94. Decentralization differs from delegation in that decentralization involves:
   a) Division of workload to lower levels
   b) **Distribution of authority to lower levels**
   c) Bureaucratic structures
   d) Centralized decision-making

95. What are the criteria proposed by Earnest Dale to measure the extent of decentralization in an organization?
   a) The number of employees at lower levels
   b) The number of decisions made at higher levels
   c) The number of areas in which decisions can be made at lower levels
   d) **The number of decisions made at lower levels, the importance of decisions made at lower levels, the number of areas in which decisions can be made at lower levels, and the fewer people to be consulted**

96. What is the process of arranging and allocating work, authority, and resources among an organization's members to achieve the organization's goals?
   a) Controlling
   b) Leading
   c) Staffing
   d) **Organizing**

97. What does "chain of command" in an organization refer to?
   a) Division of work
   b) Recruitment and selection process
   c) **Unity of command and scalar principle**
   d) Filling positions in the organization

98. Work specialization in an organization refers to:
   a) The number of workers who report to one manager
   b) The process of grouping activities into units
   c) **The division of work into separate tasks**
   d) The identification of workforce requirements

99. What is the term used for the process of identifying and putting the right person in the right job?
   a) **Staffing**
   b) Leading
   c) Controlling
   d) Organizing

100. Which sub-function of staffing involves measuring an individual's performance on the job and potential for development?

a) Recruitment b) Selection

c) Training and development d) **Performance appraisal**

101. What are the stages involved in the performance appraisal process?

a) Planning, organizing, and controlling

b) Monitoring performance, appraising, and feedback

c) Establishing standards and measures, communicating job expectations, and planning

d) **All of the above**

102. What is delegation of authority in an organization?

a) The process of assigning tasks and duties to subordinates

b) The process of filling positions in the organization

c) The process of dividing work among managers

d) **The process of devolution of authority to subordinates**

103. According to the principle of delegation, what cannot be delegated by a manager to subordinates?

a) Tasks and duties b) Goals and objectives

c) **Responsibility** d) Authority

104. Which type of delegation involves entrusting someone else to do parts of your job?

a) General delegation b) Upward delegation

c) Written delegation d) **Downward delegation**

105. What is the art of influencing and motivating people to achieve common goals called?

a) Controlling b) Staffing

c) **Leading** d) Organizing

106. Which function of management involves directing and influencing the task-related activities of group members?

a) Controlling b) Staffing

c) **Leading** d) Organizing

107. What is the main advantage of effective delegation in an organization?
   a) It minimizes workload for employees
   b) It avoids wastage of time
   c) It helps in training new incumbents
   d) **All of the above**

108. Which principle of delegation emphasizes keeping a balance between authority and responsibility?
   a) Principle of result expected
   b) Principle of absolute responsibility
   c) Principle of authority level
   d) **Principle of parity of authority and responsibility**

109. What is the process of grouping activities into units for the purpose of administration called?
   a) Work specialization
   b) **Departmentation**
   c) Span of control
   d) Staffing

110. Which leadership theory suggests that great leaders are born with intrinsic characteristics such as charisma and intelligence?
   a) Trait theory
   b) Transformational leadership theory
   c) **Great man theory**
   d) Contingency approach

111. According to the Trait theory of leadership, what is the focus of analysis to identify effective leaders?
   a) Mental abilities
   b) Physical appearance
   c) **Personal characteristics of leaders**
   d) Organizational structure

112. What does the Behavioural theory of leadership emphasize?
   a) Intrinsic characteristics of leaders
   b) **Task and people-oriented behaviors of effective leaders**
   c) The contingency approach to leadership
   d) Transactional exchange between leaders and followers

113. Contingency theories argue that effective leadership is contingent upon:
   a) The number of workers who report to one manager
   b) The organization's culture and policies
   c) The leader's charisma and confidence
   d) **Specific situational factors**

114. Which leadership theory focuses on transactional exchange between leaders and followers?
   a) **Transactional leadership theory**
   b) Transformational leadership theory
   c) Trait theory
   d) Great man theory

115. Transformational leadership is characterized by:
   a) A focus on task-oriented behaviors
   b) Rigid rules and regulations
   c) **Creating a sense of belonging and identification with the leader's purpose**
   d) A transactional exchange between leaders and followers

116. Which theory suggests that employees' motivation is influenced by their perception of rewards and outcomes?
   a) Maslow's Hierarchy of Needs theory
   b) **Vroom's Expectancy theory**
   c) Equity theory
   d) Herzberg's Two-Factor theory

117. According to Expectancy theory, what is the belief that your effort will lead to the achievement of desired goals called?
   a) Valence
   b) **Performance-outcome expectancy**
   c) Effort-performance expectancy
   d) Instrumentality

118. The Equity theory of motivation proposes that motivation is influenced by:
   a) Task requirements and employee characteristics
   b) The balance between motivator and hygiene factors
   c) **Perceived fairness in comparison to others**
   d) The expectation of outcomes from actions

119. Reinforcement theory suggests that behavior with positive consequences tends to be:

a) **Repeated**
b) Punished
c) Ignored
d) Modified

120. The Goal setting theory focuses on:

a) Identifying leaders' intrinsic characteristics
b) **Setting and striving for goals**
c) The exchange of rewards and outcomes between leaders and followers
d) Analyzing mental, physical, and social characteristics of leaders

121. Which theory proposes that leaders transform their followers through their inspirational and charismatic nature?

a) Trait theory
b) Great man theory
c) **Transformational leadership theory**
d) Contingency approach

122. What are the two main factors identified by Herzberg in his Two-Factor theory of motivation?

a) Expectancy and instrumentality
b) **Motivator factors and hygiene factors**
c) Task requirements and employee characteristics
d) Effort-performance expectancy and valence

123. According to the Contingency theories of leadership, effective leadership styles should be based on:

a) Intrinsic characteristics of leaders
b) **Specific situational factors**
c) The exchange of rewards and outcomes
d) Transactional relationships with followers

124. Which theory suggests that leaders are made, not born, and that behavior is learned?

a) Great man theory
b) Transactional leadership theory
c) Trait theory
d) **Behavioral theories**

125. The ERG theory of motivation was proposed by:

a) Maslow
b) **Alderfer**
c) Vroom
d) Skinner

126. What does the ERG theory of motivation stand for?

a) Esteem, Recognition, Growth
b) Expectancy, Rewards, Goals
c) **Existence, Relatedness, Growth**
d) Effort, Results, Goals

127. The Reinforcement theory of motivation is based on the principle of:

a) Hierarchy of needs
b) Expectancy and instrumentality
c) **Behavior and consequences**
d) Transactional exchange

128. According to the Equity theory of motivation, employees compare themselves with:

a) Other organizations
b) Their own past jobs
c) **Their peers within the organization or outside referents**
d) Their supervisors and managers

129. Controlling is defined as:

a) Setting organizational goals
b) Delegating tasks to subordinates
c) **Measuring and correcting performance**
d) Hiring new employees

130. According to Koontz, the controlling procedure consists of how many steps?

a) 1 step
b) 2 steps
c) **3 steps**
d) 4 steps

131. Traditional techniques of control include:

a) Return on investment
b) **Personal observation**
c) Ratio analysis
d) Responsibility accounting

132. Budgeting is defined as:
   a) The measurement of employee performance
   b) **Formulating plans for the future in numerical terms**
   c) Correcting deviations in performance
   d) Establishing controls for corrective action

133. Talent management includes the following processes:
   a) Budgeting, planning, and staffing
   b) Training, performance management, and promotions
   c) **Talent attraction, talent retention, and talent development**
   d) Staffing, organizing, and leading

134. How can organizations manage talent effectively?
   a) By ignoring employee strengths and interests
   b) By limiting opportunities for employees to take on new tasks
   c) **By providing challenging projects, mentoring, and recognition of merit**
   d) By enforcing rigid organizational rules and procedures

135. Conflict management is the process of:
   a) Eliminating all conflicts in the workplace
   b) Limiting positive aspects of conflicts
   c) **Limiting negative aspects of conflicts while increasing positive aspects**
   d) Encouraging conflicts to escalate for resolution

136. According to Hans Selye, stress is:
   a) **The response of the body to any demand**
   b) A state of peace and relaxation
   c) Only caused by negative events
   d) Unrelated to an individual's perception

137. Positive effects of stress include:
   a) Decreased job performance
   b) Lower job attitudes
   c) **Feeling stimulated and facing an exciting challenge**
   d) Increased turnover

138. The Transactional model of stress emphasizes:
    a) Eliminating stressors from the environment
    b) **Balancing demands and resources**
    c) Focusing on the individual's personality traits
    d) Ignoring stress and its effects on individuals

139. What are some job-related strategies for stress management?
    a) Focusing on emotional intelligence
    b) **Proper job designing and matching individuals to jobs**
    c) Implementing reactive approaches to stress
    d) Blaming employees for stress in the workplace

140. The stages of conflict include:
    a) Latent conflict, perceived conflict, and solution conflict
    b) Manifested conflict, aftermath conflict, and resolution conflict
    c) **Latent conflict, perceived conflict, felt conflict, manifested conflict, and conflict aftermath**
    d) Conflict initiation, escalation, and de-escalation

141. The sources of conflict in organizations can be categorized into:
    a) **Individual, group, and environmental sources**
    b) Task, relationship, and process sources
    c) Formal and informal sources
    d) Interpersonal and intrapersonal sources

142. Stress management models include:
    a) The proactive approach and the blaming approach
    b) The Transactional model and the Structural model
    c) **The Transactional model and the Health realization/innate health model**
    d) The problem-focused strategy and the emotion-focused strategy

143. What are the requirements for effective control?
    a) Establishing controls that lead to corrective action
    b) Tailoring control to individual managers
    c) Seeking objectivity of control
    d) **All of the above**

144. Modern techniques of control include:
 a) Personal observation
 b) **Return on investment**
 c) Budgetary control
 d) Statistical reports

145. The process of talent management starts with:
 a) Performance support
 b) **Talent attraction**
 c) Talent retention
 d) Succession planning

146. The Transactional model of stress emphasizes:
 a) Eliminating stressors from the environment
 b) **Balancing demands and resources**
 c) Focusing on the individual's personality traits
 d) Ignoring stress and its effects on individuals

147. Which of the following is NOT one of the stages of conflict?
 a) Latent conflict
 b) Manifested conflict
 c) Resolved conflict
 d) **Conflict aftermath**

148. What is the purpose of project planning?
 a) To make the project complex and challenging
 b) **To define project scope, timeframe, and resources**
 c) To involve as many stakeholders as possible
 d) Project planning is not mentioned in the text

149. What are the two most important rules in network techniques (CPM and PERT)?
 a) **All activities must be completed before the project starts**
 b) Arrows represent actual time taken for each activity
 c) Dummy activities are used to represent the critical path
 d) Network techniques do not have specific rules

150. What is the purpose of the SWOT analysis?
 a) To create complex matrices for project evaluation
 b) **To assess internal and external factors affecting project success**
 c) SWOT analysis is not mentioned in the text
 d) To measure project progress using verifiable indicators

151. When should a SWOT analysis be conducted in a project?
   a) At the end of the project
   b) **During the start-up phase of the project**
   c) After the project is completed
   d) SWOT analysis should be an ongoing process throughout the project

152. What is one of the limitations of the Logical Framework Approach (LFA)?
   a) LFA is not suitable for situations with uncertainty
   b) LFA does not involve detailed planning of projects
   c) LFA cannot be put into a log frame
   d) LFA is only used for strategic planning

153. What is a project?
   a) An activity without a specific purpose
   b) A planned work or activity with a particular objective over a period of time.
   c) A randomly organized set of tasks
   d) A repetitive and ongoing process

154. Which of the following is the essence of a project?
   a) Unlimited timeframe b) **Specific objectives**
   c) Vague deliverables d) No constraints

155. Project planning involves all of the following except:
   a) Defining project scope
   b) Identifying deliverables
   c) Setting measurable objectives
   d) **Managing resources without constraints**

156. Project management is different from general management because it:
   a) Has a longer timeframe
   b) **Involves a finite time span and has a final deliverable**
   c) Doesn't require any specific skills
   d) Deals with unrelated tasks

157. Which of the following is NOT a project management tool?
   a) Gantt chart b) PERT
   c) **SWOT analysis** d) Logical framework approach

158. What is a disadvantage of the Gantt chart?
  a) **It cannot show relationships between tasks**
  b) It is too complex to use
  c) It requires specialized software
  d) It is not suitable for small projects

159. What are the two most important rules of networking in PERT and CPM?
  a) **Arrows imply logical precedence only**
  b) The length of the arrow determines the task's duration
  c) Arrows indicate time delays between tasks
  d) Arrows indicate resources required for each task

160. What is the key difference between CPM and PERT?
  a) **CPM is probabilistic, while PERT is deterministic**
  b) PERT has a finite time span, while CPM doesn't
  c) CPM focuses on critical constraints, while PERT does not
  d) PERT emphasizes long-range planning, while CPM does not

161. What is the ultimate objective to which the programme contributes in the logical framework approach?
  a) Purpose
  b) Output
  c) **Goal**
  d) Input

162. The important assumptions in the logical framework approach are:
  a) Conditions that the project manager can control
  b) Critical factors that are not linked to project success
  c) **External factors critical to project success**
  d) Assumptions about internal resources only

163. The SWOT analysis stands for:
  a) Strengths, Weaknesses, Opportunities, Timeframes
  b) Strategies, Weaknesses, Opportunities, Threats
  c) Strengths, Weaknesses, Opportunities, Trends
  d) **Strengths, Weaknesses, Opportunities, Threats**

164. When is SWOT analysis generally conducted in a project?
   a) After the project is completed
   b) **At the start-up phase of the project**
   c) During the project execution phase
   d) After project evaluation and closure

165. Forecasting is:
   a) **The technique of estimating future events based on past or present events**
   b) A process of guessing future events without any basis
   c) A method of predicting the past events
   d) None of the above

166. Forecasting is different from prediction because:
   a) **Forecasting uses past data and present events to estimate future events**
   b) Prediction relies on historical data and future events
   c) Forecasting is a random process, while prediction is based on data analysis
   d) There is no difference between forecasting and prediction

167. The importance of forecasting in organizations includes all of the following, except:
   a) Basis for sound planning
   b) Facilitate co-ordination and control
   c) Creating uncertainty in decision making
   d) **Keeps management alert and active to face challenges of future events**

168. Quantitative forecasting methods are used when:
   a) Historical data is not available or scarce
   b) **Expert opinions are the only source of information**
   c) Both historical data and expert opinions are available
   d) None of the above

169. The Delphi method of forecasting:
   a) Uses historical data and statistical analysis for predictions
   b) **Relies on the expert opinions of a panel of geographically dispersed experts**
   c) Requires frequent face-to-face meetings with experts
   d) Is not suitable for futuristic projects

170. Characteristics of the Delphi technique include all of the following, except:
  a) Anonymity to respondents
  b) Controlled feedback process-reducing the effect of noise
  c) Limited geographical dispersion of experts
  d) **Suitability for a variety of statistical analysis techniques**

171. The total number of steps involved in the Delphi technique is:
  a) 5   b) 8
  c) **10**   d) 12

172. TQM stands for:
  a) Total Quantity Management   b) Total Quality Movement
  c) **Total Quality Management**   d) Total Quality Model

173. The key elements of TQM do not include:
  a) Ethics   b) Integrity
  c) Leadership   d) **Financial resources**

174. Six Sigma methodology improves business processes by:
  a) Avoiding any changes in the process
  b) **Constantly reviewing and reuniting the process**
  c) Implementing new processes without any analysis
  d) Focusing only on customer feedback

175. The Five-S principle that ensures there is a place for everything and everything is in place is:
  a) Sorting   b) **Simplifying**
  c) Systematic Cleaning   d) Standardizing

176 The element of Five-S that involves the implementation of common processes for consistency is:
  a) Sorting   b) Simplifying
  c) Systematic Cleaning   d) **Standardizing**

177. What is the main difference between quantitative and qualitative forecasting methods?
  a) Quantitative methods use expert opinions, while qualitative methods rely on historical data
  b) **Quantitative methods are based on past data, while qualitative methods rely on expert opinions**

c) Quantitative methods use statistical analysis, while qualitative methods use data extrapolation

d) There is no difference between quantitative and qualitative forecasting methods

178. Which of the following is NOT one of the principles of Total Quality Management (TQM)?

a) Customer focus
b) Leadership
c) Mutual exclusion
d) **Involvement of people**

179. The Six Sigma approach aims to achieve:

a) Three standard deviations
b) Five standard deviations
c) **Six standard deviations**
d) Ten standard deviations

180. Which of the following is a key element of TQM?

a) Resourcefulness
b) Negativity
c) Integrity
d) **Chaos**

181. The Delphi method of forecasting is primarily based on:

a) Historical data
b) Statistical analysis
c) **Expert opinions**
d) Random selection of variables

182. The characteristic feature of an effective relationship is:

a) Isolation
b) Unpredictability
c) **Trust and mutual respect**
d) Instability

183. The Five-S principle that ensures a neat and clean area ready for inspection is:

a) Sorting
b) Simplifying
c) **Systematic Cleaning**
d) Standardizing

184. What is the primary purpose of the Delphi method in forecasting?

a) To collect historical data
b) **To gather expert opinions and achieve convergence of opinion**
c) To use statistical analysis for predictions
d) To predict future events based on past data and trends

5

Directing Organizational Behavirour within Agricultural Extension

1. The roles of extension professionals have become more complex and challenging due to all of the following factors except:
   a) Economic liberalization
   b) Technological advances
   c) **Decreased demand for increased performance**
   d) Globalization

2. Organizational behaviour (OB) focuses on understanding, explaining, and changing human behaviour in which context?
   a) Personal relationships
   b) Social gatherings
   c) **Organizational context**
   d) Educational institutions

3. What are the two sub-fields of Organizational Behaviour (OB)?
   a) Macro-organizational behaviour and Individual psychology
   b) Group dynamics and Micro-organizational behaviour
   c) **Macro-organizational behaviour and Micro-organizational behaviour**
   d) Group dynamics and Individual psychology

4. Attitudes and values play a major role in influencing the:
   a) **Personality of an individual**
   b) Economic growth of a country
   c) Technological advancements
   d) Political climate of an organization

5. Which theory emphasizes that people seek consistency among different attitudes they hold to maintain rationality?
   a) Cognitive Dissonance theory
   b) Social Learning theory
   c) Cognitive Response theory
   d) **Consistency theory**

Bold Means Correct Answer

6. Source credibility affects attitude change, and messages coming from credible sources are more likely to produce:
   a) **Greater impact** b) No impact
   c) Negative impact d) Neutral impact

7. The basic units involved in attitude change are:
   a) Extension agents, government officials, and farmers
   b) Farmers, researchers, and extension agencies
   c) **Source, message, and receivers**
   d) Educators, students, and administrators

8. Values are defined as the worth or excellence of an object, and they serve as principles to guide:
   a) Decision-making
   b) Productivity
   c) **Attitude, action, and evaluation**
   d) Job satisfaction

9. What are the two main types of values ?
   a) Theoretical and religious b) Positive and negative
   c) Social and political **d) Economic and aesthetic**

10. Which type of value refers to preferable ways of behaving and are means for achieving terminal values?
   a) **Instrumental values** b) Terminal values
   c) Theoretical values d) Economic values

11. Attitudes and values are important in an organizational context because they affect:
   a) Personal life only
   b) **Productivity and job satisfaction**
   c) Social interactions
   d) Political affiliations

12. What is the primary focus of organizational behaviour?
   a) **Understanding and changing human behaviour as it occurs in organizations**
   b) Understanding the behaviour of individuals in isolation
   c) Understanding the impact of technology on human behaviour
   d) Understanding cultural anthropology

13. What are the dimensions of organizational behaviour?
    a) Group and Intergroup relations, Organizational structure, and Leadership
    b) **Individual in organization, Group and Intergroup relations, Organizational context, and Intervention process**
    c) Attitudes and values, Human resource management, and Work motivation
    d) Social psychology, Sociology, and Cognitive psychology

14. What skills are most needed at the top level of management?
    a) Human skills
    b) Technical skills
    c) **Conceptual skills**
    d) Problem-solving skills

15. What does OB stand ?
    a) Organizational Benefits
    b) Occupational Behaviour
    c) **Organizational Behaviour**
    d) Occupational Balance

16. What is the role of attitudes and values in extension education?
    a) They do not play any role in extension education
    b) They affect the attitudes of extension professionals
    c) **They affect the behaviour of employees in organizations**
    d) They determine the success of government policies

17. Which theory emphasizes that people maintain consistency in their attitudes in any situation?
    a) Cognitive Response theory
    b) **Balance Theory**
    c) Social Learning theory
    d) Cognitive Dissonance theory

18. What are the three components of attitudes ?
    a) **Cognitive, affective, and behavioural**
    b) Emotional, psychological, and social
    c) Observable, external, and rational
    d) Physical, mental, and perceptive

19. How are values classified ?
    a) Positive and negative
    b) Theoretical and terminal
    c) Instrumental and terminal
    d) **Economic, aesthetic, social, political, religious, and theoretical**

20. Motivation can be defined as:
    a) The process of fulfilling physiological needs
    b) **A force that helps a person move towards action**
    c) The process of persuasion and conviction
    d) The interaction of needs, drives, and incentives

21. What is the root meaning of the word "motivation"?
    a) To relax
    b) To fulfill physiological needs
    c) **To move**
    d) To persuade

22. A need refers to:
    a) **A gap or imbalance related to physiological or mental realm**
    b) A desire to achieve a specific goal
    c) An external factor that influences behavior
    d) An internal force that directs behavior

23. Drives can be defined as:
    a) External incentives that reduce the imbalance or gap
    b) Unlearned physiological needs
    c) **Deficiencies or imbalances that give direction to reduce them**
    d) External factors that activate behavior

24. In the context of motivation, incentives refer to:
    a) Unlearned physiological needs
    b) External factors that activate behavior
    c) **External incentives that reduce imbalances or gaps**
    d) Internal factors that influence thoughts and behavior

25. Which of the following is an example of intrinsic motivation?
    a) Salary and benefits
    b) Promotion and recognition
    c) **Curiosity and need for achievement**
    d) Working conditions and job security

26. External/extrinsic motivation includes:
    a) Unlearned physiological needs only
    b) **Unlearned physiological needs and other factors controlled by the manager**
    c) Internal needs and desires of an individual
    d) Incentives and drives

27. What are primary motives in the classification of human motives?
    a) Learned motives important for motivation in organizations
    b) Physiological needs based on genetic makeup and unlearned
    c) External factors controlled by the manager
    d) **Unlearned but not based physiologically**

28. Which of the following is an example of secondary motives?
    a) Hunger and sleep
    b) **Curiosity and affection**
    c) Physiological needs such as thirst and sex
    d) Unlearned motives not based on physiology

29. Maslow's hierarchy of needs suggests that:
    a) Employees are motivated only by external means such as rewards or punishment
    b) **The needs are arranged in a hierarchy, and one set of needs no longer motivates a person once they are satisfied**
    c) Intrinsic motives are more powerful than extrinsic motives
    d) Theories of motivation are based on hygiene and motivator factors

30. The hygiene factors in Herzberg's Two Factor Theory:
    a) Cause satisfaction in employees
    b) Result in increased job productivity
    c) **Cause dissatisfaction if absent**
    d) Are the same as motivator factors

31. Which of the following is an example of a motivator factor according to Herzberg's theory?
    a) Poor working conditions
    b) Inadequate salary
    c) **Challenging work and recognition for achievements**
    d) Poor job security

32. According to Herzberg, the presence of only hygiene factors:
    a) Prevents employees from being dissatisfied
    b) **Results in dissatisfaction**
    c) Creates a neutral condition for work
    d) Increases job productivity

33. What is the first step to prevent employees from getting frustrated or sick, according to Herzberg's theory?

    a) Providing motivator factors

    b) **Promoting a clean environment**

    c) Increasing salary and job security

    d) Establishing good relationships with coworkers

34. Maslow's hierarchy of needs and Herzberg's Two Factor Theory share a similar set of relationships. Which of the following statements is correct?

    a) Maslow's physiological, safety, and social needs are motivators in Herzberg's theory

    b) Herzberg's hygiene factors are motivators in Maslow's theory

    c) **Maslow's esteem and self-actualization needs are motivators in Herzberg's theory**

    d) Maslow's needs are not related to Herzberg's theory

35. Which of the following best describes intrinsic motivation?

    a) Motivation derived from external incentives

    b) Motivation influenced by physiological needs

    c) **Motivation based on internal desires and needs**

    d) Motivation influenced by external factors controlled by the manager

36. Extrinsic motivation includes:

    a) The satisfaction of self-actualization needs

    b) The fulfillment of physiological needs

    c) **Internal desires and needs**

    d) External incentives controlled by the manager

37. What is the primary focus of Maslow's hierarchy of needs?

    a) Providing employees with intrinsic motivation

    b) **Meeting physiological needs first, followed by safety, social, esteem, and self-actualization needs**

    c) Focusing on hygiene factors to prevent dissatisfaction

    d) Emphasizing the importance of motivator factors in job content

38. According to Herzberg, what differentiates hygiene factors from motivator factors?

a) Hygiene factors result in increased job productivity

b) Motivator factors cause dissatisfaction if absent

c) **Hygiene factors prevent employees from being dissatisfied**

d) Motivator factors are based on physiological needs

39. In Herzberg's Two Factor Theory, what is the role of motivator factors in employee motivation?

a) They prevent dissatisfaction and create a neutral work environment

b) They cause dissatisfaction if absent and motivate employees when present

c) They operate similarly to hygiene factors and are not good enough to act as motivators

d) **They result in satisfaction and increased job productivity**

40. Motivational studies in extension and development organizations have limited research evidence to explain the correlation between higher order of motivation of employees and their:

a) Need for affiliation

b) Work or performance orientation

c) Dependence on the organization

d) **Financial incentives**

41. The extension approach is synonymous with:

a) Benevolent approach

b) Feudalistic approach

c) Development approach by economists

d) **All of the above**

42. Feudalistic approach is characterized by a predominant concern for:

a) Concern for people with superordinate goals

b) Concern for influence and giving

c) **Keeping control of the situation**

d) Making oneself relevant for others

43. The benevolent approach defines the concern that has a high tendency of:
    a) Making community and employees dependent on the giver
    b) Supporting the people and giving generously
    c) **Achieving personal excellence**
    d) Achieving organizational goals

44. According to the text, which of the following is NOT one of Maslow's hierarchy of needs?
    a) Physiological needs
    b) Social needs
    c) Affiliation needs
    d) **Safety needs**

45. Extension motivation is best defined as:
    a) Providing rewards and punishments to motivate employees
    b) **The motivation of employees driven by higher-order needs to help others**
    c) Meeting the needs and goals of both the employer and the workforce
    d) Focusing on intrinsic rewards in the organization

46. The concept of higher-order needs assumes significance in dealing with complex human behavior to help enhance performance in:
    a) Extension and development organizations
    b) Agricultural research centers
    c) Industrial manufacturing units
    d) **Educational institutions**

47. In the realm of Indian studies, who propounded the hypothesis of extension motivation during his early work with the farming community?
    a) Frederick Herzberg
    b) Abraham Maslow
    c) **Udai Pareek**
    d) Prayag Mehta

48. The "Panchatantra of motivation factors" includes all of the following dimensions except:
    a) Dependence motivation
    b) Extension motivation
    c) Achievement motivation
    d) **Benevolent motivation**

49. The dependence motivation is characterized by:
    a) A focus on community service and support
    b) A need for control and discipline in the work system
    c) **A high need for decision-making role by few selected persons in the organization**
    d) A strong concern for social achievement

50. Extension motivation is closely related to which of the following dimensions in the "Panchatantra of motivation factors"?

a) Affiliation motivation
b) Achievement motivation
c) Power motivation
d) **None of the above**

51. Which approach is likely to kill the sense of self-drive to stand up on one's own and seek avenues to help oneself?

a) Feudalistic approach
b) Extension approach
c) **Benevolent approach**
d) Achievement approach

52. The achievement motivation is characterized by a higher need to build quality and:

a) **Focus on creating standard of excellence at every level of work system**
b) Achieve personal excellence concern
c) Support and donate to others
d) Keep harmony and coexistence of relationships

53. What is the central focus of extension-driven organizations?

a) Achieving personal excellence
b) Meeting the needs of employees
c) **Community and farmers' well-being**
d) Providing extrinsic rewards to motivate employees

54. What is the relationship between intrinsic rewards and extrinsic rewards in the organization, according to the text?

a) Intrinsic rewards tend to compete with extrinsic motivation
b) Intrinsic rewards have no impact on employee motivation
c) **Extrinsic rewards are more effective in stimulating performance**
d) Intrinsic rewards and extrinsic rewards have similar effects on employee motivation

55. Role of motivational climate in an organization is

a) It determines the strategic focus on how to evolve human resource development measures
b) It focuses on tangible reward systems
c) It directly correlates with the achievement of personal goals
d) **It measures the understanding of the organization's financial goals**

56. Who emphasized the significance of intrinsic needs of employees to drive work productivity and excellence?
    a) Frederick Herzberg
    b) Abraham Maslow
    c) Udai Pareek
    d) **Prayag Mehta**

57. What is the ulimate purpose of extension motivation?
    a) To address the needs of the giver
    b) To provide tangible rewards to employees
    c) **To reinforce intrinsic values in the workforce**
    d) To promote dependence motivation in the community

58. What is the primary purpose of communication in an organization?
    a) To direct individual action
    b) To achieve coordinated action
    c) To share information, feedback, and control
    d) All of the above

59. Downward communication in an organization flows from:
    a) Lower levels to higher levels
    b) **Higher levels to lower levels**
    c) Lateral levels within the same organization level
    d) Diagonally across different organization levels

60. Which type of communication is less formal and involves problem-solving and coordination of work flow between peers or groups?
    a) Downward communication
    b) Upward communication
    c) **Horizontal communication**
    d) Diagonal communication

61. Diagonal communication becomes most efficient in situations where:
    a) Downward communication is ineffective
    b) **Communication through other channels is not effective**
    c) Communication needs to be kept highly confidential
    d) Communication needs to flow laterally within the same organization level

62. A communication network in an organization is a group of people who:
    a) Develop and maintain contact to exchange information informally
    b) Exchange information formally through the chain of command
    c) Follow a strict hierarchical structure for communication
    d) **Communicate only through written messages**

63. In a centralized organization, the communication network often revolves around:
    a) Several pivotal persons
    b) A wheel-type of communication network
    c) A chain-type of communication network
    d) **A single pivotal person**

64. Informal communication in organizations coexists with:
    a) Grapevine communication
    b) Written communication
    c) Verbal communication
    d) **Formal communication systems**

65. The grapevine in an organization arises primarily from:
    a) Official communication channels
    b) The formal communication system
    c) **Social interaction and people's natural motivation to communicate**
    d) The organization's hierarchical structure

66. Which method of communication is most likely to have the advantage of speed and feedback?
    a) Written communication
    b) Verbal communication
    c) Non-verbal communication
    d) **Oral communication**

67. Written communication is more likely to be well thought out, clear, and logical because:
    a) It is less formal than verbal communication
    b) It can carry any information at any time
    c) **Both the sender and receiver have a record of the communication**
    d) It involves the use of non-verbal messages

68. Non-verbal communication can be expressed through all of the following EXCEPT:
    a) Gestures
    b) Body language
    c) **Written words**
    d) Facial expressions

69. What is the most important factor that can lead to distortion in communication?
    a) Selective perception
    b) **Frame of reference**
    c) Filtering of information
    d) Emotional state of the receiver

70. Distortion in communication occurs because of differing:

a) **Frames of reference**
b) Selective perception
c) Filtering of information
d) Emotional states of the sender

71. When communication is altered by a manager to make it appear more favorable to the receiver, it is called:

a) Semantic problems
b) Filtering
c) Frame of reference
d) **Noise in communication**

72. Information overload occurs when:

a) Communication is altered by a manager
b) The receiver's emotion affects message interpretation
c) **The amount of information exceeds the processing capacity**
d) Stereotypes affect communication with different individuals

73. Stereotype effect in communication occurs when managers:

a) Categorize people based on their experience
b) **Base communication on preconceived notions**
c) Use written communication exclusively
d) Rely heavily on oral communication

74. What factor influences communication in an organization when the channels of command and communication are unclear?

a) Frame of reference
b) Selective perception
c) **Organizational structure**
d) Information overload

75. When downward communication in an organization passes through various levels, it may become inaccurate due to:

a) Frame of reference
b) Filtering
c) Noise in communication
d) **All of the above**

76. Which type of communication is less formal and occurs more quickly due to fewer social barriers?

a) Downward communication
b) Upward communication
c) **Horizontal communication**
d) Diagonal communication

77. In which type of organization does the grapevine communication system grow most vigorous?
    a) Centrally controlled organization
    b) Organization with strong lateral communication
    c) Organization with a well-defined chain of command
    d) **Organization with secrecy, poor communication, and autocratic leadership**

78. Collaboration in an organization is considered a powerful value system because:
    a) It helps reduce interpersonal conflicts
    b) It leads to teaming and improved productivity
    c) It is essential for decision making by consensus
    d) **All of the above**

79. Challenges in building functional teams may arise in organizations with a competitive culture due to:
    a) Emphasis on organizational excellence over individual excellence
    b) Extrinsic reward system
    c) **Both A and B**
    d) None of the above

80. The process of consensus decision-making in a group emphasizes:
    a) Division of tasks and responsibilities
    b) Unifying the members' strengths and resources
    c) Power inequality among team members
    d) **Individual decision-making**

81. Consensus decision making can be a powerful tool for developing strong groups and excellent decisions because it:
    a) Leads to total satisfaction among all members
    b) Prioritizes individual interests over the common goal
    c) **Ensures all concerns are considered to find the optimum solution**
    d) Reduces the need for communication skills among team members

82. Which of the following factors supports consensus decision making?
    a) Power inequality among group members
    b) Avoiding discussion of disagreements
    c) **Good communication skills among members**
    d) Focusing on individual goals over the common goal

83. The concept of synergy in group decision-making means that:
   a) Individual contributions outweigh group contributions
   b) The group's performance is lower than the performance of its best members
   c) Group decision-making is less effective than individual decision-making
   d) The group outperforms even its best members

84. Which factor may impede consensus decision making in a group?
   a) Unity of purpose among members
   b) High level of participation from all members
   c) **Domination by a few members**
   d) Valuing conflict and competition among members

85. Groupthink occurs when:
   a) Group members avoid confronting differences and avoid discussions
   b) Members trade their points of view with others to get their ideas accepted
   c) **Members are influenced by a hidden agenda**
   d) Group members are highly cooperative and trusting of one another

86. The competency required for decision making through consensus that involves analyzing consequences of different alternatives is called:
   a) Task facilitation competencies
   b) **Problem-solving competencies**
   c) Group-building competencies
   d) Task alignment competencies

87. Which competency involves expressing and responding to emotions, supporting, and encouraging silent members in the group?
   a) Problem-solving competencies
   b) Task facilitation competencies
   c) **Group-building competencies**
   d) Decision-making competencies

88. Building a successful team requires clarity of mission and vision of the team within a given:
   a) Organizational structure
   b) **Time frame**
   c) Hierarchy of power
   d) Lateral communication system

89. Consensus decision making works well when group members have attitudes such as:
    a) Valuing conflict and competition
    b) **Cooperation, mutual trust, and concern for others**
    c) Exclusively valuing their own ideas and feelings
    d) Focusing only on task-oriented communication

90. Which factor impairs consensus decision making when members rush decisions due to time pressure?
    a) Low participation
    b) Hidden agenda
    c) Group polarization
    d) **Time constraints**

91. To promote consensus decision making, facilitators need to:
    a) Focus solely on task-oriented communication
    b) Use dominating strategies to lead discussions
    c) **Attend to both task and the way people are feeling**
    d) Minimize active listening to ensure efficiency

92. Which type of decision-making process involves trading and compromising between members?
    a) Decision making by consensus
    b) Decision making by division
    c) Groupthink decision making
    d) **Trading decision making**

93. The process of division in group decision making results in:
    a) Power equality among group members
    b) Synergy and creative thinking
    c) **The group getting divided**
    d) Active participation from all members

94. Which of the following attitudes hinders the consensus-building process in an organization?
    a) Cooperation, mutual trust, and idea of common ownership
    b) Valuing feelings and contributions of all members
    c) **Social prejudices, bias, and self-centeredness**
    d) Respecting and valuing conflict in group discussions

95. How can groups avoid the pitfall of groupthink in decision making?
    a) **Encourage active information seeking and reality testing**
    b) Avoid confronting differences and avoid discussions
    c) Allow polarized functions to promote diverse ideas
    d) Emphasize personal interests over group interests

96. Consensus decision making is hindered when members have:
    a) Patience and inclination to pay attention to opinions of others
    b) Skills in harmonizing differences and downplaying conflict
    c) **Attitudes like competitiveness and fostered inequality**
    d) Group members willing to actively listen to each other

97. Which competency is crucial for effective decision making through consensus as it involves analyzing the root cause and identifying solutions?
    a) Problem-solving competencies
    b) Task facilitation competencies
    c) Group-building competencies
    d) **Decision-making competencies**

98. What is the primary function of leadership?
    a) **Providing a futuristic goal or vision**
    b) Implementing existing plans
    c) Fostering competition among team members
    d) Maximizing individual achievements

99. Which leadership style involves making decisions without involving others and expects strict obedience?
    a) Democratic leadership
    b) **Autocratic leadership**
    c) Laissez-faire leadership
    d) Transformational leadership

100. What is the main difference between transformational and transactional leadership?
    a) Transformational leadership focuses on rewards and punishment.
    b) **Transactional leadership involves motivating followers to higher levels.**
    c) Transactional leadership is more people-oriented.
    d) Transformational leadership is based on formal structure.

101. Which leadership style encourages team members to participate in decision-making and values their input?
   a) Autocratic leadership
   b) **Democratic leadership**
   c) Laissez-faire leadership
   d) Transformational leadership

102. A leader who focuses on developing the potential of each individual team member is displaying which leadership style?
   a) Autocratic leadership
   b) Democratic leadership
   c) Laissez-faire leadership
   d) **Transformational leadership**

103. In the leadership style continuum, which style involves making decisions without consulting the group?
   a) Telling
   b) Selling
   c) Presenting ideas and inviting questions
   d) Presenting tentative decisions
   e) **Presenting problems and getting suggestions**

104. What type of leader believes that people are lazy and not interested in achieving organizational objectives?
   a) Autocratic leader
   b) Democratic leader
   c) Laissez-faire leader
   d) **Impoverished leader**

105. Which leadership style emphasizes maintaining healthy relationships among employees?
   a) Autocratic leadership
   b) Democratic leadership
   c) Laissez-faire leadership
   d) **People-oriented leadership**

106. Which component of transformational leadership involves challenging followers to achieve higher levels of performance?
   a) Charisma
   b) **Inspirational motivation**
   c) Intellectual stimulation
   d) Individual consideration

107. Which leadership style involves exchanging rewards and punishment to control behavior?
   a) Democratic leadership
   b) **Transactional leadership**
   c) Laissez-faire leadership
   d) Transformational leadership

108 A leader who uses rewards or praises to secure the commitment of people for his ideas follows which autocratic leadership style?

a) Hard-boiled autocrat
b) **Benevolent autocrat**
c) Manipulative autocrat
d) Democratic autocrat

109. Which leadership style involves making decisions that are tentative and subject to change?

a) Telling
b) Selling
c) Presenting ideas and inviting questions
d) **Presenting tentative decisions**

110. Which leadership style allows the group to take decisions within fixed limits?

a) Telling
b) Selling
c) Presenting ideas and inviting questions
d) **Allowing the group to take decisions within fixed limits**

111. A leader who believes in the capacity of people to take competent decisions and treats them as responsible and talented follows which leadership style?

a) Autocratic leadership
b) **Democratic leadership**
c) Laissez-faire leadership
d) Authoritarian leadership

112. Which leadership style involves minimal influence from the leaders and non-participation of leaders in task determination and rewards?

a) Autocratic leadership
b) Democratic leadership
c) **Laissez-faire leadership**
d) Authoritarian leadership

113. Which leadership style emphasizes imagination, creativity, and redefining the mission and purpose of the organization?

a) Autocratic leadership
b) Democratic leadership
c) Transactional leadership
d) **Transformational leadership**

114. Which life position in Transactional Analysis reflects a sense of defeat and viewing the world as miserable?

a) I am OK-You are OK
b) **I am OK-You are not OK**
c) I am not OK-You are OK
d) I am not OK-You are not OK

115. Which ego state in Transactional Analysis contains all the impulsive characteristics that come naturally to a child?

a) Parent ego
b) Adult ego
c) **Child ego**

116. In Transactional Analysis, what type of transactions occur when the stimulus and response lines are not parallel?

a) Complimentary transactions
b) Ulterior transactions
c) **Crossed transactions**

117. Which component of transformational leadership involves providing a vision or a sense of purpose that followers want to emulate?

a) **Charisma**
b) Inspirational motivation
c) Intellectual stimulation
d) Individual consideration

118. What does "work specialization" refer to in the context of organizational structure?

a) The process of creating multiple departments in an organization
b) The degree to which tasks are subdivided into separate jobs
c) Assigning jobs according to the location or territory
d) Combining tasks to form natural work units

119. Which form of departmentalization involves grouping activities around a specific operation or process?

a) Geographic departmentalization
b) Product departmentalization
c) Customer departmentalization
d) Process departmentalization

120. What type of organizational structure combines functional and product departmentalization?

a) Hybrid structure
b) Matrix departmentalization
c) Project departmentalization
d) Geographic departmentalization

121. The unbroken line of authority that extends from the top of the organization to the lowest levels is known as:

a) Departmentalization
b) Span of management
c) Centralization
d) Chain of command

122. What is the term used for the number of employees a manager can efficiently and effectively manage?

a) Work specialization
b) Centralization
c) Decentralization
d) Span of management

123. In a decentralized organization, where is decision making shared?

a) At the top of the organization
b) Amongst various levels of management
c) Amongst the employees
d) Amongst the customers

124. Which job design technique involves breaking down the job into smaller tasks to achieve high proficiency?

a) Job enlargement
b) Job enrichment
c) Job simplification
d) Job rotation

125. The degree to which employees are encouraged to be innovative and take risks is known as:

a) People orientation
b) Attention to detail
c) Innovation and risk-taking
d) Stability

126. What level of culture is characterized by observable artifacts and symbols of an organization?

a) Common assumptions
b) Shared values
c) Observable artifacts
d) Material artifacts

127. What is the role of leaders in maintaining and reinforcing organizational culture?

a) They should encourage employees to violate the established culture
b) They should set a poor example of behavior inconsistent with the culture
c) They should demonstrate behavior consistent with the culture
d) They should create multiple subcultures within the organization

128. What are the two types of stressors?
   a) Environmental stressors and personal stressors
   b) Challenge stressors and hindrance stressors
   c) Workplace stressors and family stressors
   d) Physical stressors and emotional stressors

129. Which of the following stressors is associated with workload, pressure to complete tasks, and time urgency?
   a) Environmental stressors
   b) Personal stressors
   c) Challenge stressors
   d) Hindrance stressors

130. Hindrance stressors are stressors that:
   a) Lead to improved performance
   b) Prevent individuals from reaching their goals
   c) Are controllable by the individual
   d) Are related to personal factors

131. How is stress associated with demands and resources?
   a) Demands are things within an individual's control, and resources are obligations and uncertainties.
   b) Demands are uncertainties, and resources are responsibilities and pressures.
   c) Demands are responsibilities and pressures, and resources are things within an individual's control.
   d) Demands and resources are unrelated to stress.

132. Which organizational factor is NOT mentioned as a cause of stress?
   a) Task demands
   b) Role demands
   c) Environmental demands
   d) Relationship demands

133. Redesigning jobs to give employees more responsibility, more meaningful work, more autonomy, and increased feedback can help reduce stress because:
   a) It increases dependence on others
   b) It lessens employees' control over work activities
   c) It reduces role ambiguity and role conflict
   d) It increases the level of organizational support

134. The interactionist view of conflict suggests that:
   a) Conflict is always dysfunctional and should be avoided at all costs
   b) Conflict is productive and necessary for group performance
   c) Conflict should be encouraged to promote creativity and innovation
   d) Conflict can only be functional if it is related to task issues

135. Which type of conflict focuses on the content and goals of the work?
   a) Relationship conflict
   b) Process conflict
   c) Task conflict
   d) Functional conflict

136. Avoiding conflict occurs when:
   a) Parties seek a mutually beneficial outcome
   b) Parties desire to fully satisfy the concerns of all parties
   c) **Parties intend to withdraw from or suppress the conflict**
   d) Parties are assertive and uncooperative

137. Negotiation is a process that occurs when:
   a) Parties compete to divide up a fixed amount of resources
   b) Parties try to find a mutually beneficial solution
   c) Parties collaborate to fully satisfy each other's concerns
   d) Parties compromise to ration the object of the conflict

138. Integrative bargaining is preferable to distributive bargaining because:
   a) It provides a win-win solution
   b) It is faster and more efficient
   c) It involves external subject matter experts
   d) It leads to competitive outcomes

139. The negotiation process includes five steps. Which of the following is NOT one of the steps?
   a) Preparation and planning
   b) Definition of ground rules
   c) Evaluation and judgment
   d) Bargaining and problem solving

140. Which postulate of change emphasizes the importance of integrating visibility and longevity of purpose?

a) Postulate one
b) Postulate two
c) Postulate three
d) Postulate four

141. What is an essential factor for the success of a change initiative?

a) Relying on external subject matter experts
b) Adapting a rigid plan throughout the process
c) Emphasizing project-driven approaches
d) Balancing planning with flexibility

142. What does the interactionist view of conflict emphasize?

a) Avoiding conflict at all costs
b) Encouraging conflict to promote creativity
c) Minimizing conflict to improve performance
d) Resolving conflict through compromise

143. Which type of conflict relates to the content and goals of the work being done?

a) Relationship conflict
b) Task conflict
c) Process conflict
d) Dysfunctional conflict

144. What are the five conflict-handling intentions mentioned in the text?

a) Competing, collaborating, avoiding, accommodating, and compromising
b) Avoiding, compromising, mediating, negotiating, and competing
c) Collaborating, accommodating, compromising, confronting, and avoiding
d) Mediating, negotiating, avoiding, competing, and accommodating

145. The negotiation process includes the following steps EXCEPT:

a) Preparation and planning
b) Definition of ground rules
c) Evaluation and judgment
d) Closure and implementation

146. What is the primary requirement for a positive outcome in change initiatives?

a) Short term programme with minimal effort
b) Sustained effort and consistent input over the long term
c) Immediate results with no need for future adjustments
d) Reactive response to external factors

147. Asthayee parivartan refers to:
   a) Temporary or tentativeness of change
   b) State of permanence in change
   c) Momentary change with quick jerk
   d) A radical and sudden change

148. What is the focus of Kshanik parivartan?
   a) Short-term gains and quick results
   b) Long-term effect and permanent change
   c) Incremental changes in the organization
   d) Radical and sudden change with quick jerk

149. Alpha change in an organization implies:
   a) Linear or non-linear shift of location with time
   b) Constant progress and incremental change
   c) Sudden and radical transformation
   d) Quick changes in variables and measurements

150. Which type of change involves a complete revolution in "how we do things" or "what results we strive to achieve"?
   a) Alpha change
   b) Beta change
   c) Gamma change
   d) Kshanik parivartan

151. Which method of organizational development involves unstructured group interaction to change behavior?
   a) Sensitivity training
   b) Survey feedback
   c) Process consultation
   d) Team building

152. Survey feedback is a tool used for:
   a) Assessing individual performance
   b) Assessing attitudes and perceptions among organizational members
   c) Evaluating the efficiency of technology systems
   d) Identifying hidden resistance to change

153. What does the process consultation (PC aim to achieve?
   a) To provide sensitivity training to employees
   b) To identify hidden resistance to change
   c) To improve organizational performance through task-directed methods
   d) To help managers understand and act upon process events they must deal with

154. The team-building process includes:
   a) Conducting surveys to gather feedback
   b) Development of interpersonal relations among team members
   c) Focusing on demographic differences among occupations
   d) Analyzing individual performance

155. What does Appreciative Inquiry focus on during the organizational development process?
   a) Identifying an organization's strengths and successes
   b) Solving problems and fixing issues in the organization
   c) Conducting sensitivity training for employees
   d) Identifying hidden resistance to change

156. Which of the following is NOT a feature of organizational development?
   a) Long-term effort
   b) Visioning process
   c) Short-term results and quick fixes
   d) Empowerment process

157. Who should initiate and support organizational development initiatives?
   a) Mid-level managers
   b) Frontline employees
   c) Customers and clients
   d) Top management

158. Organizational development values:
   a) Disregard for people's opinions and perspectives
   b) Hierarchy and control in decision-making
   c) Participation in problem-solving and decision-making
   d) Rigid structures and lack of flexibility

159. What is the focus of empowerment in organizational development?
   a) Mere delegation of authority
   b) Maintaining hierarchical authority and control
   c) Identifying leadership qualities and nurturing them
   d) Discouraging individual growth and development

160. Which method of organizational development focuses on creating new and expansive patterns of thinking?

a) Sensitivity training
b) Survey feedback
c) Appreciative inquiry
d) Team building

161. In the organizational development process, what is the role of teams?

a) Teams are not involved in the process.
b) Teams are responsible for only a specific task at hand.
c) Teams are building blocks of the organization responsible for all tasks from planning to completion.
d) Teams are temporary groups formed to address specific issues.

162. Which type of change is associated with incremental progress and constant variables?

a) Alpha change
b) Beta change
c) Gamma change
d) Kshanik parivartan

163. What is the primary focus of survey feedback in organizational development?

a) Identifying an organization's strengths
b) Assessing attitudes and perceptions of organizational members
c) Identifying hidden resistance to change
d) Enhancing employees' technical skills

164. The empowerment process in organizational development involves:

a) Setting up organization goals to hinder individual growth
b) Identifying leadership qualities in employees
c) Maintaining rigid hierarchical authority and control
d) Creating independent, self-directed, and task-oriented teams

165. Appreciative inquiry in organizational development focuses on:

a) Identifying an organization's weaknesses and problems
b) Exploring new and expansive patterns of thinking
c) Eliminating differences and conflicts among employees
d) Conducting surveys to gather feedback

6

Innovative Outreach Connecting with Farmers

1. Agricultural extension work is a significant social innovation that has evolved over nearly how many years?

   a) Two centuries
   b) Four thousand years
   c) One millennium
   d) Fifty years

2. What is the main purpose of agricultural extension work?

   a) To promote agricultural research
   b) To apply new knowledge to agricultural practices through farmer education
   c) To increase the profits of large-scale farmers
   d) To discourage the adoption of new practices by farmers

3. In which continent does agriculture employ around 60% of the population?

   a) Europe
   b) Africa
   c) Asia
   d) South America

4. Which model of agricultural extension is usually associated with the Ministry of Agriculture and is dominant worldwide?

   a) Commodity Extension and Research Model (CERM)
   b) Training and Visit (T and V) Extension Model
   c) NGO Extension Model
   d) National Public Extension Model (NPEM)

5. The Training and Visit (T and V) Extension Model was launched in which country in the early seventies and later spread to India and throughout Africa?

   a) India
   b) Mali
   c) Turkey
   d) Zambia

Bold Means Correct Answer

6. Which model of agricultural extension combines research and extension and was introduced by colonial powers in countries exporting cotton and palm oil?

   a) NGO Extension Model

   b) Commodity Extension and Research Model (CERM)

   c) Training and Visit (T and V) Extension Model

   d) National Public Extension Model (NPEM)

7. Which region in Asia has the highest rural population density and practices predominantly small-scale agriculture?

   a) East Asia **b) South Asia**

   c) Central Asia d) West Asia

8. Which Asian country has the most technically advanced agriculture with successful and vibrant extension systems?

   a) China b) Malaysia

   c) Japan **d) Saudi Arabia**

9. In which continent are Six Models of Agricultural Extension implemented in many countries, with most countries opting for the pluralism of models?

   a) Africa b) Europe

   c) Asia d) North America

10. What was the main reason for the Training and Visit (T and V) Extension Model proving to be financially unsustainable during 1975-1995?

    a) Lack of farmer interest b) Inefficient extension workers

    c) Insufficient donor assistance **d) High implementation costs**

11. The first agricultural extension service of a modern kind was established as a result of a crisis caused by what in Europe in 1845?

    a) Potato blight b) Wheat rust

    c) Locust infestation d) Coffee rust

12. In which country did the first national, wholly state-funded agricultural extension service get established in 1879?

    a) France b) United Kingdom

    c) Germany d) United States

13. The Smith-Lever Act, passed in 1914, established the Cooperative Extension Service in which country, aimed at diffusing useful and practical information on subjects relating to agriculture and home economics?

a) Canada b) United Kingdom

c) Australia **d) United States**

14. What type of agricultural extension model emerged in Asia in the 1980s and was remarkably effective in reducing pesticide use by up to 80% in rice mono-cropping areas?

a) Private Extension Model

b) Commodity Extension and Research Model (CERM)

c) Farmer Field School (FFS)

d) Training and Visit (T and V) Extension Model

15. In which continent did agricultural extension work start before 1900 in countries like Japan and some European colonies?

a) Africa b) Europe

c) Asia d) South America

16. The European colonial powers established experimental and demonstration botanical gardens in tropical areas to improve knowledge of tropical agricultural products. The earliest such garden was opened in 1821 in which country (then called Ceylon)?

a) India **b) Sri Lanka**

c) Ghana d) Nigeria

17. The Agricultural Extension work in the United States, after the passage of the Smith-Lever Act, was established as a tripartite cooperation among which entities?

a) Federal, State, and Local County Governments

b) Federal, State, and Agricultural Societies

c) Federal, State, and University Extension Services

d) Federal, State, and Farmers' Institutes

18. In which country did Horace Plunkett establish agricultural extension work in 1900 through the initiative of the Department of Agriculture and Technical Instruction?

a) Canada b) United States

c) United Kingdom (Ireland) d) Australia

19. Which model of agricultural extension is widespread in industrial countries like the Netherlands, New Zealand, and the United States, with farmers expected to pay some of the extension costs?
    a) Farmer Field School (FFS)
    b) Private Extension Model
    c) National Public Extension Model (NPEM)
    d) Commodity Extension and Research Model (CERM)

20. The extension workers appointed in the mid-1850s in Württemberg, Hesse, and western Prussia, known as Wanderlehrer, were part of the activities of which type of organizations?
    a) Agricultural societies
    b) University extension programs
    c) Government departments of agriculture
    d) Local government authorities

21. In the early years of the last century, agricultural extension services were relatively small in scale and limited in scope, organized predominantly by:
    a) Agricultural colleges
    b) Central or local governments
    c) NGOs and charitable organizations
    d) Private commercial companies

22. The work of extension services has become more bureaucratic with distinct hierarchical structures over time. What has been a major preoccupation due to this growth?
    a) Developing new agricultural technologies
    b) Improving farmer education programs
    c) Ensuring regular field contacts and supervision
    d) Managing and controlling extension activities

23. During the Pre-Independence effort of extension (1866-1947), the Famine Commission of 1880 recommended the establishment of:
    a) Agricultural colleges
    b) Cooperative marketing societies
    c) Department of Agriculture at the Centre and in every province
    d) Rural Reconstruction Institutes

24. The Famine Commission of 1901 led to the establishment of which significant agricultural research institute in India?

a) National Agricultural Research Institute (NARI)

b) Indian Council of Agricultural Research (ICAR)

c) Imperial Agricultural Research Institute at Pusa

d) Indian Institute of Agriculture and Rural Development (IIARD)

25. The Integrated Agricultural Extension approach, focusing on the major cereal crops for food security, was a characteristic of which era in India?

a) Colonial agriculture and extension

b) Broad-based or multipurpose extension

c) Area specific target group extension (The Green Revolution era)

d) Top-down extension

26. The Training and Visit (T&V) Extension Management system was introduced as a top-down approach in India. What was one of the major shortcomings of this system?

a) Inadequate funding from international donors

b) Lack of interest from farmers in the program

c) Neglecting communication skills and leadership training for extension workers

d) Overemphasis on critical feedback and self-evaluation

27. The Agricultural Technology Management Agency (ATMA) was introduced in India as a part of which project, aimed at reforming the extension system?

a) National Agricultural Technology Project (NATP)

b) National Agricultural Innovation Project (NAIP)

c) Rural Agricultural Development Project (RADP)

d) Agricultural Extension Modernization Project (AEMP)

28. ATMA is an autonomous organization registered under the Societies Registration Act of 1860 and aims to ensure:

a) Top-down approach to extension services

b) Convergence of extension services with commercial companies

c) Bottom-up planning process for technology dissemination

d) Privatization of all extension activities

29. What has been a constraint in the functioning of ATMA and its implementation?
    a) Lack of qualified manpower at the state level
    b) Overemphasis on public-private partnerships
    c) Inadequate financial support from the government
    d) Limited technical and financial support for the pilot program

30. What is the primary role of Frontline extension in agriculture?
    a) Conducting research in laboratories
    b) Disseminating agricultural technologies to farmers
    c) Marketing agricultural products
    d) Providing legal support to farmers

31. Which organization played a crucial role in the success of the Green Revolution in India?
    a) United Nations (UN)
    b) World Health Organization (WHO)
    c) Indian Council of Agricultural Research (ICAR)
    d) National Aeronautics and Space Administration (NASA)

32. When was the first Krishi Vigyan Kendra (KVK) established in India?
    a) 1965 **b) 1974**
    c) 1985 d) 1995

33. The main objective of KVKs is:
    a) To conduct large-scale agricultural technology dissemination
    b) To assess the location specificity of agricultural technologies
    c) To provide vocational training in agriculture
    d) To sell agricultural equipment to farmers

34. Which project was launched to demonstrate the genetic potentiality of new agricultural technologies to farmers?
    a) Frontline Demonstration Project (FDP)
    b) National Demonstration Project (NDP)
    c) Green Revolution Project (GRP)
    d) Agricultural Extension Project (AEP)

35. What is the primary focus of Frontline Demonstrations conducted by KVKs?

a) Providing entertainment to farmers

b) Assessing the location specificity of technologies

c) Establishing the production potential of technologies on farmers' fields

d) Promoting new fashion trends among farmers

36. The Education Commission recommended the establishment of specialized institutions for vocational education in agriculture. What were these institutions called?

a) Agricultural Colleges

b) Krishi Vigyan Kendras (KVKs)

c) Agricultural Research Institutes

d) Farm Science Centres

37. What is the primary aim of On-Farm Testing (OFT) conducted by KVKs?

a) Providing entertainment to farmers

b) Assessing the location specificity of agricultural technologies

c) Conducting large-scale technology dissemination programs

d) Conducting research in laboratories

38. Which agricultural innovation is associated with the effective utilization of land and water resources without altering groundwater levels?

a) Climate-resilient agriculture

b) Integrated Pest Management (IPM)

c) Rainwater harvesting through land shaping

d) Custom hiring of farm equipment

39. KVKs are expected to collaborate with which organization to foster the lab to land process and feedback in the agricultural sector?

a) Indian Space Research Organization (ISRO)

b) National Bank for Agricultural and Rural Development (NABARD)

c) Food and Agriculture Organization (FAO)

d) Department of Agriculture and Cooperation (DAC)

40. What is Farmer FIRST?
   a) A program to attract and retain youth in agriculture.
   b) An initiative to develop model villages for agricultural development.
   c) An innovative extension methodology involving farmers, researchers, and extension personnel.
   d) A scheme to establish technology incubation centers in agriculture.

41. What is the main objective of the Attracting and Retaining Youth in Agriculture (ARYA) program?
   a) To promote nutri-sensitive agriculture among farming communities.
   b) To empower farm youth to establish network groups for processing and value addition.
   c) To adopt villages and introduce technologies developed by ICAR.
   d) To attract and empower youth in rural areas for sustainable income in agriculture.

42. What is the purpose of the Mera Gaon Mera Gaurav (My Village, My Pride) program?
   a) To develop nutritional products from local farm produce.
   b) To promote nutri gardens and nutri villages.
   c) To adopt villages and provide technical guidance to farmers.
   d) To adopt villages and introduce technologies developed by ICAR.

43. What is the main focus of the Krishi Dak (Agri Post) model?
   a) Developing entrepreneurial skills among rural youth.
   b) Using postmen as change agents to disseminate agricultural information.
   c) Establishing value addition centers for agriculture produce.
   d) Promoting bio-fortified crop varieties for nutritional security.

44. What is the objective of the Knowledge System for Homestead Agricultural Management in Tribal Areas (KSHAMATA) program?
   a) To create awareness of nutri-sensitive agriculture among farm communities.
   b) To promote the use of indigenous fruits and vegetables for nutrition.
   c) To support technology needs for tribal farmers in remote areas.
   d) To harness traditional agricultural knowledge of tribal communities for better agricultural production.

45. What is the main goal of the Nutri-sensitive Agricultural Resources and Innovation (NARI) program?

a) To provide incubation training to rural youth in processing and value addition.

b) To narrow the nutrition gap and ensure food security.

c) To promote nutri-sensitive agriculture and develop entrepreneurship among youth.

d) To establish VATICA centers for technological interventions in agriculture.

46. What is the purpose of the Value Addition and Technology Incubation Centre in Agriculture (VATICA model)?

a) To develop nutrition gardens in rural areas.

b) To promote nutri-sensitive agricultural practices.

c) To establish centers for processing and value addition of agricultural products.

d) To provide training to farmers on modern agricultural practices.

7

Integrating and Embracing Agricultural Innovations

1. What is the crucial function of extension in bringing about desirable changes in human behavior?
   a) Informing farmers about improved practices
   b) Bridging the gap between knowledge and action through education
   c) Conducting field trials to test new ideas
   d) Measuring the efficiency of extension workers

2. What can be measured to determine an extension worker's efficiency?
   a) The number of new practices adopted by the extension worker
   b) The number of farmers and communities that adopt the innovations
   c) The speed with which the gap between knowledge and action is bridged
   d) All of the above

3. Why do extension workers often face questions about the gap between knowledge and action in farmers?
   a) Farmers are not interested in new practices
   b) Farmers lack access to information
   c) Extension workers fail to communicate effectively
   d) Extension workers lack practical application of research results

4. Where do most farmers typically get their new ideas or new practices?
   a) From neighboring farmers
   b) From agricultural universities
   c) From agricultural extension workers
   d) From online sources

Bold Means Correct Answer

5. What can help extension agents accelerate the adoption of innovations in agriculture?
   a) Conducting more field trials
   b) Providing monetary incentives to farmers
   c) Understanding adoption and diffusion processes
   d) Encouraging farmers to take quick decisions

6. Diffusion is the process by which an innovation is communicated over time among the members of a social system. What makes diffusion a special type of communication?
   a) It involves the use of mass media channels
   b) It focuses on spreading old ideas
   c) It is concerned with new ideas
   d) It is based on quantitative research methods

7. The diffusion of innovations is primarily a __________ process.
   a) Political
   b) Economic
   c) Social
   d) Technological

8. What element is responsible for the spread of a new idea from its source to its ultimate adopters?
   a) Innovation
   b) Communication channels
   c) Time
   d) Social system

9. What is an innovation in the context of diffusion research?
   a) An idea that is perceived as old by an individual
   b) A new object perceived as old by an individual
   c) A practice that is perceived as new by an individual
   d) A new idea, practice, or object perceived as new by an individual

10. What is the innovation-decision process?
   a) The process of developing new innovations through research
   b) The mental process through which an individual passes from first knowledge of an innovation to adoption or rejection
   c) The process of spreading old ideas among adopters
   d) The process of predicting the success of an innovation in the market

11. Which of the following is NOT a category of adopters based on innovativeness?

    a) Innovators
    b) Early adopters
    c) Late adopters
    d) Laggards

12. What is the role of communication channels in diffusion?

    a) To create uncertainty about expected consequences
    b) To influence opinion leaders
    c) To persuade individuals to accept new ideas
    d) To increase the speed of diffusion

13. What is the main characteristic of an innovation that creates uncertainty among potential adopters?

    a) Its complexity
    b) Its newness
    c) Its cost
    d) Its popularity

14. Which research tradition has the largest number of diffusion studies?

    a) Anthropology research tradition
    b) Rural sociology research tradition
    c) Education research tradition
    d) Marketing and management research tradition

15. In which research tradition are anthropologists known to avoid using quantitative research tools?

    a) Anthropology research tradition
    b) Rural sociology research tradition
    c) Communication research tradition
    d) General economics research tradition

16. Which research tradition focuses on the diffusion of medical innovations among health professionals or patients?

    a) Public health and medical sociology research tradition
    b) Education research tradition
    c) Geography research tradition
    d) General sociology research tradition

17. What does the diffusion research tradition in marketing and management primarily focus on?
    a) The spread of new communication technologies
    b) The adoption of educational innovations
    c) The diffusion of agricultural innovations to farmers
    d) The launch of new products by private firms

18. Which diffusion research tradition emphasizes space as a major factor affecting the diffusion of innovations?
    a) Anthropology research tradition
    b) Education research tradition
    c) Geography research tradition
    d) General sociology research tradition

19. In which diffusion research tradition are general economists mainly concerned with economic analyses of technological innovations?
    a) General economics research tradition
    b) Marketing and management research tradition
    c) Public health and medical sociology research tradition
    d) Communication research tradition

20. The diffusion of innovations follows a ________ curve over time.
    a) Straight
    b) Exponential
    c) Bell-shape
    d) d) Zigzag

21. What type of information does diffusion primarily deal with?
    a) Old ideas and practices
    b) Outdated technologies
    c) New ideas and innovations
    d) Political ideologies

22. Which element in the diffusion of innovations affects the rate of adoption?
    a) Communication channels
    b) Time
    c) Social system
    d) Innovativeness

23. In which step of the innovation-decision process does an individual decide to make full use of an innovation?
    a) Knowledge
    b) Persuasion
    c) Decision
    d) Implementation

24. What are the means by which messages get from one individual to another in the diffusion process?

a) Mass media channels **b) Communication channels**

c) Social media platforms d) Written pamphlets

25. What does diffusion research seek to understand?

a) Social change in rural areas

b) The spread of new technologies

c) The adoption of educational innovations

d) The communication of new ideas among a social system

26. Diffusion research aims to understand the ___________ of an innovation among members of a social system.

a) Source **b) Spread**

c) Invention d) Dissemination

27. Which typology of diffusion research focuses on the relative speed with which an innovation is adopted?

a) Rate of adoption of different innovations

b) Role of opinion leadership in diffusing innovation

c) Pervasiveness of diffusion networks

d) Innovativeness of members of a social system

28 Innovativeness refers to the degree to which an individual is relatively ___________ in adopting new ideas.

a) Cautious **b) Early**

c) Late d) Inflexible

29. What is the primary role of opinion leaders in the diffusion process?

a) They adopt innovations early.

b) They spread information through mass media channels.

c) They influence others to adopt innovations.

d) They play a supervisory role in diffusion programs.

30. Which channels are more important for earlier adopters in the diffusion process?

a) Mass media channels b) Cosmopolite channels

c) Interpersonal channels d) Localite channels

31. In diffusion research, the unit of analysis for studying tribes or peasant villages falls under which research tradition?

    a) Anthropology research tradition

    b) Rural sociology research tradition

    c) Education research tradition

    d) Communication research tradition

32. Which type of diffusion research focuses on the role of spatial distance in the spread of innovations?

    a) Rate of adoption of different innovations

    b) Role of opinion leadership in diffusing innovation

    c) Pervasiveness of diffusion networks

    d) Innovativeness of members of a social system

33. What are the two broad categories of channels through which diffusion may occur?

    a) Social networks and online platforms

    b) Social networks and mass communications

    c) Mass communications and telecommunication networks

    d) Telecommunication networks and print media

34. Diffusion research in marketing and management mainly focuses on the adoption of which type of innovations?

    a) Technological innovations

    b) Medical and health innovations

    c) Educational innovations

    d) News events and media innovations

35. What is the primary role of communication channels in the diffusion process?

    a) To reduce uncertainty among adopters

    b) To influence opinion leaders

    c) To classify adopters into categories

    d) To measure the consequences of an innovation

36. Which aspect of an innovation affects the rate of its adoption in different social systems?
    a) Economic rewards
    b) Compatibility with farmers' values
    c) Technological complexity
    d) Spread through mass media

37. What does diffusion research seek to understand?
    a) The process of adopting new ideas
    b) The social change within a system
    c) The characteristics of adopters
    d) The consequences of an innovation

38. Which element in the diffusion process creates a sense of uncertainty among potential adopters?
    a) Role of opinion leadership
    b) Rate of adoption
    c) Pervasiveness of diffusion networks
    d) Innovativeness of members of a social system

39. The typology of diffusion research that focuses on the role of communication channels is concerned with:
    a) Innovativeness of members of a social system
    b) Rate of adoption of different innovations
    c) Pervasiveness of diffusion networks
    d) Use of communication channel for diffusion

40. What do the consequences refer to in diffusion research?
    a) The benefits of an innovation
    b) The changes that occur as a result of adopting an innovation
    c) The motivations for adopting an innovation
    d) The challenges faced during the diffusion process

41. Which research tradition focuses on the spread of technological ideas among communities or individuals?
    a) Anthropology research tradition
    b) Rural sociology research tradition
    c) Education research tradition
    d) General sociology research tradition

42. The role of opinion leaders is especially important in which stage of the innovation-decision process?
    a) Knowledge
    b) Persuasion
    c) Decision
    d) Confirmation

43. In diffusion research, what is the focus of the rate of adoption of different innovations?
    a) The adoption of a specific innovation in different social systems
    b) The rate at which individuals adopt innovations
    c) The speed of spreading innovations through mass media channels
    d) The role of opinion leaders in adopting innovations

44. What do social networks and mass communications refer to in the context of diffusion?
    a) Political ideologies
    b) Channels through which diffusion occurs
    c) Innovations with high economic rewards
    d) The consequences of an innovation

45. What is the main difference between discovery and invention?
    a) Discovery involves experimentation, while invention involves exploration.
    b) Discovery refers to creating something completely new, while invention involves finding something unexpected.
    c) Discovery applies to things that never existed, while invention applies to those that existed for a long time.
    d) Discovery is the result of natural occurrences, while invention is a human-made artifact.

46. Which process deals with finding something that already exists but was never recognized before?
    a) Innovation
    b) Invention
    c) Discovery
    d) Development

47. An innovation is an idea, practice, or object that is perceived as ___________.
    a) Old
    b) Unpopular
    c) New
    d) Ineffective

48. Invention involves creating something new with one's own ideas and __________.

a) Experiences b) Equipment

c) Investment d) Intentions

49. What does an invention primarily focus on creating?

a) New materials **b) New technologies**

c) New discoveries d) New breeds of livestock

50. Christopher Columbus's discovery of the Americas is an example of __________.

a) Innovation b) Invention

c) Discovery d) Development

51. What is the primary characteristic of a discovery?

a) It is a human-made artifact.

b) It involves experimentation.

c) It is something that never existed before.

d) It is an outcome of natural occurrences.

52. Invention and innovation both involve the creation of __________.

a) New ideas b) New discoveries

c) New practices d) New accidents

53. Which of the following processes refers to creating something with available material using concepts like +, -, and x?

a) Invention b) Innovation

c) Discovery d) Development

54. What differentiates a discovery from an invention in terms of time?

a) Discovery involves past occurrences, while invention involves future occurrences.

b) Discovery applies to historical events, while invention applies to contemporary events.

c) Discovery refers to finding something from the past, while invention refers to creating something for the future.

d) Discovery is something that has always existed, while invention is something that will exist in the future.

55. What is the status of diffusion research today?

a) Neglected and ignored by academic scholars

b) Unpopular and irrelevant in social science knowledge

c) Prominent and incorporated in various fields of study

d) Limited to a few government agencies

56. Which bias in diffusion research implies that an innovation should be diffused and adopted by all members of a social system?

a) Pro-innovation bias

b) Individual-blame bias

c) Recall problem bias

d) Equality bias

57. How can diffusion researchers overcome the pro-innovation bias?

a) Avoid conducting research on innovations

b) Study innovations without considering their potential adopters

c) Investigate the broader context in which an innovation diffuses

d) Only focus on the perfect innovations for all potential adopters

58. What is the recall problem in diffusion research?

a) Difficulty in remembering the names of innovations

b) Inaccuracies in respondents' recollection of the time of adopting a new idea

c) Difficulty in gathering data from potential adopters

d) Inability to recall the benefits of innovations

59. What is the individual-blame bias in diffusion research?

a) Blaming individuals for their problems instead of the system

b) Holding individuals responsible for promoting innovations

c) Focusing on the faults of individual adopters

d) Considering individuals as the primary source of innovation

60. Which bias tends to side with the change agencies that promote innovations?

a) Pro-innovation bias

b) Individual-blame bias

c) Recall problem bias

d) Equality bias

61. What is the main weakness of diffusion research concerning time?
    a) Difficulty in finding enough time to conduct the research
    b) Dependence on recall data from respondents about the time of adoption
    c) Inability to measure the duration of diffusion
    d) Lack of interest in studying the process of diffusion over time

62. What does the issue of equality in diffusion research refer to?
    a) Socio-economic gaps among the members of a social system
    b) Equal distribution of innovations among potential adopters
    c) Ensuring all innovations are diffused at the same pace
    d) Promoting innovation to achieve equality in society

63. Which approach in diffusion research provides a common conceptual ground across various scientific fields?
    a) Individual-based approach
    b) Pro-innovation approach
    c) Multidisciplinary diffusion approach
    d) Time-based approach

64. What is the goal of diffusion research concerning practitioners like change agents?
    a) To promote innovations aggressively
    b) To ignore the adoption of new ideas
    c) To explore alternate research approaches
    d) To utilize diffusion research as a useful field of social science knowledge

65. What is an innovation in the context of the innovation development process?
    a) A process of generating new ideas
    b) A practice perceived as old by individuals
    c) An idea, practice, or object perceived as new by individuals
    d) A product that is well-established in the market

66. What is the initial step in the innovation-development process?
    a) Diffusion and adoption
    b) Research and development
    c) Recognition of a problem or need
    d) Consequences of an innovation

67. What is the term used as a synonym for innovation when most innovations investigated are technological in nature?
    a) Research and development
    b) Consequences of innovation
    c) Technology
    d) Commercialization

68. What is the process of putting a new idea into a form that meets the needs of potential adopters?
    a) Recognition of a problem or need
    b) Commercialization
    c) Development of an innovation
    d) Diffusion and adoption

69. What does R&D stand for in the context of the innovation development process?
    a) Research and Documentation
    b) Recognition and Development
    c) Research and Development
    d) Research and Diffusion

70. What is commercialization in the innovation development process?
    a) Recognition of a problem or need
    b) Diffusion and adoption of innovations
    c) The conversion of an idea into a product for sale in the market
    d) Tracing the consequences of an innovation

71. What is the final phase in the innovation-development process?
    a) Recognition of a problem or need
    b) Diffusion and adoption
    c) Consequences of an innovation
    d) Commercialization

72. What do tracer studies generally show about major technological advancements?
    a) They require multiple innovations in a cluster
    b) They rely on applied research rather than serendipity
    c) They have immediate impacts after development
    d) They are based on a single breakthrough innovation

73. What is the main limitation of tracer studies in the innovation development process?
    a) They lack retrospective data
    b) They focus too much on diffusion and adoption
    c) They do not consider the consequences of the innovation
    d) They rely heavily on research publications for data

74. What are the four stages for converting research into practice for the benefit of the farming community?

a) Research awareness, research evaluation, research trial, research into practice

b) Research recognition, research development, research diffusion, research implementation

c) Research dissemination, research commercialization, research adoption, research consequences

d) Research topic, research quality, research dissemination, research sustainability

75. What is the process of recognizing a need or problem that stimulates research and development activities?

a) Commercialization

b) Development of an innovation

c) Diffusion and adoption

d) Recognition of a problem or need

76. What type of research investigates scientific knowledge for the advancement of practical problems?

a) Basic research

b) Applied research

c) Commercial research

d) Development research

77. What is the term used for the production, marketing, and distribution of a product embodying an innovation?

a) Tracer studies

b) Commercialization

c) Innovation development

d) Research awareness

78. What are the changes that occur as a result of the adoption or rejection of an innovation?

a) Research outcomes

b) Consequences

c) Diffusion and adoption

d) Development of an innovation

79. What is the process of putting a new idea into a form expected to meet the needs of potential adopters?

a) Commercialization

b) Development of an innovation

c) Recognition of a problem or need

d) Research and development

80. What is the final phase in the innovation-development process?
    a) Diffusion and adoption
    b) Consequences of an innovation
    c) Commercialization
    d) Recognition of a problem or need

81. What is the term used to describe controlling the flow of messages through a communication channel during the innovation development process?
    a) Gatekeeping
    b) Tracer studies
    c) Research awareness
    d) Diffusion and adoption

82. What is adoption in the context of extension and farming community?
    a) The process of developing new technologies
    b) A decision to make partial use of an innovation
    c) A decision to make full use of an innovation as the best course of action available
    d) A decision-making process involving multiple stakeholders

83. Why do farmers take some time to adopt innovations even if they are aware of them?
    a) Lack of knowledge about innovations
    b) Pressure from extension officers
    c) The decision-making process involving mental stages
    d) Immediate acceptance of new ideas

84. Which stage in the adoption process involves seeking additional information about an innovation?
    a) Awareness stage
    b) Interest stage
    c) Evaluation stage
    d) Adoption stage

85. In which stage of the adoption process does the farmer mentally apply the new idea in present and future situations?
    a) Awareness stage
    b) Interest stage
    c) Evaluation stage
    d) Adoption stage

86. What is the purpose of the trial stage in the adoption process?
    a) To evaluate the effectiveness of an innovation on a large scale
    b) To gather more information about an innovation
    c) To make a final decision to adopt or reject an innovation
    d) To test the utility or feasibility of an innovation on a small scale

87. Which stage in the adoption process involves using the new idea continuously on a full scale?
    a) Awareness stage
    b) Interest stage
    c) Evaluation stage
    d) Adoption stage

88. How are the stages of adoption dynamic rather than static?
    a) They occur in a fixed order for all adopters
    b) Some stages may be skipped or appear more than once
    c) The process is capsule and looks like a unit act
    d) The stages are independent of social relations

89. What are the five stages of adoption process widely accepted and studied in diffusion of farm practices?
    a) Need, awareness, evaluation, trial, and adoption
    b) Awareness, interest, evaluation, trial, and adoption
    c) Awareness, conviction, acceptance, trial, and adoption
    d) Awareness, interest, evaluation, application, and adoption

90. In which stage of the seven-stage model does the farmer make an attempt to know more about the innovation?
    a) Need
    b) Awareness
    c) Interest
    d) Deliberation

91. What are the antecedents in the paradigm of adoption of innovation by an individual?
    a) The actor's identity and perception of the situation
    b) The extension officer's recommendations
    c) The results of trial and evaluation
    d) The decision-making process

92. What is the purpose of the deliberation stage in the adoption process?
    a) To obtain information about the innovation
    b) To evaluate the innovation's performance on various dimensions
    c) To accept the innovation for full-scale adoption
    d) To calculate input-output, risks, and uncertainties

93. Which term refers to the difference between what is and what ought to be, motivating farmers to change their existing practices?
    a) Evaluation
    b) Trial
    c) Need
    d) Adoption

94. Which of the following is not one of the five stages in the widely accepted adoption process?

a) Interest
b) Evaluation
c) Application
d) Awareness

95. In the adoption process, what stage involves seeking advice from opinion leaders, observing performance at different places, and discussing with family members?

a) Need
b) Evaluation
c) Deliberation
d) Trial

96. Which term refers to the process of using a new idea on a small scale to observe its performance under own conditions?

a) Awareness
b) Interest
c) Evaluation
d) Trial

97. What stage in the adoption process involves judging the utility of the innovation based on the farmer's mental application of the idea?

a) Awareness
b) Interest
c) Evaluation
d) Adoption

98. What is the decision-making process involving a period of time during which an individual goes through several mental stages before adopting an innovation?

a) Innovation process
b) Adoption process
c) Extension process
d) Diffusion process

99. How are the stages in the adoption process related to each other?

a) They occur independently without any sequence
b) They follow a fixed order for all adopters
c) Some stages may occur more than once, and the process may seem capsule-like
d) The stages are unrelated to social relations and ideology

100. Which term refers to the decision to extend the use of an innovation on a continued basis?

a) Adoption
b) Awareness
c) Evaluation
d) Interest

101. What are the three major divisions of the paradigm of adoption of innovation by an individual?

a) Antecedents, extension process, results

b) Antecedents, process, and application

c) Antecedents, process, and results

d) Antecedents, decision-making, and application

102. What is the major difference between the innovation-decision process and the diffusion process?

a) The innovation-decision process occurs among social units, while diffusion occurs within the mind of an individual.

b) The innovation-decision process is about developing new ideas, while diffusion is about adopting existing ideas.

c) The innovation-decision process involves forming attitudes toward innovations, while diffusion involves communicating new ideas to social systems.

d) The innovation-decision process is a passive process, while diffusion is an active process.

103. What is a distinctive aspect of innovation-decision making compared to other types of decision-making?

a) The decision to adopt or reject is always final and conclusive.

b) The newness of the alternative being considered for adoption.

c) The decision-making process is shorter for innovations.

d) The innovation-decision process only involves individual decisions.

104. Which of the following stages in the innovation-decision process involves forming a favourable or unfavourable attitude toward the innovation?

a) Knowledge stage

b) Persuasion stage

c) Decision stage

d) Confirmation stage

105. What is the main concern at the persuasion stage in the innovation-decision process?

a) Knowledge about the innovation's existence

b) Formation of a specific attitude toward the innovation

c) Selective exposure to innovation messages

d) The development of a general attitude toward change

106. What is the significance of selective perception at the persuasion stage of the innovation-decision process?
   a) It helps individuals to actively seek information about the innovation.
   b) It determines the receiver's communication behavior at the attitude formation stage.
   c) It influences individuals to seek only innovation messages that are in accord with their interests.
   d) It leads to a positive general attitude toward change in individuals.

107. At which stage in the innovation-decision process does the individual engage in activities that lead to a choice to adopt or reject the innovation?
   a) Knowledge stage
   b) Persuasion stage
   c) Decision stage
   d) Implementation stage

108. What is the primary consideration for individuals at the decision stage of the innovation-decision process?
   a) Whether or not to try the innovation on a probationary basis
   b) Whether or not to expose themselves to innovation messages
   c) Whether the innovation is compatible with existing beliefs
   d) Whether the innovation will be accepted by the social system

109. What is an important means to decrease the perceived risk of an innovation for the adopter?
   a) Selective exposure to innovation messages
   b) Continuous knowledge seeking about the innovation
   c) Small-scale trial as part of the decision to adopt
   d) Implementation of the innovation in local situations

110. What does "re-invention" refer to in the innovation-decision process?
   a) The process of convincing others to adopt an innovation
   b) The degree to which an innovation is changed or modified during adoption and implementation
   c) The evaluation of an innovation's performance after adoption
   d) The decision to reject an innovation after prior adoption

111. At which stage of the innovation-decision process does an individual seek reinforcement for their decision to adopt or reject the innovation?
   a) Knowledge stage
   b) Persuasion stage
   c) Decision stage
   d) Confirmation stage

112. What is the term used to describe a decision not to adopt an innovation?

a) Rejection
b) Confirmation
c) Implementation
d) Persuasion

113. What type of rejection occurs when a farmer rejects an innovation after initially adopting it, including the trial stage?

a) Passive rejection
b) Active rejection
c) Delayed rejection
d) Continuous rejection

114. What is a distinctive characteristic of the innovation-decision process compared to other types of decision-making?

a) It involves choosing between two alternatives, to adopt or reject an innovation.
b) It occurs among social units in a community.
c) It always leads to the adoption of new ideas.
d) It is a continuous and iterative process.

115. What is the primary function of the persuasion stage in the innovation-decision process?

a) To form a general attitude toward change
b) To seek information about the innovation
c) To engage in small-scale trials of the innovation
d) To form a favourable or unfavourable attitude toward the innovation

116. Why is selective exposure important in the innovation-decision process?

a) It determines the receiver's communication behavior at the attitude formation stage.
b) It helps individuals actively seek information about the innovation.
c) It influences individuals to seek only innovation messages that are in accord with their interests.
d) It leads to a positive general attitude toward change in individuals.

117. What is the significance of small-scale trials in the decision stage of the innovation-decision process?

a) It confirms the decision to adopt an innovation.
b) It decreases the perceived risk of the innovation for the adopter.
c) It leads to the implementation of the innovation on a large scale.
d) It influences the individual's general attitude toward change.

118. What does "re-invention" imply during the implementation stage of the innovation-decision process?

a) The process of convincing others to adopt an innovation

b) The evaluation of an innovation's performance after adoption

c) The decision to reject an innovation after prior adoption

d) The degree to which an innovation is changed or modified during adoption and implementation

119. How does the confirmation stage continue after the decision to adopt or reject an innovation?

a) The individual seeks reinforcement for the innovation-decision made.

b) The individual reverts to the knowledge stage to gather more information.

c) The individual seeks feedback from others about the innovation.

d) The individual seeks to avoid internal disequilibrium or dissonance.

120. What type of rejection occurs when an individual decides not to adopt an innovation without any active resistance?

a) Passive rejection

b) Active rejection

c) Delayed rejection

d) Continuous rejection

121. What is the term used to describe the series of actions and choices over time through which an individual evaluates a new idea and decides whether or not to incorporate it?

a) Diffusion process

b) Decision-making process

c) Adoption process

d) Innovation-decision process

122. Dissonance, in the context of human behavior change, refers to:

a) A state of internal harmony that motivates individuals to adopt new ideas or innovations.

b) A state of internal equilibrium that leads individuals to resist change.

c) An uncomfortable state of mind that individuals seek to reduce or eliminate by changing their knowledge, attitude, or actions.

d) A state of external conflict between individuals and their social environment.

123. When does dissonance occur during the innovation-decision process?

a) At the awareness stage when an individual becomes aware of a new idea.

b) At the knowledge stage when an individual seeks information about an innovation.

c) At the persuasion stage when an individual is exposed to pro-innovation messages.

d) At the confirmation stage when an individual seeks supportive messages to prevent dissonance.

124. Which form of discontinuance occurs when a farmer rejects an innovation in favor of adopting a better and superior idea?

a) Replacement discontinuance

b) Disenchantment discontinuance

c) Forced discontinuance

d) Passive discontinuance

125. What is over adoption in the context of agricultural innovations?

a) The process by which farmers actively influence others to adopt an innovation.

b) The decision to reject an innovation after previously adopting it.

c) The excessive and uncontrolled adoption of an innovation beyond recommended levels.

d) The process by which farmers passively adopt an innovation without influencing others.

126. Which stage in the innovation-decision process is characterized by the length of time required for an individual to pass through the process?

a) Knowledge stage

b) Persuasion stage

c) Decision stage

d) Innovation-decision period

127. How can extension workers speed up the adoption of innovations?

a) By increasing the rate of awareness-knowledge.

b) By providing financial incentives to potential adopters.

c) By imposing penalties on those who do not adopt innovations.

d) By limiting the availability of traditional practices.

128. What are interpersonal channels in the context of communication?
   a) Means of transmitting messages that involve mass media, such as radio and television.
   b) Face-to-face exchanges between two or more individuals.
   c) Channels originating from localite sources.
   d) Channels originating from cosmopolite sources.

129. Which type of source originates a message in the communication process?
   a) Channel
   b) Receiver
   c) Localite source
   d) Source

130. Mass media channels are relatively more important during which stage of the innovation-decision process?
   a) Knowledge stage
   b) Persuasion stage
   c) Decision stage
   d) Confirmation stage

131. Which type of discontinuance occurs when farmers are forced to discontinue existing practices due to government policies?
   a) Replacement discontinuance
   b) Disenchantment discontinuance
   c) Forced discontinuance
   d) Passive discontinuance

132. What is selective exposure in the context of dissonance reduction?
   a) Seeking information that confirms an already made decision.
   b) Rejecting an innovation after previously adopting it.
   c) Forcing discontinuance of existing practices due to external factors.
   d) Actively influencing other farmers to adopt an innovation.

133. Which type of source has knowledge that extends beyond the local social system and can bring in new ideas to receivers?
   a) Localite source
   b) Cosmopolite source
   c) Mass media channel
   d) Interpersonal channel

134. Discontinuance due to dissatisfaction with the performance of an innovation is known as:
   a) Replacement discontinuance
   b) Disenchantment discontinuance
   c) Forced discontinuance
   d) Passive discontinuance

135. What is the role of awareness-knowledge in the rate of adoption of innovations?

a) Awareness-knowledge leads to immediate adoption of innovations.

b) Awareness-knowledge does not affect the rate of adoption.

c) Increasing awareness-knowledge can speed up the adoption process.

d) Increasing awareness-knowledge delays the adoption process.

136. Which communication channels are relatively more important at the persuasion stage in the innovation-decision process?

a) Mass media channels

b) Interpersonal channels

c) Localite channels

d) Cosmopolite channels

137. When does active adoption occur in the innovation-decision process?

a) When a farmer influences others to adopt an innovation.

b) When a farmer adopts an innovation without influencing others.

c) When an individual becomes aware of a new idea.

d) When an individual seeks information about an innovation.

138. Which stage of the innovation-decision process involves the process of a new idea fermenting in an individual's mind?

a) Knowledge stage

b) Persuasion stage

c) Decision stage

d) Confirmation stage

139. What is the main method of speeding up the diffusion of an innovation according to extension workers?

a) Increasing the rate of awareness-knowledge

b) Imposing penalties on non-adopters

c) Restricting the availability of traditional practices

d) Limiting the number of extension workers

140. Which type of source is an example of an impersonal cosmopolite source?

a) Extension agent

b) Mass media

c) Relatives

d) Friends

141. What is the main motivation behind human behavior change, according to the concept of dissonance?

a) A desire for novelty and change

b) A state of internal equilibrium

c) An uncomfortable state of mind that seeks reduction or elimination

d) External pressures from the social environment

142. Which stage of the innovation-decision process involves seeking information about an innovation to meet a perceived need?

a) Knowledge stage

b) Persuasion stage

c) Decision stage

d) Confirmation stage

143. What is the term for the process by which a farmer actively influences others to adopt an innovation?

a) Active adoption

b) Passive adoption

c) Over adoption

d) Discontinuance

144. What are cosmopolite sources in the context of communication channels?

a) Sources that originate messages from the local social system of receivers.

b) Sources that originate messages from outside the social system of receivers.

c) Channels that involve mass media, such as radio and television.

d) Channels that involve face-to-face exchanges between individuals.

145. Which type of discontinuance occurs when farmers are forced to discontinue existing practices due to government policies?

a) Replacement discontinuance

b) Disenchantment discontinuance

c) Forced discontinuance

d) Passive discontinuance

146. What is selective exposure in the context of dissonance reduction?

a) Seeking information that confirms an already made decision.

b) Rejecting an innovation after previously adopting it.

c) Forcing discontinuance of existing practices due to external factors.

d) Actively influencing other farmers to adopt an innovation.

147. Which type of source has knowledge that extends beyond the local social system and can bring in new ideas to receivers?

a) Localite source

b) Cosmopolite source

c) Mass media channel

d) Interpersonal channel

148. What is the role of awareness-knowledge in the rate of adoption of innovations?

a) Awareness-knowledge leads to immediate adoption of innovations.

b) Awareness-knowledge does not affect the rate of adoption.

c) Increasing awareness-knowledge can speed up the adoption process.

d) Increasing awareness-knowledge delays the adoption process.

149. Which communication channels are relatively more important at the persuasion stage in the innovation-decision process?

a) Mass media channels

b) Interpersonal channels

c) Localite channels

d) Cosmopolite channels

150. What is an innovation in the context of the adoption process?

a) An idea, practice, or object that is perceived as new by an individual or unit of adoption.

b) A traditional practice that has been in use for generations.

c) A decision made by a social system collectively.

d) A process of rejecting new ideas to maintain stability.

151. What does making an innovation decision involve?

a) Choosing between alternative courses of action.

b) Rejecting all new ideas.

c) Adopting all new ideas without questioning.

d) Following the majority decision of a social system.

152. Which type of innovation decision involves choices made by an individual independent of others?

a) Optional innovation-decisions

b) Collective innovation-decisions

c) Authority innovation-decisions

d) Contingent innovation-decisions

153. What is the main difference between collective and authority innovation-decisions?
   a) The speed of adoption.
   b) The level of resistance from other members.
   c) The number of individuals involved in making the decision.
   d) The level of innovativeness of the individuals.

154. Contingent innovation-decisions are made:
   a) Before any prior innovation decision.
   b) After a prior innovation decision.
   c) Independently of any other decision.
   d) By individuals with technical expertise.

155. How are individuals classified into adopter categories?
   a) By their age and gender.
   b) By their occupation and education level.
   c) On the basis of their innovativeness.
   d) On the basis of their decision-making skills.

156. What is innovativeness?
   a) The degree to which an individual adopts all new ideas.
   b) The degree to which an individual is relatively earlier in adopting new ideas compared to others in the social system.
   c) The degree to which an individual is resistant to change.
   d) The degree to which an individual conforms to the majority decision of a social system.

157. What shape does the adopter distribution usually follow over time?
   a) Straight line
   b) S-shaped curve
   c) U-shaped curve
   d) Bell-shaped curve

158. What does the S-shaped diffusion curve represent?
   a) The adoption rate of an innovation in a social system.
   b) The resistance to change within a social system.
   c) The number of adopters over time.
   d) The number of individuals who reject an innovation.

159. Why is the S-shaped curve of adoption considered normal?
   a) Because it represents a linear increase in adoption over time.
   b) Because it represents a constant level of adoption over time.
   c) Because it follows a bell-shaped distribution when plotted on a frequency basis.
   d) Because it shows a sudden spike in adoption at the beginning.

160. What is the heart of the diffusion process in the S-shaped curve of adoption?
   a) The initial adoption phase
   b) The plateau phase
   c) The declining adoption phase
   d) The mid-adopter phase

161. How is innovativeness used for adopter categorization?
   a) By considering age and gender.
   b) By dividing individuals into discrete categories based on their level of innovativeness.
   c) By counting the number of new ideas adopted by an individual.
   d) By measuring the influence of authority figures on decision-making.

162. What is the main characteristic of an ideal set of adopter categories?
   a) Being exhaustive and mutually exclusive.
   b) Being derived from multiple classificatory principles.
   c) Being focused on external factors influencing decisions.
   d) Being based on an individual's resistance to change.

163. What is the purpose of using standard deviation in adopter categorization?
   a) To determine the number of adopter categories.
   b) To calculate the mean time of adoption.
   c) To measure the variance in innovativeness among individuals.
   d) To divide the normal adopter distribution into discrete categories.

164. Which adopter category includes the first 2.5% of individuals who adopt an innovation?
   a) Innovators
   b) Early adopters
   c) Early majority
   d) Late majority

165. Which adopter category includes approximately 34% of individuals who adopt after the innovators and early adopters?
   a) Innovators
   b) Early adopters
   c) Early majority
   d) Late majority

166. How does the S-shaped curve of adoption change as more individuals adopt the innovation?
   a) It steepens and accelerates.
   b) It plateaus and levels off.
   c) It becomes linear and constant.
   d) It slows down and declines.

167. Which parameter of distribution is used to divide a normal adopter distribution into five adopter categories?
   a) Mean (x)
   b) Standard deviation (sd)
   c) Median
   d) Mode

168. The S-shaped diffusion curve levels off after approximately what percentage of the individuals in a social system have adopted the innovation?
   a) 10%
   b) 25%
   c) 50%
   d) 75%

169. Which adopter category includes the last 16% of individuals who adopt the innovation?
   a) Innovators
   b) Early adopters
   c) Late majority
   d) Laggards

170. What is the primary criterion used for adopter categorization?
   a) Age
   b) Gender
   c) Innovativeness
   d) Occupation

171. Why is the adoption of an innovation expected to follow a normal, bell-shaped curve over time?
   a) Because individuals adopt new ideas at random intervals.
   b) Because each individual has a fixed time for adoption.
   c) Because individuals influence each other to adopt over time.
   d) Because there is no pattern to the adoption of innovations.

172. What is the area under the S-shaped curve between the mean time of adoption and one standard deviation to the right called?
   a) Innovators
   b) Early adopters
   c) Late majority
   d) Laggards

173. How does the rate of adoption change during the early majority phase in the S-shaped curve?
   a) It accelerates rapidly.
   b) It levels off.
   c) It declines sharply.
   d) It remains constant.

174. Which category of adopters is characterized by a strong resistance to change and a slow rate of adoption?

a) Innovators
b) Early adopters
c) Late majority
d) Laggards

175. How are adopter categories typically divided based on the normal adopter distribution?

a) Equal intervals of time
b) Equal proportions of the social system
c) Equal geographical regions
d) Equal number of individuals

176. Why is the concept of innovativeness important in adopter categorization?

a) It allows researchers to study the characteristics of early adopters.
b) It helps identify individuals who resist change.
c) It provides a basis for dividing individuals into discrete categories.
d) It determines the speed of adoption for an innovation.

177. Which parameter is used to measure the variation or dispersion of innovativeness among individuals in a social system?

a) Mean (x)
b) Standard deviation (sd)
c) Median
d) Mode

178. What does the plateau phase in the S-shaped curve represent?

a) The decline in the adoption rate of an innovation.
b) The initial adoption phase.
c) The peak of adoption in the social system.
d) The time when it is impossible to stop further diffusion of the innovation.

179. Which of the following adopter categories is characterized by individuals who are venturesome and have a desire for thrash, daring, and risk-taking?

a) Early Adopters
b) Innovators
c) Early Majority
d) Late Majority
e) Laggards

180. Early adopters are sought by change agents as local missionaries because they:
    a) Are highly cosmopolite and well-traveled
    b) Possess substantial financial resources for investing in innovations
    c) Are respected by peers and serve as role models for others
    d) Have the highest degree of adoption leadership in most systems
    e) Adopt new ideas just before the average member of a system

181. The early majority differs from the early adopters in that they:
    a) Have a strong pro-innovation bias
    b) Interact frequently with cosmopolite sources of information
    c) Serve as gate-keepers in the flow of new ideas into a system
    d) Tend to be skeptical and cautious about adopting innovations
    e) Are the last to adopt an innovation in a social system

182. Late majority adopt new ideas:
    a) With deliberate willingness just before the average member of a system
    b) Just after the average member of a system, often due to economic necessity
    c) By importing the innovation from outside the system's boundaries
    d) Because they possess almost no opinion leadership and rely on peer pressure

183. Laggards are the last in a social system to adopt an innovation primarily because:
    a) They possess substantial financial resources
    b) They have a strong pro-innovation bias
    c) They are venturesome and daring individuals
    d) Their innovation-decision process is relatively lengthy, with adoption lagging behind awareness

184. Innovators are generally characterized by all of the following EXCEPT:
    a) Large farms
    b) High net worth and risk capital
    c) Being past middle age
    d) Respect and prestige in progressive communities

185. Which adopter category is most likely to participate in government programs and furnish a disproportionate amount of formal leadership in the community?

a) Innovators
b) Early Adopters
c) Early Majority
d) Late Majority

186. The characteristics associated with early majority include:

a) Above-average age and education
b) More social and economic status than early adopters
c) Formal leaders in community associations
d) Mostly mentioned as neighbors and friends from whom farmers seek information

187. Late majority adopters are characterized by:

a) Greater empathy and higher aspirations
b) High social participation and more cosmopolite interpersonal networks
c) Higher social status and more years of formal education
d) Less education and older age than early majority adopters

188. Which of the following variables is NOT related to innovativeness in adopter categories?

a) Empathy
b) Intelligence
c) Dogmatism
d) Rationality
e) Fatalism

189. The innovativeness of an individual is primarily governed by:

a) Perceived attributes of the innovation
b) Socio-economic status
c) Personality values
d) Communication behavior

190. Which adopter category relies heavily on subjective evaluation to make decisions about adopting innovations?

a) Innovators
b) Early Adopters
c) Early Majority
d) Late Majority

191. Reflective appraisal and comparative appraisal are important factors in evaluating the:

a) Product use norms
b) Socio-economic status
c) Personality values
d) Communication behavior

192. The term "reservation price" refers to:
   - **a) The price an individual is willing to pay for an innovation**
   - b) The subjective evaluation of an innovation
   - c) The mental upper limit for spending on an innovation
   - d) The economic constraints that force an adopter to prioritize needs

193. Innovators are most likely to have which characteristic related to their sphere of influence?
   - a) Few formal and informal contacts outside the immediate locality
   - b) Limited participation in social activities of the community
   - **c) A high degree of interconnectedness through interpersonal networks**
   - d) Mainly associated with neighbors and friends for seeking information

194. The early majority adopters are likely to have:
   - a) Higher social and economic status than early adopters
   - b) Lower social participation and interconnectedness
   - **c) Greater exposure to mass media communication channels**
   - d) Less exposure to inter-personal communication channels

195. Innovators and early adopters are generally more _______ than later adopters.
   - **a) Empathetic**
   - b) Risk-averse
   - c) Cautious
   - d) Fatalistic

196. The characteristics associated with late majority adopters include:
   - **a) Higher social status and more education than early majority adopters**
   - b) More active in formal groups and government programs
   - c) Greater willingness to take risks
   - d) Greater exposure to mass media communication channels

197. The personality variable that refers to an individual's ability to project themselves into the role of another person is called:
   - **a) Empathy**
   - b) Rationality
   - c) Intelligence
   - d) Fatalism

198. Which category of adopters is most likely to have a greater ability to cope with uncertainty and risk?

a) Innovators

b) Early Adopters

c) Early Majority

d) Late Majority

199. The characteristic of "reservation price" in economics is important in predicting:

a) Innovativeness of potential adopters

b) The influence of mass media on early adopters

c) The age and education of innovators

d) The social participation of early majority adopters

200. The willingness to take risks is a characteristic typically associated with:

a) Innovators

b) Early Adopters

c) Early Majority

d) Late Majority

201. The socio-economic status of earlier adopters is often indicated by variables such as:

a) Age and education

b) Interconnectedness through interpersonal networks

c) Empathy and intelligence

d) Income and level of living

202. The characteristic "product use norm" refers to:

a) The perceived attributes of the innovation

b) Reflective appraisal by reference groups

c) Empathy and rationality in decision-making

d) The beliefs of reference groups about the behavior of an individual

203. Innovators are more likely to be respected and prestigious in:

a) Conservative communities

b) Early adopter communities

c) Progressive communities

d) Late adopter communities

204 Innovators are characterized by their ability to:

a) Take risks and be venturesome

b) Test untried ideas in their own situations

c) Participate in formal groups and government programs

d) Adopt innovations just before the average member of a system

205. The early majority adopters are slightly above average in all of the following characteristics EXCEPT:
   a) Age
   b) Education
   c) Farming experience
   d) Social and economic status

206. The characteristics associated with early adopters include all of the following EXCEPT:
   a) Being younger than the innovators
   b) Having large farms
   c) High income
   d) Less exposure to mass media communication channels

207. Innovators often rely on informal contacts and bypass the local extension worker to get information from:
   a) Innovators in other systems
   b) Early adopters
   c) Late adopters
   d) Change agents

208. The early majority adopters are most likely to:
   a) Participate in government programs
   b) Be formal leaders in the community
   c) Read more farm journals and bulletins
   d) Have a greater ability to cope with uncertainty

209. The characteristics associated with laggards include:
   a) Greater empathy and higher aspirations
   b) Higher social participation and more social mobility
   c) More exposure to inter-personal communication channels
   d) Being less educated and older

210. Innovators are more likely to be associated with which type of social relationship?
   a) Local and cosmopolite social relationships
   b) Informal and formal social relationships
   c) Peer networks within their community
   d) Peers from whom other farmers seek information

211. The early majority adopters have a higher degree of _______ than the early adopters.
   a) Empathy
   b) Rationality
   c) Interconnectedness
   d) Opinion leadership

212. The socio-economic status of earlier adopters is characterized by all of the following EXCEPT:

a) Possession of wealth
b) Occupational prestige
c) Level of living
d) Dogmatism

213. The inclination for adoption of innovation is primarily governed by:

a) Normative influence
b) Perceived attributes of the innovation
c) Economic factors
d) Reservation price

214. The perceived utility of an innovation is influenced by all of the following factors EXCEPT:

a) Relative advantage
b) Compatibility
c) Complexity
d) Predictability

215. The degree to which an innovation is perceived as being better than the idea it supersedes is called:

a) Relative advantage
b) Compatibility
c) Complexity
d) Trialability

216. Compatibility, as an attribute of innovations, refers to its consistency with:

a) Perceived attributes of the innovation
b) Economic factors
c) Existing values, past experiences, and needs of potential adopters
d) Trialability and observability

217. The degree to which an innovation is perceived as relatively difficult to understand and use is known as:

a) Relative advantage
b) Compatibility
c) Complexity
d) Trialability

218. Trialability, as an attribute of innovations, refers to its:

a) Compatibility with existing values
b) Ability to compete for scarce resources
c) Potential for experimentation on a limited basis
d) Observable results to others

219. Observability, as an attribute of innovations, refers to:
   a) The compatibility with existing values and past experiences
   b) The observable results of an innovation to others
   c) The relative advantage of an innovation over previous ideas
   d) The willingness to pay for the innovation

220. Predictability, as an attribute of innovations, refers to the degree of:
   a) Relative advantage over previous ideas
   b) Compatibility with existing values and needs
   c) Observable results of an innovation
   d) Certainty of receiving expected benefits from the adoption of an innovation

221. The perceived attributes of innovations influence the process of:
   a) Generating temporal data
   b) Making collective decision on adoption
   c) Predicting innovativeness of potential adopters
   d) Engaging in e-mediated communication

222. The attribute of an innovation that motivates the potential adopters based on the belief that it is better than the existing idea is:
   a) Compatibility
   b) Complexity
   c) Relative advantage
   d) Observability

223. The compatibility of an innovation is positively related to its rate of adoption because it is perceived as:
   a) Economically viable
   b) Easier to understand and use
   c) Consistent with the existing values and needs of potential adopters

224. The complexity of an innovation is negatively related to its rate of adoption because it is perceived as:
   a) Economically unviable
   b) Inconsistent with the existing values and needs of potential adopters
   c) Difficult to experiment with on a limited basis
   d) Easy to understand and use

225. The attribute of an innovation that refers to its potential for experimentation on a limited basis is:
   a) Relative advantage
   b) Compatibility
   c) Complexity
   d) Trialability

226. The observable results of an innovation to others are known as its:
   a) Relative advantage
   b) Compatibility
   c) Complexity
   d) Observability

227. The attribute of an innovation that refers to the degree of certainty in receiving expected benefits is:
   a) Compatibility
   b) Complexity
   c) Trialability
   d) Predictability

228. The rate of adoption of an innovation is influenced by various factors, including:
   a) Perceived attributes of the innovation
   b) Types of innovation-decision
   c) Normative influence and relative advantage
   d) Reservation price and observability

229. The method of decision-making for adopting an innovation that involves all members of the social system is called:
   a) Reflective appraisal
   b) Trialability
   c) Collective decision-making process
   d) Normative influence

230. The channels of communication that may be used for reaching potential adopters can be:
   a) Limited to mass media channels
   b) Limited to interpersonal channels
   c) Either traditional or electronically mediated
   d) Only based on economic factors

231. The nature of social system, including social norms and beliefs, has a significant impact on the acceptance of innovation because it influences:
   a) Reflective appraisal
   b) Economic factors
   c) Reservation price
   d) Normative influence

232. The extent of promotion efforts made by the extension professional plays a significant role in the adoption of innovation, as it affects:
   a) Reflective appraisal and observability
   b) Compatibility and complexity
   c) Trialability and reservation price
   d) Rate of adoption and predictability

233. The identification of adopter characteristics in diffusion studies is concerned with factors associated with:
   a) Economic constraints and complexity of innovation
   b) Innovativeness of farmers and rate of adoption
   c) Reflective appraisal and reservation price
   d) Predictability and trialability
   e) Normative influence and collective decision-making

234. Among the perceived attributes of innovation, which one is most likely to influence potential adopters positively?
   a) Complexity
   b) Compatibility
   c) Trialability
   d) Observability

235. The innovation attribute that may motivate potential adopters to accept an innovation based on observable and visible outcomes is:
   a) Compatibility
   b) Trialability
   c) Predictability
   d) Observability

236. The nature of communication channels plays a crucial role in diffusion because it affects the:
   a) Reflective appraisal of potential adopters
   b) Complexity of an innovation
   c) Observable results of an innovation
   d) Rate of adoption and trialability

237. The perceived attributes of innovations are essential in predicting the:
   a) Reflective appraisal of potential adopters
   b) Normative influence on adoption decisions
   c) Innovativeness of farmers
   d) Reservation price for adopting an innovation

238. The channels of communication used for reaching potential adopters can be either:

   a) Interpersonal channels or electronically mediated channels

   b) Normative channels or mass media channels

   c) Trialability channels or complex channels

   d) Observable channels or reflective channels

239. The social norms, folkways, and mores play a significant role in the acceptance of innovation because they influence:

   a) Reflective appraisal of potential adopters

   b) Compatibility of the innovation with existing values and needs

   c) Trialability and observability of the innovation

   d) Rate of adoption and innovativeness of farmers

240. The extent of promotion efforts made by the extension professional can significantly impact the rate of adoption of an innovation because it affects the:

   a) Reflective appraisal and complexity of the innovation

   b) Compatibility and trialability of the innovation

   c) Observable results and normative influence

   d) Rate of adoption and willingness to pay for the innovation

241. Which of the following personal factors may influence the adoption of innovations?

   a) Farm income b) Size of farm

   c) Tenure status **d) Education**

242. Which characteristic refers to the degree to which an innovation is consistent with existing values and past experiences of the adopters?

   a) Complexity **b) Compatibility**

   c) Cost d) Communicability

243. Which type of change involves new techniques or operations?

   a) A simple change b) Improved practice

   c) Innovation d) Change in total enterprise

244. The diffusion effect refers to:
    a) The speed with which adoption takes place
    b) The process by which an innovation is communicated to others
    c) The increasing pressure towards adoption as more individuals adopt the innovation
    d) The negative effect of over adoption

245. Over adoption occurs due to:
    a) Excessive cost of the innovation
    b) Lack of awareness about the innovation
    c) Pressure from interpersonal networks
    d) Insufficient knowledge about the innovation and its consequences

246. What is the innovation-decision period?
    a) The length of time required for an innovation to be developed
    b) The gestation period for an idea to ferment in an individual's mind
    c) The period when an innovation is introduced to the market
    d) The time it takes for an individual to be aware of an innovation

247. Active adoption occurs when:
    a) Farmers adopt an innovation but do not influence others to do the same
    b) Farmers adopt an innovation and influence other farmers to do the same
    c) Farmers are aware of an innovation but are not motivated to try it
    d) Farmers are not aware of an innovation

248. What can extension workers do to speed up the adoption of innovations?
    a) Increase the complexity of the innovations
    b) Shorten the rate of awareness-knowledge
    c) Decrease the rate of adoption
    d) Promote over adoption of innovations

249. Which situational factor is associated with higher adoption rates?
    a) High cost
    b) Complexity
    c) Compatibility
    d) Low net returns

250. Which personal factor is positively related to farm practice adoption rates?

a) Mental rigidity

b) Low emphasis on science and material comfort

c) Desire for high school or college education for children

d) Few contacts within and beyond the community

251. What type of innovation is likely to be adopted most readily?

a) Innovation with high complexity

b) Innovation with low net returns

c) Innovation with high compatibility

d) Innovation with high cost

252. The adoption of innovations is generally higher among:

a) Tenant cultivators

b) Farmers with lower education levels

c) Farmers with mental rigidity

d) Farmers with larger farm sizes

253. Which source of farm information is usually negatively associated with the adoption of new farm practices?

a) Government agencies

b) Relatives and friends

c) Agricultural universities

d) Agricultural extension workers

254. Why do some people adopt new ideas and practices more quickly than others?

a) Due to their mental rigidity

b) Because they have less education

c) Due to the characteristics of the individual

d) Because they have a high emphasis on traditionalism

255. What factor is NOT associated with the speed of adoption of an innovation?

a) Complexity of the innovation b) Cost of the inputs

c) Compatibility with existing values **d) Age of the adopter**

256. In which type of adoption does the innovation remain confined to the farmer who has adopted it?
    a) Active adoption
    b) Passive adoption
    c) Over adoption
    d) Diffusion effect

257. Which factor is NOT a situational factor affecting the adoption of innovations?
    a) Nature of the practice
    b) Complexity
    c) Values and attitudes
    d) Cost of the inputs

258. Which factor is positively related to the adoption of new farm practices?
    a) Mental rigidity
    b) High emphasis on traditionalism
    c) High farm income
    d) Low educational level

259. What is meant by the term "divisibility" in the context of innovation adoption?
    a) The degree to which an innovation may be tried on a limited basis
    b) The speed with which adoption will take place
    c) The cost of adopting the innovation
    d) The complexity of the innovation

260. Which characteristic refers to the degree to which the results of an innovation may be diffused to others?
    a) Complexity
    b) Communicability (observability)
    c) Compatibility
    d) Cost

261. What type of change involves a change in materials and equipment only, without a change in techniques or operations?
    a) A simple change
    b) Improved practice
    c) Innovation
    d) Change in total enterprise

262. Which personal factor is associated with higher adoption rates?
    a) Exposure to reliable sources of farm information
    b) Mental rigidity
    c) Low emphasis on science and material comfort
    d) Older age

263. What is the main role of a change agent in preventing over adoption of an innovation?
   a) Increasing the cost of the innovation
   b) Limiting access to the innovation
   c) Providing adequate knowledge about the innovation through training and communication
   d) Encouraging farmers to adopt the innovation regardless of its consequences

264. Which social factor provides the general framework wherein the process of change occurs?
   a) Farm income
   b) Community standards and social relationships
   c) Education level
   d) Size of the farm

265. What is the relationship between the innovation-decision period and the time of adoption?
   a) The innovation-decision period is the same as the time of adoption.
   b) The innovation-decision period is shorter for later adopters.
   c) The innovation-decision period is longer for earlier adopters.
   d) The innovation-decision period is unrelated to the time of adoption.

266. Which characteristic is positively related to the adoption of innovations?
   a) Complexity
   b) Cost
   c) Compatibility
   d) Mental rigidity

267. What does active adoption refer to?
   a) The process by which an innovation is communicated to others
   b) The speed with which adoption takes place
   c) The farmer who adopts the practice but does not influence others to do the same
   d) The farmer who adopts the practice and influences others to do the same

268. Which characteristic is associated with faster adoption rates of innovations?
   a) High complexity
   b) High cost
   c) Low compatibility
   d) High net returns

269. What is the term used for the degree to which an innovation may be tried on a limited basis?

a) Compatibility
b) Divisibility (trialability)
c) Communicability (observability)
d) Complexity

270. What is the role of opinion leaders in a social system?

a) To enforce strict rules and regulations
b) To influence others' attitudes and behaviors informally
c) To control the mass media channels
d) To create barriers to the flow of innovations

271. Which model challenged the hypodermic needle model by proposing that communication messages flow from a source to opinion leaders and then to followers?

a) Multi-step flow model
b) Diffusion of innovations model
c) Two-step flow model
d) Heterophily model

272. What characteristic makes opinion leadership an informal form of leadership?

a) Formal position or status in the system
b) Technical competence and conformity to the system's norms
c) Educational background and media coverage
d) Influence on mass media channels

273. In the multi-step flow theory of innovation, who intervenes between the media's direct message and the audience's reaction?

a) Innovators
b) Opinion leaders
c) Change agents
d) Mass media channels

274. What factor makes opinion leaders have a greater effect on those they are most similar to?

a) Their exposure to mass media channels
b) Their level of education and expertise
c) Their ability to interpret media messages
d) Similarities in personality, interests, and demographics

275. Which method of measuring opinion leadership involves obtaining data about communication patterns among individuals in a system?

a) Sociometric method
b) Informants' ratings
c) Self-designating method
d) Observation

276. What is a limitation of the sociometric method in measuring opinion leadership?

a) Requires a small number of respondents to locate opinion leaders
b) Provides only subjective perceptions of followers
c) Not applicable to small social systems
d) Requires a large number of respondents to locate opinion leaders

277. The self-designating method of measuring opinion leadership is particularly suitable for which type of sample design?

a) Random sampling
b) Systematic sampling
c) Cluster sampling
d) Stratified sampling

278. What advantage does observation have as a method of measuring diffusion networks and opinion leadership?

a) Provides the most valid data
b) Requires a small number of respondents
c) Works best in a large social system
d) Involves no interaction with the subjects

279. In terms of communication network analysis, what does homophily refer to?

a) Similarity between individuals who communicate
b) The degree of network structure
c) The occurrence of direct communication links
d) The spread of innovations in a system

280. Which type of communication network links often connect two sets of socially dissimilar individuals in a system?

a) Homophilous links
b) Heterophilous links
c) Direct links
d) Mass media channels

281. What is one drawback of homophily in diffusion networks?

a) It encourages effective communication between change agents and clients.

b) It causes new ideas to spread vertically within a system.

c) It can slow down the rate of diffusion.

d) It leads to higher social status for opinion leaders.

282. Which type of opinion leadership refers to an individual acting as an opinion leader for only a single topic?

a) Polymorphic opinion leadership

b) Heterophily opinion leadership

c) Monomorphic opinion leadership

d) Homophilous opinion leadership

283. According to the characteristics of opinion leaders, what should opinion leaders adopt before their followers?

a) Norms of the system

b) New ideas and innovations

c) The mass media channels

d) Heterophilous communication

284. What are the three major categories in which consequences of innovation can be classified?

a) Positive, negative, and neutral consequences

b) Desirable, undesirable, and unexpected consequences

c) Direct, indirect, and anticipatory consequences

d) Anticipated, unanticipated, and accidental consequences

285. Which type of consequence occurs as a result of adoption or rejection of an innovation and is intended and recognized by the members of a social system?

a) Desirable consequence

b) Direct consequence

c) Indirect consequence

d) Anticipated consequence

286. What type of consequence is characterized by changes that occur as a result of the direct consequences of innovation and are not intended or recognized by the members of a social system?

a) Unintended consequence

b) Undesirable consequence

c) Indirect consequence

d) Unanticipated consequence

287. What are the functional effects of an innovation for an individual or a social system called?
   a) Indirect consequences b) Unanticipated consequences
   c) Desirable consequences d) Unintended consequences

288. Which method of measuring opinion leadership involves asking key informants to designate opinion leaders in a system?
   a) Sociometric method **b) Informants' ratings**
   c) Self-designating method d) Observation

289. What characteristic of opinion leaders refers to their ability to influence others' attitudes and behaviors informally?
   a) Innovativeness b) Accessibility
   c) External communication d) Socio-economic status

290. Who is an individual that influences clients' innovation-decisions in a desirable direction?
   a) Innovator **b) Change agent**
   c) Opinion leader d) Mass media channel

291. What is one of the main roles of a change agent in the diffusion process?
   a) Preventing the adoption of any innovation
   b) Creating barriers to change in a client system
   c) Facilitating the flow of innovations to clients
   d) Discouraging feedback from the client system

292. Which of the following occupations can be considered as change agents?
   a) Farmers b) Engineers
   c) Athletes **d) Public health workers**

293. What does a change agent do to develop a need for change in clients?
   a) Point out new alternatives to existing problems
   b) Discourage clients from confronting their problems
   c) Hide information about innovations
   d) Isolate clients from new ideas

294. In order to be effective, a change agent must develop rapport with clients by being perceived as:
   a) Incompetent and untrustworthy
   b) Unsympathetic and judgmental
   c) Credible, competent, and trustworthy
   d) Disconnected from the clients' needs

295. What is one of the main responsibilities of a change agent during the process of introducing an innovation?
   a) To criticize the clients' existing alternatives
   b) To analyze clients' problems from the agency's perspective
   c) To motivate clients' interests in the innovations
   d) To ensure that clients adopt the innovations immediately

296. At which stage of the innovation-decision process do interpersonal network influences from near-peers become most important?
   a) Adoption stage
   b) Persuasion stage
   c) Confirmation stage
   d) Knowledge stage

297. How does a change agent stabilize new behavior in clients who have adopted innovations?
   a) By discouraging the adoption of innovations
   b) By creating barriers to the diffusion process
   c) By reinforcing messages to clients who have adopted
   d) By encouraging clients to discontinue the new behavior

298. What is the end goal for a change agent regarding their relationship with clients?
   a) To keep clients dependent on the change agent's services
   b) To maintain a long-term relationship without change
   c) To develop self-renewing behavior in clients
   d) To control clients' decisions and actions

299. What is the main objective of most change agencies in relation to their clients?
   a) To secure the adoption of new ideas
   b) To discourage clients from adopting innovations
   c) To maintain the status quo in the client system
   d) To prevent any change in clients' behavior

300. What factor is positively related to change agent success in securing the adoption of innovations?
   a) Effort spent in communication activities with clients
   b) Effort spent in communication activities with the agency
   c) Emphasis on adopting undesirable innovations
   d) Emphasis on preventing any changes in clients' behavior

301. Which orientation is positively related to change agent success in securing the adoption of innovations?
   a) Change agency orientation
   b) Client-oriented orientation
   c) Innovation-focused orientation
   d) External communication orientation

302. Change agent success in securing the adoption of innovations is positively related to the degree of compatibility with:
   a) Change agency needs
   b) The change agent's personal interests
   c) The client's needs
   d) The opinions of opinion leaders

303. What is the degree to which an individual can put themselves into the role of another person called?
   a) Client empathy
   b) Change agent empathy
   c) Client orientation
   d) Change agency perspective

304. When are change agents more likely to be effective in the long run regarding higher-quality adoptions?
   a) When they emphasize adopting as many innovations as possible
   b) When they focus on securing adoption by opinion leaders
   c) When they achieve higher-quality adoptions that satisfy clients
   d) When they discourage any changes in clients' behavior

305. Which of the following is NOT a role of a change agent in introducing an innovation in a client system?
   a) To create an intent in the client to change
   b) To diagnose problems from the agency's perspective
   c) To translate an intent to action
   d) To achieve a terminal relationship

306. What is one of the factors used to measure the degree of change agent success in securing the adoption of innovations?
   a) The rate of adoption among change agents
   b) The rate of adoption among opinion leaders
   c) The rate of adoption among clients
   d) The rate of adoption among mass media channels

307. Which type of communication is crucial for the change agent in the diffusion process?

a) One-way communication from the change agency to the clients

b) Two-way information exchange between the change agent and clients

c) One-way communication from the clients to the change agency

d) Two-way information exchange between the change agency and opinion leaders

308. What is the end goal of a change agent regarding their relationship with clients?

a) To become the sole decision-maker for the clients

b) To maintain clients' dependence on the change agent's services

c) To develop self-renewing behavior in clients

d) To prevent clients from becoming change agents themselves

309. Which role of a change agent involves analyzing clients' problems and understanding them from the clients' perspective?

a) To translate an intent to action

b) To establish an information-exchange relationship

c) To diagnose problems

d) To create a need for change

8

Collaborative Methods for Tech Advancements in Extension

1. What was the main reason for the emergence of the Farming Systems Research (FSR) movement in the 1970s?
   a) To benefit resource-poor farmers
   b) To improve research station trials
   c) To promote hybrid and genetically modified seeds
   d) To increase productivity for all farmers
2. Participatory Technology Development (PTD) emphasizes the involvement of which group in the innovation process?
   a) Scientists and extensionists
   b) NGOs and policymakers
   c) Farmers and local communities
   d) Development agencies and international organizations
3. What is the primary focus of PTD in the development of agricultural technology?
   a) Environmental sustainability
   b) Maximizing profits for farmers
   c) Increasing productivity for resource-poor farmers
   d) Introducing modern technologies to rural areas
4. Which type of farmers' experiments involves trying out a new idea purely out of curiosity?
   a) Curiosity experiments
   b) Problem-solving experiments
   c) Adaptation experiments
   d) Hypothetical experiments
5. The control of research in participatory research is jointly shared by whom?
   a) Professional researchers
   b) Farmers and other stakeholders
   c) Government agencies
   d) International organizations

Bold Means Correct Answer

6. Participatory Technology Development (PTD) is also known as:
   a) Farmer-First Research
   b) Technology Transfer Approach
   c) Top-Down Development
   d) Conventional Farming Approach

7. What are the innovation characteristics important to poor farmers?
   a) Profit maximization and risk reduction
   b) Input saving and cost reducing
   c) Resource exploitation and capital accumulation
   d) Expansion into commercial farming

8. In PTD, what is the main role of outsiders such as research scientists and extension staff?
   a) To control the research process
   b) To dictate the research agenda
   c) To facilitate and support local people in technology development
   d) To act as experts and make decisions for farmers

9. What does the term "participation" mean in the context of PTD?
   a) Farmers are forced to participate in research
   b) Farmers are merely observers in the research process
   c) Farmers actively contribute and have a say in research activities
   d) Farmers are passive recipients of research outcomes

10. What is the primary goal of farmer participatory research?
    a) To develop appropriate agricultural technology for small farmers
    b) To increase the profitability of large farms
    c) To encourage urbanization and migration from rural areas
    d) To promote the use of hybrid seeds in agriculture

11. What is the main focus of PTD during the process of experimentation?
    a) Implementing large-scale trials at research stations
    b) Conducting controlled experiments with the participation of scientists
    c) Developing farmer-led experiments in real farm conditions
    d) Outsourcing experimentation to specialized agencies

12. How does PTD contribute to the refinement of sustainable agricultural systems?
    a) By enforcing top-down development strategies
    b) By promoting the use of modern technologies
    c) By empowering farmers and incorporating local knowledge
    d) By establishing centralized agricultural management systems

13. What is the role of outsiders in the PTD process?
    a) To control and direct all research activities
    b) To serve as technical advisors and managers of development institutions
    c) To implement experiments without farmers' involvement
    d) To dictate solutions without considering farmers' perspectives

14. What is one of the key outcomes of using participatory research in technology development?
    a) Isolation of farmers from the research process
    b) Reduction in the number of farmers involved in the research
    c) Accelerated transfer and adoption of improved technology
    d) Decreased interest of farmers in experimentation

15. What is a challenge faced in implementing PTD?
    a) Lack of interest from farmers to participate in research
    b) Difficulty in enforcing top-down approaches
    c) Resistance from development agencies to support PTD initiatives
    d) Inability to involve farmers in decision-making

16. The main goal of PTD is to:
    a) Develop technology based on farmers' needs and criteria
    b) Promote modern agricultural practices only
    c) Increase profits for large-scale farmers
    d) Disregard the needs of resource-poor farmers

17. In PTD, who conducts experiments to test possible solutions to old and new problems?
    a) Professional researchers
    b) Resource-rich farmers
    c) Resource-poor farmers
    d) Extension agents

18. What is the role of "outsiders" in PTD?
    a) To control and dominate the research process
    b) To facilitate and support local farmers in technology development
    c) To impose their knowledge and solutions on farmers
    d) To discourage farmers from participating in research

19. What is the main focus of PTD in the development of agricultural technology?
    a) To promote hybrid and genetically modified seeds
    b) To increase productivity for resource-poor farmers
    c) To improve research station trials
    d) To benefit resource-rich farmers

20. How does PTD differ from conventional top-down approaches?
    a) PTD relies solely on scientific knowledge and disregards farmers' input.
    b) Conventional approaches involve more farmers in the decision-making process.
    c) PTD emphasizes the participation of farmers and local communities in research.
    d) Conventional approaches are more cost-effective and efficient in technology transfer.

21. What is participation in a group process?
    a) A static process where only a few members contribute.
    b) A dynamic process where members contribute, share, and influence each other.
    c) A process where decisions are made by a single leader.
    d) A process focused on exclusion of disadvantaged groups.

22. How does people's participation empower them in problem-solving and decision-making?
    a) By limiting their involvement in rural development.
    b) By giving them confidence and control over their decisions and actions.
    c) By excluding them from large-scale project design and evaluation.
    d) By discouraging their initiative and action.

23. What does "participatory extension" involve for extension staff?
    a) Implementing government projects without community involvement.
    b) Encouraging community-driven development planning and activity implementation.
    c) Providing development assistance to rural communities without their input.
    d) Excluding local knowledge and resources in development planning.

24. How has the FAO's experience shown the benefits of participatory programs?
    a) By increasing the cost of providing development assistance to governments.
    b) By reducing the involvement of extension staff in community planning.
    c) By mobilizing local knowledge and resources for self-reliant development.
    d) By restricting large-scale projects to centralized decision-making.

25. What role does participation play in strategies for sustainable agriculture development?
    a) It is unnecessary for sustainable agriculture development.
    b) It is essential for involving disadvantaged groups in decision-making.
    c) It restricts progress and accelerates development setbacks.
    d) It focuses solely on implementing government projects.

26. How can participatory approaches be beneficial in large-scale projects?
    a) By reducing the involvement of disadvantaged groups.
    b) By excluding the local level in the implementation process.
    c) By stimulating self-help activities at the local level.
    d) By limiting the evaluation of project progress.

27. What is the synergy between participating partners in the context of progress?
    a) A reduction in knowledge and experience base.
    b) An increase in setbacks and delays in development.
    c) An exchange of input and knowledge to accelerate development.
    d) A limitation in the planning and implementation process.

28. What is the main focus of participatory extension in development planning?
    a) Centralized decision-making by extension staff.
    b) Routine monitoring and evaluation of development progress.
    c) Mobilizing local resources without community input.
    d) Facilitating community-driven development planning and activity implementation.

29. Which approach recognizes the need to involve disadvantaged segments of the rural population in policy design?
    a) Participatory extension.
    b) Static extension.
    c) Exclusionary extension.
    d) Government-driven extension.

30. What does people's participation imply in the context of rural development?
    a) Exclusion of disadvantaged groups.
    b) Limited involvement in decision-making.
    c) Active involvement in development planning.
    d) A focus on government-led development.

31. How does participation benefit individuals in problem-solving and decision-making?
    a) By limiting their analysis and decision-making abilities.
    b) By reducing their confidence and command over actions.
    c) By empowering them to do their own analysis and make decisions.
    d) By discouraging them from planning and taking action.

32. What is the relationship between participatory approaches and sustainable development?
    a) They are unrelated and do not complement each other.
    b) They focus on excluding disadvantaged segments of the population.
    c) They recognize the need to involve disadvantaged groups in policy design.
    d) They form an essential element in strategies for sustainable development.

33. How has participatory extension reduced the cost of providing development assistance?

    a) By centralizing decision-making with government officials.

    b) By excluding community-driven planning and implementation.

    c) By mobilizing local knowledge and resources for self-reliant development.

    d) By avoiding large-scale projects and focusing only on self-help activities.

34. What is the primary focus of people's participation in development processes?

    a) To limit the involvement of rural populations.

    b) To discourage individual decision-making.

    c) To stimulate self-help activities at the local level.

    d) To involve disadvantaged groups in decision-making.

35. Why is participatory extension considered more effective than static extension?

    a) It restricts interaction and input from participating partners.

    b) It limits development planning and activity implementation.

    c) It promotes collective problem-solving through a group approach.

    d) It reduces the involvement of rural communities in decision-making.

36. What is the key benefit of interaction between participating partners in development planning?

    a) A reduction in knowledge and experience base.

    b) An increase in setbacks and delays in development.

    c) An exchange of input and knowledge to accelerate development.

    d) A limitation in the planning and implementation process.

37. How can participatory approaches be utilized in large-scale project design and evaluation?

    a) By excluding local communities from the decision-making process.

    b) By reducing the scope of the project to limit complexity.

    c) By stimulating self-help activities at the national level.

    d) By involving local communities in the design, implementation, and evaluation.

38. What does "participatory extension" mean for extension staff in development planning?
    a) Implementing government projects without community involvement.
    b) Encouraging community-driven development planning and activity implementation.
    c) Providing development assistance to rural communities without their input.
    d) Excluding local knowledge and resources in development planning.

39. How does people's participation empower them in development processes?
    a) By limiting their involvement in decision-making.
    b) By reducing their confidence and command over actions.
    c) By encouraging them to take initiatives and actions.
    d) By excluding them from development planning.

40. What role does participation play in strategies for sustainable agriculture development?
    a) It is unnecessary for sustainable agriculture development.
    b) It is essential for involving disadvantaged groups in decision-making.
    c) It restricts progress and accelerates development setbacks.
    d) It focuses solely on implementing government projects.

41. How is participation defined?
    a) The involvement of people in shaping and criticizing public programs.
    b) Involvement in decision-making, program implementation, and evaluation.
    c) Voluntary contribution to national development without involvement in shaping programs.
    d) Participation in funding agencies and donor organizations.

42. What does community participation entail in a development project?
    a) Direct control over government funding for projects.
    b) Influencing the direction and execution of the project for better well-being.
    c) Providing feedback on completed projects without influencing them.
    d) Implementing projects without considering the views of beneficiary groups.

43. Why is people's participation considered important in development projects?
    a) It reduces efficiency and cost-effectiveness.
    b) It allows people to criticize the contents of the programs.
    c) It is a fashion trend in development thinking.
    d) It is essential for sustainable and long-lasting development.

44. How does participation improve project efficiency?
    a) By assigning fewer resources and costs to local people.
    b) By reducing the involvement of people in decision-making.
    c) By working in tandem with local people to achieve objectives.
    d) By eliminating the need for routine monitoring and evaluation.

45. What can people's involvement in decision-making and implementation ensure?
    a) Less effective utilization of resources.
    b) A dependence syndrome in development interventions.
    c) Effective utilization of resources and project effectiveness.
    d) A limitation in the coverage of weaker sections of society.

46. How does people's participation promote self-reliance in development?
    a) By creating a mentality of dependence on government solutions.
    b) By limiting the utilization of local resources and solutions.
    c) By increasing awareness, self-confidence, and control of the development process.
    d) By discouraging local human resource development.

47. What is the major advantage of people's participation in ensuring wider coverage of weaker sections of society?
    a) Reduced benefits for the target groups.
    b) A dependence syndrome among the non-poor and elite.
    c) Potent way to ensure the flow of benefits to the target groups.
    d) Limited availability of resources for development.

48. How does people's participation contribute to the sustainability of development interventions?
    a) By relying on externally assisted projects for funding.
    b) By generating a sense of ownership among local people.
    c) By encouraging dependence on donor agencies.
    d) By limiting the utilization of local resources.

49. What percentage of people's participation is typically sought in projects?
    a) 25% to 50%
    b) 10% to 25%
    c) 50% to 75%
    d) 75% to 100%

50. What is the first requirement of participatory approaches?
    a) Technical expertise of the team members.
    b) Building rapport and creating an interactive environment with the villagers.
    c) Performing everyday activities alongside the villagers.
    d) Consulting external experts before initiating the process.

51. What is the purpose of DIY (Do-it-yourself) in participatory approaches?
    a) To replace the villagers in executing development activities.
    b) To provide practical ideas and feelings of complexities of activities.
    c) To minimize the involvement of the team members with the villagers.
    d) To delegate the decision-making process to the villagers entirely.

52. Why is consultation with various stakeholders essential before initiating the participatory process?
    a) To assign decision-making solely to external experts.
    b) To select a village that is inaccessible for ease of supervision
    c) To validate information obtained from the semi-structured interviews.
    d) To discourage the involvement of local people in the planning process.

53. What is the purpose of training of trainers in participatory approaches?
    a) To equip villagers with the knowledge and skills for development activities.
    b) To increase the burden of project implementation on the facilitators.
    c) To ensure capacity building and sustainability of the approach.
    d) To discourage the involvement of local people in decision-making.

54. What does diagnosis involve in the context of participatory approaches?
    a) An examination and analysis of rural resources only.
    b) An examination and analysis of the villagers' practices and problems.
    c) An examination and analysis of external funding sources.
    d) An examination and analysis of non-poor and elite groups.

55. What is the primary focus of Rapid Rural Appraisal (RRA)?

a) Quick and efficient acquisition of information about rural life.

b) A systematic approach to gather precise figures for development projects.

c) Empowering local people to take an active role in analyzing problems.

d) Supporting participatory development cooperation.

56. How does Participatory Rural Appraisal (PRA) differ from RRA?

a) PRA relies solely on external experts for analysis.

b) PRA focuses on technical feasibility of projects.

c) PRA empowers local people to own the results and implementation.

d) PRA is more suitable for conventional survey methods.

57. What is the purpose of involving local people in PRA?

a) To reduce the need for technical experts in the study.

b) To shift the focus of conventional surveys to essential aspects.

c) To rely solely on local resources for project implementation.

d) To ensure feasibility studies are conducted accurately.

58. In what areas have RRA/PRA been applied?

a) Public infrastructure development.

b) Economic planning at the national level.

c) Upliftment of weaker sections of society.

d) Governance and policy analysis.

59. What is the primary purpose of participation in development projects?

a) To criticize the contents of public programs.

b) To involve external experts in decision-making.

c) To enhance local well-being and development.

d) To reduce the efficiency of projects.

60. Why are participatory approaches widely used by public and private agencies?

a) To impose external decisions on communities.

b) To involve external experts in planning and implementation.

c) To shift the focus of development to essential aspects.

d) To empower local people and ensure sustainability.

61. What is the main difference between RRA and PRA in terms of their focus?

    a) RRA focuses on local people's knowledge, while PRA focuses on local people's analytical capabilities.

    b) RRA focuses on change of behavior and attitudes, while PRA focuses on methods.

    c) RRA is extractive in nature, while PRA is facilitating.

    d) RRA involves visual instruments, while PRA involves verbal instruments.

62. What is the ideal objective of RRA?

    a) Learning from insiders by outsiders.

    b) Empowerment of local people.

    c) Initiating and catalyzing change.

    d) Extracting information from local people.

63. In which mode does RRA operate?

    a) Facilitating **b) Extractive**

    c) Visual d) Verbal

64. What does PRA aim to achieve in terms of the insider's role?

    a) To present and analyze the gathered information.

    b) To respond to outsider's questions.

    c) To initiate and catalyze change within the community.

    d) To be the main investigator of the study.

65. What is the primary role of outsiders in RRA?

    a) Initiating and catalyzing change.

    b) Responding to local people's questions.

    c) Investigating the local people's practices.

    d) Facilitating the participatory process.

66. How does PRA differ from traditional surveys in terms of data collection?

    a) PRA relies on pre-set questions for data collection.

    b) PRA relies on visual instruments for data collection.

    c) PRA focuses on absolute measurement of data.

    d) PRA relies on comparison rather than measurement.

67. In PRA, how are various exercises and activities carried out?

a) Through individual interactions with respondents.

b) Through semi-structured interviews with local leaders.

c) Through group work involving multiple participants.

d) Through external experts conducting field visits.

68. What does the shift from tables and paper to the ground achieve in PRA?

a) Allows more people to participate simultaneously.

b) Reduces the involvement of the elite in the process.

c) Makes the use of visuals and symbols easier.

d) Enables faster and more accurate measurements.

69. How does the use of visuals in PRA benefit the participation of non-literate individuals?

a) It allows them to express themselves more openly.

b) It helps them overcome their inhibitions.

c) It facilitates quicker data collection.

d) It ensures more accurate measurements.

70. What does the shift from reserve to rapport mean in PRA?

a) Moving from verbal to visual communication.

b) Building a strong bond between outsiders and insiders.

c) Allowing the elite to participate actively.

d) Focusing on absolute measurement of data.

71. What is the primary focus of PRA in terms of the initial interactions with local people?

a) Extracting information from local people.

b) Building rapport and establishing trust.

c) Initiating and catalyzing change.

d) Shifting from visual to verbal communication.

72. How does PRA differ from traditional methods of inquiry in terms of involvement?

a) Local people get bored with PRA exercises.

b) PRA increases the level of local people's involvement.

c) PRA requires longer field work hours for the facilitators.

d) Researchers find traditional methods exhilarating.

73. What does PRA emphasize in comparison to traditional surveys?
    a) Measurement over comparison.
    b) Visuals and symbols over verbal communication.
    c) Individual respondents over group work.
    d) Paper and pen over ground-based activities.

74. What makes comparison in PRA easier than measurement?
    a) Comparison requires less effort and time.
    b) Comparison provides more accurate data.
    c) Comparison is favored by external experts.
    d) Comparison involves individual interactions.

75. What makes PRA a potent equalizer in community participation?
    a) The involvement of elite members in the process.
    b) The use of visual instruments in data collection.
    c) The focus on individual interactions in data collection.
    d) The participation of non-literate and less articulate individuals.

76. How does PRA encourage local people to express themselves more openly?
    a) By using pre-set questions for data collection.
    b) By involving external experts in facilitation.
    c) By using verbal communication in data collection.
    d) By encouraging the use of visuals and symbols.

77. What role does the outsider play in PRA?
    a) Initiator and catalyst for change.
    b) Investigator of local practices.
    c) Main presenter and analyst of data.
    d) Respondent to local people's questions.

78. What is the main advantage of conducting PRA exercises on the ground?
    a) It allows for more accurate data collection.
    b) It reduces the need for verbal communication.
    c) It involves more individuals in the process.
    d) It enables easy modifications during activities.

79. How does PRA differ from traditional surveys in terms of local people's involvement?
    a) PRA activities require less effort from local people.
    b) PRA facilitates in-depth information in less time.
    c) PRA focuses on individual interactions with respondents.
    d) PRA relies on pre-set questions for data collection.

80. What is one of the major strengths of PRA compared to traditional approaches?
    a) PRA focuses on rapid and precise measurements.
    b) PRA shifts from an open and participatory approach to a closed approach.
    c) PRA empowers local people and allows for their active involvement.
    d) PRA relies solely on visual instruments for data collection.

81. What is one of the major principles of PRA?
    a) Deduction-based learning
    b) Avoiding participatory interactions
    c) Listening and learning through interactions
    d) Seeking representativeness of results

82. Why does PRA aim to offset biases during the appraisal process?
    a) To ensure quick results
    b) To involve professionals in data collection
    c) To focus on important aspects only
    d) To involve diverse and marginalized groups

83. How does PRA utilize community time effectively?
    a) By consulting with professionals at convenient times
    b) By focusing on a quick and rushed appraisal process
    c) By seeking diversity in data collection
    d) By respecting the time and convenience of local community members

84. What does seeking diversity mean in the context of PRA?
    a) Seeking diverse events and processes to understand issues from different perspectives
    b) Focusing on representativeness of data collected
    c) Seeking opinions only from those who are better off
    d) Seeking diverse opinions from the same group of people

85. Why is triangulation/cross-checking an important principle in PRA?
    a) To minimize community time
    b) To ensure precision of information
    c) To improve trustworthiness of data
    d) To involve a multi-disciplinary team

86. What does the principle of optimal ignorance mean in PRA?
    a) Seeking appropriate imprecision to save time
    b) Knowing enough to serve the purpose and not seeking unnecessary information
    c) Seeking precision of information at all costs
    d) Avoiding the involvement of professionals in data collection

87. What role does the multi-disciplinary team play in PRA?
    a) Ensuring representativeness of data collected
    b) Facilitating participatory sessions
    c) Minimizing biases during data collection
    d) Inclusion of scientists from relevant disciplines for a comprehensive study

88. What should one member of the PRA team be responsible for during interactions with villagers?
    a) Data recording
    b) Seeking representativeness of results
    c) Developing rapport with the villagers
    d) Seeking optimal ignorance during data collection

89. Which principle of PRA involves changing the team composition and techniques applied?
    a) Seeking diversity
    b) Triangulation/cross-checking
    c) Optimal ignorance
    d) Utilizing precious community time

90. Why is listening to local people important in PRA?
    a) To gather quick results
    b) To avoid biases in data collection
    c) To portray their world view and learn progressively
    d) To focus on precision of information

91. How does PRA aim to involve the poorest people, women, and disadvantaged groups?
    a) By seeking optimal ignorance in data collection
    b) By focusing on representativeness of results
    c) By consulting with professionals during the appraisal process
    d) By visiting remote and interior locations at the convenience of local communities

92. What does seeking appropriate imprecision mean in PRA?
    a) Avoiding the involvement of professionals in data collection
    b) Knowing enough to serve the purpose without seeking unnecessary information
    c) Focusing on diverse events and processes during data collection
    d) Involving professionals for quick results

93. What is the main focus of PRA when it comes to community time?
    a) Minimizing biases in data collection
    b) Seeking optimal ignorance during data collection
    c) Respecting the time and convenience of local community members
    d) Focusing on representativeness of data collected

94. How does PRA aim to improve the trustworthiness of data?
    a) By involving a multi-disciplinary team
    b) By seeking diversity in data collection
    c) By changing the sources of information and techniques applied
    d) By seeking optimal ignorance during data collection

95. Why is seeking diversity important in PRA?
    a) To minimize biases in data collection
    b) To ensure quick and efficient data collection
    c) To involve professionals in data collection
    d) To understand issues from different perspectives

96. What is the role of the multi-disciplinary team in PRA?
    a) Seeking representativeness of results
    b) Facilitating participatory sessions
    c) Inclusion of scientists from relevant disciplines for a comprehensive study
    d) Minimizing biases during data collection

97. What does optimal ignorance mean in the context of PRA?
    a) Seeking diversity in data collection
    b) Avoiding precision of information that is not necessary
    c) Focusing on representativeness of results
    d) Involving professionals in data collection

98. Why does PRA aim to offset biases during the appraisal process?
    a) To ensure quick results
    b) To involve professionals in data collection
    c) To focus on important aspects only
    d) To involve diverse and marginalized groups

99. How does PRA utilize community time effectively?
    a) By consulting with professionals at convenient times
    b) By focusing on a quick and rushed appraisal process
    c) By seeking diversity in data collection
    d) By respecting the time and convenience of local community members

100. What does seeking diversity mean in the context of PRA?
    a) Seeking diverse events and processes to understand issues from different perspectives
    b) Focusing on representativeness of data collected
    c) Seeking opinions only from those who are better off
    d) Seeking diverse opinions from the same group of people

101. According to the behavioural principles of PRA, what does "handing over the stick" mean?
    a) Dominating the local people during data collection
    b) Encouraging local people to take control of the process
    c) Seeking diversity in data collection methods
    d) Failing forward in data analysis

102. Which component of self-critical awareness in PRA involves using errors as an opportunity to learn?
    a) Failing forward
    b) Seeking diversity
    c) Optimal ignoranced
    Triangulation

103. How do facilitators act in accordance with the local conditions and needs of the circumstances in PRA?
   a) By avoiding innovation and improvisation
   b) By seeking representativeness of data
   c) By using their best judgments
   d) By sharing information with local people

104. What is the key principle of PRA regarding information and ideas?
   a) Sharing
   b) Stealing
   c) Avoiding diversity
   d) Minimizing errors

105. What is the main focus of Participatory Learning and Action (PLA)?
   a) Local people's appraisal of their lives and livelihoods
   b) Dominance and control during data collection
   c) Seeking representativeness of data

106. What is the role of outsiders in Participatory Learning and Action(PLA)?
   a) Local people's appraisal of their lives and livelihoods
   b) Local people's data generation and analysis
   c) Dominating the participatory process
   d) Seeking representativeness of data

107. Which level is the preferred study level in Agro Ecosystem Analysis (AEA)?
   a) Global regions
   b) Rice and wheat fields
   c) Villages
   d) Countries

108. What does the Agro Ecosystem Analysis (AEA) involve?
   a) Secondary data review only
   b) Direct observation and data analysis
   c) Data collection using questionnaires
   d) Field residence and agro ecosystem diagrams

109. What are the system properties analyzed in Agro Ecosystem Analysis (AEA)?
   a) Productivity, stability, and sustainability
   b) Dominance, control, and distribution
   c) Failing forward, sharing, and triangulation
   d) Optimal ignorance, seeking diversity, and self-critical awareness

110. Which tool/technique is NOT used in Agro Ecosystem Analysis (AEA)?

a) Decision trees

b) Seasonal calendars

c) Verbal interviews

d) Venn diagrams

111. What is the focus of "handing over the stick" in PRA?

a) Seeking diversity in data collection

b) Dominance and control by outsiders

c) Encouraging local people to take control of the process

d) Sharing information and ideas at different levels

112. Which principle of PRA involves critically examining one's own behavior and attitudes?

a) Handing over the stick

b) Self-critical awareness

c) Use your best judgments

d) From stealing to sharing

113. In PRA, what is the role of outsiders to local communities during participatory appraisal?

a) They dominate the process and control the data collection.

b) They take control of the process and pass it on to the local people.

c) They seek representativeness of results from local communities.

d) They minimize errors in data collection.

114. What does Participatory Learning and Action (PLA) focus on?

a) The appraisal of local people's lives and livelihoods

b) Dominance and control during data collection

c) Seeking diversity in data collection methods

d) Failing forward in data analysis

115. How does PLA involve local communities in decision-making and project planning?

a) By minimizing errors in data collection

b) By avoiding biases in data analysis

c) By seeking diversity in data collection

d) By evoking their participation and involvement

116. What is the preferred study level in Agro Ecosystem Analysis (AEA)?

a) Global regions

b) Rice and wheat fields

c) Villages

d) Countries

117. What are some of the tools/techniques used in Agro Ecosystem Analysis (AEA)?
   a) Verbal interviews only
   b) Decision trees and seasonal calendars
   c) Venn diagrams and sharing information
   d) Avoiding diversity and triangulation

118. What are the system properties analyzed in Agro Ecosystem Analysis (AEA)?
   a) Productivity, stability, and sustainability
   b) Dominance, control, and distribution
   c) Failing forward, sharing, and triangulation
   d) Optimal ignorance, seeking diversity, and self-critical awareness

119. What is the role of outsiders to local communities during participatory appraisal?
   a) They dominate the process and control the data collection.
   b) They take control of the process and pass it on to the local people.
   c) They seek representativeness of results from local communities.
   d) They minimize errors in data collection.

120. Which organization developed the Participatory Learning Methods (PALM)?
   a) FAO **b) MYRADA**
   c) World Bank d) United Nations

121. What is the aim of PALM?
   a) To dominate and control data collection in villages
   b) To arrive at participatory analysis and a common understanding of rural conditions
   c) To minimize errors in data collection
   d) To focus on appraisal and create false expectations

122. What are the tools/techniques used in PALM?
   a) Verbal interviews and questionnaires
   b) Seasonality diagramming and triangulation
   c) Geographical and historical transects, participatory mapping, ranking and scoring
   d) Decision trees and Venn diagrams

123. What is the Participatory Action Research (PAR) approach developed from?
    - **a) Social science circles in Latin America**
    - b) Urban development in the United States
    - c) Rural organizations in India
    - d) Health care programs in Africa

124. What is the focus of PAR?
    - a) Dominating and controlling data collection
    - **b) Learning-by-doing and searching for solutions with local groups**
    - c) Minimizing errors in data analysis
    - d) Seeking diversity in data collection methods

125. What is expected of an action researcher in PAR?
    - a) Seeking representativeness of results
    - b) Avoiding biases in data collection
    - **c) Empathizing with and sharing the problems and needs of local people**
    - d) Minimizing cost and time

126. What are the tools/techniques used in PAR?
    - a) Seasonal calendars and decision trees
    - **b) Social stratification techniques and group interviews**
    - c) Verbal interviews and triangulation
    - d) Geographical and historical transects, participatory mapping, ranking and scoring

127. What do spatial PRA techniques focus on?
    - a) Appraisal of rural conditions
    - b) Dominance and control of data collection
    - **c) Spatial dimensions of people's realities**
    - d) Avoiding biases in data analysis

128. What is the chief feature of a social map in spatial PRA techniques?
    - a) It is drawn to scale by local people.
    - b) It depicts the natural resources of the area.
    - c) It is made by experts to guide interventions.
    - **d) It is made by local people and not drawn to scale.**

129. What is the objective of a social map in spatial PRA techniques?
   a) To dominate and control data collection in villages
   b) To arrive at participatory analysis and common understanding of rural conditions
   c) To serve as a monitoring and evaluating tool
   d) To seek representativeness of data

130. What is the organization MYRADA known for?
   a) Participatory Learning Methods (PALM)
   b) Participatory Action Research (PAR)
   c) Spatial PRA techniques
   d) Rural development in Latin America

131. Where was Participatory Action Research (PAR) developed as an academic discipline?
   a) United States
   b) Latin America
   c) India
   d) Africa

132. What are the tools/techniques used in PAR?
   a) Seasonal calendars and decision trees
   b) Social stratification techniques and group interviews
   c) Verbal interviews and triangulation
   d) Geographical and historical transects, participatory mapping, ranking and scoring

133. What do spatial PRA techniques focus on?
   a) Appraisal of rural conditions
   b) Dominance and control of data collection
   c) Spatial dimensions of people's realities
   d) Avoiding biases in data analysis

134. What is the chief feature of a social map in spatial PRA techniques?
   a) It is drawn to scale by local people.
   b) It depicts the natural resources of the area.
   c) It is made by experts to guide interventions.
   d) It is made by local people and not drawn to scale.

135. What is the objective of a social map in spatial PRA techniques?
    a) To dominate and control data collection in villages
    b) To arrive at participatory analysis and common understanding of rural conditions
    c) To serve as a monitoring and evaluating tool
    d) To seek representativeness of data

136. What is the distinguishing feature of the social mapping process that amazes new PRA practitioners?
    a) The involvement of old people, women, and children in mapping
    b) The use of advanced technology for mapping
    c) The accuracy of measurements to scale in the map
    d) The exclusion of marginalized sections of society from mapping

137. What should be considered while selecting the site for mapping?
    a) The availability of modern amenities at the site
    b) The exclusion of certain social groups from the site
    c) The convenience of the site for all participants
    d) The capacity of the site to hold a large gathering

138. Why is it important to transfer the social map onto paper?
    a) To make it permanent and safe
    b) To reduce the number of participants involved
    c) To minimize errors in data collection
    d) To avoid using locally available materials

139. How does social mapping involve the largest number of participants compared to other PRA methods?
    a) By minimizing the number of participants for efficient mapping
    b) By using advanced technology for mapping
    c) By actively involving old persons and young children in the process
    d) By excluding certain social groups from participation

140. What is the key characteristic of a resource map in PRA?
    a) It is drawn to scale by experts
    b) It focuses on habitation and community facilities
    c) It is not drawn to scale and done by local people
    d) It uses advanced technology for accurate measurements

141. Participatory Learning Methods (PALM) is an approach developed by:
   a) United Nations Development Programme (UNDP)
   b) World Bank
   c) FAO (Food and Agriculture Organization)
   d) MYRADA in Bengaluru, India

142. Participatory Action Research (PAR) was developed in which academic discipline of social psychology?
   a) Anthropology
   b) Sociology
   c) Political Science
   d) Economics

143. Social maps in PRA are typically drawn by:
   a) Experts from outside the community
   b) Local people
   c) Government officials
   d) Surveyors

144. What is the main objective of creating a resource map in PRA?
   a) To locate and mark historical sites in the area
   b) To identify potential sites for development projects
   c) To depict the natural resources in the locality
   d) To determine the population density of the area

145. What is the major benefit of utilizing space-related PRA methods such as social mapping and resource mapping?
   a) It minimizes the need for community participation
   b) It allows for accurate measurements of resources
   c) It creates a common understanding among participants
   d) It eliminates the need for facilitators or external help

146. Which PRA method focuses on the causal factors of a phenomenon, activity, or problem, and the effects thereof?
   a) Well-being Ranking
   b) Social Mapping
   c) Venn Diagram
   d) Cause Effect Diagram

147. Well-being ranking is based on the perception of:
   a) Government officials
   b) Local people
   c) NGOs (Non-governmental Organizations)
   d) Experts from outside the community

148. Which method in PRA is also known as Chapati diagram and uses circles to represent institutions or individuals?

a) Matrix Method
b) Cause Effect Diagram
c) Well-being Ranking
d) Venn Diagram

149. In a cause effect diagram, what do the arrows represent between causes and effects?

a) Importance
b) Closeness
c) Size
d) Accessibility

150. Which method in PRA involves arranging a list of households in descending order of well-being?

a) Well-being Ranking
b) Social Mapping
c) Matrix Method
d) Venn Diagram

151. What is the main purpose of using a Venn diagram in PRA?

a) To study natural resources in a community
b) To analyze cause-effect relationships in a problem
c) To rank households based on income and assets
d) To study institutional relationships and interactions

152. What is a common alternative name for the Cause Effect Diagram?

a) Social Mapping
b) Fishbone Diagram
c) Well-being Ranking
d) Venn Diagram

153. Which PRA method uses circles of different sizes to represent the importance of institutions or individuals?

a) Matrix Method
b) Well-being Ranking
c) Cause Effect Diagram
d) Social Mapping

154. What does the Venn diagram use overlapping circles to represent?

a) Illiteracy levels in a community
b) Interaction and interlinkages between institutions or individuals
c) Water sources in a village
d) Wealth distribution among households

155. What should an action plan in PRA explicitly answer regarding each intervention?

a) What and why
b) When and where
c) Who and which
d) All of the above

156. What is the purpose of monitoring in a development project?
    a) To implement new technologies
    b) To evaluate the success of the project
    c) To improve financial management
    d) To ensure resources are allocated appropriately

157. What are the three broad categories of results in monitoring?
    a) Inputs, outcomes, and impacts
    b) Outputs, effects, and impacts
    c) Inputs, outputs, and outcomes
    d) Inputs, effects, and outcomes

158. Process monitoring is concerned with assessing:
    a) The efficiency of resource allocation
    b) The effectiveness of project outcomes
    c) The delivery system and implementation efficiency
    d) The impact of the project on the community

159. Which of the following is not typically assessed in process monitoring?
    a) Division of tasks within the project
    b) Modes of cooperation among staff
    c) The impact of project effects
    d) Understanding and dealing with resistance

160. Participatory monitoring involves:
    a) Periodic analysis of information by insiders only
    b) Periodic analysis of information by outsiders only
    c) Recording and analysis of information by both insiders and outsiders
    d) Recording and analysis of information by outsiders only

161. What is one of the benefits of participatory monitoring?
    a) It allows for the use of specialized external evaluators
    b) It provides ongoing information to adjust project activities
    c) It requires fewer resources compared to other monitoring methods
    d) It focuses exclusively on the project's overall impact

162. Participatory monitoring is especially useful for:
    a) Conducting cost-benefit analyses
    b) Identifying long-term trends and patterns
    c) Gathering information from a community's perspective
    d) Analyzing the outcomes of a project

163. What is the purpose of a participatory evaluation?
    a) To determine the success of project implementation
    b) To provide a final judgement on project effectiveness
    c) To identify problems and seek solutions early
    d) To allocate resources more effectively

164. In a participatory evaluation, who takes the lead?
    a) External evaluators
    b) Community insiders
    c) Both outsiders and insiders
    d) Donors and funding agencies

165. Why might outsiders facilitate a participatory evaluation?
    a) To control the evaluation process
    b) To answer specific questions required by donors
    c) To ensure the evaluation is objective and unbiased
    d) To provide support and guidance to community members

166. Participatory evaluation is beneficial for better decision-making because:
    a) It helps justify project expenditures
    b) It encourages insiders to accept outsiders' objectives
    c) It provides more realistic information on outcomes
    d) It focuses on satisfying donors' requirements

167. Which aspect is NOT considered in a participatory evaluation?
    a) Overall project objectives
    b) Effectiveness of activities
    c) Financial performance of the project
    d) Relevance of activities to community needs

168. Participatory evaluation can strengthen insider-to-insider communication by:

a) Disseminating information to outsiders

b) Providing an opportunity to discuss important issues

c) Encouraging community members to evaluate the project

d) Sharing results with other communities facing similar problems

169. What is the purpose of a SWOT analysis in a participatory evaluation?

a) To assess the cost-effectiveness of project activities

b) To identify the strengths, weaknesses, opportunities, and threats of the project

c) To measure the impact of the project on the community

d) To analyze the results of participatory monitoring

170. Which group is responsible for planning and conducting a participatory evaluation?

a) Donors and funding agencies

b) External evaluators

c) The community evaluation team

d) The project implementers

171. What is the first step in preparing for a participatory evaluation?

a) Identifying the community's long-term objectives

b) Reviewing the objectives and activities of the project

c) Setting a timeline for data gathering

d) Selecting the evaluation team

172. Which of the following is NOT a potential benefit of participatory evaluation?

a) Better decision-making by insiders

b) Greater understanding of community concerns by outsiders

c) Minimization of insider perspectives and interests

d) Use of results for ongoing project management

173. Which information source can be used to identify the original objectives of a project?

a) Participatory baselines

b) Participatory assessments

c) Participatory monitoring

d) External evaluations

174. In a participatory evaluation, who decides the evaluation questions and indicators?
    a) The donors and funding agencies
    b) The community evaluation team
    c) External evaluators
    d) The project implementers

175. When should information gathering and analysis be done in a participatory evaluation?
    a) At the end of the project
    b) Only when requested by the funding agencies
    c) As soon as the evaluation team is formed
    d) Within the timeframe set by the evaluation team

176. What was the main reason for the emergence of the Farming Systems Research (FSR) movement in the 1970s?
    a) To benefit resource-poor farmers
    b) To improve research station trials
    c) To promote hybrid and genetically modified seeds
    d) To increase productivity for all farmers

177. Participatory Technology Development (PTD) emphasizes the involvement of which group in the innovation process?
    a) Scientists and extensionists
    b) NGOs and policymakers
    c) Farmers and local communities
    d) Development agencies and international organizations

178. In PTD, what is the main role of outsiders such as research scientists and extension staff?
    a) To control the research process
    b) To dictate the research agenda
    c) To facilitate and support local people in technology development
    d) To act as experts and make decisions for farmers

179. What does the term "participation" mean in the context of PTD?
    a) Farmers are forced to participate in research
    b) Farmers are merely observers in the research process
    c) Farmers actively contribute and have a say in research activities
    d) Farmers are passive recipients of research outcomes

180. What is the primary goal of farmer participatory research?
    a) To develop appropriate agricultural technology for small farmers
    b) To increase the profitability of large farms
    c) To encourage urbanization and migration from rural areas
    d) To promote the use of hybrid seeds in agriculture

181. What is the main focus of PTD during the process of experimentation?
    a) Implementing large-scale trials at research stations
    b) Conducting controlled experiments with the participation of scientists
    c) Developing farmer-led experiments in real farm conditions
    d) Outsourcing experimentation to specialized agencies

182. How does PTD contribute to the refinement of sustainable agricultural systems?
    a) By enforcing top-down development strategies
    b) By promoting the use of modern technologies
    c) By empowering farmers and incorporating local knowledge
    d) By establishing centralized agricultural management systems

183. What is the role of outsiders in the PTD process?
    a) To control and direct all research activities
    b) To serve as technical advisors and managers of development institutions
    c) To implement experiments without farmers' involvement
    d) To dictate solutions without considering farmers' perspectives

184. What is one of the key outcomes of using participatory research in technology development?
    a) Isolation of farmers from the research process
    b) Reduction in the number of farmers involved in the research
    c) Accelerated transfer and adoption of improved technology
    d) Decreased interest of farmers in experimentation

185. What is a challenge faced in implementing PTD?
    a) Lack of interest from farmers to participate in research
    b) Difficulty in enforcing top-down approaches
    c) Resistance from development agencies to support PTD initiatives
    d) Inability to involve farmers in decision-making

186. The main goal of PTD is to:

a) Develop technology based on farmers' needs and criteria

b) Promote modern agricultural practices only

c) Increase profits for large-scale farmers

d) Disregard the needs of resource-poor farmers

187. In PTD, who conducts experiments to test possible solutions to old and new problems?

a) Professional researchers

b) Resource-rich farmers

c) Resource-poor farmers

d) Extension agents

188. What is the role of "outsiders" in PTD?

a) To control and dominate the research process

b) To facilitate and support local farmers in technology development

c) To impose their knowledge and solutions on farmers

d) To discourage farmers from participating in research

189. What is the main focus of PTD in the development of agricultural technology?

a) To promote hybrid and genetically modified seeds

b) To increase productivity for resource-poor farmers

c) To improve research station trials

d) To benefit resource-rich farmers

190. How does PTD differ from conventional top-down approaches?

a) PTD relies solely on scientific knowledge and disregards farmers' input.

b) Conventional approaches involve more farmers in the decision-making process.

c) PTD emphasizes the participation of farmers and local communities in research.

d) Conventional approaches are more cost-effective and efficient in technology transfer.

9

Research in Agricultural Extension Techniques and Methodology

1. What is the primary challenge faced by Indian agriculture?
   a) Producing more from less land
   b) Meeting food and nutritional needs sustainably
   c) Implementing advanced technology
   d) Increasing agricultural workforce

2. The role of agricultural extension discipline in technology assessment and refinement was significant during which period?
   a) First Green Revolution
   b) Second Green Revolution
   c) Both first and second Green Revolutions
   d) Third Green Revolution

3. What is the current phase of the Green Revolution that emphasizes the role of agricultural extension?
   a) Third Green Revolution
   b) Fourth Green Revolution
   c) Second Green Revolution
   d) Industrial Revolution

4. The potential of agricultural extension in the National Agricultural Research System (NARS) is:
   a) Fully realized
   b) Partially realized
   c) Overestimated
   d) Yet to be fully realized

5. Why is the basic research in extension education considered neglected?
   a) Lack of qualified researchers
   b) Insufficient funding
   c) Low demand for agricultural extension
   d) Overemphasis on technological advancements

Bold Means Correct Answer

6. What is essential for assigning rigor to agricultural extension work?

   a) Clarity and accountability of scientifically accepted methodology

   b) A large number of research traditions

   c) Funding from the National Agricultural Research System

   d) Government regulations

7. The progress of a scientific field is helped by the realization of its:

   a) Assumptions, biases, and weaknesses

   b) Strengths, weaknesses, and threats

   c) Opportunities, assumptions, and biases

   d) Biases, limitations, and strengths

8. Research methodologies and outputs are more likely to be accepted if they:

   a) Prioritize commercial interests

   b) Align with government policies

   c) Meet three specific purposes

   d) Are conducted by renowned researchers

9. What are the three purposes that research methodologies and outputs should meet for higher acceptance?

   a) Financial gain, technological advancement, and commercial success

   b) Advance understanding, identify probable causes, and prescribe remedies and control outcomes

   c) Achieve government objectives, improve crop yield, and reduce expenses

   d) Ensure environmental sustainability, social equity, and international recognition

10. Which of the following is crucial for the progress of agricultural extension as a scientific discipline?

   a) Continuous introduction of new technologies

   b) Clear communication of research findings

   c) Ignoring weaknesses to promote optimism

   d) Emphasis on commercial profitability

11. Agricultural Extension Education Discipline draws knowledge and practices from various social sciences, including all of the following EXCEPT:

    a) Anthropology
    b) Human resource development
    c) Botany
    d) Educational technology

12. What are the five dimensions primarily embraced by social sciences research?

    a) Sociological, physiological, ideological, methodological, and anthropological
    b) Sociological, ontological, ideological, epistemological, and methodological
    c) Sociological, psychological, methodological, epistemological, and ecological
    d) Sociological, ontological, psychological, epistemological, and anthropological

13. Social sciences research is mostly conducted in a natural and non-manipulated social environment involving:

    a) Animals
    b) Plants
    c) Microorganisms
    d) Human beings individually or in groups

14. Which characteristics make achieving objectivity in social sciences research challenging?

    a) Inherent characteristics of the phenomena under study
    b) Involvement of animals in the research
    c) Reliance on mathematical models
    d) Lack of research funding

15. What is the primary concern for researchers regarding objectivity in social sciences research?

    a) Ensuring maximum research funding
    b) Maintaining a diverse team of investigators
    c) Deriving conclusions without bias and value judgment
    d) Demonstrating personal biases openly

16. How can researchers achieve objectivity and account for biases in their work?
    a) Ignoring biases to focus on empirical evidence
    b) Minimizing biases through appropriate understanding and training
    c) Shifting focus from empirical evidence to theoretical constructs
    d) Advocating for subjective interpretations

17. Which of the following is NOT a common bias observed in social sciences studies?
    a) Interviewer bias
    b) Response bias
    c) Sampling bias
    d) Chemical bias

18. To contribute to the existing body of knowledge, social sciences research should be all of the following EXCEPT:
    a) Systematic
    b) Empirical
    c) Controlled
    d) Opinion-based

19. Agricultural Extension Education Discipline is an applied behavioural science that deals with desirable changes in:
    a) Economic systems
    b) Political ideologies
    c) Human behavior complex
    d) Technological advancements

20. What should social science research be in order to be considered valid and reliable?
    a) Objective and theoretical
    b) Verifiable and intuitive
    c) Empirical, systematic, controlled, measureable, valid, and reliable
    d) Opinion-based and subjective

21. Which approach in social science research aims to explore and understand a phenomenon from the perspective of individuals or groups?
    a) Quantitative research
    b) Mixed methods research
    c) Descriptive study
    d) Qualitative research

22. What is the main purpose of quantitative research in social science?
    a) Exploring and understanding phenomena
    b) Building from general themes
    c) Testing objective theories and examining relationships among variables
    d) Integrating both qualitative and quantitative methods

23. Mixed methods research in social science combines which two types of research approaches?
    a) Qualitative and descriptive research
    b) Qualitative and exploratory research
    c) Quantitative and exploratory research
    d) Qualitative and quantitative research

24. Which step in the social science research process involves identifying research problem?
    a) Literature review
    b) Data collection
    c) Hypothesis development
    d) Research topic selection

25. What is the main purpose of conducting an extensive literature review in social science research?
    a) To develop hypotheses
    b) To analyze data
    c) To understand past research results and methodological issues
    d) To formulate research questions

26. What is the core assumption behind mixed methods research?
    a) Combining qualitative and quantitative methods improves the reliability of data.
    b) Quantitative methods are more effective than qualitative methods.
    c) Qualitative methods are superior to quantitative methods.
    d) The combination of qualitative and quantitative methods enhances understanding of a research problem.

27. In which approach of social science research, variables are measured using statistical procedures?
    a) Descriptive study
    b) Qualitative research
    c) Quantitative research
    d) Mixed methods research

28. The template for a research problem statement includes all of the following elements EXCEPT:
    a) Research topic
    b) Research questions
    c) Justification of the problem's importance
    d) Preferred data collection methods

29. What is the purpose of formulating hypotheses in social science research?
    a) To provide a justification for the research topic
    b) To determine the appropriate research design
    c) To identify research gaps
    d) To test objective theories

30. What is the primary characteristic of qualitative research in social sciences?
    a) Testing objective theories
    b) Use of statistical procedures
    c) Understanding meanings from participants' perspectives
    d) Strict control of intervening variables

31. Which approach in social science research involves examining the relationship among variables?
    a) Descriptive study
    b) Quantitative research
    c) Qualitative research
    d) Mixed methods research

32. What is the core assumption of mixed methods research?
    a) Qualitative research is more reliable than quantitative research.
    b) Combining qualitative and quantitative methods improves the rigor of research.
    c) Quantitative research is more suited for exploratory studies.
    d) Mixed methods research is only applicable to historical research.

33. The social science research process begins with:
    a) Data analysis
    b) Literature review
    c) Hypothesis development
    d) Identifying a research problem

34. Which element is NOT part of the template for a research problem statement?
    a) Research topic
    b) Research questions
    c) Justification of the problem's importance
    d) Preferred data collection methods

35. Which principle should be followed when writing research objectives?

a) SMART principle b) Intelligent principle

c) Complex principle d) Specific principle

36. A well-written research objective should be all of the following EXCEPT:

a) Brief b) Precise

c) Vague d) Comprehensive

37. What type of verbs should be used when formulating research objectives?

a) Abstract verbs b) Passive verbs

c) Action verbs d) Future tense verbs

38. Which category of concepts includes directly observable objects that are close to reality and concrete?

a) Abstract concepts

b) Concrete concepts

c) Observable concepts

d) Indirectly observable concepts

39. Constructs are mental processes used to make fuzzy and imprecise notions:

a) Specific and measurable b) Concrete and observable

c) Abstract and indirectly observable d) Theoretical and interpretive

40. What are empirically observable manifestations of a concept?

a) Constructs **b) Variables**

c) Propositions d) Hypotheses

41. What are statements of prediction or conjectural relationships between concepts in a theory?

a) Hypotheses b) Constructs

c) Variables **d) Propositions**

42. Which type of hypothesis does not specify the direction of the relationship between variables?

a) Null hypothesis b) Alternate hypothesis

c) Causal hypothesis d) Hypothesis in question form

43. What does the construct conceptualization process begin with?
    a) Data analysis
    b) Hypothesis formulation
    c) Research objectives
    d) Research questions

44. Which type of hypothesis states a conjectural relationship between variables?
    a) Alternate hypothesis
    b) Causal hypothesis
    c) Hypothesis in question form
    d) Null hypothesis

45. What is the primary purpose of concepts in social science research?
    a) To provide specific data points
    b) To make research objectives measurable
    c) To serve as building blocks for hypotheses and theories
    d) To represent theoretical interpretations

46. Which category of concepts is directly used in agricultural extension research?
    a) Directly observable objects
    b) Concrete and indirectly observable
    c) Abstract and indirectly interpreted
    d) Abstract and indirectly observable through multiple observable entities

47. What is the purpose of using action verbs in research objectives?
    a) To create abstract objectives
    b) To emphasize theoretical concepts
    c) To clearly indicate the action to be taken in the research
    d) To make objectives vague and imprecise

48. In which approach of social science research, variables are measured using statistical procedures?
    a) Descriptive study
    b) Qualitative research
    c) Quantitative research
    d) Mixed methods research

49. What is the purpose of formulating hypotheses in social science research?
    a) To provide a justification for the research topic
    b) To determine the appropriate research design
    c) To identify research gaps
    d) To test objective theories

50. What is the primary characteristic of qualitative research in social sciences?
    a) Testing objective theories
    b) Use of statistical procedures
    c) Understanding meanings from participants' perspectives
    d) Strict control of intervening variables

51. Which approach in social science research involves examining the relationship among variables?
    a) Descriptive study
    b) Quantitative research
    c) Qualitative research
    d) Mixed methods research

52. What is the core assumption of mixed methods research?
    a) Qualitative research is more reliable than quantitative research.
    b) Combining qualitative and quantitative methods improves the rigor of research.
    c) Quantitative research is more suited for exploratory studies.
    d) Mixed methods research is only applicable to historical research.

53. The social science research process begins with:
    a) Data analysis
    b) Literature review
    c) Hypothesis development
    d) Identifying a research problem

54. What is the main purpose of conducting a literature review in research?
    a) To summarize the findings of the research study
    b) To critically analyze past and current knowledge related to the research topic
    c) To create new research questions
    d) To promote a specific research methodology

55. Which type of literature review involves analyzing journal articles and books related to a specific theme?
    a) Thematic review
    b) Study-by-Study review
    c) Quantitative review
    d) Qualitative review

56. How is the review of literature different between quantitative and qualitative studies?

a) The extent of literature is greater in qualitative studies.

b) Qualitative studies use literature only at the beginning of the study.

c) Quantitative studies use literature only at the end of the study.

d) Literature review is the same for both quantitative and qualitative studies.

57. What is the primary purpose of using literature at the beginning of a quantitative study?

a) To support or modify existing findings in the literature

b) To document the need for the study and provide a rationale for the direction of the study

c) To confirm or disconfirm prior predictions from the literature

d) To justify the use of specific statistical analysis

58. Which type of research design includes defining the information needed, specifying measurement procedures, and developing a plan of data analysis?

a) Literature review design

b) Exploratory design

c) Descriptive design

d) Research design

59. What is the main function of a research design?

a) To control variance

b) To select participants

c) To interpret data

d) To analyze data

60. What are the two types of experimental designs in quantitative research?

a) True experiments and longitudinal designs

b) Factorial designs and correlational designs

c) Randomized experiments and quasi-experiments

d) Single-subject designs and non-experimental designs

61. In a cross-sectional survey design, data is collected:

a) At multiple time periods from the same sample

b) At multiple time periods from different samples

c) At one point in time from the same sample

d) At one point in time from different samples

62. Which type of longitudinal design assesses trends in a specific aspect over the years with a different sample each year?
    a) Trend study
    b) Cohort study
    c) Panels study
    d) Successive independent samples study

63. What is the primary advantage of using a longitudinal design in survey research?
    a) It allows researchers to infer individual changes over time
    b) It requires a smaller sample size compared to other designs
    c) It is more suitable for cross-sectional analysis
    d) It uses randomized experiments for data collection

64. What is the purpose of using literature at the end of a quantitative study?
    a) To provide a rationale for the direction of the study
    b) To support or modify existing findings in the literature
    c) To confirm or disconfirm prior predictions from the literature
    d) To justify the use of specific statistical analysis

65. Which type of review of literature involves analyzing individual research studies one by one?
    a) Thematic review
    b) Study-by-Study review
    c) Quantitative review
    d) Qualitative review

66. In which type of quantitative research design does the researcher manipulate a specific treatment and observe its effect on an outcome?
    a) Non-experimental design
    b) Quasi-experimental design
    c) Correlational design
    d) Experimental design

67. Which type of quantitative research design does not involve manipulation of conditions?
    a) Experimental design
    b) Non-experimental design
    c) Causal-comparative design
    d) Survey research design

63. In a successive independent samples design, the researcher conducts a series of cross-sectional surveys:
    a) At different time periods from different samples
    b) At different time periods from the same sample
    c) At one point in time from different samples
    d) At one point in time from the same sample

69. What is the main purpose of using literature at the beginning of a qualitative study?
    a) To justify the use of specific statistical analysis
    b) To confirm or disconfirm prior predictions from the literature
    c) To support or modify existing findings in the literature
    d) To document the need for the study and provide a rationale

70. Which type of quantitative research design focuses on determining the effect of a specific treatment on an outcome?
    a) Non-experimental design
    b) Causal-comparative design
    c) Correlational design
    d) Experimental design

71. What are the two key aspects of a successive independent samples design?
    a) Use of multiple interventions and different sample sizes
    b) Use of identical questions and samples drawn from different populations
    c) Use of the same set of questions and different samples from the same population
    d) Use of randomized assignments and random sampling

72. Which type of survey research design collects data at one point in time to describe the characteristics of a population or differences among populations?
    a) Cross-sectional design
    b) Successive independent samples design
    c) Longitudinal design
    d) Trend study

73. In the longitudinal design, the same respondents are surveyed over a long period of time to examine changes in:
    a) The research questions
    b) The treatment conditions
    c) The dependent variables
    d) Some characteristics of individual respondents

74. What is the main purpose of using literature at the end of a qualitative study?
    a) To justify the use of specific statistical analysis
    b) To confirm or disconfirm prior predictions from the literature
    c) To support or modify existing findings in the literature
    d) To document the need for the study

75. Which type of review of literature provides a quantitative description of trends, attitudes, or opinions of a population?

a) Thematic review
b) Study-by-Study review
c) Quantitative review
d) Qualitative review

76. In a cross-sectional survey design, data is collected:

a) At multiple time periods from the same sample
b) At multiple time periods from different samples
c) At one point in time from the same sample
d) At one point in time from different samples

77. What is the primary advantage of using a longitudinal design in survey research?

a) It allows researchers to infer individual changes over time
b) It requires a smaller sample size compared to other designs
c) It is more suitable for cross-sectional analysis
d) It uses randomized experiments for data collection

78. What is the purpose of using literature at the end of a quantitative study?

a) To provide a rationale for the direction of the study
b) To support or modify existing findings in the literature
c) To confirm or disconfirm prior predictions from the literature
d) To justify the use of specific statistical analysis

79. Ex-post facto research is also known as:

a) Quasi-experimental research
b) Experimental research
c) Descriptive research
d) Longitudinal research

80. What is the main difference between ex-post facto research and true experimental research?

a) Ex-post facto research involves manipulation of the independent variable.
b) Ex-post facto research uses random assignment to treatment conditions.
c) Ex-post facto research begins after the phenomenon has occurred.
d) Ex-post facto research allows for generalization to a larger population.

81. Which type of qualitative research design involves studying an intact cultural group in a natural setting over a prolonged period of time?

a) Grounded theory
b) Phenomenological research
c) Ethnography
d) Narrative research

82. In a narrative research design, the researcher collects and narrates:

a) Statistical data from a sample population
b) Stories about people's lives
c) Observational data in a controlled setting
d) Experiences of the researcher

83. Concept analysis is a research strategy used to:

a) Investigate the relationship between two variables
b) Study the history of a phenomenon
c) Identify different meanings of the same concept
d) Measure changes in attitudes over time

84. Which type of mixed methods design collects both quantitative and qualitative data simultaneously, analyzing and interpreting them for a comprehensive view?

a) Convergent parallel design
b) Explanatory sequential design
c) Exploratory sequential design
d) Embedded design

85. In an explanatory sequential design, which data is collected first?

a) Quantitative data
b) Qualitative data
c) The data is collected simultaneously
d) No data is collected

86. The MAXMINCON principle for variance control focuses on controlling variance in which types of variables?

a) Independent variables in experimental research
b) Dependent variables in correlational studies
c) Both independent and dependent variables in experimental research
d) Neither independent nor dependent variables

87. In which type of research design is there no control group and subjects are presented with a treatment followed by outcome measurement?
 a) One-group design
 b) Two-group design
 c) Experimental design
 d) True experimental design

88. The major limitation of the one-group design is:
 a) The lack of a control group
 b) The lack of pre-testing
 c) The lack of random assignment
 d) The lack of post-testing

89. In a simulated before-after design, how are the measures obtained from the two groups?
 a) Measures are obtained from one group at different time points.
 b) Measures are obtained from one group before and after intervention, and from another comparable group after the intervention.
 c) Measures are obtained from two groups before intervention and compared after intervention.
 d) Measures are obtained from two groups simultaneously.

90 In a two-group, no control design, what is the purpose of the control group?
 a) To receive the treatment
 b) To be compared to the experimental group
 c) To manipulate the independent variable
 d) To control the extraneous variables

91. Which type of research design begins after the phenomenon has occurred, without any intervention from the researcher?
 a) Experimental research
 b) Quasi-experimental research
 c) Ex-post facto research
 d) Descriptive research

92. In a narrative research design, what kind of data does the researcher collect and write narratives about?
 a) Experimental data
 b) Qualitative data
 c) Survey data
 d) Quantitative data

93. What is the purpose of using a non-interactive qualitative research design?
 a) To manipulate conditions and observe the effect on the phenomenon
 b) To describe or interpret a phenomenon without intervention
 c) To collect both quantitative and qualitative data simultaneously
 d) To gather data from different samples at different time points

94. Which type of research design involves studying the past through a systematic analysis of artifacts, texts, images, and old buildings?

a) Policy analysis
b) Concept analysis
c) Historical analysis
d) Ethnography

95. What is the primary difference between quantitative and qualitative research designs?

a) The use of statistics in data analysis
b) The manipulation of variables
c) The control over the research process
d) The use of random sampling

96. What is the main purpose of the MAXMINCON principle for variance control in research design?

a) To maximize control over independent variables
b) To minimize measurement errors in the data
c) To control for extraneous variables
d) To maximize generalization to the population

97. Which type of research design is used to develop theories by deriving abstract theories from the views of participants?

a) Grounded theory
b) Ethnography
c) Phenomenological research
d) Concept analysis

98. In a successive independent samples design, data is collected at different time periods from:

a) The same sample
b) Different samples from the same population
c) Different samples from different populations
d) The control group only

99. Which type of research design focuses on describing the current state of a population or comparing attitudes between different groups?

a) Experimental design
b) Non-experimental design
c) Cross-sectional survey design
d) Longitudinal survey design

100. In a convergent parallel design, what is the purpose of collecting both quantitative and qualitative data simultaneously?

a) To compare the results of the two data sets
b) To validate the quantitative findings with qualitative insights
c) To offset biases and errors in data collection
d) To explain the results of quantitative analysis using qualitative data

101. Which of the following is NOT a factor affecting internal validity of experimental/quasi-experimental designs?

a) History b) Maturation

c) Sampling procedures d) Instrumentation

102. Which class of extraneous variables is caused by specific events occurring between the first and second measurement in an experiment?

a) History b) Maturation

c) Instrumentation d) Statistical regression

103. What is the main purpose of random assignment in experimental research?

a) To control for extraneous variables

b) To ensure equal representation of all groups

c) To eliminate maturation effects

d) To control for statistical regression

104. In non-probability sampling, how are samples selected?

a) Each unit in the population has an equal probability of being selected.

b) Samples are selected based on subjective criteria and represent specific characteristics.

c) Samples are selected using random sampling techniques.

d) Each unit in the population has an unequal probability of being selected.

105. Which type of sampling method is most suitable for a large population with a known size?

a) Quota sampling b) Convenience sampling

c) Simple random sample d) Cluster random sample

106. In the formula for sample size in probability sampling, what does "N" represent?

a) Sampling error b) Variance

c) Size of population d) Confidence level

107. Which postulate of measurement deals with the establishment of order?

a) Either $a < b$ or $a = b$ b) If a - b, then b - a

c) If $a < b$, and $b < c$, then $a < c$ d) If $a < b$, then $b < a$

108. In social sciences research, measurement process begins after identifying:
    a) Extraneous variables
    b) Randomized groups
    c) Constructs and their relationships
    d) Maturation effects

109. What is the main purpose of probability sampling?
    a) To ensure equal representation of all groups in the population
    b) To control for extraneous variables in the research design
    c) To select samples based on subjective criteria and specific characteristics
    d) To give each unit in the population an equal chance of being selected

110. In non-probability sampling, how are samples selected?
    a) Each unit in the population has an equal probability of being selected.
    b) Samples are selected based on subjective criteria and represent specific characteristics.
    c) Samples are selected using random sampling techniques.
    d) Each unit in the population has an unequal probability of being selected.

111. Which factor affects the selection of the appropriate sample size for a research study?
    a) The size of the population
    b) The number of surveys mailed, or interviews planned
    c) The desired statistical power
    d) The type of statistical analysis to be applied

112. In the MAXMINCON principle for variance control, what does "MAX" stand for?
    a) Maximum effect size of the independent variable
    b) Maximum control over extraneous variables
    c) Maximum sample size
    d) Maximum representation of the population

113. What is the main purpose of random assignment in experimental research?
    a) To control for extraneous variables
    b) To ensure equal representation of all groups
    c) To eliminate maturation effects
    d) To control for statistical regression

114. Which factor affects the selection of the appropriate sample size for a research study?
   a) The size of the population
   b) The number of surveys mailed or interviews planned
   c) The desired statistical power
   d) The type of statistical analysis to be applied

115. Which level of measurement involves classifying objects into mutually exclusive categories based on a property?
   a) Interval
   b) Ordinal
   c) Nominal
   d) Ratio

116. In which level of measurement are objects ranked based on the degree of possessing a property?
   a) Interval
   b) Nominal
   c) Ratio
   d) Ordinal

117. Which level of measurement provides a true zero point and allows for ratios of magnitude?
   a) Ratio
   b) Interval
   c) Nominal
   d) Ordinal

118. Which scaling characteristic indicates the relative sizes or positions of the descriptors without any absolute value?
   a) Distance
   b) Origin
   c) Order
   d) Description

119. Which measurement approach assumes that causality of a phenomenon flows from items or variables to the latent variable?
   a) Classical test theory
   b) Formative models
   c) The C-OAR-SE approach
   d) Item response theory

120. Which measurement approach focuses on individual responses to particular items rather than aggregate statistics?
   a) Classical test theory
   b) Formative models
   c) The C-OAR-SE approach
   d) Item response theory

121. What does the C-OAR-SE approach stand for in measurement modeling?
   a) Construct-object-attribute-rater entity
   b) Classical test theory, ordinal measurement, and statistical error
   c) Cluster analysis, origin characterization, and statistical estimation
   d) Content validity, ordinal attributes, and regression analysis

122. Which level of measurement is used primarily for classification purposes and does not involve ordering or ranking?
   a) Nominal
   b) Ratio
   c) Interval
   d) Ordinal

123. Which characteristic of scaling means that the scale has a unique or fixed beginning or true zero point?
   a) Description
   b) Order
   c) Distance
   d) Origin

124. What is the main purpose of scaling in research?
   a) To convert qualitative constructs into quantitative metric units
   b) To summarize multiple measures into an index
   c) To test the reliability of measurement instruments
   d) To determine the statistical significance of differences between groups

125. Which measurement approach assumes that a person's observed score is the sum of a true score and an error score?
   a) Formative models
   b) Item response theory
   c) The C-OAR-SE approach
   d) Classical test theory

126. Which level of measurement allows for measuring attribute distances among objects but does not provide a true zero point?
   a) Interval
   b) Ratio
   c) Nominal
   d) Ordinal

127. Which scaling characteristic involves the assignment of unique labels or descriptors to scale values?
   a) Description
   b) Order
   c) Distance
   d) Origin

128. In which level of measurement are variables measured at nominal and ordinal levels converted to standard scores?
   a) Ratio
   b) Interval
   c) Nominal
   d) Ordinal

129. What is the main purpose of probability sampling?
   a) To ensure equal representation of all groups in the population
   b) To control for extraneous variables in the research design
   c) To select samples based on subjective criteria and specific characteristics
   d) To give each unit in the population an equal chance of being selected

130. What is the primary purpose of converting variables measured at ordinal or interval levels to standard scores?

   a) To make data amenable for analysis

   b) To convert continuous variables to categorical variables

   c) To eliminate outliers from the data

   d) To calculate the mean and standard deviation of the data

131. Which scale development strategy employs reasoning and deductive logic to determine the meaning of a scale response?

   a) Subject-centred b) Response scale

   c) Deductive d) Empirical

132. In the stimulus-centred scale development strategy, what are the two main stages involved in scale construction?

   a) Subject scaling and person scaling

   b) Item analysis and theoretical basis

   c) Stimulus scaling and person scaling

   d) Item scaling and response scaling

133. Which method of stimulus scaling involves adjusting the differences between stimuli so that the differences in magnitudes appear equal, producing an interval scale?

   a) Method of equal-appearing intervals

   b) Method of successive intervals

   c) Method of paired comparisons

   d) Method of expert judges

134. How many expert judges are typically asked to rate each potential scale item in the equally appearing interval method?

   a) 10 to 15 **b) 20 to 30**

   c) 50 to 100 d) 80 to 100

135. What is the purpose of computing the interquartile range in the equally appearing interval method?

   a) To determine the mean rating for each scale item

   b) To select the final scale items based on their median values

   c) To adjust the differences between stimuli to appear equal

   d) To identify the scale values for each item

136. Which scale development strategy follows a systematic data collection process and statistical analyses to determine the meaning of a test response to items representing a specific construct?

a) Deductive
b) Empirical
c) Response scale
d) Subject-centred

137. In Thurstone's scaling methods, what are the two main stages of scale construction?

a) Subject-centred scaling and person-centred scaling
b) Item scaling and response scaling
c) Stimulus scaling and person scaling
d) Expert judgment and item analysis

138. What is the main purpose of stimulus scaling in Thurstone's scaling methods?

a) To locate subjects on the continuum of the specific construct
b) To estimate the scale value for each object or item representing a psychological construct
c) To select the final scale items based on their median values
d) To adjust the differences between stimuli to appear equal

139. Which method of stimulus scaling involves comparing each stimulus with every other stimulus to determine their relative rankings?

a) Method of equal-appearing intervals
b) Method of successive intervals
c) Method of paired comparisons
d) Method of expert judges

140. In the empirical scale development strategy, what follows the systematic data collection process?

a) Theoretical basis
b) Expert judgment
c) Statistical analyses
d) Deductive logic

141. Which scaling strategy employs reasoning and deductive logic to determine the meaning of a scale response?

a) Subject-centred
b) Response scale
c) Deductive
d) Empirical

142. Q methodology is a combination of conceptual framework, data collection technique, and method of analysis used to study:

a) Objective phenomena

b) Human subjectivity expressed through viewpoints and opinions

c) Physical properties of objects

d) Statistical relationships

143. In Q methodology, participants are asked to rank and sort a series of statements representing a specific phenomenon. What method of analysis is used to analyze participant responses?

a) Regression analysis
b) Factor analysis
c) Correlation analysis
d) T-test

144. What is the main purpose of using Q methodology?

a) To identify statistical relationships among variables

b) To investigate perspectives of participants on specific phenomena

c) To conduct experiments in a controlled environment

d) To measure physical properties of objects

145. Which type of scale is used in Likert scaling to measure attitudes, opinions, or perceptions?

a) Nominal scale
b) Ordinal scale
c) Interval scale
d) Ratio scale

146. In a Likert scale, what does a score of "1" represent?

a) Strongly agree
b) Agree
c) Neutral
d) Strongly disagree

147. The Semantic Differential (SD) scale focuses on three dimensions: evaluation, potency, and activity. How many points are there on the rating continuum of the SD scale?

a) 3
b) 5
c) 7
d) 10

148. Which scale is considered ordinal in nature, but is often treated as an interval scale for analysis purposes?

a) Likert scale
b) Guttman's scalogram analysis
c) Rasch method
d) Semantic Differential scale

149. Guttman's scalogram analysis is used to measure:

a) Attitudes and public opinion
b) Human subjectivity
c) Objective phenomena
d) Physical properties of objects

150. In Guttman's scalogram analysis, respondents are asked to indicate their agreement or disagreement on a series of attitudinal statements arranged in:

a) A random order
b) A hierarchical order
c) An alphabetical order
d) A reverse order

151. Which method of scale development uses the Item Response Theory and postulates that item response is a function of item characteristics and a person's attributes?

a) Likert scale
b) Guttman's scalogram analysis
c) Rasch method
d) Semantic Differential scale

152. Which of the following statements describes the relationship between reliability and validity?

a) Reliability and validity are unrelated concepts.
b) Reliability and validity are closely inter-dependent.
c) Reliability is more important than validity in research.
d) Validity can exist without reliability.

153. Which of the following statements is true regarding the relationship between reliability and validity?

a) Reliability and validity are completely independent of each other.
b) High reliability guarantees high validity.
c) Low reliability always results in low validity.
d) Reliability can be present even if validity is low.

154. What is the maximum validity of a test in relation to its reliability coefficient?

a) Equal to the reliability coefficient
b) Twice the reliability coefficient
c) Three times the reliability coefficient
d) Square root of the reliability coefficient

155. Which method of observation and data collection uses unstructured, indirect questioning to access underlying motivations and feelings?

a) Content analysis
b) Case study
c) Projective methods
d) Social network analysis

156. Content analysis is used for:

a) Systematic data collection in field experiments
b) Measuring attitudes and opinions using a Likert scale
c) Categorizing qualitative textual data into clusters of similar entities
d) Observing and recording natural behavior in a controlled environment

157. Which of the following is NOT one of the key dimensions that distinguish observational methods?

a) Control
b) Observer status
c) Time duration of observation
d) Concealment of observation

158. Which method of observation involves collecting impressions of the world using the senses in a systematic and purposeful way?

a) Content analysis
b) Ego-centric analysis
c) Case study
d) Observation

159. Social Network Analysis (SNA) is used to:

a) Analyze individual networks of a single actor
b) Investigate in-depth case studies
c) Conduct surveys for data collection
d) Identify consistent patterns in qualitative data

160. Ego-centric analysis (ECA) deals with:

a) Identifying consistent patterns in qualitative data
b) Analyzing the complete network of a single actor
c) Conducting meta-analysis on research studies
d) Mapping social relationships among multiple actors

161. What is the primary objective of research synthesis?

a) To create new theories
b) To generalize research findings
c) To design new research studies
d) To collect primary data

162. Systematic reviews and meta-analysis (SRMA) are used for:
    a) Observational data collection
    b) Content analysis
    c) Combining and summarizing data from multiple studies
    d) Analyzing social network relationships

163. Which method is a versatile approach used for collecting information from people to describe, compare, or explain their knowledge, attitudes, and behavior?
    a) Case study
    b) Content analysis
    c) Social Network Analysis (SNA)
    d) Survey

164. Surveys are commonly used in extension education science because they allow researchers to collect:
    a) Qualitative data only
    b) Quantitative data only
    c) Both quantitative and qualitative data
    d) Observational data

165. Which method of observation uses unstructured, vague, and ambiguous stimuli to indirectly project respondents' behaviors, motivations, beliefs, attitudes, or feelings?
    a) Content analysis
    b) Likert scale
    c) Projective methods
    d) Case study

166. What are the three types of content analysis based on the mode of analysis?
    a) Summarising content analysis, Predictive content analysis, and Descriptive content analysis
    b) Explicative content analysis, Structuring content analysis, and Predictive content analysis
    c) Summarising content analysis, Explicative content analysis, and Structuring content analysis
    d) Descriptive content analysis, Predictive content analysis, and Structuring content analysis

167. In Social Network Analysis (SNA), what do the nodes represent in the network map?
    a) The relationships between actors
    b) The strength of the relationships between actors
    c) The various actors in the network
    d) The level of social influence

168. What is the primary goal of Ego-centric analysis (ECA)?
   a) To analyze complete networks of multiple actors
   b) To analyze the complete network of a single actor
   c) To analyze social relationships using statistical techniques
   d) To analyze the complete network of a single research study

169. What is the main objective of systematic reviews and meta-analysis (SRMA)?
   a) To identify consistent patterns in qualitative data
   b) To conduct observational research in natural settings
   c) To analyze the complete network of a single actor
   d) To combine and synthesize data from multiple studies into a single quantitative estimate or summary effect size

170. Questionnaires are documents designed to solicit information for:
   a) Descriptive analysis only
   b) Ethical considerations
   c) Systematic observation
   d) Appropriate analysis

171. What is a major advantage of personally administered questionnaires?
   a) Quick data collection process
   b) No need for interviewer bias
   c) Easy to reach respondents in remote areas
   d) Researcher can regulate the data collection process

172. Which type of questionnaire is mailed to respondents along with a self-addressed envelope for returning it back to the researchers?
   a) Personally administered questionnaire
   b) Electronic and online questionnaire
   c) Mailed questionnaire
   d) Structured questionnaire

173. Online questionnaires are created as "web forms" and stored in a database to:
   a) Analyze qualitative data
   b) Efficiently process mailed questionnaires
   c) Reach respondents dispersed in a large geographical area
   d) Reduce the number of questions in the questionnaire

174. What is the formula for calculating the minimum item to total correlation in a given dimension?
   a) **1 / N, where N is the number of items in the given dimension**
   b) 1 / n, where n is the number of respondents in the sample
   c) N / 1 + (n-1)r, where N is the number of items and r is the correlation coefficient
   d) $r\pi$ = N(r) / 1+(n-1)r, where N is the number of items and r is the correlation coefficient

175. Which type of questionnaire is prone to nonresponse due to the absence of the researcher?
   a) Personally administered questionnaire
   b) **Mailed questionnaire**
   c) Electronic and online questionnaire
   d) Structured questionnaire

176. The personally administered questionnaire can be time-consuming, especially when collecting data from:
   a) **Remote areas**
   b) High-income respondents
   c) University students
   d) Large urban cities

177. What does the formula rtt represent?
   a) **Item to total correlation of a specific item with the total score**
   b) The coefficient of correlation for each item in descending order
   c) Total correlation among all items in the questionnaire
   d) The selection criteria for choosing items for the questionnaire

178. Which type of questionnaire is appropriate when the research team intends to collect data from areas at their proximity?
   a) **Personally administered questionnaire**
   b) Mailed questionnaire
   c) Electronic and online questionnaire
   d) Structured questionnaire

179. In a mailed questionnaire, respondents are asked to return the completed questionnaire:
   a) Via email
   b) In person to the researchers
   c) **By mail along with a self-addressed envelope**
   d) Through a web form

180. Which type of questionnaire can suffer from nonresponse due to the absence of the researcher?
   a) Personally administered questionnaire
   b) Mailed questionnaire
   c) Electronic and online questionnaire
   d) Structured questionnaire

181. What is the formula for calculating rtt (item 2, 4, 5, 3)?
   a) 4(0.442) / 1+(4-1)0.442
   b) 3(0.570) / 1+(3-1)0.570
   c) 2(0.660) / 1+(2-1)0.660
   d) N(r) / 1+(n-1)r

182. Which method is used to facilitate the selection of items for a questionnaire based on their correlation with the total score?
   a) Content analysis
   b) Factor analysis
   c) Social Network Analysis (SNA)
   d) Survey

183. What is the primary disadvantage of personally administered questionnaires?
   a) Time-consuming and cumbersome process
   b) High cost compared to other types of questionnaires
   c) Limited reach to respondents in remote areas
   d) Absence of researcher control

184. Which formula is used to calculate $r\pi$, representing the minimum item to total correlation?
   a) N / 1 + (n-1)r
   b) 1 / n
   c) 1 / N
   d) N(r) / 1+(n-1)r

185. Factor analysis is used to:
   a) Regulate the data collection process
   b) Facilitate the selection of items for a questionnaire
   c) Calculate the total correlation among all items in the questionnaire
   d) Analyze qualitative data obtained from interviews

186. Participatory research is a collaborative process aimed at:
   a) Collecting data from remote areas
   b) Encouraging social transformation
   c) Developing standardized technologies
   d) Conducting experiments on the research farm

187. Which of the following is an example of participatory research in agriculture?
   a) Social Network Analysis (SNA)
   b) Critical Incident Technique (CIT)
   c) Programme evaluation
   d) On-farm adaptive research

188. Participatory Rural Appraisal (PRA) enables local communities to:
   a) Conduct experiments on the research farm
   b) Collect systematic analysis of village resources
   c) Conduct joint consultation with researchers
   d) Develop standardized technologies

189. Critical Incident Technique (CIT) is used to:
   a) Assess the impact of technological interventions
   b) Improve the job performance of farmers
   c) Conduct systematic analysis of village resources
   d) Collect data on seasonal calendars and trends

190. Programme evaluation is a process of:
   a) Collecting evidence to determine the success of a task
   b) Identifying the tasks or behaviors that lead to ineffective job performance
   c) Systematically assessing the operation and outcomes of a program or project
   d) Conducting experiments on the research farm

191. Formative evaluation is conducted during which phase of a program?
   a) Planning
   b) Implementation
   c) Conclusion
   d) Impact assessment

192. Grounded theory building is a part of which research tradition?
   a) Quantitative research tradition
   b) Meta-analytic theory building
   c) Social constructionist theory building
   d) Qualitative research tradition

193. The critical incident technique collects incidents that lead to the success or failure of a:

a) Task b) Interview

c) Questionnaire d) Survey

194. Which approach in theory building is inductively derived from the study of the phenomenon it represents?

a) Grounded theory building

b) Meta-analytic theory building

c) Social constructionist theory building

d) Dubin's theory-building method

195. Participatory research in agriculture involves enabling stakeholders to participate in:

a) Standardized experiments on the research farm

b) Technology map creation

c) Randomized control trials

d) Experiments designed in joint consultation

196. Theory includes two components, one that specifies relationships between theoretical constructs and another that describes relationships between constructs and:

a) Research findings b) Researchers

c) Measures d) Technologies

197. Which type of evaluation focuses on programme implementation?

a) Formative evaluation b) Summative evaluation

c) Process evaluation d) Impact assessment

198. The meta-analytic theory building approach seeks general conclusions across multiple studies as the basis for:

a) Collecting evidence

b) Conducting interviews

c) Building theories

d) Monitoring extension programs

199. Which theory-building method uses a hypothetical-deductive approach for creating and using knowledge?

a) Grounded theory building

b) Meta-analytic theory building

c) Social constructionist theory building

d) Dubin's theory-building method

200. Theory vs facts: A theory is a set of inter-related concepts that presents a systematic view of the phenomenon with the purpose of:
   a) Observing the real world
   b) Identifying empirical observations
   c) Explaining and predicting phenomena
   d) Collecting qualitative data

201. Participatory research involves conducting experiments jointly with:
   a) Researchers
   b) External experts
   c) Stakeholders and farmers
   d) Extension professionals

202. Theory construction in agricultural extension education includes theories related to adult learning and:
   a) Human resource management
   b) Programme evaluation
   c) On-farm adaptive research
   d) Participatory technology dissemination

203. Which type of evaluation focuses on long-term sustained changes as a result of planned interventions?
   a) Formative evaluation
   b) Output evaluation
   c) Impact evaluation
   d) Process evaluation

204. Which theory-building approach emphasizes the understanding of how people perceive the real world and give meaning to social experience?
   a) Dubin's theory-building method
   b) Grounded theory building
   c) Meta-analytic theory building
   d) Social constructionist theory building

205. Case study research focuses on understanding dynamics within a:
   a) Multiple settings
   b) Single setting
   c) Controlled environment
   d) Controlled group

206. Data exploration in data analysis involves:
   a) Identifying patterns in the data
   b) Conducting experiments on the research farm
   c) Summarizing main characteristics of a dataset
   d) Estimating population parameters

207. Construction of strata involves grouping raw data to form contingency tables based on:

a) Homogeneous groups b) Random sampling
c) Sample statistics d) Standard deviation

208. Population parameters are constants that summarize characteristics of:

a) Sample data b) Case study research
c) A population d) Data exploration

209. Descriptive statistics are used to:

a) Develop generalizations about population characteristics
b) Summarize large amounts of numerical data
c) Test statistical hypotheses
d) Estimate population parameters

210. Inferential statistics develop generalizations about population characteristics based on:

a) Sample data b) Descriptive statistics
c) Sample parameters d) Sample statistics

211. Which method is used to test the presence or absence of relationships between two sets of variables?

a) Exploratory factor analysis b) Cluster analysis
c) Canonical correlation d) Case study research

212. Predictive statistical methods are used for:

a) Dimension reduction b) Exploratory analysis
c) Predicting dependent variables d) Creating contingency tables

213. Configurational analysis is an alternate method of predictive analysis that:

a) Uses linear regression models
b) Analyzes variables independently
c) Involves bifurcation of heterogeneous groups
d) Focuses on exploratory factor analysis

214. Scales and indexes are both used to measure a social phenomenon, but they are different in terms of:

a) Data exploration techniques **b) Accumulation of scores**
c) Data processing methods d) Hypothesis testing procedures

215. Appraisal involves a critical examination of a program or project proposal:
  a) After implementation
  b) Before implementation
  c) During evaluation
  d) During data exploration

216. Monitoring is a process that starts and ends with a program or project and is required for:
  a) Hypothesis testing
  b) Impact assessment
  c) Mid-course corrections
  d) Data exploration

217. Impact assessment focuses on longer-term and wider-ranging outcomes:
  a) Beyond the immediate results of a program or project
  b) During the data exploration phase
  c) During evaluation
  d) Before implementation

218. Which method in multivariate analysis analyzes associations between two or more sets of measurements?
  a) Exploratory factor analysis
  b) Confirmatory factor analysis
  c) Canonical correlation
  d) Principal components

219. Data exploration and editing involves variable identification, missing values treatment, outlier treatment, and:
  a) Descriptive statistics
  b) Factor analysis
  c) Hypothesis testing
  d) Assumption testing

220. Which statistical method is used to summarize a group of data by describing how they are spread out?
  a) Measures of central tendency
  b) Measures of spread
  c) Exploratory factor analysis
  d) Confirmatory factor analysis

221. The basic consideration in the formation of strata is to create groups that are:
  a) Randomly selected
  b) Internally homogeneous
  c) Externally homogeneous
  d) Homoscedastic

222. Multivariate methods are procedures for analyzing associations between two or more sets of measurements made on:
  a) Randomly selected samples
  b) Each object in one or more samples
  c) Different settings
  d) Independent variables

223. Descriptive statistics reduce large amounts of numerical data into a more manageable form:
    a) For exploratory factor analysis
    b) For inferential statistics
    c) To create contingency tables
    d) To summarize information from a sample

224. Inferential statistics are used to make generalizations about population characteristics based on:
    a) Sample data
    b) Case study research
    c) Sample parameters
    d) Descriptive statistics

225. The technique used for exploratory analysis of groupings from object similarities is called:
    a) Principal components analysis
    b) Cluster analysis
    c) Confirmatory factor analysis
    d) Canonical correlation analysis

226. Configurational analysis proceeds by a successive bifurcation of heterogeneous groups into smaller, homogeneous:
    a) Samples
    b) Populations
    c) Subgroups
    d) Strata

227. Appraisal involves a critical examination of a program or project proposal:
    a) Before implementation
    b) After implementation
    c) During data exploration
    d) During impact assessment

228. Which method in multivariate analysis is used to create spatial representation of object similarities?
    a) Principal components analysis
    b) Confirmatory factor analysis
    c) Multi-dimensional scaling
    d) Canonical correlation analysis

229. Monitoring is a process that is required for immediate use and:
    a) Descriptive statistics
    b) Case study research
    c) Inferential statistics
    d) Mid-course corrections

230. The process of identifying patterns in the data and summarizing main characteristics of a dataset is known as:
    a) Data exploration
    b) Case study research
    c) Inferential statistics
    d) Hypothesis testing

231. Which type of data are appropriate for cases involving amount or magnitude, including interval and ratio levels?
   a) Non-metric data
   b) Metric data
   c) Descriptive data
   d) Exploratory data

232. Impact assessment focuses on:
   a) Exploratory factor analysis
   b) Inferential statistics
   c) Short-term outcomes
   d) Longer-term outcomes

233. Which method is used to test statistical hypotheses and make inferences about how well a particular model might describe the relationship between variables in a population?
   a) Exploratory factor analysis
   b) Confirmatory factor analysis
   c) Descriptive statistics
   d) Parameter estimation

234. The statistical method that develops generalizations about population characteristics based on sample data is called:
   a) Descriptive statistics
   b) Exploratory factor analysis
   c) Inferential statistics
   d) Principal components analysis

235. The Adoption Quotient in agricultural extension research includes which of the following components?
   a) Extent of adoption and Speed of adoption
   b) Socio-demographic profile
   c) Livelihood strategies

236. The Livelihood Vulnerability Index (LVI) is used to estimate the impacts of climate change on communities and includes how many major components?
   a) Three
   b) Five
   c) Seven
   d) Ten

237. The Household Commercialization Index (HCI) is used to assess the level of commercialization among smallholder farmers in which country?
   a) India
   b) Mozambique
   c) Zimbabwe
   d) North India

238. What is the range of values for the Household Commercialization Index (HCI)?
   a) 0 to 10
   b) 0 to 50
   c) 0 to 100
   d) 0 to 500

239. The Adoption Quotient is based on the final scale tried in a village in which region of India?

a) South India
b) East India
c) North India
d) West India

240. The Livelihood Vulnerability Index (LVI) uses which approach to calculate the index?

a) Balanced weighted average approach
b) Proportional index approach
c) Linear regression approach
d) Factor analysis approach

241. Which component is NOT included in the Livelihood Vulnerability Index (LVI)?

a) Health
b) Water
c) Agricultural practices
d) Climate Variability

242. The Household Commercialization Index (HCI) assumes a value between 0 and 100, with zero signifying:

a) Subsistence-oriented household
b) Fully commercialized household
c) High level of education
d) Low level of income

243. The Adoption Quotient in agricultural extension research is aimed at:

a) Estimating household income
b) Assessing the level of education
c) Understanding the decision-making process for technology adoption
d) Evaluating social networks

244. The Livelihood Vulnerability Index (LVI) was developed to estimate the impacts of climate change in which country?

a) India
b) Mozambique
c) Zimbabwe
d) North India

10

The Role of Psychometry in Extension Research

1. Which of the following best describes psychometrics?
   a) The study of physiological measurements
   b) The measurement of attitudes, knowledge, skills, personality traits, and educational achievements
   c) The analysis of psychophysical theory
   d) The study of the mind-body connection

2. Which two theoretical approaches are essential in psychometrics?
   a) Cognitive Behavioral Theory and Social Learning Theory
   b) Classical Test Theory (CTT) and Psychophysical Theory
   c) Item Response Theory (IRT) and Behavioral Theory
   d) Classical Test Theory (CTT) and Item Response Theory (IRT)

3. According to Classical Test Theory (CTT), a person's observed test score consists of:
   a) True score only
   b) Error score only
   c) Both true score and error score
   d) None of the above

4. Which theory of psychometrics predicts outcomes of psychological testing as the difficulty of items?
   a) Cognitive Test Theory (CogTT)
   b) Item Response Theory (IRT)
   c) Behavior Response Theory (BRT)
   d) Classical Test Theory (CTT)

5. How does Item Response Theory (IRT) differ from Classical Test Theory (CTT)?
   a) IRT assumes all test items have equal difficulty, while CTT considers varying item difficulties.
   b) IRT predicts outcomes based on true score and error score, while CTT relies on ability and item difficulty.

Bold Means Correct Answer

c) IRT focuses on cognitive abilities, while CTT focuses on personality traits.

d) IRT predicts outcomes based on personality traits, while CTT relies on ability and item difficulty.

6. Who was the founder and first President of the Psychometrics Society in 1936?

a) Gustav Fechner

b) Ernst H. Webber

c) L.L. Thurstone

d) Sigmund Freud

7. L.L. Thurstone's theoretical approach to measurement is based on:

a) The Law of Comparative Judgment

b) The Theory of Multiple Intelligences

c) The Law of Cognitive Development

d) The Law of Classical Conditioning

8. Before psychometrics, behavioral scientists relied on the psychophysical theory of which two individuals?

a) L.L. Thurstone and Sigmund Freud

b) Ernst H. Webber and Gustav Fechner

c) Abraham Maslow and B.F. Skinner

d) Carl Rogers and Ivan Pavlov

9. What contribution did L.L. Thurstone make to psychometrics?

a) He developed the Theory of Multiple Intelligences.

b) He introduced the concept of classical conditioning.

c) He provided a theoretical framework for a psychological continuum through the Law of Comparative Judgment.

d) He discovered the Law of Effect in operant conditioning.

10. What is the main focus of psychometrics?

a) Analyzing the relationship between body and mind

b) Studying physiological measurements

c) Measuring attitudes, knowledge, skills, personality traits, and educational achievements

d) Understanding cognitive biases and heuristics

11. What is one of the essential applications of psychometrics in agricultural extension research?
   a) Analyzing cognitive biases
   b) Constructing and validating scales and tests
   c) Studying physiological variables
   d) Assessing personality disorders

12. The main purpose of psychological scaling methods is to:
   a) Measure cognitive abilities
   b) Evaluate stimulus objects on non-linear scales
   c) Assess physiological variables
   d) Evaluate stimulus objects on linear scales

13. What is a scale in the context of psychometrics?
   a) A continuum with no specific endpoints
   b) A continuum with fixed endpoints representing different characteristics
   c) A non-linear representation of stimuli
   d) A set of psychological variables

14. In extension research, attitude scales are popularly used to:
   a) Measure cognitive abilities
   b) Study physiological attributes
   c) Make distinctions of degree between individuals
   d) Assess memory and learning

15. What does a scaling study involve?
   a) Analyzing cognitive biases
   b) Assigning numerical values to psychological attributes
   c) Measuring physiological variables
   d) Studying cognitive abilities

16. Which of the following is NOT a psychological variable commonly measured using scales in agricultural extension research?
   a) Achievement motivation
   b) Entrepreneurial orientation
   c) Emotional intelligence
   d) Risk orientation

17. How is a scale like a measuring instrument?
    a) It measures physical attributes
    b) It measures psychological variables
    c) It has a defined range of values
    d) It measures cognitive abilities

18. What is the purpose of constructing and validating scales and tests in agricultural extension research?
    a) To predict future crop yields
    b) To evaluate stimulus objects on nonlinear scales
    c) To measure psychological attributes
    d) To analyze environmental variables

19. Which aspect of a scale refers to the highest and lowest points in terms of a characteristic?
    a) Continuum
    b) Endpoints
    c) Numerals
    d) Rules

20. What is the primary focus of psychometrics in agricultural extension research?
    a) Understanding cognitive processes
    b) Studying physiological variables
    c) Measuring and assessing psychological attributes using scales and tests
    d) Analyzing behavioral patterns

21. What are the four levels of measurement commonly used in behavioral sciences?
    a) Dichotomous, trichotomous, ordinal, and ratio
    b) Nominal, ordinal, interval, and ratio
    c) Low, medium, high, and very high
    d) Classificatory, ranking, known magnitude, and absolute zero

22. At which level of measurement are numbers assigned to objects or events without having a numerical meaning?
    a) Nominal level
    b) Ordinal level
    c) Interval level
    d) Ratio level

23. Which of the following operations are NOT possible at the nominal level of measurement?

    a) Addition and subtraction

    b) Multiplication and division

    c) Counting frequencies and calculating percentages

    d) Establishing rank order

24. What is the primary requirement of nominal measurement for a set of objects?

    a) All objects must have the same numeral assigned to them

    b) Each object must have a different numeral assigned to it

    c) The numerals must represent more or less of a property

    d) Objects must be ranked in order

25. Which level of measurement defines the relative position of objects with respect to a particular characteristic?

    a) Nominal level **b) Ordinal level**

    c) Interval level d) Ratio level

26. Ordinal numbers in measurement indicate:

    a) The actual distance between objects

    b) The rank order of objects

    c) The additivity of objects

    d) The ratio of objects

27. Why does the ordinal level of measurement lack information about the distance between objects?

    a) It does not provide numerical values

    b) It only provides a rank order

    c) It assumes an arbitrary zero point

    d) It lacks mutual exclusivity

28. Which level of measurement provides numerically equal distances on the continuum measuring a particular property of objects?

    a) Nominal level b) Ordinal level

    c) Interval level d) Ratio level

29. What assumption is made in interval level of measurement?
    a) Variables follow normal distribution
    b) Arithmetic operations are not applicable
    c) There is a true zero point
    d) The categories must be exhaustive and non-overlapping

30. Which level of measurement has all the characteristics of nominal, ordinal, and interval measures, along with a true zero point as its origin?
    a) Nominal level
    b) Ordinal level
    c) Interval level
    d) Ratio level

31. What is the primary advantage of ratio level of measurement over the other levels?
    a) It is the lowest level of measurement
    b) It provides numerical values without rank order
    c) All arithmetic operations are possible
    d) It assumes an arbitrary zero point

32. Can data obtained at a higher level of measurement be brought down to a lower level without any loss of information?
    a) Yes, data conversion is always lossless
    b) No, data conversion always results in a loss of information
    c) Yes, but only from ratio to ordinal level
    d) No, data can only be converted from nominal to ordinal level

33. In which level of measurement are mathematical operations like mean, standard deviation, and Pearson correlation applicable?
    a) Nominal level
    b) Ordinal level
    c) Interval level
    d) Ratio level

34. What is the lowest level of measurement in behavioral sciences?
    a) Nominal level
    b) Ordinal level
    c) Interval level
    d) Ratio level

35. Which level of measurement lacks the ability to measure differences between classes, but provides information about the order or ranking of objects?
    a) Nominal level
    b) Ordinal level
    c) Interval level
    d) Ratio level

36. Which level of measurement provides numerically equal distances on the continuum and also allows for the interpretation of less than or more than relationships?

a) Nominal level | b) Ordinal level
c) Interval level | d) Ratio level

37. At which level of measurement are objects classified based on a characteristic without implying any distance or order?

a) Nominal level | b) Ordinal level
c) Interval level | d) Ratio level

38. In behavioral sciences, which level of measurement is commonly used for most attitudinal measurements?

a) Nominal level | **b) Ordinal level**
c) Interval level | d) Ratio level

39. Which level of measurement includes characteristics of both nominal and ordinal measures, along with numerically equal distances on the continuum?

a) Nominal level | b) Ordinal level
c) Interval level | d) Ratio level

40. What is the highest level of measurement possible in behavioral sciences with some assumptions?

a) Nominal level | b) Ordinal level
c) Interval level | d) Ratio level

41. Which approach involves developing a scale with an arbitrary collection of statements based on subjective judgment of the researcher?

a) Differential scale approach | b) Item analysis approach
c) Arbitrary approach | d) Factor analysis approach

42. What is the primary purpose of a rating scale?

a) To measure unobservable traits
b) To rank order individuals based on a particular characteristic
c) To ascertain the difference in the degree of response
d) To assign numerical values to individuals

43. Which form of rating scale uses descriptive phrases or terms instead of numerical values?

a) Graphical rating scale
b) Numerical rating scale
c) Differential rating scale
d) Descriptive rating scale

44. Which type of rating scale orders individuals from high to low degree of traits by comparing them with each other?

a) Numerical rating scale
b) Graphical rating scale
c) Rank order scale
d) Differential scale

45. What is the primary concern when using rating scales to avoid common errors?

a) Avoiding ambiguity in guidelines for rating
b) Ensuring generosity in rating
c) Using differential scales for evaluation
d) Discerning two closely related concepts or traits

46. What are differential scales in scale development?

a) Scales where items are selected and rank ordered by a group of experts
b) Scales based on factor analysis
c) Scales that use descriptive phrases
d) Scales where statements are selected based on their discriminatory power

47. Which approach involves selecting statements for a scale based on their discriminatory power?

a) Factor analysis approach
b) Cumulative scale approach
c) Item analysis approach
d) Differential scale approach

48. What is another term for summated scales?

a) Differential scales
b) Factor scales
c) Cumulative scales
d) Likert scales

49. Which scale approach emphasizes the unidimensionality of a scale?

a) Factor analysis approach
b) Cumulative scale approach
c) Item analysis approach
d) Differential scale approach

50. In a cumulative scale, how are the items ordered or related to one another?

a) They are randomly arranged

b) They are ranked by experts

c) They are unidimensional

d) Favorable responses to one item imply favorable responses to all previous items

51. What does factor analysis help determine in scale development?

a) The number of latent variables

b) The discriminatory power of statements

c) The difference in degree of response

d) The number of experts required for ranking

52. Which approach uses semantic differential and multidimensional scaling based on factor analysis?

a) Factor analysis approach b) Cumulative scale approach

c) Item analysis approach d) Differential scale approach

53. Which scale approach involves developing a continuum with numerical points marked along it?

a) Cumulative scale approach b) Item analysis approach

c) Differential scale approach **d) Numerical rating scale**

54. What type of scale is characterized by a continuum with descriptive phrases or terms marked along it?

a) Descriptive rating scale b) Rank order scale

c) Factor scale d) Graphical rating scale

55. Which approach involves ordering individuals on a continuum based on their responses to a set of statements?

a) Rank order scale b) Cumulative scale approach

c) Factor analysis approach d) Differential scale approach

56. Which level of measurement is associated with numerical rating scales?

a) Interval level b) Ordinal level

c) Nominal level d) Ratio level

57. What does the interval level of measurement provide along the continuum?

a) Rank order of objects
b) Numerically equal distances
c) Arbitrary collection of statements
d) Summated scale scores

58. What type of scale is used when a person is compared with another already rated person and then assigned a place on the continuum?

a) Cumulative scale
b) Rank order scale
c) Differential scale
d) Man-To-Man scale

59. Which type of scale involves ordering subjects from high to low degree of traits by comparing one individual with others?

a) Cumulative scale
b) Rank order scale
c) Differential scale
d) Factor scale

60. What is a Guttman scale?

a) A scale with arbitrary collection of statements
b) A scale with numerical points marked along a continuum
c) A scale that fulfills the criterion of unidimensionality
d) A scale based on factor analysis

61. Which scaling technique involves direct comparison of stimulus objects?

a) Comparative scale
b) Non-comparative scale
c) Likert scale
d) Semantic differential scale

62. What is another term for non-comparative scale?

a) Metric scaling
b) Ordinal scaling
c) Likert scaling
d) Non-metric scaling

63. Under which scaling technique is a respondent presented with two objects and asked to select one according to some criterion?

a) Rank order scaling
b) Constant sum scaling
c) Q-sort scaling
d) Paired comparison scaling

64. What type of data is obtained from rank order scaling?

a) Metric data
b) Ordinal data
c) Nominal data
d) Continuous data

65. How are scores allocated to objects in constant sum scaling?

a) Based on their importance b) Based on their similarity
c) Based on direct comparison d) Based on their rank order

66. What is the primary characteristic of data obtained from paired comparison scaling?

a) It is continuous data **b) It is ordinal data**
c) It is metric data d) It is nominal data

67. What does Q-sort scaling involve?

a) Placing a mark on a line to rate objects
b) Allocating scores based on importance
c) Sorting objects into piles based on similarity
d) Ranking objects simultaneously

68. What type of scale is a continuous rating scale?

a) Metric scale b) Ordinal scale
c) Likert scale d) Non-metric scale

69. How do respondents rate objects in a continuous rating scale?

a) By selecting a specified category **b) By placing a mark on a line**
c) By ranking objects d) By allocating scores

70. What is the primary characteristic of data obtained from continuous rating scales?

a) It is continuous data b) It is ordinal data
c) It is metric data d) It is non-metric data

71. What type of scale provides respondents with a scale that has a number or brief description associated with each category?

a) Continuous rating scale b) Likert scale
c) Itemised rating scale d) Q-sort scale

72. How many response categories are typically present in a Likert scale?

a) 3 **b) 5**
c) 7 d) 9

73. What does the semantic differential scale use as response categories?

a) Numbers b) Brief descriptions
c) Bipolar adjectives d) Piles

74. What is the range of response categories in a typical semantic differential scale?

a) 3-point continuum **b) 7-point continuum**

c) 9-point continuum d) 11-point continuum

75. What is the distinctive feature of the Stapel scale?

a) It is a continuous scale b) It has 10 response categories

c) It is presented horizontally **d) It lacks a neutral point**

76. How are response categories presented in a Stapel scale?

a) Vertically with 10 categories b) Horizontally with 5 categories

c) Vertically with 7 categories d) Horizontally with 3 categories

77. What type of data is obtained from non-comparative scales?

a) Continuous data **b) Ordinal data**

c) Metric data d) Nominal data

78. What does a Likert scale require respondents to indicate for each statement?

a) A preference

b) A rank order

c) A degree of agreement or disagreement

d) A numerical score

79. In a continuous rating scale, how do respondents rate objects?

a) By selecting a specified category **b) By placing a mark on a line**

c) By ranking objects d) By allocating scores

80. Which scaling technique involves respondents rating objects by selecting a specified category associated with each category on a scale?

a) Rank order scaling b) Non-comparative scaling

c) Continuous rating scaling **d) Itemised rating scaling**

81. What is attitude defined as?

a) The degree of physical fitness

b) The degree of positive or negative effect associated with a psychological object

c) The level of intelligence

d) The degree of physical attractiveness

82. What distinguishes attitude scales from other tests?
   a) Attitude scales involve direct questioning
   b) Attitude scales measure physical attributes
   c) Attitude scales assess behavior
   d) Attitude scales involve endorsement of opinions on a continuum

83. Why can direct questioning sometimes result in untrue responses about attitudes?
   a) Respondents fear losing marks
   b) Respondents want to please others
   c) Respondents may want to remain out of controversy
   d) All of the above

84. What is the primary purpose of attitude scales?
   a) To classify people into different categories
   b) To observe behavior in specific conditions
   c) To assess attitudes of individuals in large groups
   d) To measure physical attributes accurately

85. What are the items in an attitude scale called?
   a) Statements
   b) Questions
   c) Answers
   d) Categories

86. What is the class of all possible statements that could be made about a given psychological object called?
   a) Scale continuum
   b) Scale range
   c) Scale spectrum
   d) Universe of content

87. What is the initial step of scale development process?
   a) Item analysis
   b) Scalogram analysis
   c) Item generation
   d) Reliability assessment

88. Which approach for item generation is used when there is lack of theoretical background?
   a) Deductiye approach
   b) Factor analysis approach
   c) Inductive approach
   d) Item analysis approach

89. What is the next step after item generation in scale construction?

a) Scalogram analysis
b) Reliability assessment
c) Item analysis
d) Validity assessment

90. What is the purpose of in scale construction?

a) To remove favorable statements
b) To ensure each item contains only one complete thought
c) To add factual statements
d) To increase the number of items in the scale

91. How many criteria are used for editing items in scale construction?

a) 7
b) 10
c) 14
d) 20

92. What does scalogram analysis check for in attitude scale construction?

a) Internal consistency
b) Validity
c) Unidimensionality
d) Reliability

93. Which method of scale construction involves using paired comparisons to determine the order of items?

a) Method of summated rating
b) Successive interval methodology
c) Method of paired comparison
d) Equal appearing interval methodology

94. Which technique of scale construction orders items based on judgments of experts?

a) Method of summated rating
b) Scalogram analysis
c) Method of paired comparison
d) Equal appearing interval methodology

95. What is the primary goal of attitude scale construction?

a) To observe overt behavior
b) To classify individuals into categories
c) To assess the degree of affect associated with psychological objects
d) To study the universe of content

96. Which psychometric approach involves assessing the reliability and internal consistency of the scale?

a) Scalogram analysis
b) Item Response Theory (IRT)
c) Classical Test Theory (CTT)
d) Factor analysis approach

97. Which type of attitude scale can be used to assess attitudes of a large group quickly and conveniently?

a) Comparative scale
b) Non-comparative scale
c) Summated scale
d) Differential scale

98. What is the main purpose of generating items in scale construction?

a) To classify individuals into categories
b) To ensure unidimensionality of the scale
c) To assess the validity of the scale
d) To obtain a clear understanding of the universe of content

99. Which type of scale construction approach is used when theoretical definitions of constructs are available?

a) Inductive approach
b) Factor analysis approach
c) Deductive approach
d) Item analysis approach

100. What does an attitude scale consist of?

a) Answers
b) Questions
c) Statements
d) Categories

101. What is the primary goal of the method of paired comparison?

a) To observe behavior in specific conditions
b) To classify individuals into categories
c) To measure physical attributes accurately
d) To assess the relative favorableness of statements

102. How are statements/items selected for the paired comparison method?

a) Each statement is paired with one other statement
b) Each statement is paired with all others
c) Each statement is paired with two others
d) Each statement is paired with the statement before and after it

103. What is the optimum number of statements to be included in a scale constructed using paired comparison methodology?
   a) 5 to 7
   b) 7 to 10
   c) 10 to 15
   d) 15 to 20

104. How is the data collected in the paired comparison method?
   a) By observing behavior
   b) By asking direct questions
   c) By asking judges to make comparative judgments on pairs of statements
   d) By conducting surveys with large groups

105. What is the formula to calculate the number of pairs of statements when there are 'n' statements?
   a) nx(n-1)/2
   b) (n-1)/2
   c) n(n-1)
   d) 2n

106. How are the judges/experts asked to provide judgment in the paired comparison method?
   a) By ranking the statements in order of favorableness
   b) By selecting the most favorable statement in each pair
   c) By rating each statement on a scale of 1 to 10
   d) By categorizing the statements into different groups

107. What is the purpose of the frequency matrix in the paired comparison method?
   a) To determine the total number of judges
   b) To determine the mean value for each statement
   c) To present the data collected from judges in a tabular form
   d) To calculate the standard deviations of the statements

108. What is the next step after obtaining the frequency matrix in the paired comparison method?
   a) Internal consistency check
   b) Scalogram analysis
   c) Reliability assessment
   d) Factor analysis

109. How is the internal consistency check performed in the paired comparison method?
   a) By conducting a pilot study
   b) By calculating the absolute average discrepancy
   c) By using the chi-square test of significance
   d) By obtaining the theoretical normal deviates

110. What does the absolute average discrepancy measure in the paired comparison method?

a) The number of pairs of statements

b) The degree of agreement between observed and theoretical proportions

c) The number of judges/experts

d) The total number of statements

111. What is the degree of freedom for the chi-square test in the paired comparison method?

a) (n-1)(n-2)/2

b) n/2

c) n-1

d) n(n-1)

112. How are the statements presented to respondents in the paired comparison method?

a) In random order

b) In ascending order of their scale values

c) In alphabetical order

d) In descending order of their scale values

113. What is the scale value of the statement chosen by a respondent in the paired comparison method?

a) The highest scale value

b) The lowest scale value

c) The mean of the scale values of all statements

d) The scale value of the statement with which the respondent agrees the most

114. What is the purpose of using the method of paired comparison?

a) To measure physical attributes

b) To classify individuals into categories

c) To assess attitudes towards psychological objects

d) To observe behavior in specific conditions

115. How are the judges asked to make judgments in the paired comparison method?

a) By selecting the most unfavorable statement in each pair

b) By ranking the statements from 1 to n

c) By categorizing the statements into groups

d) By selecting the more favorable statement in each pair

116. What is the number of pairs of statements for 10 statements in the paired comparison method?

a) 45 b) 50

c) 55 d) 60

117. What is the mean value for each column entry in the Z-matrix for 4 statements in the paired comparison method?

a) 0.342 b) 0.203

c) 0.876 **d) -0.369**

118. How is the scale value of a statement obtained in the paired comparison method?

a) By dividing the entry in the Z-matrix by the mean value of all entries

b) By adding the entry in the Z-matrix to the mean value of all entries

c) By multiplying the entry in the Z-matrix by the mean value of all entries

d) By subtracting the entry in the Z-matrix from the mean value of all entries

119. What is the purpose of the chi-square test in the paired comparison method?

a) To determine the number of judges

b) To check the normality of the data

c) To assess the internal consistency of the scale

d) To calculate the mean value of the scale

120. What is the primary focus of the method of paired comparison?

a) To measure physical attributes accurately

b) To assess the internal consistency of the scale

c) To observe behavior in specific conditions

d) To compare and rank statements in terms of favorableness

121. What is the primary advantage of the method of equal appearing interval?

a) It requires fewer judges to provide judgments

b) It allows for a large number of statements to be scaled

c) It provides more accurate judgments than other methods

d) It is quicker to administer than the paired comparison method

122. In the method of equal appearing interval, how are the selected statements presented to judges for sorting?

a) On separate cards marked A to I

b) On separate cards marked A to K

c) On a 9 or 11-point continuum marked A to K

d) On a 9 or 11-point continuum marked 1 to 11

123. How many sorting categories are there in the method of equal appearing interval?

a) 9

b) 10

c) 11

d) 12

124. What does the frequency table for each statement in the method of equal appearing interval represent?

a) The number of judges who gave favorable judgments to each statement

b) The proportion of judges who gave judgments within each interval

c) The cumulative proportion of judges who gave judgments within each interval

d) The number of judges who sorted each statement into different categories

125. How are the scale values of the statements calculated in the method of equal appearing interval?

a) By dividing the cumulative proportion by the proportion within the interval

b) By adding the cumulative proportion to 1

c) By finding the median of the cumulative proportion distribution

d) By subtracting the cumulative proportion from 1

126. What does the Q value represent in the method of equal appearing interval?

a) The proportion of judges who sorted the statement into the first interval

b) The extent of spread of responses of judges on the continuum

c) The proportion of judges who sorted the statement into the last interval

d) The proportion of judges who sorted the statement into the middle interval

127. How is the width of the interval on the psychological continuum calculated in the method of equal appearing interval?

a) By taking the median value of all intervals

b) By subtracting the upper limit from the lower limit of the interval

c) By dividing the sum of proportions below the interval by the width of the interval

d) By assuming all intervals are equal and assigning a value of 1

128. What is the range of possible values for the scale values in the method of equal appearing interval?

a) 0 to 9

b) 0 to 11

c) 1 to 11

d) 1 to 10

129. What does it indicate if a statement in the method of equal appearing interval has a high Q value?

a) The statement has a small spread of responses from judges

b) The statement has a large spread of responses from judges

c) The statement is well-suited for inclusion in the scale

d) The statement is not worthy of inclusion in the scale

130. How is the interquartile range (Q value) calculated in the method of equal appearing interval?

a) By subtracting the lower quartile from the upper quartile

b) By dividing the cumulative proportion by the proportion within the interval

c) By adding the cumulative proportion to 1

d) By finding the median of the cumulative proportion distribution

131. How are the statements selected for inclusion in the final scale in the method of equal appearing interval?

a) Based on the total number of judges

b) Based on the correlation coefficient between individual scores and total scores

c) Based on the number of intervals each statement represents

d) Based on the width of the interval on the continuum

132. What does the correlation coefficient measure in the method of equal appearing interval?

   a) The agreement among judges in judging the position of a statement on the continuum

   b) The number of judges who gave favorable judgments to each statement

   c) The proportion of judges who gave judgments within each interval

   d) The extent of spread of responses of judges on the continuum

133. In the method of equal appearing interval, what does the width of the interval represent?

   a) The range of possible values for the scale

   b) The distance between all intervals on the continuum

   c) The proportion of judges who gave favorable judgments to each statement

   d) The proportion of judges who sorted the statement into the first interval

134. How many judges typically provide judgments in the method of equal appearing interval?

   a) 100 b) 50

   c) 25 d) 10

135. How are the statements sorted by judges in the method of equal appearing interval?

   a) According to their personal attitude or belief

   b) According to the content of each statement

   c) According to the number of intervals they represent

   d) According to the scale values already assigned to them

136. What is the range of the continuum in the method of equal appearing interval?

   a) A to G b) A to H

   c) A to I **d) A to K**

137. What is the primary difference between the method of equal appearing interval and the paired comparison method?

   a) The number of statements that can be included in the scale

   b) The amount of time required to administer the method

   c) The range of the continuum used for sorting

   d) The type of judges involved in the process

138. How are the statements presented to the judges for sorting in the method of equal appearing interval?

a) On separate cards marked 1 to 11

b) On separate cards marked A to K

c) On a 9 or 11-point continuum marked A to I

d) On a 9 or 11-point continuum marked 1 to 11

139 What is the scale value of a statement in the method of equal appearing interval?

a) The proportion of judges who sorted the statement into the first interval

b) The median of the cumulative proportion distribution

c) The extent of spread of responses of judges on the continuum

d) The number of judges who sorted the statement into different categories

140. What is the width of the interval on the psychological continuum in the method of equal appearing interval?

a) 1

b) 2

c) 9

d) 11

141. The Method of Successive Intervals intends to consider possible inequalities in the widths of intervals on the psychological continuum. What is the primary goal of this method?

a) To determine the scale values of statements based on the judgments of judges.

b) To identify the most favorable statement among a set of options.

c) To obtain the cumulative proportion distribution for a given set of statements.

d) To compare statements using the Chi-square test.

142. What data is tabulated in the fashion of the earlier method of equal appearing interval in the Method of Successive Intervals?

a) The judgments of judges for each statement on a 9 or 11-point continuum.

b) The frequencies, cumulative frequencies, and cumulative proportions for each statement.

c) The widths of the intervals making up the psychological continuum.

d) The proportions of judges who gave favorable judgments to each statement.

143. In the Method of Successive Intervals, how are the proportion (P) values converted to normal deviates (Z)?

a) By adding the value of P to a constant.

b) By subtracting the value of P from a constant.

c) By using a table of standard normal deviates.

d) By dividing the value of P by the total number of judges.

144. What does the difference between successive entries in each row of the normal deviates table represent in the Method of Successive Intervals?

a) The interval widths of the psychological continuum.

b) The median values of the cumulative proportion distribution.

c) The proportion of judges who sorted the statement into each interval.

d) The extent of spread of responses of judges on the continuum.

145. How are the scale values of the statements calculated in the Method of Successive Intervals?

a) By summing the cumulative proportions and dividing by the width of the interval.

b) By finding the median of the cumulative proportion distribution.

c) By adding the value of P to the upper limit of the interval.

d) By taking the difference between the lower and upper limits of the interval.

146. What is the primary purpose of performing the internal consistency test in the Method of Successive Intervals?

a) To determine the absolute average deviation.

b) To ensure that the scale values are valid and reliable.

c) To estimate the width of each interval on the psychological continuum.

d) To compare the judgments of judges for different statements.

147. How are the statements sorted by judges in the Method of Successive Intervals?

a) According to their personal attitude or belief.

b) According to the content of each statement.

c) According to the cumulative mean width of intervals.

d) According to the width of the interval they represent.

148. What are the cumulative mean width values used for in the Method of Successive Intervals?

   a) To determine the proportion of judges who gave favorable judgments to each statement.

   b) To calculate the sum of the cumulative proportion and divide by the width of the interval.

   c) To obtain the scale values of statements based on the judgments of judges.

   d) To estimate the interval widths making up the psychological continuum.

149. What is the range of possible values for the scale values in the Method of Successive Intervals?

   a) 0 to 9 b) 1 to 11

   c) -2.054 to 2.054 **d) -1 to 1**

150. In the Method of Successive Intervals, how are the width estimates obtained for the intervals on the psychological continuum?

   a) By dividing the mean width by the number of intervals.

   b) By finding the difference between the upper and lower limits of the interval.

   c) By summing the successive differences in each row of the normal deviates table.

   d) By taking the difference between the lower and upper limits of each successive interval.

151. The Method of Successive Intervals intends to take into account possible inequalities in the widths of intervals on the psychological continuum. What is the primary goal of this method?

   a) To determine the scale values of statements based on the judgments of judges.

   b) To identify the most favorable statement among a set of options.

   c) To obtain the cumulative proportion distribution for a given set of statements.

   d) To compare statements using the Chi-square test.

152. What data is tabulated in the fashion of the earlier method of equal appearing interval in the Method of Successive Intervals?

a) The judgments of judges for each statement on a 9 or 11-point continuum.

b) The frequencies, cumulative frequencies, and cumulative proportions for each statement.

c) The widths of the intervals making up the psychological continuum.

d) The proportions of judges who gave favorable judgments to each statement.

153. In the Method of Successive Intervals, how are the proportion (P) values converted to normal deviates (Z)?

a) By adding the value of P to a constant.

b) By subtracting the value of P from a constant.

c) By using a table of standard normal deviates.

d) By dividing the value of P by the total number of judges.

154. What does the difference between successive entries in each row of the normal deviates table represent in the Method of Successive Intervals?

a) The interval widths of the psychological continuum.

b) The median values of the cumulative proportion distribution.

c) The proportion of judges who sorted the statement into each interval.

d) The extent of spread of responses of judges on the continuum.

155. How are the scale values of the statements calculated in the Method of Successive Intervals?

a) By summing the cumulative proportions and dividing by the width of the interval.

b) By finding the median of the cumulative proportion distribution.

c) By adding the value of P to the upper limit of the interval.

d) By taking the difference between the lower and upper limits of the interval.

156. What is the primary purpose of performing the internal consistency test in the Method of Successive Intervals?

a) To determine the absolute average deviation.

b) To ensure that the scale values are valid and reliable.

c) To estimate the width of each interval on the psychological continuum.

d) To compare the judgments of judges for different statements.

157. How are the statements sorted by judges in the Method of Successive Intervals?
    a) According to their personal attitude or belief.
    b) According to the content of each statement.
    c) According to the cumulative mean width of intervals.
    d) According to the width of the interval they represent.

158. What are the cumulative mean width values used for in the Method of Successive Intervals?
    a) To determine the proportion of judges who gave favorable judgments to each statement.
    b) To calculate the sum of the cumulative proportion and divide by the width of the interval.
    c) To obtain the scale values of statements based on the judgments of judges.
    d) To estimate the interval widths making up the psychological continuum.

159. What is the range of possible values for the scale values in the Method of Successive Intervals?
    a) 0 to 9
    b) 1 to 11
    c) -2.054 to 2.054
    d) -1 to 1

160. In the Method of Successive Intervals, how are the width estimates obtained for the intervals on the psychological continuum?
    a) By dividing the mean width by the number of intervals.
    b) By finding the difference between the upper and lower limits of the interval.
    c) By summing the successive differences in each row of the normal deviates table.
    d) By taking the difference between the lower and upper limits of each successive interval.

161. Scalogram analysis is a procedure used for evaluating sets of statements or existing scales to determine whether they meet the requirements of a particular kind of scale called:
    a) Likert scale
    b) Thurstone scale
    c) Guttman scale
    d) Rasch scale

162. According to Guttman's definition of a genuine scale, a set of statements is considered unidimensional if:

   a) There is complete homogeneity among the statements.

   b) There is complete heterogeneity among the statements.

   c) Each statement measures multiple factors.

   d) Each statement is rated independently.

163. What is the primary purpose of Guttman's technique and scale discrimination technique of Edwards and Kilpatrick?

   a) To determine the reliability of a scale.

   b) To assess the validity of a set of statements.

   c) To evaluate the internal consistency of a scale.

   d) To determine whether a set of statements forms a unidimensional scale.

164. The Cornell technique and Goodenough technique are two techniques used for conducting:

   a) Correlation analysis   b) Factor analysis

   c) Scalogram analysis   d) Reliability analysis

165. In scalogram analysis, the coefficient of reproducibility indicates:

   a) The accuracy with which responses to the various statements can be reproduced for the total scores.

   b) The correlation between different scales.

   c) The number of Guttman errors in the data.

   d) The percentage of judges who gave favorable judgments to each statement.

166. Mokken scale is a non-parametric, probabilistic version of which scale?

   a) Thurstone scale   b) Likert scale

   c) Guttman scale   d) Rasch scale

167. The key difference between a Guttman scale and a Mokken scale is that Mokken scaling is:

   a) Hierarchical in nature   b) Deterministic in nature

   c) Probabilistic in nature   d) Parametric in nature

168. In Mokken scaling, what does Loevinger's coefficient H measure?
    a) The extent to which pairs of items conform to Guttman criteria
    b) The correlation between different scales
    c) The number of Guttman errors in the data
    d) The percentage of respondents who answered the questions affirmatively

169. The assumption in Mokken scaling is that respondents who answere dadifficult question affirmatively are:
    a) Less likely to answer an easy question affirmatively
    b) More likely to answer an easy question affirmatively
    c) More likely to answer an easy question negatively
    d) Unlikely to answer an easy question affirmatively

170. The Dominance theory of order is used with dichotomously scored items that suggest:
    a) The dominance of one choice over the other
    b) The equality of choices in a scale
    c) The hierarchical order of choices
    d) The inconsistency of choices in a scale

171. In the Order Dominance Model, what does the logical pattern of the number of correctly answered questions versus the number of incorrectly answered questions help determine?
    a) The total score of each respondent
    b) The sequence of skills necessary for reading
    c) The percentage of respondents who answered each item affirmatively
    d) The correlation between different items in the scale

172. Fisher's exact probability is used to study the degree of:
    a) Dominance in the responses to the statements
    b) Guttman errors in the data
    c) Homogeneity among the items in the scale
    d) Reproducibility in the responses to the statements

172. Extremely easy or very difficult items in the scale may result in a deflated number of (0-1) responses. What is the likely reason for this?
    a) The respondents are avoiding answering these items.
    b) The items are not ordered hierarchically.
    c) The items have low validity and reliability.
    d) The likelihood of A>B increases as A and B are different in item difficulty.

173. What does Loevinger's coefficient H compare in the Mokken scaling process?

a) The actual Guttman errors to the expected number of errors

b) The number of (1-1) responses to the number of (0-0) responses

c) The responses of different judges to the same set of statements

d) The item response function to the item difficulty level

174. What is the primary purpose of conducting scalogram analysis?

a) To determine the scale values of statements.

b) To assess the reliability of a scale.

c) To evaluate the internal consistency of a scale.

d) To determine whether a set of statements forms a unidimensional scale.

175. In scalogram analysis, what is the coefficient of reproducibility used for?

a) To determine the reliability of a scale.

b) To evaluate the internal consistency of a scale.

c) To assess the validity of a set of statements.

d) To measure the accuracy with which responses to the statements can be reproduced for the total scores.

176. Mokken scaling is based on the assumption that the items are hierarchically ordered by:

a) The percentage of respondents that answers the question affirmatively.

b) The total scores of each respondent.

c) The frequency of each item in the scale.

d) The correlations between different items.

177. What is the key difference between a Guttman scale and a Mokken scale?

a) Guttman scaling is hierarchical, while Mokken scaling is deterministic.

b) Mokken scaling is probabilistic, while Guttman scaling is deterministic.

c) Guttman scaling is probabilistic, while Mokken scaling is hierarchical.

d) Mokken scaling is deterministic, while Guttman scaling is probabilistic.

178. In the Dominance theory of order, which type of items are utilized for analysis?

   a) Items that suggest dominance of one choice over the other (e.g., right > wrong).

   b) Items that suggest equality of choices in a scale.

   c) Items that are not hierarchically ordered.

   d) Items that have a high degree of Guttman errors.

179. Edwards and Kilpatrick devised a method for constructing attitude scales that combines the techniques of Thurstone, Likert, and Guttman. What is this method called?

   a) Guttman scaling

   b) Thurstone scaling

   c) Likert scaling

   d) Scale discrimination method

180. The Scale Discrimination method involves using Thurstone's scaling procedure and Likert's procedure for evaluating the discriminatory power of individual items. What is the main purpose of this method?

   a) To determine the reliability of a scale

   b) To eliminate the least discriminating items in a large sample

   c) To assess the validity of a set of attitude statements

   d) To measure the internal consistency of a scale

181. In the Scale Discrimination method, what is plotted on the Y-axis of the graph used to eliminate statements with low discriminant power?

   a) Scale values

   b) Q values

   c) Response categories

   d) Phi-coefficient values

182. After obtaining the scale and Q values for each statement, what is the next step in the Scale Discrimination method?

   a) Administering the statements to a new group of subjects

   b) Eliminating statements with Q values below the median

   c) Tabulating the frequencies under various response categories

   d) Plotting Thurstone's continuum on the graph

183. How are the response categories in the Scale Discrimination method given weights?

   a) The largest weight is given to the response category indicating the least favorable attitude.

b) The largest weight is given to the response category indicating the most favorable attitude.

c) The weights are assigned randomly for each response category.

d) The weights are not considered in this method.

184. What is the Phi coefficient used for in the Scale Discrimination method?

a) To determine the scale values of the statements

b) To evaluate the internal consistency of the scale

c) To measure the discriminatory power of the statements

d) To assess the validity of the responses

185. How is the Phi coefficient calculated in the Scale Discrimination method?

a) (bc - ad / (a + b + c + d

b) (bc-ad)/√(a+b(b+d(a+c(c+d

c) (a + b / (c + d

d) (b + d / (a + c

186. In the Scale Discrimination method, what is plotted on the horizontal axis of the graph?

a) Scale values

b) Response categories

c) Phi-coefficient values

d) Thurstone's continuum

187. What is the main advantage of the Scale Discrimination method over Thurstone's method alone?

a) It offers greater assurance of scalability.

b) It eliminates the most discriminating items in a large sample.

c) It provides a wider range of content in the selected statements.

d) It uses a larger group of subjects for item analysis.

188. After selecting statements with the highest Phi-coefficients from each half scale interval, what is the final step in the Scale Discrimination method?

a) Calculating the coefficient of reproducibility

b) Administering the selected statements to a new group of subjects

c) Dichotomizing the response categories for each statement

d) Using Fisher's exact probability to study response patterns

189. The Scale Discrimination method combines which three scaling techniques?
    a) Guttman, Thurstone, and Rasch scaling
    b) Thurstone, Likert, and Rasch scaling
    c) Guttman, Thurstone, and Likert scaling
    d) Guttman, Likert, and Rasch scaling

190. The Scale Discrimination method uses a new group of about 200 to 300 subjects to indicate their agreement or disagreement with each statement. What are these subjects called?
    a) Judges
    b) Experts
    c) Participants
    d) Respondents

191. What does the Phi-coefficient value indicate about a statement in the Scale Discrimination method?
    a) The total number of subjects who agreed with the statement
    b) The discriminatory power of the statement
    c) The scale value of the statement
    d) The total score of each respondent on the statement

192. How are the statements selected in the Scale Discrimination method after plotting Thurstone's continuum?
    a) The statements with the highest scale values are selected.
    b) The statements with the lowest scale values are selected.
    c) The statements with the highest Phi-coefficient values from each half scale interval are selected.
    d) The statements with the lowest Phi-coefficient values from each half scale interval are selected.

193. The Scale Discrimination method uses the coefficient of reproducibility to test:
    a) The reliability of the scale
    b) The internal consistency of the scale
    c) The validity of the scale
    d) The accuracy of reproducing responses to the statements

194. Edwards and Kilpatrick's Scale Discrimination method is a synthesis of which three methods?
    a) Thurstone, Guttman, and Rasch methods
    b) Thurstone, Likert, and Rasch methods
    c) Guttman, Thurstone, and Likert methods
    d) Guttman, Likert, and Rasch methods

195. What is the main advantage of the Scale Discrimination method over Guttman's intuitive technique?

a) **It offers greater assurance of scalability.**

b) It eliminates the least discriminating items in a large sample.

c) It provides a wider range of content in the selected statements.

d) It uses a larger group of subjects for item analysis.

196. In the Scale Discrimination method, what is used to evaluate the discriminatory power of the individual items?

a) Thurston's scaling procedure

b) Likert's procedure

c) Guttman's scaling procedure

d) Rasch's procedure

197. A psychological test is a systematic and standardized method used to obtain information about:

a) Human behavior

b) Mental disorders

c) Personality disorders

d) Cognitive abilities

198. What is the primary purpose of a psychological test?

a) To diagnose mental disorders

b) To measure cognitive abilities

c) To obtain information about human behavior

d) To evaluate personality traits

199. Which type of test is designed for mass-testing and can be administered to more than one individual at a time?

a) Individual test

b) Group test

c) Speed test

d) Power test

200. What is the main difference between speed tests and power tests?

a) **Speed tests are timed tests, while power tests offer enough time to attempt all questions.**

b) Speed tests are designed for group testing, while power tests are for individual testing.

c) Speed tests measure personality traits, while power tests measure cognitive abilities.

d) Speed tests have a higher level of difficulty, while power tests have uniform difficulty.

201. Which type of test is used to assess an individual's personality traits and predict their future behavior?

a) Achievement tests
b) Power tests
c) Personality tests
d) Speed tests

202. A psychological test that places the testee in a situation closely resembling real-life conditions is known as a:

a) Criterion-referenced test
b) Culture-specific test
c) Norm-referenced test
d) Situational test

203. What is the main purpose of item analysis in test development?

a) To assess the validity of the test
b) To determine the difficulty level of test items
c) To evaluate the construct validity of the test
d) To calculate the discrimination index of the test items

204. The difficulty index of a test item is calculated using which formula?

a) (Number of respondents correctly answered the item) / (Total number of respondents)
b) (Total number of respondents) / (Number of respondents correctly answered the item)
c) (Number of correct responses) - (Number of incorrect responses) / (Total number of respondents)
d) (Total number of respondents) - (Number of respondents correctly answered the item) / (Total number of respondents)

205. What does the discrimination index of a test item indicate?

a) The proportion of correct answers in different groups
b) The proportion of correct answers in the entire test
c) The difficulty level of the test item
d) How well the item discriminates well-informed respondents from poorly informed respondents

206. In item analysis, what is considered a good discrimination index score?

a) 0.10
b) 0.25
c) 0.50
d) 0.75

207. Which type of validity ensures that the test measures what it is supposed to measure?

a) Content validity
b) Criterion validity
c) Construct validity
d) Face validity

208. To ensure content validity, the test items are evaluated based on:

a) Their difficulty level
b) Their discriminative ability
c) Their relevance and appropriateness to the subject matter
d) Their correlation with other test items

209. What is the purpose of using the point bi-serial correlation in test development?

a) To assess the reliability of the test
b) To evaluate the construct validity of the test
c) To determine the difficulty level of the test items
d) To measure the internal consistency of the test items

210. Which type of test is administered to one person at a time and provides comprehensive information about the testee?

a) Group test
b) Situational test
c) Individual test
d) Criterion-referenced test

211. A test designed to measure cognitive abilities and predict performance in specific tasks is known as a:

a) Personality test
b) Power test
c) Culture-specific test
d) Criterion-referenced test

212. Which classification of tests is based on the nature of the test items, such as verbal and non-verbal tests?

a) Administration-wise
b) Performance-wise
c) Medium-wise
d) Scoring-wise

213. What is the primary purpose of item analysis in test development?

a) To evaluate the internal consistency of test items
b) To assess the reliability of the test
c) To calculate the discrimination index of test items
d) To determine the difficulty level of test items

214. A test that measures an individual's unique traits and behavior can be classified as:
 a) Achievement test
 b) Power test
 c) Speed test
 d) Personality test

215. Which type of test is best suited for measuring cognitive abilities and intelligence?
 a) Speed test
 b) Power test
 c) Personality test
 d) Situational test

216. The test items should promote thinking rather than mechanical memorization. This is an example of ensuring:
 a) Construct validity
 b) Content validity
 c) Face validity
 d) Criterion validity

217. Reliability refers to the:
 a) Degree to which a measuring instrument measures what it is supposed to measure
 b) Accuracy and precision of the measuring instruments
 c) Consistency and stability of the measuring instruments
 d) Logical relationship between theoretical and operational definitions

218. Which type of error is cumulative in nature and occurs in one known direction (positive or negative)?
 a) Systematic error
 b) Random error
 c) External error
 d) Construct error

219. What is the formula for calculating reliability (rtt) using error variance (Ve) and total variance (Vt)?
 a) rtt = Ve / Vt
 b) rtt = 1 - Ve / Vt
 c) rtt = Ve * Vt
 d) rtt = Vt - Ve

220. Test-retest method is used to assess which aspect of reliability?
 a) Internal consistency
 b) Equivalence
 c) Stability
 d) Content validity

221. The time gap between test and retest in the test-retest method should be:
 a) At least a year
 b) Between 3 to 6 months
 c) 15 to 30 days
 d) A few days

222. The parallel form method is also known as the method of:

a) Split halves
b) Test-retest
c) Equivalence
d) Content validity

223. The split-half method is based on the assumption of:

a) Random errors in measurement
b) Systematic errors in measurement
c) Internal consistency and homogeneity of test items
d) Unreliability of test items

224. Content validity is concerned with the:

a) Logical relationship between theoretical and operational definitions
b) Stability and consistency of the measuring instrument
c) Adequacy and representativeness of the test items
d) Degree of association between two variables

225. What type of validity is based on the degree of association between the theoretical definition and the operational definition?

a) Content validity
b) Concurrent validity
c) Predictive validity
d) Construct validity

226. Predictive validity is assessed by:

a) Correlating test scores with an external criterion measured at a future time
b) Correlating test scores with an external criterion measured simultaneously
c) Evaluating the logical relationship between theoretical and operational definitions
d) Correlating test scores with an external criterion measured in the past

227. Concurrent validity is evaluated by comparing test scores with:

a) An external criterion measured at a future time
b) An external criterion measured simultaneously
c) A known group of participants with varying degrees of a trait
d) An expert judgment on the adequacy of the test items

228. Construct validity is useful in validating:
    a) The stability and consistency of the measuring instrument
    b) The logical relationship between theoretical and operational definitions
    c) The degree of association between two variables
    d) The theory behind the test and the adequacy of the test to measure the theory

229. Content validity is evaluated by:
    a) Correlating test scores with an external criterion
    b) Comparing test scores with a known group
    c) Determining the relevance and adequacy of test items to the concept being measured
    d) Predicting future performance based on test scores

230. Which type of validity refers to the appropriateness of the instruments/ test?
    a) Internal validity
    b) External validity
    c) Content validity
    d) Face validity

231. The validity that expresses an empirical relationship between the theoretical definition and the operational definition is:
    a) Internal validity
    b) External validity
    c) Content validity
    d) Face validity

232. When two separate scales comprising similar items are used simultaneously and their scores are correlated, it is known as:
    a) Test-retest method
    b) Parallel form method
    c) Split-half method
    d) Concurrent validity method

233. The split-half method requires:
    a) Correlation between test scores at two different times
    b) Correlation between test scores on two separate but equivalent forms
    c) Correlation between test scores on one half of the scale with scores on the other half
    d) Comparison of test scores with an external criterion

234. Validity is the degree to which a measuring instrument measures:
    a) What it is supposed to measure
    b) Accuracy and precision
    c) Stability and consistency
    d) Systematic and random errors

235. Which type of validity is useful in evaluating the theory behind the test and the adequacy of the test to measure the theory?

a) Content validity
b) Concurrent validity
c) Predictive validity
d) Construct validity

236. The statistical form of validity that involves correlating test scores with an external criterion is:

a) Content validity
b) Concurrent validity
c) Predictive validity
d) Construct validity

11

Assessing the Impact and Performance of Extension Initiatives

1. Which of the following best defines Monitoring?
   a) A rigorous and independent assessment of ongoing activities to determine the extent to which they are achieving stated objectives.
   b) An ongoing process by which stakeholders obtain regular feedback on the progress being made towards achieving their goals and objectives.
   c) A methodology designed to understand the outcomes and impacts of a given program or policy.
   d) An assessment that is primarily summative in nature.

2. Evaluation is typically:
   a) Conducted during or after the programme.
   b) An ongoing process without any specific timeline.
   c) Focused solely on the implementation of actions or activities.
   d) Limited to tracking the use of an agency's resource.

3. Which statement best differentiates Monitoring from Evaluation?
   a) Monitoring is always summative in nature, whereas evaluation is always formative.
   b) Monitoring tracks the progress of strategies and actions by partners and non-partners, while evaluation does not consider partners.
   c) Monitoring is an ongoing process, while evaluation is a rigorous and independent assessment.
   d) Monitoring is done by external agencies, while evaluation is an internal process.

4 Which of the following can be both formative or summative in nature?
   a) Monitoring
   b) Evaluation
   c) Both Monitoring and Evaluation
   d) Neither Monitoring nor Evaluation

Bold Means Correct Answer

5. Which of the following is NOT true about Monitoring as per the table?
   a) Monitoring can focus on tracking projects and the use of an agency's resource.
   b) Monitoring is sufficient for evaluation.
   c) Monitoring is formative in nature.
   d) Monitoring provides feedback on the progress being made towards achieving goals.

6. From which Latin word is the term 'monitor' derived, and what does it mean?
   a) Monitus - to guide
   b) Monetarius - to manage
   c) Monito - to measure
   d) Monitor - to warn

7. According to UNDP 2002, what is the main aim of monitoring?
   a) To provide stakeholders with a final evaluation of results.
   b) To give an early indication of progress or lack thereof in the achievement of results.
   c) To measure the financial inputs of an ongoing intervention.
   d) To assess the final outcomes of a project after its completion.

8. Outcome monitoring should be:
   a) Occasional and random.
   b) Continual and systematic.
   c) Conducted only at the end of a project.
   d) Disconnected from the baseline for outcome indicators.

9. Which entity defined monitoring as the systematic process of collecting, analyzing, and using information to track a programme's progress?
   a) United Nations Security Council
   b) United Nations Educational, Scientific and Cultural Organization
   c) United Nations Entity for Gender Equality and the Empowerment of Women
   d) World Health Organization

10. Monitoring in contemporary times has shifted its focus to assess:
   a) Only the inputs and implementation process.
   b) Primarily the financial aspects of a project.
   c) The individual performance of team members.
   d) Outputs, partnerships, policy advocacy, brokering, and coordination for a given outcome.

11. One of the main objectives of result-oriented monitoring is:
    a) To limit the involvement of external stakeholders.
    b) To reduce organizational learning.
    c) To ensure informed decision-making.
    d) To avoid accountability.

12. Which principle emphasizes that a good program design is crucial for successful monitoring?
    a) Principle of indicators and baseline **b) Principle of design**
    c) Principle of results and follow up d) Principle of regularity

13. For objectivity in assessing progress, what should be clearly defined?
    a) Only the financial indicators b) Only the outcome indicators
    c) Criteria and indicators d) The principles of monitoring

14. Which principle states that stakeholder participation in the monitoring process ensures commitment, ownership, follow-up, and feedback on performance?
    a) Principle of regularity
    b) Principle of results and follow up
    c) Principle of participation
    d) Principle of design

15. What ensures the success of a program by allowing for follow-up, verification, and validation of progress?
    a) Occasional analysis of reports **b) Regular visit to the locales**
    c) Singular stakeholder meetings d) Sporadic evaluations

16. Which of the following is NOT a predominant approach in monitoring literature?
    a) Result oriented approach b) Constructivist approach
    c) Reflexive approach **d) Analytical approach**

17. The result oriented approach is based on which assumption?
    a) Causality and randomness
    b) Collective learning and shared understanding
    c) Causality and linearity
    d) Exchange of experiences and development

18. Which planning methods are best suited for the result oriented approach?
    a) Reflexive monitoring in action
    b) Learning histories
    c) Log frames or logic charts
    d) Most significant change

19. The constructivist approach heavily focuses on:
    a) Results and objectives
    b) Strategy and planning
    c) Progress in the collective learning process
    d) Linearity of interventions

20. Which approach values collective learning and development of a shared understanding the least?
    a) Result oriented approach
    b) Constructivist approach
    c) Reflexive approach
    d) None of the above

21. Which approach is known to question current practices and aims to bring a complete change?
    a) Result oriented approach
    b) Constructivist approach
    c) Reflexive approach
    d) Analytical approach

22. In which approach is reality thought to be constructed through interaction and negotiation?
    a) Result oriented approach
    b) Constructivist approach
    c) Reflexive approach
    d) None of the above

23. What is the primary objective of the reflexive approach?
    a) Learning from each other
    b) Accountability of managing
    c) Learning, change of practices, and their institutional setting
    d) Setting a predefined procedure

24. The strength of which approach lies in strategy and planning?
    a) Result oriented approach
    b) Constructivist approach
    c) Reflexive approach
    d) None of the above

25. Which approach has the highest potential for projects aiming at system innovation?
    a) Result oriented approach
    b) Constructivist approach
    c) Reflexive approach
    d) Analytical approach

26. Which of the following is NOT a major element of project monitoring?
    a) Monitors use of project inputs
    b) Monitors the project's budgeting
    c) Monitors the effectiveness of the project implementation process
    d) Monitors the production of project outputs

27. Project monitoring is primarily concerned with:
    a) End results and impact
    b) Process evaluation
    c) Long term sustainability
    d) Summative evaluation

28. What does monitoring seek answers to regarding program staff and volunteers?
    a) Their personal opinions about the project
    b) Use of allocated funds for the planned work
    c) Their personal history and background
    d) Their future career goals

29. Monitoring functions include all EXCEPT:
    a) Verification of whether the programme is on target
    b) Assisting in external marketing
    c) Assisting programme management in the decision-making process
    d) Supporting mutual learning among programme staff

30. Which of the following is a qualitative method of monitoring?
    a) Financial auditing
    b) Review meetings
    c) Analysis of man-hours spent
    d) Resource auditing

31. Monitoring tools and methods are typically decided during:
    a) The implementation phase
    b) The conclusion phase
    c) The evaluation phase
    d) The planning phase

32. Which of the following tools is associated with an external perspective in monitoring?
    a) Field visit
    b) Annual project report
    c) Quarterly report
    d) Work plan

33. Why is it crucial to choose appropriate monitoring methods and tools?
    a) To ensure the project is marketed well
    b) To ensure the information produced is useful and consistent
    c) To ensure a larger budget allocation
    d) To ensure a higher number of project beneficiaries

34. According to UNDP 2002, what is the main aim of monitoring?
    a) To provide stakeholders with a final evaluation of results.
    b) To give an early indication of progress or lack thereof in the achievement of results.
    c) To measure the financial inputs of an ongoing intervention.
    d) To assess the final outcomes of a project after its completion.

35. Outcome monitoring should be:
    a) Occasional and random.
    b) Continual and systematic.
    c) Conducted only at the end of a project.
    d) Disconnected from the baseline for outcome indicators.

36. Which entity defined monitoring as the systematic process of collecting, analyzing, and using information to track a programme's progress?
    a) United Nations Security Council
    b) United Nations Educational, Scientific and Cultural Organization
    c) United Nations Entity for Gender Equality and the Empowerment of Women
    d) World Health Organization

37. Monitoring in contemporary times has shifted its focus to assess:
    a) Only the inputs and implementation process.
    b) Primarily the financial aspects of a project.
    c) The individual performance of team members.
    d) Outputs, partnerships, policy advocacy, brokering, and coordination for a given outcome.

38. One of the main objectives of result-oriented monitoring is:
    a) To limit the involvement of external stakeholders.
    b) To reduce organizational learning.
    c) To ensure informed decision-making.
    d) To avoid accountability.

39. Which principle emphasizes that a good program design is crucial for successful monitoring?
    a) Principle of indicators and baseline **b) Principle of design**
    c) Principle of results and follow up d) Principle of regularity

40. For objectivity in assessing progress, what should be clearly defined?

a) Only the financial indicators
b) Only the outcome indicators
c) Criteria and indicators
d) The principles of monitoring

41. Which principle states that stakeholder participation in the monitoring process ensures commitment, ownership, follow-up, and feedback on performance?

a) Principle of regularity
b) Principle of results and follow up
c) Principle of participation
d) Principle of design

42. What ensures the success of a program by allowing for follow-up, verification, and validation of progress?

a) Occasional analysis of reports
b) Regular visit to the locales
c) Singular stakeholder meetings
d) Sporadic evaluations

43. According to the Food and Agriculture Organisation in 1990, participatory monitoring is defined as:

a) Periodic analysis of information chosen by outsiders only.
b) Systematic recording and analysis of information chosen by insiders with the help of outsiders.
c) Solely focusing on the end results of a project.
d) Outsiders deciding what should be monitored by insiders.

44. The main aim of participatory monitoring is to:

a) Evaluate the project after its completion.
b) Record information annually.
c) Gather information during the life of the program and make adjustments if necessary.
d) Solely focus on the community's needs.

45. Who primarily decides the terms of measurement (like kilogram, quintal) in participatory monitoring?

a) Outsiders
b) Project managers
c) Insiders or community
d) Stakeholders

46. The turnout at community meetings can be misleading as an indicator of participation because:

    a) People might not be interested in meetings.

    b) Meetings are usually long and tedious.

    c) As committees take over decision making, the larger community might only need to be kept informed.

    d) People often prefer digital communication.

47. For monitoring participation, which indicator might communities prefer?

    a) Hours spent

    b) Skill and quality of work

    c) Number of meetings attended

    d) Amount of money invested

48. When should participatory monitoring ideally be introduced?

    a) At the middle stage of activities.

    b) After all activities are completed.

    c) At the beginning stage before activities are implemented.

    d) Periodically, without any fixed time.

49. Which step involves discussing the estimated benefits of the monitoring activity?

    a) Review of objectives and activities

    b) Developing monitoring questions

    c) Sharing monitoring purposes with insiders

    d) Deciding upon information gathering tools

50. In participatory monitoring, which tool might be useful for gathering information?

    a) Formal project reports only

    b) Community environmental assessment

    c) Digital trackers

    d) Outsider evaluations

51. What is an integral and important part of a management information system?

    a) Monitoring

    b) Financial forecasting

    c) Market analysis

    d) Project design

52. Monitoring standards can be best described as:
    a) Optional guidelines for monitoring.
    b) Rules imposed by outsiders.
    c) Principles for undertaking monitoring.
    d) Detailed steps for project execution.

53. According to the Food and Agriculture Organisation in 1990, participatory monitoring is defined as:
    a) Periodic analysis of information chosen by outsiders only.
    b) Systematic recording and analysis of information chosen by insiders with the help of outsiders.
    c) Solely focusing on the end results of a project.
    d) Outsiders deciding what should be monitored by insiders.

54. The main aim of participatory monitoring is to:
    a) Evaluate the project after its completion.
    b) Record information annually.
    c) Gather information during the life of the program and make adjustments if necessary.
    d) Solely focus on the community's needs.

55. Who primarily decides the terms of measurement (like kilogram, quintal) in participatory monitoring?
    a) Outsiders
    b) Project managers
    c) Insiders or community
    d) Stakeholders

56. The turnout at community meetings can be misleading as an indicator of participation because:
    a) People might not be interested in meetings.
    b) Meetings are usually long and tedious.
    c) As committees take over decision making, the larger community might only need to be kept informed.
    d) People often prefer digital communication.

57. For monitoring participation, which indicator might communities prefer?
    a) Hours spent
    b) Skill and quality of work
    c) Number of meetings attended
    d) Amount of money invested

58. When should participatory monitoring ideally be introduced?
    a) At the middle stage of activities.
    b) After all activities are completed.
    c) At the beginning stage before activities are implemented.
    d) Periodically, without any fixed time.

59. Which step involves discussing the estimated benefits of the monitoring activity?
    a) Review of objectives and activities
    b) Developing monitoring questions
    c) Sharing monitoring purposes with insiders
    d) Deciding upon information gathering tools

60. In participatory monitoring, which tool might be useful for gathering information?
    a) Formal project reports only
    b) Community environmental assessment
    c) Digital trackers
    d) Outsider evaluations

61. What is an integral and important part of a management information system?
    a) Monitoring
    b) Financial forecasting
    c) Market analysis
    d) Project design

62. Monitoring standards can be best described as:
    a) Optional guidelines for monitoring.
    b) Rules imposed by outsiders.
    c) Principles for undertaking monitoring.
    d) Detailed steps for project execution.

63. Monitoring aims at identifying the:
    a) Results of a programme after it ends.
    b) Initial setup of a programme.
    c) Progress of a programme or project towards results.
    d) The number of participants in a programme.

64. Which of the following is NOT a scope or usefulness of monitoring?
    a) Progress towards results.
    b) Identification of factors impeding achievement.
    c) Number of meetings held during the project.
    d) Partnership strategy understanding.

65. For effective monitoring, it is recommended to:
    a) Reinvent processes every time.
    b) Start with large complex projects.
    c) Start small with pilot schemes.
    d) Ignore existing monitoring methods from other organizations.

66. When considering a monitoring method, which is NOT one of the guiding questions to ponder?
    a) Is it repeatable?
    b) Does it provide a means of measuring what is happening?
    c) How popular is the method among stakeholders?
    d) Will it provide information related to management?

67. According to monitoring standards, monitoring must be:
    a) Complex to cover every aspect.
    b) Simple and easily understandable.
    c) Time-consuming for accuracy.
    d) Exclusively for top management.

68. Why is flexibility an essential characteristic for monitoring standards?
    a) Because it is repetitive and reutilized over time.
    b) Because flexibility leads to complexity.
    c) To make monitoring more popular.
    d) To keep the monitoring process static.

69. Which of the following is NOT included in the Project Completion Report (PCR)?
    a) Achievement of objectives of the project.
    b) The initial blueprint of the project.
    c) Monitoring and auditing.
    d) Financial and physical programme.

70. Which of the following is a tip for effective monitoring?
   a) Use 'one-off' research only for ongoing monitoring.
   b) Use the most complex measures available.
   c) Start big and reduce scale over time.
   d) Understand the systemic context of particular issues and indicators.

71. What does the monitoring standard "Monitoring must be timely" emphasize?
   a) Monitoring should be done at the end of the project.
   b) Monitoring should be done only when problems arise.
   c) Monitoring requires input for timely actions and decisions.
   d) Timely monitoring means doing it every day.

72. Why should monitoring be action-oriented according to monitoring standards?
   a) Because it leads to action and should use practical approaches.
   b) So that more data can be generated.
   c) To make the monitoring process more complicated.
   d) So that all participants can have meetings regularly.

73. What is the primary aim of evaluation?
   a) To document the meetings of a project.
   b) To determine the relevance and fulfillment of objectives.
   c) To record the number of participants in a programme.
   d) To only assess immediate outputs.

74. How did the World Bank define evaluation?
   a) As a selective exercise assessing an outcome.
   b) As a simple tally of participants in a project.
   c) As a systematic and objective assessment of an ongoing or completed project, programme, and policy.
   d) As a review of the financial aspects of a project only.

75. When is formative evaluation primarily conducted?
   a) After the programme has ended.
   b) During the initial setup of a programme.
   c) During programme development and implementation
   d) Only when the programme faces issues.

76. What is the main focus of summative evaluation?
    a) On how to achieve goals.
    b) On examining the delivery of the programme.
    c) On the effects or outcomes of some object.
    d) On rectifying errors in real-time.

77. Which of the following is a type of formative evaluation?
    a) Impact evaluation.
    b) Cost-effectiveness analysis.
    c) Evaluability assessment.
    d) Meta-analysis.

78. What is the purpose of outcome evaluation in summative evaluation?
    a) To re-examine existing data.
    b) To monitor the fidelity of the programme.
    c) To integrate the outcome estimates from multiple studies.
    d) To investigate into the demonstrable effects of the programme on defined target outcomes.

79. Which country is mentioned as having program evaluation gain ground in the 1960s?
    a) USA.
    b) India.
    c) Australia.
    d) Germany.

80. In terms of evaluation, what does the term "fidelity" refer to?
    a) The cost of the programme.
    b) The integrity with which the programme, project, and technology is delivered.
    c) The number of participants in the programme.
    d) The final outcomes of a project.

81 Which of the following is NOT included in summative evaluation?
    a) Cost-benefit analysis.
    b) Structured conceptualization.
    c) Impact evaluation.
    d) Secondary analysis.

82. Based on the provided text, how is formative evaluation primarily directed?
    a) Towards development and past achievements.
    b) Exclusively towards cost analysis.
    c) Towards initial planning of a project.
    d) Only towards final outcomes.

83. Which type of evaluation is conducted during programme development and implementation?

a) Summative evaluation
b) Retrospective evaluation
c) Formative evaluation
d) Outcome evaluation

84. The main purpose of a summative evaluation is to

a) Strengthen and improve the object being evaluated.
b) Monitor the fidelity of the programme, project, and technology delivery.
c) Assess the causal effect of an object leading to an outcome.
d) Determine who needs the programme.

85. Which of the following evaluations focuses on determining the feasibility of an evaluation and how stakeholders can shape its usefulness?

a) Evaluability assessment
b) Impact evaluation
c) Process evaluation
d) Outcome evaluation

86. What does the outcome evaluation primarily investigate?

a) The overall effects of the programme or technology.
b) Costs and values associated with the programme.
c) Direct outputs of programmes in terms of exposure, reach, etc.
d) Demonstrable effects of the programme or technology on specific target outcomes.

87. The type of evaluation that re-examines existing data to address new questions is known as:

a) Meta-analysis
b) Secondary analysis
c) Impact evaluation
d) Process evaluation

88. What does "meta-analysis" involve in evaluation typologies?

a) Investigating the process of delivering the programme.
b) Standardizing outcomes in terms of costs and values.
c) Integrating the outcome estimates from multiple studies to arrive at an overall judgment.
d) Determining who needs the programme and how important the need is.

89. The formative evaluation that helps stakeholders define a programme, target population, and possible outcomes is:

a) Need assessment
b) Implementation evaluation
c) Structured conceptualization
d) Process evaluation

90. Which evaluation method is retrospective in nature and produces descriptions of final outcomes and general trends?
    a) Formative evaluation
    b) Summative evaluation
    c) Process evaluation
    d) Impact evaluation

91. Cost-effectiveness and cost-benefit analysis in summative evaluation are primarily used to:
    a) Monitor the fidelity of the programme.
    b) Address questions of efficiency by standardizing outcomes in terms of costs and values.
    c) Define a programme and its target population.
    d) Determine the overall effects of the programme or technology.

92. In the context of formative evaluation, what does "implementation evaluation" primarily monitor?
    a) The overall impact of the programme.
    b) The fidelity of the programme, project, and technology delivery.
    c) The demonstrable effects of the programme on specific outcomes.
    d) The feasibility of an evaluation.

93. Which method can be used to determine the scope and nature of a problem under formative evaluation?
    a) Econometric methods
    b) Brainstorming
    c) Observational methods
    d) Evaluability assessment

94. Under summative evaluation, which method is best suited to determine the effectiveness of a programme or technology?
    a) Brainstorming
    b) Flow charting
    c) Observational and correlation methods
    d) Stakeholder analysis

95. What is the primary aim of the evaluation process?
    a) To generate new knowledge
    b) To classify evaluation models
    c) To define the issue in terms of structure
    d) To select a suitable method for evaluation

96. Which step in the evaluation process involves defining the structure, design, and intended results of a programme?

a) First **b) Second**

c) Third d) Fourth

97. How can a problem be solved through program/technology delivery in formative evaluation?

a) Using econometric methods

b) Using the Delphi technique

c) Using flow charting and PERT/CPM

d) Through evaluability assessment

98. Under formative evaluation, to understand how well a programme or technology was delivered, which method is appropriate?

a) Need assessment survey

b) Qualitative and quantitative monitoring techniques

c) Observational methods

d) Econometric methods

99. Most authors agree on classifying evaluation models into how many categories?

a) Two **b) Three**

c) Four d) Five

100. What are the categories of evaluation models as mentioned?

a) Functionality models, economic models, and procedural models

b) Effectiveness models, economic models, and professional models

c) Qualitative models, quantitative models, and hybrid models

d) Stakeholder models, process models, and outcome models

101. Evaluation operates within multiple domains but is often subject to constraints such as:

a) Budget, time, and data

b) Stakeholders, time, and resources

c) Methods, data, and stakeholders

d) Models, budget, and resources

102. The main reason for undertaking an evaluation is:

  a) To get feedback and improve future programs

  b) To classify different evaluation models

  c) To set a budget for a program

  d) To determine the stakeholders of a program

103. Which of the following best describes the primary concern of effectiveness/result models?

  a) The methods used in a programme

  b) The stakeholders involved in a programme

  c) The results of a programme or project

  d) The budget allocated for a programme

104. Which of the following does an effectiveness/result model reveal about a programme?

  a) Only the goals specified by the implementing agency

  b) The reasons behind the failure of the programme

  c) The duration of the programme

  d) Both foreseen and unforeseen effects of the programme

105. If an evaluation focuses solely on the set goals specified by the implementing agency, it can be termed as:

  a) Goal-free evaluation

  b) Goal-bound evaluation

  c) Result-bound evaluation

  d) Process evaluation

106. In which type of evaluation does one measure the effectiveness of a program exclusively by its actual effects, irrespective of set goals?

  a) Goal-bound evaluation

  b) Goal-free evaluation

  c) Process evaluation

  d) Feedback evaluation

107. The goal-free evaluation is distinct from goal-bound evaluation in that:

  a) It is only concerned with the previously set goals

  b) It considers only the actual effects of the program, without considering the set goals

  c) It focuses solely on the unforeseen effects of the programme

  c) It is strictly bound by the implementing agency's recommendations

108. Which of the following statements about effectiveness/result models is TRUE?
   a) They are primarily concerned with the budget of a programme
   b) They only evaluate based on pre-set goals
   c) They evaluate both the intended and unintended outcomes of a programme
   d) They are always goal-free

109. The principle which evaluates a program based on the goals provided by the implementing agency is called:
   a) Goal-unbiased evaluation
   b) Goal-centered evaluation
   c) Goal-bound evaluation
   d) Goal-based assessment

110. Goal-free evaluation can be described as:
   a) Always prioritizing the goals set by the implementing agency
   b) Ignoring the actual results and focusing only on goals
   c) Evaluating the outcomes without being restricted by pre-set goals
   d) An evaluation that has no specific objectives

111. Which of the following best represents a drawback of goal-bound evaluation?
   a) It only measures against set goals, potentially missing unforeseen results
   b) It cannot be used for large projects
   c) It always provides negative feedback
   d) It does not consider the goals at all

112. An implementing agency wishes to solely evaluate the unexpected outcomes of their program. Which evaluation model should they use?
   a) Goal-based evaluation
   b) Process evaluation
   c) Goal-bound evaluation
   d) Goal-free evaluation

113. Evaluation that is conducted during the program development and implementation is known as:
   a) Summative evaluation
   b) Formative evaluation
   c) Process evaluation
   d) Impact evaluation

114. Which of the following evaluations examines the effects or outcomes of a program?
   a) Implementation evaluation
   b) Formative evaluation
   c) Summative evaluation
   d) Needs assessment

115. Which evaluation type focuses on determining who needs the program and how to satisfy this need?
   a) Process evaluation
   b) Outcome evaluation
   c) Need assessment
   d) Impact evaluation

116. What is the main purpose of an impact evaluation?
   a) To monitor the fidelity of the program
   b) To assess the overall intended or unintended net effects of the project
   c) To determine feasibility of an evaluation
   d) To measure effort and the direct outputs of programs

117. Which of the following is a methodology used to determine the scope and seriousness of a problem under formative evaluation?
   a) Evaluability assessment
   b) Brainstorming
   c) Econometric methods
   d) Observational methods

118. Under summative evaluation, which methodology is used to assess the impact of a program/project/technology?
   a) Brainstorming
   b) Evaluability assessment
   c) Econometric and qualitative methods
   d) Multi attribute utility

119. Which of the following evaluation models is concerned about whether the program project goals have been reached?
   a) Economic models
   b) Effectiveness/result models
   c) Professional/Actors' model
   d) CIPP model

120. Goal-free evaluation measures the effectiveness of a program:
   a) Based on goals set by the implementing agency
   b) Exclusively in terms of its actual effects regardless of the goals set
   c) Based on the cost-effectiveness ratio
   d) By comparing it to other programs

121. In economic models of evaluation, what does the cost-benefit analysis compare?
   a) Different programs in terms of relative benefits
   b) The relative monetary benefits of a program to its costs
   c) The budgeting and accounting systems
   d) Outcomes on a common scale

122. The CIPP model developed in the 1960s was originally intended for:
    a) Improving business strategies
    b) Analyzing technological advancements
    c) Improving United States school programs
    d) Implementing healthcare reforms

123. Which level of the Kirkpatrick/Phillips model measures the trainees' reaction to the training programme?
    a) Learning
    b) Behaviour
    c) Results
    d) Reaction

124. In the Kirkpatrick/Phillips model, which level focuses on the change in trainees' behaviour after undergoing the training?
    a) Level 1
    b) Level 2
    c) Level 3
    d) Level 4

125. At which level in the Kirkpatrick/Phillips model is the Return on Investment (ROI) calculated?
    a) Level 1
    b) Level 2
    c) Level 3
    d) Level 5

126. The formula for calculating ROI in the Kirkpatrick/Phillips model is:
    a) ROI = (Total Programme Benefits / Total Programme Costs) * 100%
    b) ROI = (Total Programme Benefits - Total Programme Costs) * 100%
    c) ROI = (Total Programme Costs / Total Programme Benefits) * 100%
    d) ROI = (Total Programme Benefits - Total Programme Costs) / Total Programme Costs * 100%

127. Which level of the Kirkpatrick/Phillips model analyzes the final results of the training programme to see if it aligns with the organization's objectives?
    a) Level 1
    b) Level 2
    c) Level 3
    d) Level 4

128. What does the Logic Model in programme evaluation illustrate?
    a) Sequence of cause-and-effect relationship
    b) Reaction of trainees
    c) Financial analysis of the training
    d) ROI percentages

129. In Bennett's hierarchy, as you ascend the hierarchy:
   a) The complexity of the evaluation decreases.
   b) The emphasis is laid on knowledge and attitudes only.
   c) Evidence of programme impact becomes stronger.
   d) The program's objectives become less clear.

130. The major emphasis of Bennett's hierarchy model is on:
   a) Knowledge
   b) Attitudes
   c) Skills
   d) Practice change and end results

131. Which method of evaluation primarily relies on observing the daily behavior, conversations, and in-depth interviews?
   a) Unstructured interview
   b) Semi-structured interview
   c) Ethnography
   d) Focus group

132. In which type of interview are neither the questions nor the answer categories predetermined?
   a) Unstructured interview
   b) Semi-structured interview
   c) Ethnography
   d) Participant observation

133. Which method involves discussing with groups of people in an interactive setting to understand their responses about a product or program?
   a) Unstructured interview
   b) Semi-structured interview
   c) Ethnography
   d) Focus group

134. If an evaluator wishes to delve deep into a particular topic during an interview, they would most likely use:
   a) Unstructured interview
   b) Semi-structured interview
   c) Ethnography
   d) Participant observation

135. Which evaluation method primarily involves gaining insights through close involvement with people in their natural settings?
   a) Ethnography
   b) Analytic induction
   c) Participant observation
   d) Focus group

136. Analytic induction is best described as
   a) Analyzing personal documents of a group
   b) Observing daily behaviors and conversations
   c) Systematically examining similarities between social phenomena
   d) Interacting with groups of people in structured discussions

137. Which method is the primary method of social and cultural anthropology?
   a) Unstructured interview
   b) Semi-structured interview
   c) Ethnography
   d) Analytic induction

138. The kind of interview where the evaluator can probe more based on the respondent's answer is:
   a) Unstructured interview
   b) Semi-structured interview
   c) Ethnography
   d) Participant observation

139. Which of the following is NOT a basic data gathering technique for qualitative methods?
   a) Participant observation
   b) Personal interviews
   c) Documents or artefact analysis
   d) Analytic induction

140. If you wanted to understand the culture of a community deeply and holistically, which method would you most likely use?
   a) Unstructured interview
   b) Semi-structured interview
   c) Ethnography
   d) Focus group

141. Which quantitative method is efficient in collecting information from a large number of respondents and can be administered through structured interviews or questionnaires?
   a) Content or textual analysis
   b) Statistical descriptive techniques
   c) Statistical survey
   d) Statistical inferential techniques

142. What does the method of content analysis primarily focus on?
   a) Detecting structures in textual information
   b) Testing hypotheses from sample data
   c) Graphical representation of data
   d) Direct interaction with the participants

143. Which standard ensures that an evaluation is both trustworthy and competent to perform?

a) U1 Stakeholder identification

b) U2 Evaluator credibility

c) U3 Information scope and selection

d) U4 Values identification

44. Which standard emphasizes that the evaluation procedures should be practical to keep disruption to a minimum?

a) FI Practical procedures

b) F2 Political viability

c) F3 Cost effectiveness

d) Pl Service orientation

145. To ensure that human subjects involved in an evaluation are treated ethically and their rights are protected, which standard should be followed?

a) P2 Formal agreements

b) P3 Rights of human subjects

c) P4 Human interactions

d) P5 Complete and fair assessment

145. Which accuracy standard ensures that the information-gathering procedures provide valid interpretations for the intended use?

a) A4 Defensible information sources

b) A5 Valid information

c) A6 Reliable information

d) A7 Systematic information

147. In ensuring that personal biases do not distort the results of an evaluation, which standard is most appropriate?

a) A10 Justified conclusions

b) A11 Impartial reporting

c) A12 Meta evaluation

d) A8 Analysis of quantitative information

148. The method that involves drawing inferences for the entire population from a sample based upon testing hypothesis is:

a) Content or textual analysis

b) Statistical descriptive techniques

c) Statistical survey

d) Statistical inferential techniques

149. Which standard ensures that evaluations are designed to assist organizations in serving the needs of the targeted participants?
   a) Pl Service orientation
   b) P2 Formal agreements
   c) P3 Rights of human subjects
   d) P4 Human interactions

150. For a systematic analysis of qualitative information to effectively answer evaluation questions, one should adhere to:
   a) A7 Systematic information
   b) A8 Analysis of quantitative information
   c) A9 Analysis of qualitative information
   d) A10 Justified conclusions

151. Which of the following is NOT a qualitative evaluation method?
   a) Unstructured interview
   b) Semi-structured interview
   c) Statistical survey
   d) Focus group

152. The unstructured interview technique is also known as all of the following EXCEPT:
   a) Informal conversational interview
   b) Non-standardized interview
   c) Structured interview
   d) Ethnographic interview

153. Which method is based on the diversity of culture and involves hands-on, on-the-scene learning, direct observation of daily behavior, and conversations?
   a) Unstructured interview
   b) Participant observation
   c) Ethnography
   d) Analytic induction

154. Which of the following quantitative evaluation methods involves collecting information from a large number of respondents and can be self-administered?
   a) Content or textual analysis
   b) Statistical descriptive techniques
   c) Statistical survey
   d) Analytic induction

155. The Joint Committee on Standards for Educational Evaluation (JCSEE) 2010 specified which of the following standards for programme evaluation?
   a) Utility standards
   b) Practicality standards
   c) Feasibility standards
   d) Both a and c

156. What is the main purpose of the Logical Framework Approach (LFA) in evaluation?
  a) To analyze stakeholder feedback
  b) To evaluate the project timeline
  c) To plan and design projects in a systematic way
  d) To allocate resources for the project

157. Impact evaluation primarily focuses on:
  a) The total number of beneficiaries from a program.
  b) The causal effect or relationship between a program and outcomes.
  c) The amount of resources spent on a program.
  d) The number of activities conducted in a program.

158. Which qualitative method is characterized by gaining close and intimate familiarity with a group in their natural settings?
  a) Ethnography
  b) Analytic induction
  c) Participant observation
  d) Focus group

159. Which standard of the JCSEE ensures that an evaluation is conducted legally, ethically, and with due regard for the welfare of those involved in the evaluation?
  a) Utility standards
  b) Feasibility standards
  c) Propriety standards
  d) Accuracy standards

160. Which step in the Logical Framework Approach focuses on understanding the core problems and determining the best ways to solve them?
  a) Stakeholder analysis
  b) Problem analysis
  c) Solution analysis
  d) Strategy analysis

161. Why is impact evaluation significant for development programmes and policies in sectors like agriculture and health?
  a) To measure the inputs and outputs of a programme.
  b) To check how much budget has been spent.
  c) To ascertain whether the intended changes or outcomes have occurred.
  d) To decide how many training programmes should be organized.

162. In which country did the programme evaluation gain momentum after the Government Performance and Results Act of 1993 was passed?
  a) India
  b) Australia
  c) USA
  d) Europe

163. The process of deciding what to evaluate, developing hypotheses, and choosing indicators falls under which step of implementing an impact evaluation?

   a) Prepare for the evaluation

   b) Choose the sample

   c) Collect data

   d) Produce and disseminate findings

164. What is the primary distinction between formative and summative evaluation?

   a) Formative evaluation deals with understanding the outcomes, whereas summative evaluation deals with the input, activities, and output.

   b) Formative evaluation deals with the input, activities, process, and output, while summative evaluation focuses on understanding the outcomes.

   c) Both deal with understanding the outcomes of the programme.

   d) Both focus on input, activities, process, and output.

165. Which type of impact evaluation model relies on the judgment of an expert and is primarily qualitative and subjective in nature?

   a) Goal-free model

   b) Participatory impact evaluation

   c) Expert model

   d) Experimental model

166. How can the success of a programme be defined in terms of evaluation?

   a) By the number of participants

   b) By how much budget was used

   c) Using indicators that are observable evidence of accomplishments or changes made

   d) By the objectives of the programme

167. In the table provided for the IPM programme evaluation, what does an immediate outcome focus on?

   a) Number of participants practicing IPM

   b) Number of participants who developed IPM skills

   c) Money saved on pesticide reduction

   d) Reduced levels of pesticide residues in water-ways

168. Which type of impact evaluation is done to determine if the goals or objectives of a programme have been achieved?
    a) Expert model
    b) Goal-free model
    c) Goal-based model
    d) Experimental model

169. In a goal-free impact evaluation, what is crucial for an evaluator?
    a) To rely on expert judgments
    b) To identify observable impact evaluation indicators carefully
    c) To focus on the budgetary aspects
    d) To solely focus on the objectives of the programme

170. Which outcome evaluation focuses on reduced levels of pesticide residues in water-ways for an IPM programme?
    a) Immediate outcome evaluation
    b) Intermediate outcome evaluation
    c) End result (Impact) evaluation
    d) Output evaluation

171. Which of the following describes the first level of impact evaluations according to Bennett's hierarchy (1975)?
    a) Economic benefits
    b) Change in practices adopted by the participants
    c) Change in the participants' knowledge, attitude, skills, and aspirations
    d) Improved social conditions

172. In Bennett's hierarchy, what represents the third level of impact evaluations?
    a) Change in practices adopted by the participants
    b) Change in the participants' knowledge, attitude, skills, and aspirations
    c) Improved social, economical, and environmental conditions
    d) None of the above

173. What is the main difference between experimental and ex-post facto in terms of research design?
    a) In experimental, the independent variable X is manipulated and then Y is observed; in ex-post facto, Y is observed after or concomitant to the observation of X.
    b) In experimental, the outcome Y is only observed; in ex-post facto, the independent variable X is manipulated.
    c) Both involve manipulation of the independent variable X.
    d) There is no difference between the two.

174. In a one-short case study design for research, which of the following is true for its ex-post-facto form?
   a) The outcome is examined or analyzed.
   b) The independent variable 'X' is manipulated.
   c) It has high scientific validity.
   d) It is always conducted post-program.

175. Which research design is an improvement over the one group design and observes the difference between O1 and O2 to determine intervention's cause?
   a) Static group comparison
   b) Pre-test post-test
   c) One group post-test only design
   d) One-short case study

176. What is the primary concern with the static group comparison design?
   a) Randomization can be easily employed.
   b) The post-test O measures are compared to ascertain the effect of X.
   c) The experimental group is administered pre-treatment for the purpose of establishing the effect of X.
   d) There's potential for uncontrolled variables to emerge since randomization cannot be used.

177. Quasi-experimental designs lack:
   a) A control group
   b) A treatment group
   c) Full control over scheduling of experimental stimuli
   d) Data collection procedures

178. In the Time series design:
   a) Only one pre-test and post-test is conducted
   b) 2-3 pre-tests and post-tests are conducted
   c) No pre-test is required
   d) No post-test is conducted

179. In the Non-equivalent/equivalent control group design, the two selected sites should be:
   a) Very different from each other
   b) In close proximity to each other
   c) Comparable in terms of farming, agro-ecology, and socio-economic background
   d) Located on different continents

180. What does the Difference-in-differences quasi-experimental design help to address?
   a) Bias introduced by a fully random sampling procedure
   b) The need for a control group
   c) The treatment effects over a short period of time
   d) Bias introduced by non-random sampling procedure

181. In the Difference-in-differences quasi-experimental design table, what does ΔΔYt represent?
   a) The difference between post-tests in treatment and control groups
   b) The difference between pre-tests in treatment and control groups
   c) The difference in differences between the treatment and control groups
   d) The overall impact of the programme

182. What is a major concern with quasi-experiments?
   a) They always produce accurate results
   b) They frequently lead to causal inferences
   c) They are always based on a random sampling procedure
   d) They lack a treatment group

183. Which of the following designs is time-consuming due to multiple data collection points?
   a) One-short case study design
   b) Static group comparison design
   c) Time series design
   d) Pre-test post-test design

184. Which of the following falls under short-term impact evaluation indicators?
   a) Economic benefits
   b) Change in participant's knowledge, skills, attitude and aspiration
   c) Adoption of practices disseminated in the program
   d) Improved environmental conditions

185. According to Bennett's hierarchy (1975), what is the first level of impact evaluations?
   a) Change in practices
   b) Improved social conditions
   c) Economic benefits
   d) Change in the participants' knowledge, attitude, skills and aspirations

186. Which among these is NOT a type of impact evaluation research design?

a) Pre-experimental
b) Experimental
c) Quasi experimental
d) Hypothesis testing

187. In the case of experimental impact evaluation, what is manipulated over time and space to observe variation?

a) Y (dependent variable)
b) X (independent variable)
c) Both X and Y
d) Neither X nor Y

188. For an agricultural program like a mushroom vocational training program conducted by a Krishi Vigyan Kendra (KVK), which of the following can be considered an intermediate outcome?

a) Farmers' participation in the program
b) Trained farmers setting up of mushroom units
c) Change in farmers' attitude towards mushroom enterprise
d) Augmenting on-farm income

189. Which of the following is essential in selecting a design for impact evaluation?

a) It should fit within the budgetary provisions.
b) It should be open-ended.
c) It should prioritize subjective over objective data.
d) It should allow for manipulation of both dependent and independent variables.

190. Propensity score matching (PSM) is employed when:

a) Subjects are randomized in a treatment and control group.
b) A large group of nonparticipants is not available.
c) One tries to develop a counterfactual group observationally similar to the treatment group.
d) Treatment groups are solely based on observed characteristics.

191. What problem does propensity score matching aim to address?

a) Lack of randomization between treatment and control groups.
b) The randomization between treatment and control groups.
c) Finding a match for each program non-participant.
d) Determining the score for propensity.

192. Which regression model is most often used to estimate the propensity score?
   a) Linear regression
   b) Probit regression
   c) Ridge regression
   d) Logistic regression

193. In the context of the given text, which of the following best describes "caliper or radius matching"?
   a) A method to calculate propensity score.
   b) A method to form matched pairs based on propensity score.
   c) A technique to ensure randomness in treatment and control groups.
   d) A tool to measure the effectiveness of a treatment.

194. In the example provided, what data was used to construct an equivalent control group?
   a) The number of faculty in the university
   b) The amount of funding received for the program
   c) Village characteristics before the program was implemented
   d) The number of students enrolled in the agri-clinic program

195. Which of the following is a source of invalidity due to unanticipated events occurring between the 1st and 2nd measurement?
   a) Maturation
   b) Selection
   c) History
   d) Contamination

196. Which experimental design has a potential threat from "Instrumentation"?
   a) Case study
   b) Static group
   c) Time series
   d) One group pre-test/post-test

197. Which of the following best describes the purpose of evaluation syntheses in the context of the text?
   a) To randomize participants in treatment and control groups.
   b) To resolve the internal and external validity of impact evaluation results.
   c) To calculate the propensity score of participants.
   d) To match participants based on observed characteristics.

198. In the context of economic impact assessment, how is the profit at farm level primarily expressed?
   a) Difference between the output prices and land costs.
   b) Difference between gross revenue and the cost of adopting an intervention/programme.
   c) Sum of gross revenue and output prices.
   d) Ratio of input prices to output prices.

199. Participatory need assessment primarily aims to:

a) Quantify the daily earnings of the local population.

b) Prioritize the needs of professionals over local communities.

c) Understand the needs of the community through a collaborative approach.

d) Provide the local people with a predefined action plan.

200. Which of the following is NOT mentioned as a source of gathering information on a participatory basis?

a) Informal discussion with groups

b) Regular community meetings

c) Interview with key informants and services users

d) Household survey

201. Which of the following describes "Their culture" in the context of elements of social impact assessment?

a) How they live, work, and play.

b) Shared beliefs, customs, values, and language or dialect.

c) Quality of the air and water people use.

d) The level of democratisation that is taking place.

202. Which approach in economic impact assessment is widely used in both ex-ante and ex-post evaluation of economic benefits?

a) Profit function approach

b) Demand-supply equilibrium approach

c) Economic surplus approach

d) Econometric approach

203. Social impact assessment primarily deals with:

a) Monitoring the physical changes in infrastructure.

b) Overseeing the economic fluctuations in a region.

c) Analyzing and managing the social consequences of planned interventions.

d) Proposing new interventions for community development.

204. Which of the following is NOT mentioned as a social change process in the text?

 a) **Environmental processes**

 b) Demographic processes

 c) Economic processes

 d) Institutional and legal processes

205. What is a primary objective of the principles for social impact assessment mentioned in the International Association for Impact Assessment (IAIA document?

 a) Propose new impact assessment methods.

 b) **Provide standards for SIA practice in international contexts**.

 c) Quantify the social and economic impacts separately.

 d) Develop new social interventions for communities

12

Fundamentals of Change Driven Communication and Growth

1. The Latin word from which "communication" is derived means:

   a) To inform
   b) To deliver
   c) To speak
   d) To share

2. Which of the following is NOT necessarily a part of the communication process?

   a) Encoding
   b) Decoding
   c) Shouting
   d) Exchanging information

3. Communication in extension education primarily focuses on:

   a) Providing entertainment to farmers
   b) Making sure everyone hears a message
   c) Reaching mutual understanding with farmers
   d) Broadcasting news about agriculture

4. Which statement best describes communication?

   a) A one-way transmission of information
   b) A process in which participants create and share information to reach mutual understanding
   c) A method for imposing ideas on others
   d) An activity restricted to verbal interaction

5. In the context of agriculture extension, why is communication important?

   a) It is solely a way to broadcast new farming techniques
   b) It helps in receiving feedback to understand if the message has been understood
   c) It is only for the benefit of the extension officers
   d) It is meant to entertain the farmers

Bold Means Correct Answer

6. Which statement is true regarding definitions of communication?
   a) All experts have a single, unified definition of communication
   b) No definition of communication exists
   c) Communication experts have never agreed on a single definition of communication
   d) Communication is strictly defined by verbal exchange

7. In the context of agriculture extension, what happens if there isn't proper communication with farmers?
   a) There is no effect
   b) Farmers get entertained
   c) The message may get distorted or lost
   d) Farmers automatically understand the message

8. How many elements are involved in the communication process?
   a) Three
   b) Five
   c) Seven
   d) Ten

9. What does the source in the communication process do?
   a) Decodes the message
   b) Sends the feedback
   c) Encodes or creates the message
   d) Acts as a barrier

10. What do symbols in communication stand for?
   a) Objects they represent
   b) Words which represent things
   c) Only non-verbal cues
   d) The message itself

11. Which of the following is NOT a dimension of a message?
   a) Code
   b) Content
   c) Channel
   d) Treatment

12. A good message should be:
   a) Vague and general
   b) Only entertaining
   c) Clear, understandable, and accurate
   d) Always long and detailed

13. Which of the following best describes fog distortion?
    a) Information is changed systematically
    b) Gives an extra or unwanted message
    c) Information is lost due to encoding and decoding errors
    d) All messages remain the same

14. Channels in the communication process refer to:
    a) Types of messages
    b) Forms through which messages are transmitted
    c) Barriers in communication
    d) Feedback mechanisms

15. Which of the following channels has the LOWEST information richness?
    a) Face-to-face conversation
    b) Telephone conversation
    c) Blogs
    d) Spreadsheets

16. The act of interpreting the message is known as:
    a) Encoding
    b) Feedback
    c) Decoding
    d) Transmitting

17. Feedback is used to:
    a) Create barriers in communication
    b) Alter messages so the intent is understood
    c) Ensure the sender speaks more
    d) Make sure the receiver is quiet

18. Which of the following is NOT a type of feedback?
    a) Fire feedback situation
    b) No feedback or zero feedback
    c) Distorted feedback
    d) Yes/no feedback

19. What is the main limitation of feedback in mass media channels like radio and television?
    a) It is more immediate.
    b) It is maximum in interpersonal communication.
    c) There is less feedback.
    d) It varies with the situation.

20. Which feedback situation allows the respondent to only see without the ability to ask questions?

    a) No feedback or zero feedback
    b) Visual appearance system
    c) Yes/no feedback
    d) Fire feedback situation

21. In which feedback situation can students ask questions and the teacher can only respond with a "Yes" or "No"?

    a) No feedback or zero feedback
    b) Visual appearance system
    c) Yes/no feedback
    d) Fire feedback situation

22. Which feedback situation does not place any restrictions on asking questions?

    a) No feedback or zero feedback
    b) Visual appearance system
    c) Yes/no feedback
    d) Fire feedback situation

23. Feedback that introduces action-reaction interdependence and affects the source is known to:

    a) Exert control over future messages.
    b) Vary with the situation.
    c) Emphasize too much on the source.
    d) Be source-oriented.

24. What does feedback do for the source in terms of understanding the receiver's emotions and perspective?

    a) It helps the source to empathize with the receiver.
    b) It increases the confidence interval of the source.
    c) It helps in the decision-making process.
    d) It exerts control over future messages.

25. One limitation of feedback is that:

    a) It always introduces errors in communication.
    b) It helps in the learning process.
    c) It affects the source-receiver relation.
    d) It is never useful in interpersonal communication.

26. Which of the following is NOT a limitation of feedback?

    a) It emphasizes too much on the source.
    b) It helps in the learning process.
    c) It diminishes the confidence interval.
    d) It varies with the situation.

27. In which communication type is feedback maximized?
    a) Mass communication
    b) Organizational communication
    c) Intrapersonal communication
    d) Interpersonal communication

28. What is message distortion?
    a) When the message remains consistent and unchanged.
    b) The exaggeration of the original message.
    c) The amplification of the message volume.
    d) When the message sent by a communicator is interpreted differently by the person receiving it.

29. Which form of message distortion involves the loss of information due to encoding and decoding issues?
    a) Systematic or stretch distortion
    b) Fog distortion
    c) Mirage distortion
    d) Both a and c

30. Which of the following techniques is NOT mentioned as a way to reduce message distortion?
    a) Communicate only the essential parts of the message.
    b) **Use as many channels as possible to send the message.**
    c) Check that the receiver has interpreted the message correctly.
    d) Check that the other person has understood what has been said.

31. In the context of communication, what is a channel?
    a) The length of the message.
    b) The device or medium used to store the message.
    c) The means by which messages are communicated.
    d) The time taken to decode a message.

32. When the receiver is interpreting the message, what is this process referred to as?
    a) Encoding
    b) Channelling
    c) Processing
    d) Decoding

33. Which of the following is NOT a type of communication barrier?
    a) Semantic barriers
    b) Physical barriers
    c) Language barriers
    d) Music barriers

34. Traffic signals and gestures by traffic policemen primarily help in overcoming which type of barrier?
    a) Behavioral barriers
    b) Attitudinal barriers
    c) Physical barriers
    d) Semantic barriers

35. Which type of barrier occurs when there is an inability of the receiver to decode a message?
    a) Encoding barrier
    b) Decoding barrier
    c) Language barrier
    d) Cultural barrier

36. What can cause a breakdown in communication due to differences in values and attitudes?
    a) Physical distractions
    b) Technical disruptions
    c) Discrimination
    d) Noise

37. Which of the following is essential for overcoming cultural barriers in communication?
    a) Use of loudspeakers
    b) Using a common language
    c) Empathy
    d) Avoiding jargon

38. Jargon should be avoided primarily to overcome which barrier?
    a) Language barrier
    b) Semantic barrier
    c) Physical barrier
    d) Environmental barrier

39. Which level of communication primarily happens within an individual?
    a) Interpersonal communication
    b) Mass communication
    c) Intrapersonal communication
    d) Group communication

40. In organizational communication, which type of communication involves the exchange of messages within the same level of hierarchy?
    a) Vertical communication
    b) Horizontal communication
    c) Upward communication
    d) Downward communication

41. What do generalizations and stereotyping cause in communication?
    a) Language barriers
    b) Communication enhancemen
    c) Communication barriers
    d) Message encoding

42. Who defined and practiced the principles of 'RHETORIC'?
    a) Socrates
    b) Plato
    c) Pythagoras
    d) Aristotle

43. Who among the following defined and practiced the principles of 'RHETORIC' in ancient Greece?

a) Socrates
b) Plato
c) Aristotle
d) Pythagoras

44. What is the art of public speaking known as?

a) Dialectic
b) Discourse
c) Rhetoric
d) Prose

45. Compared to other speaking situations, public speaking:

a) Requires entirely different communication skills.
b) Is always easier for everyone.
c) Involves many of the same communication skills.
d) Is only practiced in modern times.

46. Some individuals might feel _______ in a public speaking setting, even if they are comfortable in small group communication.

a) Excited
b) Anxious
c) Indifferent
d) Overconfident

47. Public communication involves:

a) Only the content of the message.
b) Only the delivery of the message.
c) Both content and delivery of the message.
d) Neither content nor delivery.

48. Organisational communication encompasses which forms of communication?

a) Only written communication
b) Only oral communication
c) Both written and oral communication
d) Neither written nor oral communication

49. Which of the following is the most prominent example of oral communication in organisational communication?

a) Email correspondence
b) Written reports
c) Formal presentations
d) Text messages

50. In a formal presentation, a speaker transmits a message with the help of:
    a) Only visual materials
    b) Only audio materials
    c) Both visual and audio-visual materials
    d) Neither visual nor audio materials

51. What does vertical communication in an organization entail?
    a) Only upward movement of messages
    b) Only downward movement of messages
    c) Both upward and downward movement of messages
    d) Neither upward nor downward movement of messages

52. Horizontal communication in an organization primarily occurs between:
    a) Different departments
    b) Supervisor and subordinate
    c) Individuals at the same hierarchical level
    d) Outside stakeholders

53. Who is the originator or sender of a message in a communication process?
    a) Receiver
    b) Medium
    c) Communicator
    d) Listener

54. Extension education mainly involves which two processes?
    a) Writing and Speaking
    b) Getting information to people and assisting them to use it
    c) Innovating and Testing
    d) Reading and Writing

55. How is communication behavior primarily defined?
    a) Communicator's listening skills
    b) Communicator's expression of information dissemination
    c) Communicator's reading skills
    d) Communicator's physical presence

56. Key communicators or opinion leaders are individuals who:
    a) Follow the majority opinion
    b) Are sought out for advice on specific topics
    c) Avoid communication
    d) Prefer to stay isolated

57. What percentage of communication efforts, as per research, are often misunderstood or distorted?

a) 20% **b) 70%**

c) 40% d) 50%

58. Which form of communication involves the use of symbols with generally universal meaning?

a) Non-verbal communication b) Informal communication

c) Verbal communication d) Formal communication

59. If a teacher uses a cold, fixed stare to indicate silence, which form of communication is being used?

a) Written communication b) Verbal communication

c) Formal communication **d) Non-verbal communication**

60. Which type of communication focuses on precise language use and careful attention to grammar?

a) Informal communication b) Oral communication

c) Formal communication d) Non-verbal communication

61. What distinguishes human beings from other animals in terms of communication?

a) Their use of symbols

b) Their ability to communicate

c) Their use of verbal and non-verbal forms

d) Their physical gestures

62. Fidelity in communication refers to:

a) Purity of communication b) The volume of the message

c) The speed of the communication d) The type of media used

63. What does a high fidelity encoder do?

a) Reduces the speed of the message

b) Translates the message with minor errors

c) Decreases the clarity of the source

d) Expresses the meaning of the source completely

64. Which factor negatively affects fidelity in communication?

a) Short messages **b) Increasing noise**

c) Clarity of source d) Effective decoders

65. Communication effectiveness is determined by the relationship between:
    a) The length and clarity of a message
    b) The communicator and a specific message
    c) The medium and the receiver
    d) The speed and accuracy of delivery

66. Which of the following is NOT a component of effective oral communication?
    a) Comprehension
    b) Rapid speaking
    c) Validity
    d) Effective delivery

67. The word "empathy" was first used in the context of:
    a) Social interactions in adults
    b) Understanding beliefs and motivations
    c) Motor mimicry observed in one-year-olds
    d) Effective communication practices

68. According to Katz, empathy is a process of:
    a) Understanding only the emotions of people
    b) People's communication about their past
    c) People's communication about their future goals
    d) People's communication about their current experiences

69. Empathetic understanding is essential for:
    a) Only understanding our own feelings
    b) Communicating well with others
    c) Avoiding social situations
    d) Speaking loudly and clearly

70. What is empathy fundamentally related to?
    a) Persuading others to agree with us
    b) Our cognitive abilities
    c) How we comprehend and interact with the world
    d) Our ability to memorize facts

71. When was the word "empathy" first introduced?
    a) 1980s
    b) 1940s
    c) 1920s
    d) 1960s

72. Who first used the word "empathy"?
   a) Sigmund Freud
   b) Carl Rogers
   c) E.B. Titchner
   d) B.F. Skinner

73. Which profession did E.B. Titchner belong to?
   a) Sociologist
   b) Biologist
   c) Psychologist
   d) Anthropologist

74. Which of the following best defines communication effectiveness?
   a) The quality of the message sent.
   b) The relationship between communicator, message, receiver, and situation.
   c) The clarity of oral communication.
   d) The mode of communication used.

75. What does EOC stand for?
   a) Effective Oral Communication
   b) Essential Objective Communication
   c) Effective Online Chat
   d) Essential Oral Content

76. Which of the following is NOT a part of effective oral communication?
   a) Comprehension
   b) Rapport
   c) Persuasion
   d) Validity

77. A good functional relationship in communication includes all EXCEPT:
   a) Positive attitude
   b) Language proficiency
   c) Ability to speak quickly
   d) Pleasing personality

78. What does effective delivery in communication suggest?
   a) Speaking fast and constantly
   b) Speaking less, true, slow, and loud
   c) Using complex vocabulary to impress
   d) Avoiding the use of examples

79 Communication effectiveness can be represented as:
   a) Comprehension + Validity + Utility
   b) Comprehension + Relevance + Validity
   c) Rapport + Attitude + Delivery
   d) Language + Rapport + Comprehension

80. Which of the following best describes the core principle of Communication for Social Change (CSC)?

a) Outsiders dictating change to communities.

b) Using mass media to influence individual behavior.

c) Placing community members at the center of the communication process.

d) Leveraging only new technologies for spreading information.

81. In CSC, what role do community members play?

a) Passive listeners.

b) Agents of change.

c) Just technology users.

d) Receivers of instructions from outsiders.

82. Which of the following is NOT a communicative method to invoke social change mentioned in the text?

a) Behavior change communication. **b) Passive communication.**

c) Mass communication. d) Advocacy communication.

83. In the context of communication networks, what does a 'Network' signify?

a) A pattern of technology use.

b) A pattern of connection of different people in a social system.

c) The number of devices connected in a system.

d) The hierarchy of an organization.

84. Which network type gives the greatest amount of satisfaction and is good for cognitive tasks?

a) Star network. b) Chain network.

c) Wheel network. d) Mesh network.

85. Homophily refers to:

a) A preference for diversity within one's associations.

b) The degree to which pairs of individuals who interact are different.

c) A preference in associating with people who are similar in some way.

d) The strength of weak ties in a network.

86. Which of the following is associated with successful businesses and organizations, representing a preference for diversity within associations?
    a) Homophily
    b) Heterophily
    c) Star network
    d) Passive communication

87. What best describes communication competency?
    a) Just the knowledge of the language.
    b) The ability to convey accurate meaning and adapt messages.
    c) Solely based on the context of the message.
    d) Focused on changing the behavior of clients without considering context.

88. Which are the two dimensions of communication competency?
    a) Knowledge and Credibility.
    b) Trustworthiness and Expertise.
    c) Knowledge and Skill.
    d) Language and Perception.

89. How is credibility in communication best defined?
    a) The perceived trustworthiness and competence of the source by the audience.
    b) The actual expertise of the communicator.
    c) The intention of the communicator.
    d) The number of people who follow the communicator.

90. Which term is sometimes used interchangeably with credibility?
    a) Pathos
    b) Ethos
    c) Logos
    d) Kairos

91. Why is credibility an essential component of communication?
    a) It enhances the entertainment value.
    b) It helps in marketing products better.
    c) It influences the receiver's perception and acceptance of the message.
    d) It ensures the message is short and concise.

92. Which of the following traits does NOT increase the credibility of an extension worker?
    a) Personal appearance.
    b) Consistency in giving factual information.
    c) Being passive.
    d) Honesty and straightforwardness.

93. What is traditional media primarily used for?
    a) Broadcasting the news.
    b) Transmitting tradition from one generation to another.
    c) Digital advertising.
    d) Reading news articles.

94. Which of the following does NOT require electricity?
    a) Television.
    b) Folk songs.
    c) Radio receiver.
    d) Internet.

95. Folk theatre primarily focuses on themes related to:
    a) Modern urban life.
    b) Outer space exploration.
    c) People's own suffering, daily work, dreams, and mythology.
    d) Global politics.

96. What differentiates street theatre from other traditional forms of performance?
    a) It requires a formal stage.
    b) It requires tickets for entrance.
    c) Performers and the audience are on the same level.
    d) Performers avoid making eye contact with the audience.

97. In puppetry, who does the actual work of conveying the story or message?
    a) The audience.
    b) The puppet.
    c) The puppeteer.
    d) The background music.

98. Storytelling is significant because it:
    a) Connects past, present, and future.
    b) Only focuses on fictional tales.
    c) Primarily uses written scripts.
    d) Relies on digital media for propagation.

99. Which of the following is NOT a form of traditional media?
    a) Radio broadcasting.
    b) Folk music and song.
    c) Puppetry.
    d) Fairs and festivals.

100. How are folk songs primarily transmitted?

a) Through written documents. **b) Through oral tradition.**

c) Through television broadcasts. d) Through the internet.

101. What is the primary purpose of proverbs?

a) To tell elaborate stories.

b) To express a truth based on common sense or practical experience.

c) To provide news updates.

d) To advertise products.

102. Mass communication involves sending a message to:

a) A specific, targeted group of people.

b) Large, anonymous, and scattered heterogeneous masses.

c) A small group of friends.

d) A single individual.

103. Which of the following is NOT considered a mass medium based on the provided definition?

a) Radio. b) Television.

c) Personal letter. d) Internet.

104. Who are the gatekeepers in mass communication?

a) The audience members.

b) The sources of the messages.

c) Reporters, sub-editors, editors, producers, writers.

d) The technology operators.

105. Which of the following is NOT a function of a gatekeeper?

a) Limiting the information through editing.

b) Expanding the amount of information.

c) Directly broadcasting the raw information.

d) Reorganizing or reinterpreting the information.

106. Feedback in mass communication is characterized by being:

a) Immediate. b) Instant.

c) Delayed. d) Not required.

107. Which of the following sensory channels is NOT utilized in mass communication?

a) Sight.
b) Hearing.
c) Touch.
d) Taste.

108. Which of the following best describes the nature of messages in mass communication?

a) Personal.
b) Impersonal.
c) Physical.
d) Imaginary.

109. To be considered a mass medium, it must reach how many adopters?

a) One million.
b) Ten million.
c) Fifty million.
d) A hundred million.

110. How do television executives often infer feedback on their programming?

a) Instant viewer feedback.
b) Personal visits from viewers.
c) Ratings measured by the number of viewers.
d) Direct phone calls from viewers during broadcasting.

111. What is a primary assumption of the linguistic theory of communication?

a) Meanings can easily be communicated.
b) Words are multidimensional when written.
c) Meanings are in the minds of people.
d) Words have no additional dimension when spoken.

112. Which step is NOT part of the linguistic theory of communication process?

a) Encoding into physical signals.
b) Sending messages through a telepathic channel.
c) Decoding linguistic forms into messages.
d) Interpreting and acting upon messages.

113. What is the main focus of the psycholinguistic theory?

a) The social context of language use.
b) The behavior of an individual in the use of language.
c) The variation of language across different cultures.
d) The way language is written.

114. According to the sociolinguistic theory, communication does NOT take place independently of:

   a) Physical barriers.

   b) Factors of the person or social context.

   c) Word count.

   d) Biological factors.

115. What does the theory of individual differences in mass media effect suggest?

   a) Everyone interprets media messages in the same way.

   b) Only a few individuals pay attention to media messages.

   c) People's exposure to mass media is ever shrinking.

   d) The effect of any mass media may vary from person to person.

116. Which theory emphasizes that there are broad social categories of people who may respond similarly to a given stimulus?

   a) Theory of social relationship.

   b) Theory of individual differences.

   c) Theory of social categories.

   d) Sociolinguistic theory.

117. According to the theory of social relationship, who are the first individuals to receive a message from mass media?

   a) General public.

   b) Opinion leaders.

   c) Psychologists.

   d) Government officials.

118. Selective attention and selective perception are key parameters in which theory?

   a) Theory of individual differences.

   b) Psycholinguistic theory.

   c) Sociolinguistic theory.

   d) Theory of social relationship.

119. What primary function do communication models serve?

   a) Predict future communication trends.

   b) Enhance the channel of communication.

   c) Describe the process of communication visually.

   d) Increase the speed of communication.

120. Which model of communication considers communication as a one-way process?
    a) Transactional model.
    b) Interactive model.
    c) Linear model.
    d) Both a and b.

121. In which model is the sender most prominent?
    a) Linear model.
    b) Interactive model.
    c) Transactional model.
    d) None of the above.

122. Which of the following is NOT a component of the linear model of communication?
    a) Field of experience.
    b) Encoding.
    c) Decoding.
    d) Message.

123. The Interactive model of communication emphasizes on:
    a) One-way communication.
    b) Two-way communication with feedback.
    c) Simultaneous communication.
    d) Communication without feedback.

124. What affects the message formation and interpretation in the interactive model?
    a) Encoding process.
    b) Decoding process.
    c) Channel.
    d) Field of experience.

125. In the transactional model, both sender and receiver are termed as:
    a) Transmitters.
    b) Decoders.
    c) Communicators.
    d) Interactors.

126. Which model assumes that communication affects both parties simultaneously?
    a) Linear model.
    b) Interactive model.
    c) Transactional model.
    d) None of the above.

127. Which model potentially has the most noise due to simultaneous communication?
    a) Linear model.
    b) Interactive model.
    c) Transactional model.
    d) None of the above.

128. Feedback is considered most important in which communication process?
   a) Linear model.
   b) Interactive model.
   c) Transactional model.
   d) Both b and c

129. Aristotle's model of communication emphasizes on:
   a) Interpersonal communication.
   b) The speaker's role in public speaking.
   c) Receiver's active participation.
   d) Feedback mechanism.

130. Which model proposed the concept: "Who says what in which channel to whom with what effect?"
   a) Aristotle's model
   b) Lasswell's model
   c) Newcomb model
   d) Schramm model

131. The ABX model is also known as:
   a) Schramm model
   b) Shannon and Weaver's model
   c) Newcomb model
   d) Berlo's model

132. Which model emphasizes the importance of feedback in communication and depicts it as an interactive process?
   a) Aristotle's model
   b) Lasswell's model
   c) Schramm model
   d) Shannon and Weaver's model

133. In Shannon and Weaver's model, what factor can potentially distort the intended message during transmission?
   a) Speaker
   b) Receiver
   c) Noise
   d) Feedback

134. According to Berlo's model, which among the following is NOT a component of the message?
   a) Content
   b) Channel
   c) Code
   d) Structure

135. Westley and MacLean's mass media model suggests that communication begins when:
   a) A person starts to talk.
   b) A person responds selectively to his/her physical surroundings.
   c) A person gives feedback.
   d) A message is transmitted.

136. Which model illustrates sociological implications in communication and suggests that communication is a two-way proposition?

a) Gerbner's model
b) Leagan's model
c) Riley and Riley model
d) Aristotle's model

137. In Gerbner's model, the perceptual dimension suggests that:

a) 'M' perceives the whole event.
b) 'M' perceives only part of the event.
c) 'M' has total control over the event.
d) 'E' is the message sent by 'M'.

138. Which model suggests that communication involves a skilled communicator, sending a useful message, through a proper channel, to an appropriate audience?

a) Leagan's model
b) Berlo's model
c) Aristotle's model
d) Lasswell's model

139. Communication games are primarily used to:

a) Waste time in a training session.
b) Challenge and strengthen communication skills.
c) Promote individualism.
d) Avoid learning real communication techniques.

140. Which game involves participants acting out roles to resolve conflicts, practice appropriate behavior, or entertain?

a) Emotion cards.
b) Role-playing.
c) Face to face interview.
d) Video conferencing.

141. The primary focus of "emotion cards" is:

a) Verbal communication.
b) Written communication.
c) Non-verbal communication.
d) Media communication.

142. The advent of information communication technology (ICT) has:

a) Made communication more difficult.
b) Reduced the pace of communication.
c) Brought about no significant change.
d) Taken modern media communication to a new height.

143. Which of the following is NOT a form of e-communication?
   a) Fax.
   b) Cellular phone.
   c) Role-playing.
   d) E-mails.

144. Which communication method allows both parties to see each other's body language and facial expressions?
   a) Teleconferencing.
   b) Email.
   c) Social media posts.
   d) Video conferencing.

145. Social media can be described as:
   a) A traditional way of sending letters.
   b) A means of conducting official business meetings.
   c) Tools that allow users to create online communities and share content.
   d) Only computer-assisted communication.

146. Which among the following is a communication tool that receives alert signals and/or short messages?
   a) Internet.
   b) Video conferencing.
   c) Pager.
   d) Emotion cards.

147. Which communication method primarily uses electric impulses to transmit typed messages?
   a) Face to face interview.
   b) Video conferencing.
   c) E-mails.
   d) Emotion cards.

148. How is modern communication mostly characterized?
   a) Formal.
   b) Slow.
   c) Informal.
   d) Paper-based.

149. What is Development Communication?
   a) Using communication for entertainment
   b) Using communication for business
   c) Using communication to promote development
   d) Using communication for politics

150. Which of the following is NOT a core area of development?
   a) Agriculture
   b) Music
   c) Health and sanitation
   d) Education

151. What abbreviation can Development Communication be referred to as?
   a) DEVC
   b) DEVCOM
   c) DEVCON
   d) COMMDEV

152. Which method of communication focuses on the professional facilitation of dialogue methods among stakeholders?
   a) Diffusion model
   b) One-way communication
   c) Development communication
   d) Broadcasting

153. Development communication is best used:
   a) Only after project objectives have been defined
   b) In the middle of the project
   c) At the end of the project
   d) Before objectives have been defined

154. Which of the following is NOT a feature of development communication?
   a) Innovation and creativity
   b) About sustainability and continuity
   c) One-way and top-down communication
   d) About community participation

155. Development communication primarily plays which two roles?
   a) Transforming and socializing
   b) Entertaining and teaching
   c) Reporting and analyzing
   d) Broadcasting and relaying

156. Which medium played a significant role in development communication in India during the 1940s?
   a) Television
   b) Newspapers
   c) Internet
   d) Radio

157. Which theory of development views the world economy as an international hierarchy of unequal relations?
   a) Modernization theory
   b) Dependency theory
   c) World systems theory
   d) Diffusion of innovation theory

158. What did the diffusion of innovation model originally focus on?
   a) Broadcasting entertainment
   b) Extension of agricultural practices
   c) Internet technologies
   d) Political campaigns

159. Development communication aims at creating an atmosphere for:

a) Change and innovation
b) Reporting and analysis
c) Entertainment and leisure
d) Commercial advertising

160. What is the main scope of development communication?

a) Technology advancement
b) Entertainment broadcasts
c) Proper dialogue for knowledge sharing leading to change
d) Commercial promotions

161. Which technology has transformed the communication landscape in rural India?

a) Television
b) Internet
c) Mobile phones
d) Radio

162. Which communication theory focuses on cultural change directed at institutional structures in non-industrialized countries?

a) Modernization theory
b) Dependency theory
c) World systems theory
d) Diffusion of innovation theory

163. In development communication, feedback is:

a) Discouraged
b) Optional
c) Essential
d) Unimportant

164. Which of the following focuses on the enhancement of agricultural and rural development through improved information and communication processes?

a) E-commerce
b) E-agriculture
c) E-governance
d) E-education

165. For whom does Development Communication create opportunities primarily?

a) Urban dwellers
b) Business tycoons
c) Farmers
d) Politicians

166. What tool of electronic communication allows users to exchange information and ideas in various forms like text, pictures, and videos?

a) Radios
b) Newspapers
c) Social media
d) Television broadcasts

167. When it comes to development communication, which of the following is true regarding government's role in community development?

a) Government should be a distant entity

b) Government should remain an unknown entity

c) Government should be highly visible

d) Government should not interfere

168. What is the primary goal of Development Communication?

a) To entertain the masses

b) To promote political agendas

c) To bring about positive developmental change in society

d) To report news events

13

Educative Techiques in Agricultural Extension

1. What does the extension method refer to in the context of technology dissemination?
   a) The method of extending the use of a particular technology.
   b) The role played by a channel or method of communication.
   c) The method of extending the lifespan of a technology.
   d) The method of increasing the productivity of a technology.

2. Which factors influence the choice of an extension method?
   a) Number and location of the target audience, availability of time for communication, funds, urgency of message, and background of receiver.
   b) The complexity of the technology to be disseminated.
   c) The popularity of the technology to be disseminated.
   d) The market value of the technology to be disseminated.

3. Extension methods are generally classified as:
   a) Modern method, traditional method and advanced method.
   b) Individual method, group method and mass method.
   c) Slow method, fast method and superfast method.
   d) Basic method, intermediate method and complex method.

4. Who is responsible for selecting a particular extension method or combination of methods?
   a) The target audience
   b) The creators of the technology
   c) The investors of the technology
   d) Extension functionaries

5. Does each extension method have both advantages and limitations?
   a) Yes, each method has both advantages and limitations.
   b) No, some methods have only advantages and no limitations.
   c) No, some methods have only limitations and no advantages.
   d) It's not clear if each method has both advantages and limitations.

Bold Means Correct Answer

6. When is the individual method of extension usually suitable?
   a) When the people to be contacted are many and far away from the extension agent.
   b) When the people to be contacted are few, are conveniently located close to the extension agent and sufficient time is available for communication.
   c) When there is limited time available for communication.
   d) When the people to be contacted are spread across a large geographical area.

7. What is one of the advantages of the individual method of extension?
   a) It helps in building rapport with clients by the extension agent.
   b) It reaches a large number of people at once.
   c) It is less time-consuming and less expensive.
   d) It prevents the development of favouritism or bias towards some persons by extension agents.

8. What is a limitation of the individual method of extension?
   a) It is time-consuming and relatively expensive.
   b) It facilitates transfer of technology.
   c) It enhances effectiveness of mass and group methods for technology transfer.
   d) It helps in selecting local leaders for field extension.

9. When is the group method of extension typically used?
   a) When it is necessary to communicate with a number of people simultaneously, who are located not too far off from the communicator and availability of time for communication is reasonably adequate.
   b) When the target audience is very large and dispersed.
   c) When there is limited time available for communication.
   d) When individual attention is required for each participant.

10. Which of the following is an advantage of the group method of extension?
   a) It enables the extension agent to have face-to-face contact with a number of people at a time.
   b) It provides an opportunity for personal contact with each participant.
   c) It allows for widespread coverage of a large audience.
   d) It allows for individual attention to be given to each participant.

11. What is a limitation of the group method of extension?

a) It facilitates sharing of knowledge and experience.

b) It satisfies the basic urge of people for social contacts and relationship.

c) Wide diversity in the interest of group members may hinder the effective learning situation.

d) It enables the extension agent to reach a select part of the target group.

12. When is the mass method of extension typically used?

a) When a large and widely dispersed audience is to be communicated within a short time.

b) When personal contact with each participant is required.

c) When the target audience is small and located close to the extension agent.

d) When detailed feedback from each participant is required.

13. Which of the following is an advantage of the mass method of extension?

a) It allows for intensive personal contact with each participant.

b) It allows for detailed feedback from each participant.

c) Large number of people may be communicated within a short time.

d) It allows for a lot of interaction with and amongst the audience.

14. What is a limitation of the mass method of extension?

a) It facilitates quick communication in times of emergency.

b) It reinforces previous learning.

c) Limited scope for personal contact with target audience.

d) It helps in transferring knowledge, forming and changing opinions.

15. In the group method of extension, how many people typically form a small group?

a) 5 to 10 **b) 10 to 20**

c) 20 to 30 d) 30 to 40

16. Which of the following extension methods involves direct, face-to-face contact with farmers or homemakers at their farm or home?

a) Telephone call or farmers' call b) Farm clinic (Agriclinic)

c) Personal letter **d) Farm and home visit**

17. The method of motivating farmers to adopt a new practice by showing its distinct superior results in their own situation is known as:

    a) Farm clinic (Agriclinic)
    b) Result demonstration
    c) Telephone call or farmers' call
    d) Personal letter

18. What is the main advantage of the result demonstration method?

    a) It helps to build a rapport with farmers.
    b) It helps to identify local leadership.
    c) It helps to produce positive results for extension workers by creating confidence in their judgment and ability.
    d) It helps in teaching complex practices.

19. Which extension method is suitable for contacting few people conveniently located close to the extension agent, and when sufficient time is available for communication?

    a) Farm clinic (Agriclinic)
    b) Result demonstration
    c) Telephone call or farmers' call
    d) Farm and home visit

20. What is a limitation of the farm clinic (Agriclinic extension method?

    a) It can be costly in terms of time, effort, and funds for the extension work.
    b) It may not be possible for the extension agent to be available in the office all the time.
    c) The extension agent may find it difficult to understand the problem by verbal description.
    d) It helps to build good rapport with the farmer.

21. Which extension method is used to show a group of farmers how an entirely new technique or an old practice in an improved way is carried out step-by-step?

    a) Field day or farmers' day
    b) Farmers Field School (FFS)
    c) Method demonstration
    d) Study tours

22. What is the main advantage of the "Method demonstration" extension method?

    a) Requires less preparation, equipment, and skill of the extension agent.
    b) Very effective in persuading people to acquire the skill due to knowing the results within a relatively short time.
    c) Suitable mainly for practices not involving skills.
    d) All the participants get the opportunity to practice the skill.

23. Which extension method is preferred when pooling knowledge and experience of a number of people is desired in arriving at collective decisions through shared opinion?

a) Group meeting or interaction meets

b) Farmers Field School (FFS)

c) Field day or farmers' day

d) Method demonstration

24. What is the limitation of the "Group meeting or interaction meets" extension method?

a) Requires understanding of group dynamics and skill of extension agent.

b) Suitable mainly for practices involving skills.

c) Village factions may hinder successful use of this method.

d) It is a slow process and may not be suitable in crisis or emergency situations.

25. Which extension method involves a season-long group-based training/ learning program conducted in a designated field, where farmers carry out experimental learning activities to understand the ecology of their farms?

a) Farmers Field School (FFS) b) Result demonstration

c) Study tours d) Method demonstration

26. What is an advantage of the "Farmers Field School (FFS)" extension method?

a) Opportunity for farmers to socialize and to acquaint themselves with outside experts.

b) Opportunity to develop expertise among farmers in a farmers community and thereby promote good management practices and a possible increase in profits.

c) Suitable mainly for practices involving skills.

d) Requires a good deal of preparation, equipment, and skill of the extension agent.

27. Which extension method is used to motivate people to adopt a new practice by showing them what has actually been achieved by applying the practice under field conditions?

a) Group meeting or interaction meets b) Method demonstration

c) Field day or farmers' day d) Study tours

28. What is the limitation of the "Field day or farmers' day" extension method?
    a) Requires good deal of preparation, equipment, and skill of the extension agent.
    b) Suitable mainly for practices not involving skills.
    c) Participants cannot visually observe the benefits of the practice.
    d) Field days cannot be held frequently.

29. Which extension method involves farmers visiting farms in other districts and states to see methods of cultivation and the problems farmers face?
    a) Method demonstration
    b) Farmers Field School (FFS)
    c) Study tours
    d) Field day or farmers' day

30. What is the advantage of the "Study tours" extension method?
    a) Requires less preparation, equipment, and skill of the extension agent.
    b) Farmers can integrate their knowledge and experiences into the program through experimentation without personal risks.
    c) Suitable mainly for practices involving skills.
    d) Very effective in persuading people to acquire the skill due to knowing the results within a relatively short time.

31. Which of the following broadcast media is a useful medium to circulate news or warnings more quickly to a larger number of people than through posters, extension agents, or newspapers?
    a) Television
    b) Print media
    c) Radio
    d) Campaign

32. What is the benefit of recording programs for playing back later in radio broadcasts?
    a) It reduces the production costs of radio programs.
    b) It increases the number of listeners.
    c) It allows for live interactions with the audience.
    d) It requires less equipment for broadcasting.

33. Which extension method involves a systematic display of models, specimens, charts, photographs, pictures, posters, and information in a sequence around a theme to create awareness and interest in the community?
    a) Campaign
    b) Print media
    c) Exhibition
    d) Projected media

34. A campaign is a planned set of activities that people carry out over a period of time in order to achieve targets such as social or political change. What is one of the strengths of a strategic extension campaign (SEC) methodology?
    a) It relies solely on mass media for dissemination.
    b) It focuses on short-term goals.
    c) It emphasizes people's participation in planning and implementation.
    d) It is not suitable for agricultural extension programs.

35. What is the usefulness of a campaign in agricultural extension services?
    a) It is based on a supply-driven approach.
    b) It does not require multimedia materials for effective implementation.
    c) It focuses on general issues rather than specific needs.
    d) It advocates a participatory planning approach and provides specific extension support materials and training.

36. Strategic planning aims to achieve the greatest returns through the best possible use of available resources. What is the major outcome of a strategic extension campaign?
    a) Increase in the number of extension agents
    b) Reduction in the number of campaign phases
    c) Enhancement of agricultural extension planning
    d) Elimination of feedback results

37. In the process of developing a strategic extension campaign plan, which phase involves identifying the technology, problems, and information needs?
    a) Phase 1: Technology and problems identification
    b) Phase 3: Strategy development and information positioning
    c) Phase 6: Message design, development, pretesting, and materials production
    d) Phase 9: Field implementation

38. What is the primary role of media and audio-visual aids in making extension teaching effective?
    a) Enhancing social integration in rural societies
    b) Providing entertainment to farmers
    c) Reducing the workload of extension agents
    d) Substituting classroom teaching or textbooks

39. Media planning helps to determine the best combination of media to achieve objectives. What is the first stage of a media plan?
    a) Setting up media objectives
    b) Strategy development and implementation
    c) Situational analysis
    d) Evaluation and follow-up

40. In media planning, what is the purpose of setting up media objectives?
    a) To evaluate the effectiveness of the media plan
    b) To synchronize all contributing elements
    c) To create a positive brand image
    d) To identify the target audience

41. How can media and audio-visual aids encourage farmers to adopt new technologies?
    a) By providing classroom teaching and textbooks
    b) By replacing traditional media sources
    c) By creating awareness about development programs
    d) By reducing the coverage of media target clients

42. Which phase in the media plan considers factors such as media mix, target group, and geographic coverage?
    a) Situational analysis
    b) Setting up of media objectives
    c) Strategy development and implementation
    d) Evaluation and follow-up

43. What is the primary purpose of a media mix in media planning?
    a) To evaluate the effectiveness of the media plan
    b) To identify the target audience
    c) To synchronize all contributing elements
    d) To achieve extension objectives through a combination of communication and media channels

44. What is the definition of performance appraisal?
    a) Evaluating a teacher's performance based on student feedback
    b) Identifying and measuring an individual's performance in line with organizational goals
    c) Conducting regular classroom observations without providing feedback
    d) Assessing a teacher's academic qualifications

45. What is the purpose of the Teacher Performance Appraisal (TPA)?
    a) To provide feedback to students about their teachers' performance
    b) To guide effective teaching practices throughout a teacher's career
    c) To replace pre-service teacher education programs
    d) To solely hold teachers accountable for their performance

46. Which of the following is a key component of the performance appraisal process for teachers?
    a) College Development Plan
    b) Budget Allocation
    c) Yearly Plans
    d) Payroll Management

47. What should instructional technology do in the context of teaching and learning?
    a) Supplement the instruction
    b) Replace traditional teaching methods
    c) Act as a substitute for student records
    d) Manage payroll and finance

48. What is the primary focus of the phase "Reflection and goal setting" in effective performance appraisal?
    a) Identifying the domain of teacher performance
    b) Measuring performance against identified competencies
    c) Setting measurable goals related to performance and development
    d) Conducting formal and informal feedback sessions

49. Which phase of the teacher performance appraisal involves access to professional learning to support teachers in achieving their goals?
    a) Reflection and goal setting
    b) Professional learning and practice
    c) Feedback and review
    d) Initial planning meeting

50. What does research suggest about the effects of technology-based instructional methods on students' learning?
    a) Students perform equally well with different instructional techniques
    b) Multimedia-based classes result in significantly higher final examination scores
    c) Technology has no impact on students' perceptions of their courses
    d) Students' attitudes toward instruction become less favorable with technology

51. How do students perceive the use of multimedia materials in comparison to other teaching resources?
    a) Multimedia materials are considered the least effective teaching resource
    b) Multimedia materials are perceived as equally effective as traditional methods
    c) Multimedia materials are perceived as the most effective teaching resource
    d) Students have a negative attitude toward using multimedia in their courses

52. What is a negative impact of social media on education?
    a) Improved student motivation and engagement
    b) Easy access to reliable information and resources
    c) Reduced reliance on technology for communication
    d) Addiction leading to reduced focus on studies and real-life communication

53. How does social media affect students' ability to communicate effectively in person?
    a) Social media improves face-to-face communication skills
    b) Social media provides students with more non-verbal cues for communication
    c) Students who use social media are better at multitasking in person
    d) Spending more time on social media reduces students' face-to-face communication skills

54. What are the three phases of communication research in India?
    a) Radio broadcasting, family planning, and education
    b) Planned development, family planning, and television networks
    c) Print media, family planning, and satellite technology
    d) Communication studies, television networks, and audio cassettes

55. What is the Bandwagon approach in communication research?
    a) Focusing on medium rather than messages
    b) Neglecting program areas in research
    c) Lack of methodological innovations
    d) Scrambling from one field of study to another

56. What has been neglected in studies associated with mass media?
    a) Potential of a medium
    b) Messages conveyed
    c) Social situation
    d) Indigenous communication system

57. What is the immediate feedback in programmed instruction?
    a) Group discussions with peers
    b) Response from the teacher
    c) Testing the utility of models
    d) Knowledge of results after answering a question

58. What is one advantage of programmed instruction?
    a) Large chunks of information are learned at once.
    b) The teacher is actively involved in the learning process.
    c) Data emerging from research are utilized efficiently.
    d) Students are continuously active and engaged in learning.

59. What is team-teaching?
    a) Instruction by a single teacher with the help of technology
    b) Instruction by multiple teachers working together as a group
    c) Individualized instruction using computer-assisted learning
    d) Instruction by a teacher with the assistance of a teaching aide

60. How is the college day divided in the modules system?
    a) 20 minutes time blocks called "mods"
    b) 50-minute periods for different activities
    c) 5-hour segments with specific subjects
    d) 30-minute intervals for independent work

61 In computer-assisted instruction, how does the student interact with the computer?
    a) By speaking to the computer
    b) By typing on a specially designed electric typewriter
    c) By submitting written assignments to the computer
    d) By answering questions verbally

62. What aspect of computer-assisted instruction allows it to adapt to different student needs?

    a) Time-sharing
    b) Simultaneous instruction
    c) Conversational interaction
    d) Typing speed of the student

63. What should extension workers recognize in instructional methods for farmers?

    a) Experiences of farmers
    b) Theoretical concepts
    c) Overall control of the computer
    d) Adaptability to different needs

64. What is the purpose of programmed instruction?

    a) To provide immediate feedback to the student
    b) To treat all students in an identical way
    c) To allow students to seek free time for individual conference
    d) To present materials in small, simple units for effective learning

65. In which phase of communication research in India was there a tremendous expansion in television and radio networks?

    a) First phase
    b) Second phase
    c) Third phase
    d) Fourth phase

66. What is the main advantage of utilizing computer-assisted instruction?

    a) Teachers can control the computer completely.
    b) All students receive identical instruction.
    c) Immediate feedback is given to the teacher.
    d) Instruction can be adapted to individual needs.

67. What is a major issue in communication research regarding mass media studies?

    a) Lack of understanding of community's communication system
    b) Neglecting program areas in research
    c) Concentration on medium rather than messages
    d) Inadequate assessment of models and theories

68. How are the units of instructional materials presented in programmed instruction?

    a) In large, complex frames
    b) In small, simple frames called "mods"
    c) In hour-long sessions
    d) In group discussions

69. What is the role of the teacher in computer-assisted instruction?

a) The teacher controls the computer.

b) The teacher types out the questions for the student.

c) The teacher provides immediate feedback to the student.

d) The teacher adapts instruction to individual needs.

70. What is the main focus of team-teaching?

a) Utilizing technological equipment in instruction

b) Allowing students to have independent work time

c) Providing immediate feedback to students

d) Teachers working together as a group

71. What is an advantage of utilizing time modules in teaching?

a) It allows for intensive research at the field level.

b) It provides immediate feedback to the student.

c) It enables students to rotate activities.

d) It allows for storage of multiple programs at once.

72. How is computer-assisted instruction similar to human tutoring?

a) It gives immediate feedback to the student.

b) It presents lessons step by step.

c) It provides supplementary instructional material.

d) It requires students to type out answers.

73. What is one reason for the lack of methodological innovations in communication research?

a) Lack of understanding of community's communication system

b) Neglecting program areas in research

c) Insufficient access to mass media

d) Lack of initiative in researches on fundamental issues

14

Leveraging ICT for Knowledge Dissemination in Agricultural Extension

1. What does ICT stand for?
   a) International Communication Technologies
   b) Integrated Computing Technologies
   c) Information and Communication Technologies
   d) Internet and Computer Technologies

2. How have ICTs impacted economies worldwide?
   a) They have restricted access to high-end research and development.
   b) They have made significant improvements in all sectors of the economy.
   c) They have only benefited the service sector.
   d) They have limited efficiency levels in the economy.

3. What does the term ICT include?
   a) Only information technology (IT)
   b) Telecommunication and enterprise software
   c) Unified communications and wireless signals
   d) Telecommunications, computers, and various other components

4. Why is there no universal definition of ICT?
   a) Because it is an outdated technology
   b) Because ICT only includes digital television and email
   c) Because the concepts and applications are constantly evolving
   d) Because ICT is limited to high-end research

5. What does ICT cover in terms of products?
   a) Products that store and manipulate only analog information
   b) Products that store, retrieve, manipulate, transmit, or receive information electronically
   c) Products that store and retrieve information through printed media
   d) Products that transmit and receive information through telecommunication lines

Bold Means Correct Answer

6. What does ICT stand for in the context of agriculture?
   a) Integrated Crop Techniques
   b) Information and Communication Technologies
   c) International Cultivation Tools
   d) Innovative Crop Testing

7. Which of the following is true about ICT in agriculture?
   a) It is limited to high-end research and development.
   b) It has no impact on service sectors in the economy.
   c) It involves the use of unified communications and telecommunications.
   d) It is only used for storage and retrieval of information.

8. What does AgTube refer to in the context of agriculture?
   a) A platform for agricultural research and development staff
   b) A video-sharing platform for general users
   c) A farming community for exchanging best agricultural practices
   d) A digital radio platform for farmers

9. How can mobile phones be used in agriculture?
   a) To provide feedback on extension services
   b) To serve as a substitute for television and radio
   c) To conduct on-farm research experiments
   d) To support commercial agriculture only

10. What is the potential benefit of community radio in agriculture?
    a) It can provide internet-based agricultural services.
    b) It can give voice to marginalized communities in their local languages.
    c) It can replace television as a means of disseminating information.
    d) It can connect farmers directly with potential buyers.

11. What is the primary purpose of computer and Internet use in extension work?
    a) To diagnose farmers' problems and opportunities
    b) To provide specific information needed for change
    c) To facilitate access to credit and inputs
    d) To train farmers in modern farming techniques

12. Which technology is particularly helpful in providing visuals to farmers?
    a) Mobile phones
    b) Radio
    c) Television
    d) Computers

13. What is the additional potential of smart devices compared to simple cell phones in agriculture?
    a) Smart devices have better call and text options.
    b) Smart devices can be used for mobile banking.
    c) Smart devices can access the internet and play videos.
    d) Smart devices have GPS for data collection.

14. How can radio be enhanced in agriculture to provide more information?
    a) By allowing farmers to call in and provide feedback
    b) By integrating videos into the radio programs
    c) By using smart devices instead of traditional radios
    d) By providing interactive programming

15. What is the role of extension function in agriculture?
    a) To demonstrate or train farmers in modern techniques
    b) To inform farmers of available services through one-way communication
    c) To collect and respond to farmer feedback
    d) To facilitate access to credit and inputs

16. Which of the following is NOT an example of new media tools?
    a) Television programs
    b) Internet
    c) Video games
    d) CD-ROMS

17. What is an example of a social media mode where most users are also participants?
    a) Wikipedia
    b) Facebook
    c) Wikitude
    d) CD-ROMS

18 Why do conventional modes of communication for technology transfer not serve the purpose in modern agriculture?
    a) They focus on individual farm-based issues
    b) They are too expensive
    c) They do not use multimedia options
    d) They are only accessible to small farmers

19. What advantage does mobile-based technology advisory have over computer-based systems?
    a) Better reach to remote areas
    b) Faster speed of communication
    c) Lower costs
    d) All of the above

20. What is the key merit of using ICTs in agricultural extension?
    a) Improved reach to international resources
    b) Free access to information What is one of the factors contributing to differences in crop productivity?
    a) Lack of access to credit for investing in new agricultural tools
    b) Excessive rainfall in rural areas
    c) Limited availability of smartphones among farmers
    d) Overuse of fertilizers and pesticides

21. How have mobile phones impacted the productivity of crops in rural areas?
    a) Reduced communication and information costs
    b) Increased dependency on traditional farming methods
    c) Hindered farmers from accessing market information
    d) Limited the use of agricultural apps

22. Farmers directly exchange market information among each other using:
    a) Mobile phones
    b) Landline phones
    c) Fax machines
    d) Pigeon messengers

23. What are some of the knowledge-related constraints faced by rural communities in using ICT tools?
    a) Slow internet speed and poor connectivity
    b) Lack of access to mobile phones
    c) Language barrier and lack of understanding of app usage
    d) Limited access to credit for investing in ICT devices

24. What is one of the content-related constraints in using ICT applications for agriculture?
    a) High cost of smartphones
    b) Difficulty in accessing accurate, timely, and reliable information
    c) Overdependence on social media apps
    d) Lack of interest in agricultural information

25. How can the issue of accessibility be addressed for farmers who do not use smartphones?
    a) Introducing video conferencing services
    b) Providing free smartphones to all farmers
    c) Developing applications that provide information through SMS
    d) Expanding the network coverage in urban areas

26. What is one of the strategies to enhance the use of ICT applications in agriculture?
    a) Encouraging farmers to use smartphones for social purposes only
    b) Creating awareness programs on the potential of mobile phones
    c) Discouraging the use of smartphones among illiterate farmers
    d) Limiting technical training for farmers on app usage

27. What is the core technology used in a video conferencing system?
    a) Mobile networks
    b) Interactive Voice Response (IVR)
    c) Digital compression of audio and video streams
    d) Satellite connections

28. What does KM stand for in the context of knowledge management?
    a) Knowledge Making **b) Knowledge Memorization**
    c) Knowledge Management d) Knowledge Mastery

29 What is the ultimate objective of Agricultural Knowledge, Science, and Technology (AKST) activities?
    a) To increase agricultural taxes
    b) To develop new smartphones for farmers
    c) To increase production and conserve the environment
    d) To reduce the use of mobile phones in agriculture

30. What is the purpose of building a National Agriculture Research Information System (NARIS)?
    a) To promote international agricultural research only
    b) To document indigenous agricultural practices
    c) To encourage the use of traditional farming methods
    d) To eliminate the need for extension documents

31. How can the digital divide be overcome in agriculture?
    a) By providing smartphones to all farmers
    b) By training farmers and extension workers in ICT
    c) By eliminating the use of video conferencing
    d) By reducing the number of research papers published internationally

32. What technology is needed to make national and regional agricultural information systems available globally?
    a) Satellite connections
    b) Telephones with video capability
    c) Internet and Web technology
    d) Interactive Voice Response (IVR) systems

33. What does information represent in the hierarchy of data, information, knowledge, and wisdom?
    a) A collection of data
    b) A collection of knowledge
    c) A collection of wisdom
    d) A collection of principles

34. What is the primary objective of knowledge management in an organization?
    a) To ensure that all employees are well-trained
    b) To transform information into enduring value
    c) To encourage employees to memorize facts
    d) To eliminate the need for sharing information

35. What is the role of video conferencing in agriculture?
    a) To replace face-to-face meetings between farmers
    b) To provide access to the Internet in rural areas
    c) To create a national agriculture research information system
    d) To enable communication between multiple locations simultaneously

36. How does knowledge differ from information in terms of context and meaning?
    a) Knowledge is more linear in nature, while information is self-contextualizing
    b) Knowledge lacks meaning without context, while information is always meaningful
    c) Knowledge is without reference to space or time, while information is static
    d) Knowledge is based on data relationships, while information is based on principles

37. What should be done to manage indigenous agricultural practices for sustainable development?

    a) Develop an information system and record matured technologies

    b) Eliminate the use of digital networks in agriculture

    c) Promote the use of smartphones among farmers

    d) Increase the digital divide in rural areas

    c) Instant access to important resources AI

38. How does the use of mobile phones benefit farmers in acquiring information?

    a) Reduces transaction cost

    b) Provides information at their fields

    c) Improves market connectivity

    d) All of the above

39. What do new media tools have in common?

    a) They are digital   b) They are interactive

    c) They are manipulated   **d) All of the above**

40. What is an example of an application developed specifically for small wireless computing devices?

    a) Internet   b) CD-ROMS

    c) Mobile app   d) Television programs

41. How does ICT enhance access to information for extension personnel?

    a) Through on-line expert systems

    b) Through e-mails and chat groups

    c) Through multimedia options

    d) All of the above

42. What is the main advantage of using ICTs for communication in agriculture?

    a) Reduced information distortion

    b) Access to global information

    c) Lower communication costs

    d) Improved lab-to-market connections

43. Which type of network is used for communicating among computer devices within an office building or home?

    a) Metropolitan Area Network (MAN)

    b) Wide Area Network (WAN)

    c) Local Area Network (LAN)

    d) Personal Area Network (PAN)

44. What is the main advantage of a LAN?

    a) High speed

    b) Large geographical coverage

    c) Low cost

    d) Multiple access points

45. Which network spans a city or a large campus and allows sharing of regional resources?

    a) Wide Area Network (WAN)

    b) Metropolitan Area Network (MAN)

    c) Personal Area Network (PAN)

    d) Local Area Network (LAN)

46. Which type of network covers a large geographic area, such as a country or continent?

    a) Personal Area Network (PAN)

    b) Local Area Network (LAN)

    c) Wide Area Network (WAN)

    d) Metropolitan Area Network (MAN)

47. Which network allows communication among computer devices in close proximity, typically within a room?

    a) Wide Area Network (WAN)

    b) Personal Area Network (PAN)

    c) Metropolitan Area Network (MAN)

    d) Local Area Network (LAN)

48. What technology is used for wireless local area networking with devices based on IEEE 802.11 standards?

    a) Wi-Fi

    b) Wi-MAX

    c) MAN

    d) WSN

49. Which network technology is used to provide internet access within a range connected to a wireless network?
    a) Wi-Fi
    b) Wi-MAX
    c) MAN
    d) WSN

50. What does the term Wi-Fi certified refer to?
    a) Devices connected to the Internet
    b) Devices using IEEE 802.11 standards
    c) Devices connected to a wireless network
    d) Devices with successful interoperability certification testing

51. What family of wireless communication standards provides multiple physical layer and Media Access Control (MAC options?
    a) Wi-Fi
    b) Wi-MAX
    c) PAN
    d) LAN

52. Which type of network technology is promising for issues like soil management, pest management, and precision agriculture?
    a) Wi-MAX
    b) WSN
    c) LAN
    d) MAN

53. What is the purpose of K-Seva?
    a) To integrate services with the existing national Kisan SMS Portal
    b) To provide pre-recorded voice responses to callers
    c) To interact with users on social networking platforms
    d) To broadcast short messages to friends

54. How does the Department/Organization register for K-Seva?
    a) Through a designated officer on the website http://mkisan.gov.in/ksewa/registrationForm.aspx
    b) Through the head of the department or organization
    c) By sending an email to the K-Seva administrator
    d) By white-listing the server

55. What is the purpose of the Authentication Code for Integration in K-Seva?
    a) To access the "How to Integrate" tab
    b) To log in to the service
    c) To link the service with the Kisan SMS Portal
    d) To approve the registration request

56. What is the main function of the Interactive Voice Response System (IVRS)?
    a) To broadcast short messages to friends
    b) To provide pre-recorded voice responses to callers
    c) To integrate services with the Kisan SMS Portal
    d) To gather information and route calls to the appropriate recipient

57. How can farmers give feedback through the IVRS for the services provided?
    a) By calling the feedback number (022-67870177)
    b) By sending SMS messages to the Kisan SMS Portal
    c) By interacting with users on social networking platforms
    d) By accessing the "How to Integrate" tab

58. What is the purpose of Social Networking Tools in agriculture?
    a) To broadcast short messages to friends
    b) To provide pre-recorded voice responses to callers
    c) To interact with users on social networking platforms
    d) To integrate services with the Kisan SMS Portal

59. Which social networking platform allows users to broadcast short messages to their friends or followers?
    a) Facebook
    b) Twitter
    c) Blogger
    d) YouTube

60. What is the main function of YouTube in social networking?
    a) To broadcast short messages to friends
    b) To interact with users in new ways
    c) To share videos with millions of other users
    d) To maintain blogs with regular entries

61. What is the distinguishing feature of blogs that differentiates them from other static websites?
    a) They allow visitors to leave comments
    b) They enable users to send and receive SMS messages
    c) They provide pre-recorded voice responses to callers
    d) They integrate services with the Kisan SMS Portal

62. What is the purpose of Short Message Services (SMS)?
   a) To broadcast short messages to friends
   b) To provide pre-recorded voice responses to callers
   c) To interact with users on social networking platforms
   d) To send and receive text messages

63. What is the main objective of the Farm Crop Management System in AGRISNET?
   a) To provide pre-recorded voice responses to farmers
   b) To bring the Second Green Revolution using Information Technology
   c) To maintain a record of benefits provided to farmers
   d) To provide farm machineries on rental to small farmers

64. What is the purpose of the Scheme Benefits Tracking Module in AGRISNET?
   a) To provide pre-recorded voice responses to farmers
   b) To maintain a record of benefits provided to farmers
   c) To monitor and upload photographs of capital assets
   d) To provide farm machineries on rental to small farmers

65. What is the purpose of the Online Hiring System of Farm Machineries in AGRISNET?
   a) To bring the Second Green Revolution using Information Technology
   b) To maintain a record of benefits provided to farmers
   c) To provide pre-recorded voice responses to farmers
   d) To provide farm machineries on rental to small farmers

66. What is the key component that distinguishes GIS from other information systems?
   a) Hardware
   b) Software
   c) Data
   d) Spatial analysis functions

67. What is the main purpose of Agricultural Decision Support Systems (AgriDSS)?
   a) To provide pre-recorded voice responses to farmers
   b) To bring the Second Green Revolution using Information Technology
   c) To help farmers tackle complex problems in crop production
   d) To provide farm machineries on rental to small farmers

68. Remote sensing is used in agriculture for:
    a) Photography
    b) Surveying
    c) Geology
    d) Crop production forecasting

69. What does remote sensing technology help determine in the event of crop damage?
    a) Soil moisture content
    b) Crop health analysis
    c) Crop yield forecasting
    d) Progress of the remaining crop

70. Remote sensing plays a vital role in identifying:
    a) Water resources
    b) Horticulture patterns
    c) Crop nutrient deficiency
    d) Land cover mapping

71. Which of the following is NOT an application of remote sensing in agriculture?
    a) Determination of water content of field crops What are the advantages of using IoTs in agriculture?
    a) Increased cost
    b) Limited resource allocation
    c) Reduced water usage
    d) Decreased yield

72. Which of the following is NOT a category of popular applications of AI in agriculture?
    a) Agricultural robots
    b) Crop and soil monitoring
    c) Predictive analytics
    d) Timing plantings

73. What does AI enable farmers to easily visualize and take action on?
    a) Water usage data
    b) Crop and soil health
    c) Pest and disease outbreaks
    d) Market conditions for inputs and outputs

74. Why is there a need for credit support and policy environment for IoT adoption in agriculture?
    a) To invest in high-end technology solutions
    b) To focus on subsistence farming
    c) To reduce water wastage
    d) To switch to smart farming

75. What is the main objective of the Farm Crop Management System using IoT?
    - **a) Bringing Second Green Revolution**
    - b) Automating on-farm activities
    - c) Identifying pests and disease outbreaks
    - d) Predicting crop yields based on climate data

76. How can IoT help in agriculture?
    - a) By increasing soil fertility
    - **b) By automating on-farm activities**
    - c) By decreasing fertilizer usage
    - d) By reducing the cost of inputs

77. Which application of IoT involves monitoring crop and soil health using drones and/or software-based technology?
    - a) Water resources mapping
    - b) Crop acreage estimation
    - **c) Crop and soil monitoring**
    - d) Irrigation monitoring and management

78. What does AI enable in agriculture?
    - a) Improved crop yield
    - b) Efficient usage of inputs
    - c) Reduced costs
    - **d) Predictive analysis of crop yield**

79. Which technology plays an important role in determining the water content of field crops?
    - a) Internet of Things (IoTs)
    - **b) Remote sensing**
    - c) Artificial intelligence (AI)
    - d) Precision farming

80. What can AI do in agriculture with the help of historical data and climate information?
    - a) Predict market conditions
    - b) Automate farming tasks
    - c) Monitor crop and soil health
    - **d) Track and predict crop yield impacts**

81. Remote sensing technology is important in monitoring:

a) Weather patterns
b) Soil management practices
c) Compliance of farmers
d) Water resources mapping

82. Remote sensing helps in mapping out the areas that are likely to be hit by:

a) Crop damage
b) Pests infestation
c) Floods
d) Droughts

83. What does remote sensing technology assist in determining for precision farming?

a) Crop yield modeling
b) Soil mapping
c) Water content in field crops
d) Cropping patterns

84. Remote sensing is used to identify problematic soils that have difficulty in:

a) Yield estimation
b) Drainage
c) Crop identification
d) Soil moisture estimation

85. Which application of remote sensing is related to determining the overall expected yield of a crop?

a) Crop acreage estimation
b) Crop health analysis
c) Reflectance modeling
d) Crop yield modelling and estimation

15

Reporting and Journalism in the Agricultural Domain

1. What is one of the main objectives of extension education in agriculture?
   a) Crop yield prediction
   b) Knowledge sharing
   c) Radio and television production
   d) Farm magazine printing

2. What role does agricultural journalism play in agricultural communication?
   a) Printing and dissemination of extension literature
   b) Conducting Intensive Agricultural District Programme (IADP)
   c) Transmitting farm messages through mass media
   d) Establishing Package Press in agriculture departments

3. Who are the contributors of agricultural articles in media?
   a) Extension personnel and farmers
   b) Scientists and researchers only
   c) Farm reporters and journalists
   d) Only farmers with extensive experience

4. What knowledge is essential for agricultural communicators involved in media reporting?
   a) Technical farming skills
   b) Knowledge of journalism
   c) Radio and television production
   d) Printing and dissemination techniques

5. What is the aim of the chapter that explores the historical background of new journalistic ventures?
   a) Understanding media reporting techniques
   b) Highlighting the importance of radio and television programmes
   c) Discussing current agricultural practices
   d) Providing basic knowledge of extension education

Bold Means Correct Answer

6. What is the primary function of journalism?
   a) Entertainment
   b) Shaping public opinion
   c) Informing the public
   d) Advocacy for government policies

7. Which theory of journalism advocates that journalists should seek truth and monitor the government's activities independently?
   a) Authoritarian theory
   b) Libertarian theory
   c) Social responsibility theory
   d) Soviet Communist theory

8. According to the social responsibility theory, what are the responsibilities of reporters?
   a) Serving the political system and promoting advertisements
   b) Being propagandists and agitators for the government
   c) Providing factual reporting and being neutral observers
   d) Encouraging public debate and protecting individual rights

9. What is the main idea behind the democratic elite theory?
   a) Democracy is best served by highly educated elites and specialized technicians.
   b) The press should create a domination-free environment for public debate.
   c) Journalists should promote grassroots citizen movements through diverse viewpoints.
   d) Journalists should operate only under government protection and censorship.

10. Which theory emphasizes promoting reasoned and civil public debate among ordinary citizens?
   a) Democratic participatory theory
   b) Public sphere theory
   c) Development theory
   d) Social responsibility theory

11. Which theory of journalism is associated with the concept of being a "watchdog" against government abuse of power?
   a) Authoritarian theory
   b) Social responsibility theory
   c) Libertarian theory
   d) Soviet Communist theory

12. What is the main idea behind the development theory of journalism?

    a) Promoting grassroots citizen movements

    b) Supporting economic development and nation-building efforts

    c) Fostering a domination-free environment for public debate

    d) Operating as propagandists for the government

13. According to the libertarian theory, what should the state's role be in media?

    a) Full control and censorship

    b) Limited interference and autonomy for journalists

    c) Providing syndicated materials for entertainment

    d) Strict regulation of media content

14. Which theory advocates for the press to examine competing elite perspectives and monitor the activities of powerful social institutions?

    a) Development theory

    b) Public sphere theory

    c) Democratic elite theory

    d) Authoritarian theory

15. What is the main objective of the public sphere theory in journalism?

    a) Promoting reasoned and civil public debate

    b) Supporting economic development in impoverished societies

    c) Advocating for government policies and programs

    d) Creating a domination-free environment for media coverage

16. What is agricultural journalism?

    a) Journalism that focuses on issues related to agriculture

    b) Journalism about fashion and lifestyle

    c) Journalism that covers international news

    d) Journalism that deals with sports and entertainment

17. How is the training of agriculture journalists different from traditional journalists?

    a) Agriculture journalists focus on politics and current affairs.

    b) Agriculture journalists understand agricultural systems.

    c) Agriculture journalists work only for advertising firms.

    d) Agriculture journalists cover entertainment and celebrity news.

18. What are the career options for those with a course in agriculture journalism?
    a) Becoming a chef in a renowned restaurant
    b) Working as a software developer in a tech company
    c) Becoming an agricultural client for advertising firms
    d) Pursuing a career in law or medicine

19. What type of organizations and businesses might require the services of agricultural journalists?
    a) Fashion and beauty companies
    b) Agricultural commodity organizations and businesses
    c) IT and software companies
    d) Automotive and manufacturing industries

20. Which universities in India offer courses in agricultural journalism?
    a) Only IARI, New Delhi
    b) Only GBPUAT, Pant Nagar, Uttarakhand
    c) Only PAU, Ludhiana
    d) Several agricultural universities in India

21. What is the main purpose of farm journalism?
    a) To promote agricultural products
    b) To entertain farmers with music and movies
    c) To provide timely reporting and editing of farm-related information
    d) To create advertisements for agricultural businesses

22. Which was the first farm periodical published in India?
    a) KrishiJagat b) Gaon
    c) KrishiSudhar (Hindi) d) Kheti

23. When was the periodical 'Krishi' published from Agra?
    a) 1914 **b) 1918**
    c) 1946 d) 1953

24. What were some of the outstanding farm periodicals during the pre-Independence period?
    a) Agriculture and Livestock, Journal of Animal Science, and Gaon
    b) KrishiSudhar and Sevagram
    c) KrishiJagat and Basundhara
    d) Kheti and Krishi

25. Which organization ventured into publishing the farm monthly 'Kheti' in Hindi in May 1947?

a) Indian Council of Agricultural Research (ICAR)

b) Directorate of Extension

c) Ministry of Agriculture and Farmers' Welfare

d) Farm Information Unit

26. What type of media does farm journalism primarily focus on?

a) Radio and television

b) Newspapers and magazines

c) Social media platforms

d) Music and movies

27. Why do farmers, extension workers, and Panchayat officials need farm journalism?

a) To promote entertainment events in rural areas

b) To share gossip and rumors

c) To access timely information for their work

d) To report on political developments

28. Which government department started publishing farm periodicals in 1931?

a) Ministry of Agriculture and Farmers' Welfare

b) Indian Council of Agricultural Research

c) Directorate of Extension

d) Ministry of Rural Development

29. What was the result of a survey conducted in 1972 regarding farm magazines in India?

a) Fifty farm magazines were published in various languages

b) One hundred farm magazines were published in various languages

c) Two hundred farm magazines were published in various languages

d) Five hundred farm magazines were published in various languages

30. How does farm journalism contribute to the agricultural community?

a) By promoting advertising for agricultural products

b) By providing entertainment to farmers

c) By supplying essential information through periodicals and magazines

d) By focusing on political news and controversies

31. What is one of the problems faced in farm journalism?
    a) Lack of interest in agricultural news
    b) Overemphasis on economic news related to farming
    c) Paucity of skilled science writers
    d) Excessive coverage of agricultural content in newspapers

32. Why do farm journalists lack adequate knowledge about farming and farmers?
    a) They are not interested in agriculture-related issues
    b) They focus more on economic news than new technology in farming
    c) They are not given specialized training in agriculture journalism
    d) They are not exposed to the problems faced by the farming community

33. What is a challenge faced by farm journalists when covering agriculture news?
    a) Lack of interest from the farming community
    b) Difficulty in exploring cases from villages
    c) Overemphasis on crime and politics in media
    d) Inadequate knowledge about farm technologies

34. Why do journalists shy away from covering agriculture news?
    a) Lack of specialized training in agriculture journalism
    b) Farming is not considered important by the media
    c) Farming news is always positive and lacks controversy
    d) Journalists prefer covering sports and entertainment news

35. What is one reason for low coverage of agriculture news in the media?
    a) Lack of interest from the farming community
    b) Farming news is not considered newsworthy
    c) Journalists are not interested in covering agriculture
    d) Lack of skilled science writers in the media

36. What is one problem faced by farm journalists in writing news stories and feature articles?
    a) Inadequate knowledge about farming and farmers
    b) Excessive coverage of agricultural content in newspapers
    c) Lack of interest from the media in agriculture news
    d) Lack of training in media skills

37. What is one aspect of farm journalism that needs improvement?
    a) Coverage of sports and crime news
    b) Training of journalists in specialized agricultural reporting
    c) Focus on economic news related to farming
    d) Relegation of agricultural news to the background

38. What is one consequence of low priority to agricultural news?
    a) Lack of skilled science writers in the media
    b) Excessive coverage of farming funds in the media
    c) Lack of interest in agricultural journalism
    d) Inadequate knowledge about farming among journalists

39. What is one of the problems faced in farm journalism?
    a) Lack of interest in agricultural news
    b) Overemphasis on economic news related to farming
    c) Paucity of skilled science writers
    d) Excessive coverage of agricultural content in newspapers

40. Why do farm journalists lack adequate knowledge about farming and farmers?
    a) They are not interested in agriculture-related issues
    b) They focus more on economic news than new technology in farming
    c) They are not given specialized training in agriculture journalism
    d) They are not exposed to the problems faced by the farming community

41. What is a challenge faced by farm journalists when covering agriculture news?
    a) Lack of interest from the farming community
    b) Difficulty in exploring cases from villages
    c) Overemphasis on crime and politics in media
    d) Inadequate knowledge about farm technologies

42. Why do journalists shy away from covering agriculture news?
    a) Lack of specialized training in agriculture journalism
    b) Farming is not considered important by the media
    c) Farming news is always positive and lacks controversy
    d) Journalists prefer covering sports and entertainment news

43. What is one reason for low coverage of agriculture news in the media?

    a) Lack of interest from the farming community

    b) Farming news is not considered newsworthy

    c) Journalists are not interested in covering agriculture

    d) Lack of skilled science writers in the media

44. What is one problem faced by farm journalists in writing news stories and feature articles?

    a) Inadequate knowledge about farming and farmers

    b) Excessive coverage of agricultural content in newspapers

    c) Lack of interest from the media in agriculture news

    d) Lack of training in media skills

45. What is one aspect of farm journalism that needs improvement?

    a) Coverage of sports and crime news

    b) Training of journalists in specialized agricultural reporting

    c) Focus on economic news related to farming

    d) Relegation of agricultural news to the background

46. What is one consequence of low priority to agricultural news?

    a) Lack of skilled science writers in the media

    b) Excessive coverage of farming funds in the media

    c) Lack of interest in agricultural journalism

    d) Inadequate knowledge about farming among journalists

47. Which skill is essential for a successful journalist?

    a) Speaking ability **b) Writing ability**

    c) Analytical skills d) Technical knowledge

48. Which writing style is suitable for news stories and feature articles?

    a) Impersonal style b) Scholarly style

    c) Technical style **d) Conversational style**

49. What does a good style of writing depend upon?

    a) Author's interests and preferences

    b) Length of the article

    c) Complexity of the subject matter

    d) Availability of reference books

50. Why is it advised to use simple words in writing?
    a) Simple words make the writing look more professional
    b) Simple words are easier to understand for readers
    c) Complex words add variety to the writing
    d) Simple words make the writing more formal

51. How should sentences be structured in writing?
    a) They should be long and complex to provide more information
    b) They should be short and straightforward for clarity
    c) They should include slang expressions for a casual tone
    d) They should be lengthy to impress readers

52. What is the importance of keeping a dictionary handy while writing?
    a) It helps in improving vocabulary
    b) It serves as a reference for spellings and word usage
    c) It provides inspiration for writing ideas
    d) It prevents the use of informal language

53. Why should sentences be clear and unambiguous in writing?
    a) To impress readers with complex language
    b) To add mystery and intrigue to the writing
    c) To avoid annoying the readers
    d) To make the writing sound more academic

54. Which writing approach is suitable for newspaper reports and magazine articles?
    a) Technical and scholarly approach
    b) Conversational and informal approach
    c) Slang and colloquial approach
    d) Formal and impersonal approach

55. What is the purpose of writing simply in journalism?
    a) To impress the readers with complex language
    b) To make the writing sound more academic
    c) To ensure clarity and easy understanding for readers
    d) To maintain a formal tone in the writing

56. Which writing style is similar to talking with readers in journalism?
    a) Scholarly style
    b) Impersonal style
    c) Technical style
    d) Conversational style

57. What is a feature article?
    a) A piece of writing that informs readers with facts
    b) A piece of writing that provides information and entertainment
    c) A piece of writing that reports breaking news
    d) A piece of writing that analyzes current events

58. How does a feature article differ from a news story?
    a) Feature articles are written in a hurry, while news stories are written leisurely.
    b) Feature articles compete for newspaper space, while news stories have a clear structure.
    c) Feature articles entertain readers, while news stories only inform.
    d) Feature articles assume an inverted pyramid structure, while news stories have a clear ending.

59. What is the primary purpose of a process feature in a feature article?
    a) To entertain the readers
    b) To provide biographical information
    c) To inform and educate the readers
    d) To criticize or analyze a subject

60. What type of lead is commonly used in feature articles?
    a) Narrative lead
    b) Inverted pyramid lead
    c) Question lead
    d) Informative lead

61. Why is pre-writing important in writing a feature article?
    a) It helps in finding the right publisher for the article.
    b) It ensures the article is written in a hurry.
    c) It makes the writing process less complicated.
    d) It allows the writer to gather supporting information.

62. What are the two or three essential types of feature articles?
    a) Biographic and analytical features
    b) Process and informational features
    c) Narrative and interview features
    d) Utility and biographic features

63. What is the primary difference between a news lead and a feature lead?
   a) News leads are interesting, while feature leads are monotonous.
   b) News leads provide background information, while feature leads summarize the story.
   c) News leads are written leisurely, while feature leads are written in a hurry.
   d) News leads have a clear structure, while feature leads are unpredictable.

64. What is the purpose of leaving the article for a day or two before revising it?
   a) To gather more facts and information
   b) To ensure the article is entertaining enough
   c) To allow the writer to work on other projects
   d) To read the article with fresh eyes during revisions

65. What should be the main focus when organizing key points in a feature article?
   a) Chronological order
   b) Order of priority and supporting the main point
   c) Reverse order
   d) Alphabetical order

66. What is the last step in writing a feature article before submitting it to the editor?
   a) Gathering facts and information
   b) Writing a compelling lead
   c) Rewriting or retyping the whole draft
   d) Sending it for peer review

67. What is the primary purpose of approaching agricultural scientists and researchers for a farm journalist?
   a) To get opinions on current events
   b) To gather reliable and accurate information for news stories
   c) To learn about local customs and traditions
   d) To promote sales of agricultural inputs

63. Why is it essential for a journalist to develop contacts with reliable sources?
   a) To promote sales of agricultural inputs
   b) To have a wider social circle
   c) To bring stories into the office on their own initiative
   d) To gather gossip and rumors for articles

69. What can farm journalists gain from regular visits to agricultural research stations and agricultural colleges?
    a) Sales promotions for agricultural inputs
    b) Accurate information for success stories
    c) Inspiration for writing fiction
    d) Contacts with marketing and sales promotion staff

70. What is the primary focus when writing a success story?
    a) Highlighting problems and issues in agriculture
    b) Describing the positive impact of an extension intervention
    c) Focusing on the research design and sampling process
    d) Analyzing the financial success of farmers

71. How does the Cloze Procedure differ from other readability measurements?
    a) It measures the ease of understanding due to the style of writing
    b) It uses mechanical characters like words per sentence and syllables per hundred words.
    c) It measures the ability of a reader to fill in the blanks in a piece of writing.
    d) It gives a score of reading ease based on average sentence length and polysyllable count.

72. What is the main purpose of using a readability formula in writing?
    a) To measure the length of a piece of writing
    b) To determine the interest value of a piece of writing
    c) To assess the ease of understanding or comprehension of a piece of writing
    d) To evaluate the legibility of handwriting or typography

73. What part of a success story is considered the most crucial?
    a) Situation
    b) Intervention
    c) Results
    d) Evidences

74. What writing style is preferred for success stories?
    a) Narrative and descriptive
    b) Conversational and humorous
    c) Analytical and technical
    d) Objective and factual

75. Why should a farm journalist write in the local mother tongue of the farmers?

   a) To show off their language skills

   b) To entertain readers during leisure time

   c) To ensure their articles are read and understood by the farmers

   d) To avoid making mistakes in spelling and grammar

76. How can farm journalists ensure their articles have a clear structure?

   a) By using an inverted pyramid style

   b) By including personal opinions and anecdotes

   c) By writing in a hurry to meet deadlines

   d) By including a lead, body, and ending in their feature articles

77. What does the Gunning Fog Index measure?

   a) The complexity of a piece of writing

   b) The number of words in a piece of writing

   c) The readability of a piece of writing

   d) The length of sentences in a piece of writing

78. How is the Gunning Fog Index typically presented?

   a) A score between 0 and 20

   b) A grade level required to understand the text

   c) A percentage indicating readability

   d) A count of complex words in the text

79. What does a Gunning Fog Index score of 6 mean?

   a) The text is suitable for 6th-grade students

   b) The text is suitable for graduate-level readers

   c) The text is suitable for general public readers

   d) The text is suitable for 17-year-old readers

80. What does the Gunning Fog Index formula consider as complex words?

   a) Words with five or more syllables

   b) Words with four or more syllables

   c) Words with three or more syllables

   d) Words with two or more syllables

81. Who developed the Gunning Fog Index?
    a) Robert Flesch
    b) Robert Gunning
    c) Robert Associates
    d) Robert Fog

82. What was the aim of Robert Gunning Associates when developing the Gunning Fog Index?
    a) To help businesses improve their marketing strategies
    b) To create a test of writing complexity for authors
    c) To identify and clear writing complexity or "fog"
    d) To improve the readability of newspapers

83. What age group of readers should a text with a Gunning Fog Index score of 8 be suitable for?
    a) Children aged 8
    b) College students
    c) General public readers
    d) Graduates

84. How does the Gunning Fog Index compare to other readability formulae?
    a) It provides more accurate measurements
    b) It is more complex to calculate
    c) It is easier and simpler to calculate
    d) It gives a percentage score instead of a grade level

85. What does the Gunning Fog Index help writers to identify and clear in their writing?
    a) Spelling mistakes
    b) Sentence length issues
    c) Complex words
    d) Readability "fog"

86. What is photojournalism?
    a) Communicating through pictures and photos
    b) Writing news stories with a lot of pictures
    c) Using symbols and icons to tell a story
    d) Creating illustrations for farm magazines

87. Why do editors prefer using photos in news stories?
    a) Photos are cheaper than hiring a reporter
    b) Photos can replace lengthy write-ups
    c) Photos attract more advertisers
    d) Photos make the story more complex

88. What is the significance of the phrase "A picture is worth a thousand words" in photojournalism?
   a) Photos are easier to understand than words
   b) Photos can replace the need for words in a story
   c) Photos are cheaper to produce than words
   d) Photos can be misleading in a story

89. How do pictures contribute to the storytelling process in photojournalism?
   a) Pictures attract illiterate readers
   b) Pictures brighten up the story and make it realistic
   c) Pictures are easier to produce than written stories
   d) Pictures are just symbols and not useful for storytelling

90. What makes photographs preferred illustrations for farm magazines?
   a) They are more appealing to readers
   b) They are cheaper than hiring a professional photographer
   c) They can be used as substitutes for formal education
   d) They can replace the need for radio journalism

91. Why is radio considered a powerful medium of communication in Indian rural settings?
   a) It is the cheapest medium of communication
   b) It reaches a vast audience in rural areas
   c) It provides formal education to farmers
   d) It replaces the need for extension workers

92. What is one of the latent functions performed by radio journalism in rural areas?
   a) It encourages farmers to become journalists
   b) It enables communities to critically examine issues affecting their lives
   c) It provides a substitute for formal education
   d) It replaces the need for agricultural research

93. What role can radio play in disseminating agricultural research?
   a) It can be a substitute for formal education
   b) It can serve as a link between research and extension workers
   c) It can replace the need for academic institutions
   d) It can be used to collect feedback from communities

94. Why is establishing a radio station difficult?
    a) It is expensive and hard to manage
    b) Radio signals are hard to transmit in rural areas
    c) Radio stations are not allowed in rural communities
    d) Radio is not as effective as TV journalism

95. What alternative option can be used if establishing a radio station is difficult?
    a) Hiring more extension workers
    b) Translating messages into foreign languages
    c) Using television for communication
    d) Establishing a community radio

96. What is a key advantage of radio as a medium of communication?
    a) It is more informative than newspapers
    b) It allows for a faster reading pace
    c) It can be enjoyed while doing other activities
    d) It is easier to understand than written content

97. How does writing for radio differ from writing for newspapers?
    a) Radio writing requires shorter scripts
    b) Radio writing should focus on headlines
    c) Radio writing is more formal and structured
    d) Radio writing must suit the medium of broadcasting and be listenable

98. What are the three popular modes of presentation on radio?
    a) News, articles, and interviews
    b) Talk show, interviews, and features
    c) Straight talk, interview, and feature or dramatic presentation
    d) Drama, music, and talk show

99. What is a key guideline for writing interviews for radio?
    a) The interviewer should use technical jargon
    b) The interview should be like a monologue
    c) Speakers should not be introduced with names and designations
    d) The interview should appear like a conversation

100. Why should sentences in radio writing be kept simple and direct?
   a) It makes the script easier to print
   b) It allows for more complex information
   c) It helps the speaker to talk faster
   d) It ensures clear understanding by the listener

101. What is the main objective of radio talks on serious science topics?
   a) To give brief information in a boring manner
   b) To cover as many topics as possible in one presentation
   c) To provide complex scientific explanations
   d) To give brief information clearly and in an interesting manner

102. How should radio presenters use their voice effectively?
   a) Speak in a formal and distant manner
   b) Use unfamiliar words to impress the audience
   c) Make the presentation informal and sincere
   d) Cover many topics in one presentation

103. Why is it important to avoid confusing statistics and numbers in radio writing?
   a) Listeners cannot ask for repetitions
   b) Radio shows have time constraints
   c) The audience prefers narratives over data
   d) Statistics are not relevant in radio writing

104. What is the main difference between a television/video script and a radio script?
   a) Television scripts have more visuals and sound
   b) Radio scripts require more research
   c) Television scripts are longer than radio scripts
   d) Radio scripts focus on visuals shot by shot

105. What is the first step in script writing for television/video?
   a) Gathering all relevant information
   b) Conducting research on the subject
   c) Finalizing the treatment and format
   d) Identifying the location for shooting

106. What is the purpose of carrying out research on the subject for television/ video script?
   - **a) To gather all relevant information and data**
   - b) To decide on the target audience
   - c) To identify the location for shooting
   - d) To consult an expert on the subject

107. What is the role of the story board in video script writing?
   - a) It describes the format and style of the video production
   - b) It presents the educational objectives of the video
   - **c) It gives a shot by shot description of sequences with accompanying sound track**
   - d) It serves as a proposal for the video shooting script

108. What is the final stage in video script writing?
   - a) Gathering all relevant information
   - b) Finalizing the treatment and format
   - c) Writing the proposal for the video shooting script
   - **d) Presenting the video to the audiences**

109. Why is it important for farm journalists to understand both radio, television, and video?
   - a) They need to specialize in all forms of journalism
   - **b) They need to use all potential mass media for educating farmers**
   - c) They need to become experts in electronic journalism
   - d) They need to provide digital information services to farmers

110. What is the role of a consultant in video script writing?
   - a) To finalize the treatment and format of the video
   - b) To conduct research on the subject
   - **c) To provide technical expertise on the subject**
   - d) To write the proposal for the video shooting script

111. What is the purpose of a video shooting script?
   - a) To present the video to the audiences
   - b) To finalize the treatment and format of the video
   - c) To gather all relevant information and data
   - **d) To serve as a detailed plan for video shooting and editing**

112. What is the main purpose of an advertisement?
   a) To promote products and services among the farmers
   b) To create awareness of existence of a product or brand
   c) To provide information about competitive products
   d) To advertise non-profit organizations

113. What is the key characteristic of a good advertisement?
   a) Being entertaining and humorous
   b) Making exaggerated claims about the product
   c) Being truthful, believable, and fair in presenting product's claims
   d) Using complex language to impress the audience

114. Which type of advertisement focuses on promoting the brand image and various products across the country?
   a) National advertising
   b) Retail advertising
   c) Business advertising
   d) Product advertising

115. What is the purpose of a retentive stage advertisement?
   a) To show consumers what the product is and how it works
   b) To remind consumers about the product they are already familiar with
   c) To create awareness about a new product
   d) To introduce consumers to a superior product

116. What is the advantage of personal selling in rural regions?
   a) Proficiency in foreign languages
   b) Good human relations skills and persuasive communication
   c) Use of modern digital platforms for advertising
   d) Familiarity with urban areas and consumers

117. Which type of advertising focuses on promoting social marketing of ideas, practices, and policies?
   a) National advertising
   b) Retail advertising
   c) Non-profit advertising
   d) Industrial advertising

118. What is the main challenge faced in promoting agricultural products in rural areas?
   a) Lack of transport facilities
   b) Lack of advertising agencies
   c) Lack of foreign investment
   d) Lack of proper marketing structures in urban areas

119. What is the primary purpose of an advertisement spiral?
   a) To create a desirable response in the receiver
   b) To adapt marketing efforts over time as consumers become familiar with the product
   c) To change the advertising campaign based on consumer feedback
   d) To launch a new product to multiple audiences simultaneously

120. What is the primary purpose of a layout in graphic design?
   a) To use as many colors as possible to make the design vibrant
   b) To make reading easy and appealing for the audience
   c) To include as many illustrations and photographs as possible
   d) To use various font styles to create an interesting format

121. Which of the following visual elements is NOT included in a layout?
   a) Illustration
   b) Typography
   c) Shape
   d) Audio elements

122. Why is the choice of typeface important in a layout design?
   a) It affects the overall cost of printing the layout
   b) It can influence the message's impact and readability
   c) It determines the size of the layout
   d) It affects the printing quality of the layout

123. Which of the following is true about serif and sans serif fonts?
   a) Sans serif fonts are difficult to read, while serif fonts are easy on the eye.
   b) Serif fonts are uniformly thick and easy to read.
   c) Arial is an example of a serif font, while Times New Roman is a sans serif font.
   d) Upper and lower case letters should always be used instead of all upper case letters.

124. What does "hue" refer to in the context of colors?
   a) The addition of white, greys, and black to a color to get various tints and shades
   b) The saturation of a color, either rich and vibrant or dull and pale
   c) Any color on the color spectrum
   d) The four basic colors of printing: cyan, yellow, magenta, and black (CYMK)

125. How can leaving open unused space (blank space) benefit a layout design?
   a) It makes the design vibrant and lively
   b) It provides relief to the layout and highlights the clarity of visual elements
   c) It allows for more illustrations and photographs to be included
   d) It reduces the cost of printing the layout

126. Which type of color scheme involves using colors that are close to each other on the color wheel?
   a) Contrast color scheme
   b) Adjacent color scheme
   c) Complementary color scheme
   d) Monochromatic color scheme

127. Why does a wise designer spend more time in planning and visualizing a layout?
   a) To save time in the actual design process
   b) To create a more complex and elaborate layout
   c) To ensure the layout is appealing to the eye
   d) To make the final finished layout easier and more effective

128. Which field does agricultural journalism primarily form a part of?
   a) Agricultural research
   b) Agricultural communication and mass media
   c) Farming techniques
   d) Agricultural development

129. Who were among the first individuals to conduct research studies in agricultural journalism?
   a) Agricultural researchers
   b) Farm magazine editors and publishers
   c) Agricultural extension communicators
   d) Social researchers

130. What is the purpose of the readership survey in agricultural journalism research?
   a) To understand the preferences of agricultural researchers
   b) To evaluate the effectiveness of farm magazines
   c) To assess the impact of agricultural policies on farmers
   d) To identify the readers and their preferences for farm magazines

131. What does the readership survey provide in terms of research data?
    a) Feedback responses from readers
    b) Effectiveness of farm magazines
    c) Readership scores for articles
    d) Development reporting criteria

132. What were the researchable issues identified in emerging areas of agricultural journalism?
    a) Effectiveness of agricultural policies
    b) Coverage of space and time in mainstream media
    c) Media literacy for agricultural information
    d) Writing skills for development reporting

133. Which group of individuals are identified as a new set of clients for agricultural information?
    a) Agricultural researchers
    b) Freelance farmers
    c) Urban enthusiasts
    d) Social researchers

134. What are the research questions asked by farm magazine editors and publishers to understand their readers?
    a) Who are my subscribers?
    b) How to improve agricultural practices?
    c) What are the latest farming techniques?
    d) How to increase agricultural production?

135. What is the main purpose of content analysis in agricultural journalism research?
    a) To assess the effectiveness of farm magazines
    b) To analyze the content of mainstream media
    c) To evaluate the ecological impact of farming practices
    d) To assess whether content in farm magazines is harmonious and socially responsible

136. Which group of farmers are identified as a new client for agricultural information?
    a) Peri-urban agriculturists
    b) Retired farmers
    c) Agricultural researchers
    d) Mainstream media journalists

137. What type of training programs are needed for farm journalists?
   a) Agricultural research training
   b) Skill-oriented training programs
   c) Farming techniques training
   d) Media production training

138. What is the focus of the studies on message treatment for farmers?
   a) Writing skills for development reporting
   b) Coverage of space and time in agricultural journalism
   c) Media production and dissemination studies
   d) Effectiveness of farm magazines

139. What type of farmers are looking for value addition and agro-processing enterprises?
   a) Freelance farmers
   b) Young organic farmers
   c) Urban enthusiasts
   d) Peri-urban agriculturists

140. Which principle of agricultural journalism research involves assessing whether content is personally empowering and humanistic?
   a) Coverage of space and time
   b) Content analysis
   c) Understanding media literacy
   d) Writing skills for development reporting

141. What is the research focus for understanding information needs of stakeholders in agriculture?
   a) Media literacy for agricultural information
   b) Message treatment for farmers
   c) Coverage of farm content in local newspapers
   d) Media production and dissemination studies

142. What is the primary goal of agricultural journalism research in relation to emerging clients for agricultural information?
   a) Identifying freelance farmers
   b) Analyzing the content of farm magazines
   c) Addressing the needs of new agricultural information seekers
   d) Developing textual and format criteria for an effective farm magazine

143. What is the purpose of studying media production and dissemination in agricultural journalism?

a) To improve writing skills for development reporting

b) To understand media literacy for agricultural information

c) To identify new clients for agricultural information

d) To assess the effectiveness of farm magazines

144. What is the primary goal of research studies in agricultural journalism according to the text?

a) To improve agricultural practices

b) To evaluate farm journals

c) To understand the preferences of agricultural researchers

d) To assess the ecological impact of farming practices

145. What type of research questions were asked by farm magazine editors and publishers?

a) Content analysis questions

b) Research questions about experimental stations

c) Feedback questions from readers

d) Questions about agricultural policies

146. What is the importance of readership scores in agricultural journalism research?

a) To assess the effectiveness of agricultural policies

b) To evaluate the readership patterns of farm magazines

c) To analyze the writing skills of farm journalists

d) To understand the ecological impact of farming practices

147. What is the primary purpose of research in agricultural journalism?

a) To assess the effectiveness of mainstream media

b) To evaluate the ecological impact of farming practices

c) To understand the preferences of urban enthusiasts

d) To improve agricultural communication and mass media

148. Which step of printing involves page-composition and typesetting?

a) Pre-printing activities

b) Press operations

c) Post-press operations

d) Printing methods

149. What is the measurement unit for the thickness of paper used in printing?

a) Square inch
b) Square foot
c) Grams per square inch (gsm)
d) Kilograms per square inch

150. Which printing method is typically used for multi-color printing?

a) Gravure printing
b) Flexography printing
c) Letterpress printing
d) Offset printing

151. In which printing process is the image transferred directly from the image carrier to the paper?

a) Offset printing
b) Gravure printing
c) Screen printing
d) Letterpress printing

152. What is the main purpose of post-press operations in printing?

a) Page-composition and typesetting
b) Actual printing operations
c) Assembly of printed materials and finishing
d) Plate making

153. Which printing method involves the use of minute etched or engraved wells of differing depth?

a) Offset printing
b) Screen printing
c) Gravure printing
d) Lithography

154. What type of plates are used in letterpress and flexography printing?

a) Relief plates
b) Planographic plates
c) Intaglio plates
d) Screen plates

155. Which type of printing uses plates where the image and non-image areas remain on the same plane?

a) Relief printing
b) Planographic printing
c) Intaglio printing
d) Screen printing

156. What is the printing method where the image is transferred first to the blanket cylinder and then to the paper?

a) Offset printing
b) Gravure printing
c) Flexography printing
d) Lithography

157. What is the name given to the process where the image is transferred to the substrate by pushing ink through a perforated mesh?
   a) Relief printing
   b) Intaglio printing
   c) Screen printing
   d) Planographic printing

158. Which step of printing involves plate making and image carrier preparation?
   a) Post-press operations
   b) Press operations
   c) Pre-printing activities
   d) Printing methods

159. Which type of paper is used for leaflets?
   a) Thicker paper
   b) Matte finish paper
   c) Silky paper
   d) Thinner paper

160. What is the advantage of offset printing over direct printing?
   a) Faster printing speed
   b) Lower printing cost
   c) Better image quality
   d) More color options

161. Which type of printing method is suitable for banners, stickers, diary covers, and file covers?
   a) Gravure printing
   b) Offset printing
   c) Screen printing
   d) Flexography printing

162. What is the primary consideration for selecting paper quality for printing?
   a) Paper size
   b) Paper weight
   c) Paper quality
   d) Paper color

163. In which printing method is the image area recessed from the non-printing area?
   a) Offset printing
   b) Screen printing
   c) Gravure printing
   d) Letterpress printing

164. Which step of printing involves binding and finishing operations?
   a) Press operations
   b) Post-press operations
   c) Printing methods
   d) Pre-printing activities

165. Which printing process uses photo-processing chemicals and solutions in pre-press operations?
   a) Offset printing
   b) Gravure printing
   c) Screen printing
   d) Letterpress printing

166. Which type of printing method uses image carriers that define image and non-image areas by differing physio-chemical properties?

a) Relief printing
b) Planographic printing
c) Intaglio printing
d) Screen printing

167. What is the printing process where the image is transferred from the image carrier to the paper directly?

a) Offset printing
b) Gravure printing
c) Screen printing
d) Lithography

168. What is the primary purpose of editing in journalism?

a) Correcting spelling and punctuation errors
b) Adding images and illustrations to the article
c) Improving the writer's style and intentions
d) Formatting the article for publication

169. What is the term used for editing at a broader level, focusing on completeness and organization of content?

a) Micro-editing
b) Proofreading
c) Macro-editing
d) Galley proofing

170. Which step of editing involves checking language, grammar, and style of writing?

a) Micro-editing
b) Proofreading
c) Macro-editing
d) Galley proofing

171. What should an editor consider while editing to meet the comprehension level of the readers?

a) Adding technical terms
b) Using complex sentences
c) Ensuring the use of simple words
d) Including acronyms and abbreviations

172. What is the purpose of proofreading after editing?

a) Correcting mistakes in typing and designing
b) Adding more content to the article
c) Rearranging paragraphs for better flow
d) Rewriting the entire article

173. What is the primary focus of macro-editing in journalism?
   a) Grammar and punctuation
   b) Style and writing flow
   c) Context and coherence of subject matter
   d) Page layout and design

174. What does the editor aim to achieve in micro-editing?
   a) Ensuring completeness and organization of content
   b) Checking for spelling and typographical errors
   c) Maintaining the writer's style while making necessary changes
   d) Evaluating the article's conformance with the newspaper's nature

175. What technique is suggested for detecting spelling mistakes effectively during proofreading?
   a) Reading the text backwards
   b) Reading the text out loud
   c) Using the computer's spell check
   d) Skipping the proofreading step

176. What step should be taken after editing to ensure that the writer's statements are not changed?
   a) Proofreading
   b) Micro-editing
   c) Retyping the entire article
   d) Consulting a Thesaurus

177. Which type of editing involves reorganizing paragraphs to fit into a logical sequence and structure?
   a) Proofreading
   b) Micro-editing
   c) Galley proofing
   d) Macro-editing

178. Why is it essential to keep the writer's style intact during editing?
   a) To make the article longer
   b) To add more technical terms
   c) To maintain the writer's voice and tone
   d) To simplify the language

179. What is the purpose of re-typing the article after editing?
   a) To get a clean copy for publishing
   b) To add more content to the article
   c) To change the writer's style
   d) To correct punctuation errors

180. What should be checked during proofreading to ensure accuracy?
    a) The writer's intentions
    b) The clarity of illustrations
    c) Names, places, and dates
    d) Page numbers and citations

181. What technique is suggested to avoid skipping mistakes during proofreading?
    a) Reading the text backwards
    b) Taking breaks while editing
    c) Using the computer's spell check
    d) Having another person read the text out loud

182. What is the primary purpose of micro-editing in journalism?
    a) Correcting spelling errors
    b) Checking language and style of writing
    c) Rearranging paragraphs for better flow
    d) Evaluating completeness of content

183. What should an editor consider while editing to meet the comprehension level of the readers?
    a) Adding technical terms
    b) Using complex sentences
    c) Ensuring the use of simple words
    d) Including acronyms and abbreviations

184. What is the purpose of proofreading after editing?
    a) Correcting mistakes in typing and designing
    b) Adding more content to the article
    c) Rearranging paragraphs for better flow
    d) Rewriting the entire article

185. What is the primary focus of macro-editing in journalism?
    a) Grammar and punctuation
    b) Style and writing flow
    c) Context and coherence of subject matter
    d) Page layout and design

186 What is the term used for checking and correcting mistakes in the final print-out of an article?
    a) Macro-editing
    b) Proofreading
    c) Micro-editing
    d) Galley proofing

187. What is desktop publishing?
   a) A process of designing newspapers
   b) A method of creating printed materials on microcomputers
   c) A way to publish books online
   d) A technique for typesetting using traditional machines

188. What is the purpose of desktop publishing accessories like scanners and graphics software?
   a) To generate text and insert graphics
   b) To produce camera-ready copy
   c) To create layouts and page designs
   d) To allow for graphical designs and formats

189. What is one advantage of desktop publishing for authors and publishers?
   a) Reduced design control
   b) Increased production costs
   c) Limited access to typesetting machines
   d) Ability to provide camera-ready copy to printers

190. What is the role of media management in agricultural communication?
   a) Sending agricultural news to media houses
   b) Developing formal and informal linkages with media persons
   c) Arranging press conferences and briefings
   d) Gathering media in a single media center

191. What recent developments have fueled growth in media applications for development?
   a) Introduction of traditional typesetting machines
   b) Growing popularity of mobile and broadband channels
   c) Decline in digital media access
   d) Decreased demand for internet services

192. What career opportunities have emerged in the digital media sector?
   a) Traditional journalism and print media
   b) Web content development and web marketing
   c) Typesetting and traditional advertising
   d) Graphic designing for print materials

193. What is the primary focus of many agencies in the digital media industry?
   a) Creating traditional newspapers and magazines
   b) Developing mobile applications for gaming
   c) Providing information and entertainment online
   d) Designing advertisements for television

194. What type of professionals are responsible for creating valuable content for websites?
   a) Print designers
   b) Graphic designers
   c) E-journalists
   d) Web content developers

195. What has allowed users to interact and access information from any location?
   a) Traditional media channels
   b) Web marketing campaigns
   c) Digital media revolution
   d) Internet and digital media

196. What field is experiencing a rise in demand for candidates with technical knowledge?
   a) Typesetting and printing
   b) Traditional advertising
   c) Mobile application development
   d) Desktop publishing using traditional machines

16

Understanding Agri-Business and Entrepreneurial Development Theories

1. What does Entrepreneurship Development (ED) aim to integrate?
   a) Sociological nature of agricultural sector with cooperative entrepreneurship
   b) Sociological nature of agricultural sector with traditional entrepreneurship
   c) Sociological nature of agricultural sector with capitalistic entrepreneurship
   d) Sociological nature of agricultural sector with socialist entrepreneurship

2. Entrepreneurship Development (ED) is primarily focused on which sector?
   a) Industrial sector
   b) Service sector
   c) Agricultural sector
   d) Educational sector

3. What is the main objective of Entrepreneurship Development (ED)?
   a) To promote cooperative farming in the agricultural sector
   b) To encourage government control and management of agricultural enterprises
   c) To foster a capitalist approach to agricultural entrepreneurship
   d) To discourage private investment in the agricultural sector

4. Which of the following statements is true about Entrepreneurship Development (ED)?
   a) It discourages any form of private entrepreneurship in the agricultural sector.
   b) It solely focuses on the technological aspects of agriculture.
   c) It aims to merge sociological perspectives with cooperative entrepreneurship.
   d) It attempts to integrate sociological perspectives with capitalistic entrepreneurship.

Bold Means Correct Answer

5. Entrepreneurship Development (ED) has been compared to an imaginary creature named Heffalumf because:
   a) It is a mythical concept with no practical application in the real world.
   b) Different people have diverse viewpoints, resulting in varying definitions of entrepreneurship.
   c) ED is based on fictional narratives and stories.
   d) Heffalumf is a symbol of success in the field of entrepreneurship.

6. Which field of study focuses on studying the causes (why) of Entrepreneurship Development (ED) by examining entrepreneurs' characteristics and traits?
   a) Economics
   b) Sociology
   c) Psychology
   d) Management

7. According to the passage, what does the French root "entreprendre" mean in the context of the word entrepreneur?
   a) To create something new and innovative
   b) To achieve high profits in business ventures
   c) To take moderate risks in business undertakings
   d) To begin something or undertake a venture

8. How is an entrepreneur described in terms of their need for achievement (N-Ach) and risk-taking behavior?
   a) High need for achievement and high-risk taker
   b) Low need for achievement and low-risk taker
   c) High need for achievement and moderate risk taker
   d) Low need for achievement and high-risk taker

9. According to the passage, what is entrepreneurship considered to be in terms of its role in the economy and society?
   a) A stagnant force that preserves the status quo
   b) A means to transform the society and economy
   c) A random and unpredictable phenomenon
   d) A byproduct of cultural and religious practices

10. In a stratified society like India, why might the indicators of entrepreneurship vary among different strata of the population?
   a) Due to government regulations that restrict certain business activities
   b) Because entrepreneurship is not encouraged in certain cultural backgrounds
   c) Due to differences in economic opportunities available to different strata
   d) Because entrepreneurship is considered illegal in certain strata

11. Which of the following is a main concept studied in the entrepreneurial personality type approach?
    a) Risk aversion
    b) Conformity
    c) Innovativeness
    d) Reliance on others' decisions

12. Entrepreneurial attitudes and behavior include all of the following EXCEPT:
    a) Persistence
    b) Dependence on others' decisions
    c) Openness to new information and people
    d) Motivation to achieve

13. According to psychological trait theories of entrepreneurship, what differentiates entrepreneurs from non-entrepreneurs and successful entrepreneurs from unsuccessful ones?
    a) Technical expertise
    b) Locus of control
    c) Attitudinal and psychological attributes
    d) Political affiliations

14. Which perspective of entrepreneurship views it as the process of extracting profits from new, unique, and valuable combinations of resources in an uncertain environment?
    a) Sociological perspective
    b) Behavioral perspective
    c) Process perspective
    d) Psychological perspective

15. What do sociological theories of entrepreneurship assume to influence entrepreneurial behavior?
    a) Individual's interaction with the society
    b) Personal wealth accumulation
    c) Genetic inheritance
    d) Entrepreneur's technical know-how

16. According to the behavioral perspective, entrepreneurs are individuals who:
    a) Avoid taking risks and maintain the status quo
    b) Break with existing ways to create new things
    c) Rely solely on government support for their ventures
    d) Focus solely on marketing products and services

17. The six common behaviors of entrepreneurs include all of the following EXCEPT:
    a) Accumulating resources
    b) Responding to the environment
    c) Relying solely on the government for support
    d) Locating a business opportunity

18. Which of the following is NOT considered a key quality of an entrepreneur?
    a) Risk-taking
    b) Motivation to achieve
    c) Reliance on others' decisions
    d) Leadership

19. According to the process perspective, entrepreneurship is defined as the creation of:
    a) New enterprises and organizations
    b) Personal wealth and power
    c) Uncertain and ambiguous environments
    d) Traditional and conventional businesses

20. Which perspective provides a framework for examining how an entrepreneur's personal attributes interact with other variables to affect the organization's actions and performance?
    a) Sociological perspective
    b) Psychological perspective
    c) Interactionist perspective
    d) Behavioral perspective

21. What is one of the basic problems the world is faced with in the contex of agriculture?
    a) Low agricultural productivity
    b) Declining population in rural areas
    c) Unemployment and under-employment
    d) Excessive urbanization

22. How does unemployment affect food security in society?
    a) It leads to a shortage of food supplies in the market.
    b) Unemployed individuals lack purchasing power to buy enough food.
    c) Food prices increase due to excessive demand from the unemployed.
    d) Unemployment has no direct impact on food security.

23. What proportion of Indian farmers are considered small and marginal farmers?
    a) 30%
    b) 50%
    c) 65%
    d) 85%

24. Project ARYA (Attracting Rural Youth in Agriculture) aims to address which issue?
    a) Low agricultural productivity
    b) Lack of education among rural youth
    c) Unemployment in rural areas
    d) Overpopulation in rural regions

25. What is the role of micro-enterprises based on agriculture in the society?
    a) Increasing urbanization and industrialization
    b) Promoting rural transformation
    c) Reducing the land-man ratio
    d) Accelerating the decline in agricultural productivity

26. How can farmers tackle the challenges of unemployment and rural farm distress?
    a) By pursuing agribusiness and entrepreneurship
    b) By relying solely on government support
    c) By leaving agriculture for other jobs in cities
    d) By advocating for better agricultural policies

27. What is the objective of the post-graduate course on Entrepreneurship Development in Agriculture initiated by IARI?
    a) Training farmers to become agricultural researchers
    b) Encouraging job seekers to find employment in urban areas
    c) Fostering the development of agricultural entrepreneurs
    d) Introducing new technologies for agricultural production

28. Why are small and medium enterprises (SMEs) considered major sources of employment generation?
    a) They receive preferential treatment from the government
    b) They are exempt from taxes
    c) They are more numerous in non-agricultural sectors
    d) They have strong inter-linkages with agriculture

29. What is the main challenge faced by farmers, leading some to leave agriculture for other jobs?
    a) Lack of access to agricultural resources
    b) Declining agricultural markets
    c) The need to become agripreneurs
    d) Diminishing agricultural land and high unemployment rate

30. What is the main factor on which the development of a nation depends?
    a) Economic policies
    b) Physical infrastructure
    c) Human capital
    d) Natural resources

31. According to empirical studies, what has made a larger contribution to economic development than non-human capital?
    a) Physical infrastructure
    b) Natural resources
    c) Entrepreneurs as human capital
    d) Government policies

32. What is the role of entrepreneurs in the process of economic development?
    a) Setting government policies
    b) Managing physical infrastructure
    c) Perceiving new opportunities and taking risks
    d) Controlling natural resources

33. To convert a farm into a business or enterprise, what must the identity of the person managing it change into?
    a) Agricultural operator
    b) Agricultural engineer
    c) Farm entrepreneur or agripreneur
    d) Agricultural scientist

34. How can farmers be motivated to become entrepreneurial and move away from subsistence farming?
    a) Through systematic motivational training
    b) By providing more natural resources
    c) By implementing government-sponsored schemes
    d) By increasing population in rural areas

35. Which step is essential in developing entrepreneurship among farmers after motivation?
    a) Increasing government subsidies **b) Awareness spread program**
    c) Land redistribution d) Population control

36. Who plays a crucial role in spreading awareness about the potential of entrepreneurship in agriculture among rural masses?
    a) Government officials
    b) Agricultural scientists
    c) Field-level extension workers
    d) Entrepreneurs from other sectors

37. Why is developing competent human resources important for a developing economy?
    a) To reduce the population
    b) To manage natural resources effectively
    c) To enhance overall national development
    d) To limit entrepreneurial activities

38. What is the first and foremost step to achieve the goal of developing competent human force in the present context?
    a) Implementing economic policies
    b) Providing physical infrastructure
    c) Encouraging entrepreneurship development
    d) Enhancing natural resources

39. Which group of people are considered the architects of every conceivable material project and a motivating force behind national development?
    a) Agricultural scientists b) Field-level extension workers
    c) Entrepreneurs d) Government officials

40. Which type of entrepreneur is involved in conceiving a new product or service and creating a business to materialize their idea?
    a) Trading entrepreneur
    b) Manufacturing entrepreneur
    c) Business entrepreneur
    d) Agricultural entrepreneur

41. What do manufacturing entrepreneurs convert into finished products?
    a) Raw materials
    b) Potential markets
    c) Agricultural crops
    d) Services

42. Which type of entrepreneur starts a business due to policy measures of the government providing assistance and incentives?
    a) Pure entrepreneur
    b) Induced entrepreneur
    c) Spontaneous entrepreneur
    d) Growth entrepreneur

43. Which type of entrepreneur exhibits cleverness in converting established products or services into something new and utilitarian?
    a) Innovating entrepreneur
    b) Imitative entrepreneur
    c) Women entrepreneur
    d) Agricultural entrepreneur

44. What distinguishes an intrapreneur from an entrepreneur?
    a) Intrapreneurs work only in established organizations.
    b) Intrapreneurs do not have access to corporate resources.
    c) Intrapreneurs are not self-motivated.
    d) Intrapreneurs do not respond to corporate rewards.

45. What is the main characteristic of an imitative entrepreneur?
    a) Willingness to take risks in creating a new venture
    b) Eagerness to experiment with new ideas
    c) Ability to collaborate and network inside and outside the enterprise
    d) Readiness to adopt successful innovations by other entrepreneurs

46. Which type of entrepreneur focuses on agricultural activities such as raising and marketing crops?
    a) Pure entrepreneur
    b) Trading entrepreneur
    c) Agricultural entrepreneur
    d) Growth entrepreneur

47. Who are considered super growth entrepreneurs?
    a) First-generation entrepreneurs
    b) Women entrepreneurs
    c) Entrepreneurs who have shown enormous growth in their ventures
    d) Intrapreneurs within established organizations

48. What is the main objective of a first-generation entrepreneur?
    a) Converting established products into something new
    b) Utilizing corporate resources to innovate
    c) Combining different technologies to produce a marketable product
    d) Providing assistance and incentives for starting a venture

49. What distinguishes a woman entrepreneur from other types of entrepreneurs?
    a) Having a minimum financial interest of 51% in the capital
    b) Being more adoptive and flexible in their approach
    c) Being goal-oriented and self-motivated
    d) Employing at least 51% women employees in the enterprise

50. What are the three stages of establishing an enterprise in entrepreneurship development?
    a) Idea generation, product development, marketing
    b) Planning, execution, expansion
    c) Introduction, growth, maturity
    d) There is not enough information provided to answer this question.

51. What is the key similarity between an entrepreneur and a self-employed person?
    a) They both take on extraordinary financial risks in their business.
    b) They both work for someone else as employees.
    c) They both own a business.
    d) They both avoid risks and challenges in their ventures.

52. What distinguishes an entrepreneur from a self-employed person?
    a) An entrepreneur works for someone else, while a self-employed person works independently.
    b) An entrepreneur has a growth orientation and undertakes challenges and risks.
    c) An entrepreneur is less passionate about their business compared to a self-employed person.
    d) An entrepreneur focuses solely on income generation activities.

53. Which term refers to activities undertaken for monetary returns and livelihood?
    a) Entrepreneurship
    b) Self-employment
    c) Income generation
    d) Business development

54. What drives entrepreneurs every day according to the passage?
   a) Desire for low-profit activities
   b) Passion for their start-up and leading something to success
   c) Avoidance of challenges and risks
   d) Financial rewards from income generation activities

55. How do entrepreneurs approach risks and challenges in their ventures?
   a) They avoid taking any risks or challenges.
   b) They think outside the box and look for ways to succeed.
   c) They prioritize low-profit activities over high-profit ventures.
   d) They focus solely on income generation without any risks.

56. What is the primary focus of self-employment?
   a) Undertaking challenges and risks for growth
   b) Pursuing activities for monetary returns and livelihood
   c) Selling the business or starting a new venture
   d) Generating passive income with minimal effort

57. What is the additional attribute that a self-employed person possesses to be classified as an entrepreneur?
   a) Low-risk taking behavior
   b) Ownership of a business
   c) Growth orientation
   d) Desire for low-profit activities

58. Which term refers to working for oneself as an independent owner of a business?
   a) Entrepreneurship
   b) Income generation
   c) Self-employment
   d) Business development

59. What drives entrepreneurs to move on to their next venture or sell their current business?
   a) Desire for low-profit activities
   b) Avoidance of risks and challenges
   c) Passion for start-up and leading to success
   d) Focus on income generation activities only

60. In which stage of establishing an enterprise does the individual potential entrepreneur get motivated to take up enterprise activities?
   a) Enterprise launching
   b) Entrepreneurial stimulation
   c) Enterprise sustenance
   d) Social responsibility

61. What activities are involved in the second stage of establishing an enterprise, known as "Enterprise launching"?

a) Financial, marketing, and labor management

b) Running the enterprise's day-to-day operations

c) Market survey, product identification, and project report preparation

d) Social responsibility and ecological care

62. During which stage of the entrepreneurship development cycle does the actual running and long-term operations of the enterprise occur?

a) Social responsibility

b) Enterprise launching

c) Enterprise sustenance

d) Entrepreneurial stimulation

63. What are the major activities involved in the "Enterprise sustenance" stage?

a) Financial, marketing, and labor management

b) Market survey, product identification, and project report preparation

c) Motivating potential entrepreneurs

d) Exhibiting a sense of social responsibility

64. In which stage of the entrepreneurship development cycle, do successful entrepreneurs exhibit a sense of social responsibility?

a) Enterprise sustenance

b) Enterprise launching

c) Social responsibility

d) Entrepreneurial stimulation

65. What is the purpose of the "Enterprise launching" stage in establishing an enterprise?

a) To manage and operate the enterprise in the long term

b) To motivate potential entrepreneurs

c) To exhibit a sense of social responsibility

d) To prepare all the necessary requirements for enterprise launch

66. Which stage involves financial analysis, subsidies, certifications, and legal requirements for launching an enterprise?

a) Enterprise sustenance

b) Entrepreneurial stimulation

c) Enterprise launching

d) Social responsibility

67. What is the key objective of the "Entrepreneurial stimulation" stage?
    a) To prepare the project report for the enterprise
    b) To motivate the potential entrepreneur to take up enterprise activities
    c) To exhibit a sense of social responsibility
    d) To sustain the long-term operations of the enterprise

68. Which stage of establishing an enterprise involves client/customer relations and growth orientation?
    a) Social responsibility
    b) Enterprise sustenance
    c) Entrepreneurial stimulation
    d) Enterprise launching

69. What are the self-made rules that successful entrepreneurs exhibit as part of their social responsibility?
    a) Financial, marketing, and labor management
    b) Care for ecology and environment
    c) Market survey and product identification
    d) Legal requirements and certifications

70. Thematic Apperception Test (TAT) is a psychological test that involves:
    a) Identifying colors based on pictures shown
    b) Writing imaginative stories based on pictures shown
    c) Solving math problems based on pictures shown
    d) Memorizing sequences of numbers based on pictures shown

71. TAT is used to assess which specific need related to achievement in the stories written by participants?
    a) Need for affiliation
    b) Need for power
    c) Need for recognition
    d) Need for achievement

72. In TAT scoring, which component reflects a character's desire for success in relation to some standard of excellence?
    a) Goal anticipation
    b) Obstacles or blocks
    c) Help seeking
    d) Desire for unique achievement

73. Which category is scored in TAT when a story contains indications of activity leading to the achievement goal, with successful, unsuccessful, or doubtful outcome?
    a) Activity leading to achievement goal (Act)
    b) Stated need for achievement (N)
    c) Obstacles or blocks (Bp/Bw)
    d) Goal anticipation (Ga+/Ga-)

74. In TAT scoring, which category is scored when the character visualizes success as a consequence of their efforts?

a) Goal anticipation positive (Ga+)

b) Goal anticipation negative (Ga-)

c) Stated need for achievement (N)

d) Achievement theme (Th)

75. Which simulation exercise focuses on creativity awareness and innovation competencies?

a) Ring toss exercise

b) TAT

c) Tower building exercise

d) Nine dot exercise

76. The "Motivation cycle" refers to the cyclical process of:

a) Need, want, tension, action, and satisfaction

b) Training participants in entrepreneurial competencies

c) Scoring stories in the Thematic Apperception Test

d) Implementing institutional support for entrepreneurship development

77. In the motivation cycle, what creates an inner state of dissatisfaction or tension?

a) Action

b) Need

c) Anticipation

d) Satisfaction

78. Which element is NOT a part of the motivation cycle described in the passage?

a) Need

b) Satisfaction

c) Goal anticipation

d) Action

79. The "Motivation cycle" helps us understand:

a) Entrepreneurial competencies

b) How to prioritize action taken by individuals

c) The scoring system of TAT

d) The dynamics of human behavior and motivation

80 What does an entrepreneurial opportunity refer to?

a) A business idea with high profitability

b) A project idea accepted as a basis for financial investment and time allocation

c) A socially acceptable business idea

d) An idea that is technically and economically feasible

81. What are the major ingredients of a business opportunity?
    a) Technical feasibility, government priority, and strategic fit
    b) Economic viability, risk exposure, and profitability
    c) Technical feasibility, economic viability, and social acceptability
    d) Market availability, ease of implementation, and profitability

82. Which tool is used for analyzing business opportunities and involves documentation and analysis of strengths, weaknesses, opportunities, and threats?
    a) Micro screening
    b) SWOT analysis
    c) Decision matrix
    d) Feasibility study

83. In SWOT analysis, which element refers to the basic assets or qualities of an organization that provide a competitive advantage?
    a) Weakness
    b) Strength
    c) Opportunity
    d) Threat

84. Micro screening helps in the final selection of a business opportunity by:
    a) Conducting a detailed market analysis
    b) Assessing the government's priority for the project
    c) Rating different projects based on specific criteria
    d) Comparing the profitability of different projects

85. What does the "government priority" factor in micro screening indicate?
    a) The government's willingness to invest in the project
    b) The level of government regulation in the industry
    c) The project's alignment with the government's investment priorities
    d) The ease of obtaining government subsidies for the project

86. Which factor in micro screening assesses the availability of skilled labor for the project?
    a) Availability of market
    b) Availability of technology
    c) Availability of skills
    d) Ease of implementation

87. What does the "ease of implementation" factor in micro screening refer to?
    a) The simplicity of the project's technology
    b) The short gestation period of the project
    c) The availability of government incentives for the project
    d) The project's ability to control unforeseen difficulties

88. Which factor in micro screening assesses the profitability and return on investment of the project?
    a) Risk exposure
    b) Profitability
    c) Cost/benefit
    d) Strategic fit

89. What does the "cost/benefit" factor in micro screening represent?
    a) The overall impression of the project's feasibility
    b) The tangible benefits of the project to the community
    c) The economic viability of the project without government intervention
    d) The ease of implementation of the project

90. Which method seeks to develop forecasts based on cause-effect relationships specified in a quantitative manner?
    a) Trend projection method
    b) Chain ratio method
    c) Exponential smoothing method
    d) Moving average method

91. Consumption level method in demand analysis estimates consumption level based on:
    a) Price elasticity of demand
    b) Income elasticity of demand
    c) Aggregate demand
    d) Elasticity coefficients

92. What does the marketing strategy cover in a marketing plan?
    a) Market segmentation and price
    b) Product line and promotion
    c) Target segment and sales force
    d) Distribution and advertising

93. Which phase of the project life cycle involves the actual work and is considered the most time-consuming stage?
    a) Project initiation phase
    b) Project planning phase
    c) Project implementation phase
    d) Project closing phase

94. Which financial analysis method calculates the time taken for complete recovery of initial cash investment in a project?
    a) Break even point
    b) Payback period
    c) Proceeds per unit outlay
    d) Ranking by inspection

95. What is the ratio used to calculate the Debt Service Coverage Ratio?
    a) Net profits/sales
    b) Net profits/capital employed
    c) Debt/Equity
    d) Net profit after tax + Depreciation + Interest for one year / Instalments + Interest (for one year)

96. Social cost-benefit analysis in project feasibility considers:
    a) Profitability and return on investment
    b) Debt and equity ratios
    c) Infrastructure creation and employment opportunities
    d) Market segmentation and price elasticity

97. What is the primary objective of econometric analysis in demand forecasting?
    a) To assess the potential market share
    b) To identify opportunities and issues
    c) To forecast future behavior of economic variables
    d) To conduct market surveys

98. Which phase of the project life cycle involves analyzing the interrelation of different project activities and financial analysis?
    a) Project planning phase
    b) Project implementation phase
    c) Project closing phase
    d) Project design and network analysis

99. What does the Break Even Point (BEP) represent?
    a) The level of production where the enterprise will make a profit
    b) The level of production where the enterprise will break even
    c) The time required for complete recovery of initial cash investment
    d) The time taken for a project to reach completion

100. What is a value chain in business management?
    a) A set of activities that a firm performs to deliver a valuable product or service
    b) A chain of suppliers and customers in the market
    c) A sequence of unrelated business functions
    d) A process of outsourcing different functions

101. Which of the following is NOT a primary activity in the value chain?
    a) Inbound logistics
    b) Operations
    c) Technology development
    d) Outbound logistics

102. What is the goal of value chain management?
    a) To maximize profits
    b) To ensure communication between different stages of the value chain
    c) To minimize costs
    d) To increase market share

103. What are the support activities in the value chain?
    a) Inbound logistics, operations, and outbound logistics
    b) Marketing, sales, and service
    c) Procurement, technology development, human resource management, and firm infrastructure
    d) Distribution and promotion

104. Which type of agricultural value chain involves linkages between different levels such as seed suppliers, farmers, traders, processors, exporters/importers, retailers, and consumers?
    a) Vertical value chain
    b) Horizontal value chain
    c) Market value chain
    d) Organic value chain

105. What is the process where a firm identifies its activities that add value to its final product and then analyzes these activities to reduce costs or increase differentiation?
    a) Market analysis
    b) Supply chain management
    c) Value chain analysis
    d) Cost-benefit analysis

106. Which step in value chain analysis involves mapping the flow of activities and identifying agents in the chain?
    a) Commodity value chain prioritization
    b) Identifying the distribution of benefits of actors in the chain
    c) Examining the role of value and quality upgrading within the chain
    d) Mapping the value chain

107. What does MSME stand for in the context of enterprises?
    a) Major Small and Medium Enterprises
    b) Micro, Small, and Medium Enterprises
    c) Medium Scale Manufacturing Enterprises
    d) Major Services and Marketing Enterprises

108. What is the classification of micro-enterprises in the manufacturing sector in terms of investment in plant and machinery?

a) **Less than 25 lakh**

b) More than 25 lakh but does not exceed 5 crore

c) More than 5 crore but does not exceed 10 crore

d) More than 10 lakh but does not exceed 2 crore

109. What role do micro, small, and medium enterprises (MSMEs) play in the economy?

a) They provide employment to highly skilled people

b) **They contribute to exports and raise manufacturing sector production**

c) They are primarily involved in the service sector

d) They focus on outsourcing various functions

110. What is contract farming?

a) Agricultural production carried out solely by farmers without any external involvement

b) An agreement between the government and farmers for procurement of agricultural products

c) **An agreement between a buyer and farmers for the production and marketing of farm products**

d) A contract between farmers and suppliers for the purchase of agricultural inputs

111. What is the basic objective of contract farming?

a) To promote government-led procurement systems

b) To ensure government subsidies for farmers

c) **To achieve backward integration and assure the supply of produce**

d) To restrict private investment in the agricultural sector

112. Which of the following is NOT an element typically included in contract farming agreements?

a) Quality standards of the agricultural product

b) **Government regulations on land preparation**

c) Agreed quantities and timing of product supply

d) Pre-agreed prices for the farm produce

113. Which contract farming model involves a centralized processor and packaging agency buying from numerous small farmers?

a) Nucleus estate model
b) Informal model
c) Centralized model
d) Intermediary model

114. What is the benefit of contract farming for farmers?

a) Reduced need for market focus in crop selection
b) Guaranteed government procurement of their produce
c) Access to private investment and stable income
d) Exemption from legalities and regulations

115. What is the main problem associated with contract farming in India due to the small size of landholdings?

a) Difficulty in maintaining the quality of produce due to interactions with neighboring fields
b) Lack of interest from buyers in procuring products from small landholders
c) Excessive reliance on government subsidies for contract farming operations
d) Inability to meet government regulations on crop insurance

116. Which contract farming model involves a sponsor managing a central estate or plantation?

a) Informal model
b) Multipartite model
c) Nucleus estate model
d) Intermediary model

117. What is the potential risk associated with the intermediary model of contract farming?

a) Inability to ensure compliance with government regulations
b) Greater reliance on government support services for research and extension
c) Subcontract linkages may result in losing control over production and quality
d) Difficulty in maintaining centralized processing and packaging facilities

118. Why is contract farming considered a viable approach to meet market challenges?

a) It reduces private investment in the agricultural sector

b) It focuses on government-led procurement systems

c) It assures a stable and consistent income for farmers

d) It relies solely on informal production contracts

119. What is the main advantage of contract farming for the government?

a) Reduced involvement in the agricultural sector

b) Access to quality agricultural products through private investment

c) Centralized control over the entire agricultural supply chain

d) Elimination of the need for farmer support services

17

Building Competences Framework and Models

1. What is the primary aim of capacity building?
   a) Financial Development
   b) Infrastructure Enhancement
   c) Improving the abilities of individuals in various professional fields
   d) Political Development

2. According to the World Economic Forum's Global Human Capital Index (2017), what rank did India achieve in terms of knowledge and skill development out of 130 countries?
   a) 65th
   b) 77th
   c) 87th
   d) 103rd

3. In the context of skill development in 2017, India was ranked:
   a) 65th
   b) 77th
   c) 87th
   d) 105th

4. Which country among the BRICKS was ranked 16th in the WEF report?
   a) Brazil
   b) Russia
   c) India
   d) China

5. What is one of the primary challenges of rural development?
   a) Political Alliances
   b) Effective Skill Inculcation
   c) Financial Investments
   d) Infrastructure Expansion

6 Which of the following does NOT affect the training process?
   a) Training theories
   b) Infrastructure
   c) Types of training
   d) Training methods

7. Which two countries ranked higher than India in terms of knowledge in the WEF report?
   a) China and Brazil
   b) Nepal and Sri Lanka
   c) Russia and South Africa
   d) Brazil and South Africa

Bold Means Correct Answer

8. What is the main difference between education and training?
   a) Education is formal while training is informal.
   b) Education is only for children while training is for adults.
   c) Education provides knowledge, while training focuses on skill development.
   d) There is no difference between the two.

9. Why is agriculture crucial for India?
   a) It is the primary source of the nation's GDP.
   b) It offers employment opportunities to the majority.
   c) It holds the key to reducing poverty and increasing livelihood security.
   d) It contributes to the nation's exports.

10. In the context of gender development issues in the WEF report, how is India's performance described?
   a) Excellent
   b) Moderate
   c) Low
   d) Very high

11. The Latin word 'educare' means:
   a) To come out
   b) To lead forth
   c) To rear and to bring up
   d) Act of teaching or training

12. According to Upanishads, the end product of education is:
   a) Realization of the Self
   b) Training for the country
   c) Getting salvation
   d) All-round drawing out of the best in the child

13. Who said, "Education enables the mind to find out the ultimate truth, which gives us the wealth of inner light and love and gives significance to life."?
   a) Plato
   b) Mahatma Gandhi
   c) Rabindra Nath Tagore
   d) Dayananda

14. According to Michel Armstrong, training is:
   a) The complete development of the individuality of the child
   b) Systematic development of the knowledge, skills, and attitudes required by an individual to perform adequately a given task or job
   c) The act of increasing knowledge and skills of an employee for doing a particular job
   d) The process involved in improving the aptitudes, skills, and abilities of the employees to perform specific jobs

15. The primary difference between education and training is:
    a) Education is more about developing attitudes, while training is about developing knowledge.
    b) Education gives more knowledge and less of skill, while training promotes more of skill and less of knowledge.
    c) Education and training both aim at developing only skills.
    d) Training is only for new employees, while education is for everyone.

16. Which thinker believed that "Education is the process of living through a continuous reconstruction of experiences"?
    a) John Dewey b) Plato
    c) Ross d) Aristotle

17. The term 'training' is derived from which language?
    a) Latin b) Ancient Greek
    c) Middle English d) Old French

18. In Old French, the word "train" means:
    a) To teach b) To pull out
    c) A delay, a drawing out d) To push

19. The Latin words "traho, trahere" translate to:
    a) To teach and to learn **b) To pull, to draw**
    c) To train, to instruct d) To push, to press

20. Which word is a direct precursor to the Middle English term for "training"?
    a) Tragere **b) Train**
    c) Traho d) Trainer

21. The word "trainer" in Old French means:
    a) To push b) To instruct
    c) To pull out, to draw d) A teacher

22. From which language is the term "traginare" derived?
    a) Old French b) Latin
    c) Vulgar Latin d) Middle English

23. In the development of the word "training," what was derived from the noun in Middle English?

    a) An adjective
    b) A verb
    c) An adverb
    d) A preposition

24. Training effectiveness refers to the extent to which:

    a) Trainees attend classes.
    b) Trainees gain new knowledge and skills and improve job performance.
    c) Training costs are minimized.
    d) Trainers receive positive feedback.

25. Which of the following is NOT a trainee characteristic affecting training effectiveness?

    a) Motivational level
    b) Training need
    c) Self-efficacy
    d) Personal characteristics

26. The ___________ refers to the mental processes of awareness, knowing, and reasoning that affects trainee performance.

    a) Self-efficacy
    b) Career orientation
    c) Cognitive ability
    d) Motivational level

27. Which factor ensures that a training topic is actively engaged and willingly learned by trainees?

    a) Training design and implementation
    b) Type of training
    c) Training need
    d) Management support

28. The effectiveness of training is decided by the quality of the:

    a) Trainees work environment
    b) Classroom facilities
    c) Training design
    d) Training syllabus or content

29. Which of the following best describes the significance of "Management support" in training effectiveness?

    a) It helps in selecting the best trainers.
    b) It impacts the growth of an organization.
    c) It fosters a climate conducive to learning.
    d) It guarantees trainee participation.

30. What role does a trainee's work environment play in training effectiveness?

   a) It solely depends on the availability of modern equipment.

   b) It's influenced by opportunities to experiment and time/resources provided.

   c) It is unrelated to training effectiveness.

   d) It depends only on the feedback from colleagues.

31. Which of the following is NOT an essential component of a smart classroom?

   a) Comfortable chairs

   b) Note pad

   c) Web camera

   d) Internet connectivity

32. What can discourage training transfer in an organization?

   a) Adequate need analysis

   b) High motivational levels

   c) Stagnation in pay and promotion

   d) Active management support

33. The difference between education and training in terms of purpose is:

   a) Education prepares students for specific jobs while training prepares them for the future.

   b) Education deals with application of theories while training deals with theories and concepts.

   c) Education is about the complete development of an individual while training is about improving job performance.

   d) Education is about preparing students for the future, while training is about inculcating specific skills for specific jobs.

34. Which of the following trainings is provided by an employer to new recruits to help them get accustomed to the work environment?

   a) Refresher training

   b) Induction training or orientation training

   c) Apprenticeship training

   d) Soft skills training

35. What type of training involves learning while earning, often at a reduced wage?

   a) Management training

   b) Job training

   c) Apprenticeship training

   d) Vestibule training

36. Coaching differs from training in terms of:
    a) Function
    b) Duration
    c) Intensity
    d) Method

37. Who usually provides mentoring in an organization?
    a) An external consultant
    b) A junior employee
    c) A senior or more experienced individual
    d) A newly hired employee

38. Remedial training is given to:
    a) Acquaint employees with new skills
    b) Train new employees
    c) Overcome specific shortcomings in employee behavior and performance
    d) Familiarize employees with organizational policies

39. What type of training enables employees to work safely and minimize risks?
    a) Soft skills training
    b) Safety training
    c) Technical training
    d) Promotional training

40. The training which focuses on improving interpersonal skills, communication, and other related skills is called:
    a) Technical training
    b) Soft skills training
    c) Job rotation training
    d) Management training

41. Training that occurs directly on the job site while performing the actual job is known as:
    a) Off-the-job training
    b) On-the-job training
    c) Apprenticeship training
    d) Vestibule training

42. If training is conducted for farmers within the institute that organizes the training, it is termed as:
    a) Off-campus training
    b) On-campus training
    c) Off-the-job training
    d) On-the-job training

43. Which training technique exposes employees to a variety of skills by moving them between different jobs?
    a) Remedial training
    b) Vestibule training
    c) Job rotation training
    d) On-the-job training

44. What does Vestibule Training refer to?

a) Training provided outside the organization at specialized training centers.

b) Training in a special environment within the organization that closely simulates the actual work site.

c) Training provided on the actual job site while performing tasks.

d) Training provided only by external experts in specialized fields.

45. What is the primary purpose of assessing training needs?

a) To find new trainers for the program.

b) To discover problems and identify future challenges that can be addressed by training interventions.

c) To evaluate the results of a training program.

d) To decide the location of the training program.

46. Which of the following circumstances indicates an individual may require training?

a) When an individual receives a promotion.

b) When an individual moves to a different city.

c) When an individual's job performance meets the organization's expectations.

d) When an individual's job performance falls short of the organization's expectations.

47. What is the main aim of enumerating training objectives?

a) To determine the budget for training.

b) To spell out the direction for designing an effective training program.

c) To select the trainers for the program.

d) To choose the training methods to be used.

48. In the training design phase, which of the following is NOT a characteristic of a well-designed training activity?

a) The cost of the training.

b) Who are the participants of the training?

c) Where should the training be organized?

d) What is the training curriculum?

49. Which of the following methods is NOT commonly used in training?
    a) Lecture
    b) Microlab
    c) Podcasting
    d) Role play

50. Where might training programs typically be organized?
    a) Only at the training institute organizing the training.
    b) Only at a neutral place convenient for both trainers and trainees.
    c) Either at the training institute, client institute, or a neutral place.
    d) Only at the client institute whose employees need to be trained.

51. In the four levels of the training evaluation model, which level measures the extent to which participants find the training engaging and relevant to their jobs?
    a) Behaviour
    b) Result
    c) Reaction
    d) Learning

52. Which type of evaluation focuses on the assessment of the soft skills such as teamwork and interpersonal communication?
    a) Task Evaluation
    b) Process Evaluation
    c) Behaviour Evaluation
    d) Learning Evaluation

53. Which is the LAST stage in the training process?
    a) Training evaluation
    b) Implementing the training
    c) Assessing training needs
    d) Developing training design

54. In which phase of the training process are decisions regarding the curriculum and selection of trainers made?
    a) Enumerating training objectives
    b) Assessing training needs
    c) Developing training design
    d) Implementing the training

55. What is a training curriculum best defined as?
    a) A fixed set of subjects taught across all institutions.
    b) A brief guideline on what topics to cover in a training session.
    c) A plan comprising a systematic set of courses or subjects, designed to provide the best learning experiences.
    d) A sequence of activities to engage participants during training.

56. Which of the following is NOT a primary component examined when developing a training curriculum?
    a) The expenses incurred for the training.
    b) Content or information to be transmitted.
    c) Structure of the curriculum.
    d) Training methods to be used.

57. In an in-service training program, why is content important?
    a) To keep the participants engaged.
    b) Content must be applicable to direct practice.
    c) To fill the training schedule.
    d) To ensure participants pass their exams.

58. What does 'structure' in the context of curriculum refer to?
    a) The type of content to be delivered.
    b) The materials and resources required for the training.
    c) The scheduling of topics or contents in a proper sequence during the training period.
    d) The teaching methods and styles applied.

59. Which learning theory emerged in the 1970s and 1980s and emphasizes learners' active role in constructing knowledge?
    a) Behaviourism
    b) Cognitivism
    c) Constructivism
    d) Action learning

60. According to the facilitation theory, which of the following is NOT a characteristic of facilitative trainers?
    a) Being protective of their constructs and beliefs.
    b) Willingness to listen to learners.
    c) Interest in their relationship with learners.
    d) Encouraging learners to take responsibility for their own learning.

61. Which learning theory suggests that learning is most effective when the senses are stimulated?
    a) Sensory stimulation theory
    b) Constructivism
    c) Behaviourism
    d) Cognitivism

62. According to the theory of sensory stimulation, which sense is responsible for the majority of knowledge held by adults?
    a) Hearing
    b) Taste
    c) Touch
    d) Seeing

63. Bloom's taxonomy of learning classifies learning into how many domains?
    a) Two
    b) Three
    c) Four
    d) Five

64. What does the 'Q' represent in the equation L = P + Q in the context of Action learning?

a) Quality b) Quantity

c) Questioning insight d) Quantitative analysis

65. Systems thinking is primarily about:

a) Focusing on individual parts of a system.

b) Thinking about the system as a whole.

c) Avoiding interconnections and relationships.

d) Emphasizing only the human subsystem.

66. A hard systems approach is characterized by:

a) Ill-defined situations.

b) Interactions based on interests of the family.

c) Clear-cut quantitative goals.

d) Human interactions in an environment.

67. Which example best illustrates a soft systems approach?

a) A pesticide factory.

b) An isolated machinery.

c) A farm system with various sub-systems.

d) Engineers managing machinery.

68. The spiral model is useful for visualizing:

a) Only the pre-training phase.

b) Only the post-training phase.

c) A training program as an entity.

d) The independent variables.

69. For effective adult learning, what plays a crucial role before even entering the training?

a) The duration of the training.

b) The kind of food provided during training.

c) The general reputation of the course and the institution.

d) The attire to be worn during training.

70. The process of traning what has been learnt into a habitual pattern of behaviour is referred to as:
   a) Initial trial.
   b) Reinforcement.
   c) Internalizing.
   d) Feedback.

71. What plays a significant role in determining the success of post-training?
   a) The location of the training.
   b) The duration of breaks during training.
   c) Organizational support or lack of it.
   d) The design of training certificates.

72. At what stage is the risk of a break in participants' learning the highest?
   a) During the reinforcement stage.
   b) During the initial trial stage.
   c) While internalizing what has been learnt.
   d) During feedback from the initial trial.

73. Who decides the focus of attention and expectations during training?
   a) The training institution.
   b) The trainer.
   c) The participant.
   d) The organization sending the participant.

74. In the post-training phase, what is a clear indicator of training success?
   a) Verbal support from peers.
   b) Participants' job effectiveness improvement.
   c) Duration of the training.
   d) Design of the training program.

75. Traditional training is based on which of the following assumptions?
   a) Trainers and learners are on equal footing.
   b) Learners are empty vessels to be filled by the trainer.
   c) Participatory training is the conventional method.
   d) All knowledge transfer is value neutral.

76. Participatory training aims at:
   a) Simply transferring knowledge.
   b) Just knowing more.
   c) Behaving differently and process of analysis.
   d) Keeping the trainer as the center of the process.

77. In the participatory approach to training, learners are seen as:
    a) Passive recipients.
    b) Know-it-alls.
    c) Active participants with knowledge of reality.
    d) Only relevant in group settings.

78. Which of the following best describes the alternative view of training mentioned in the passage?
    a) Training for copying.
    b) Training for tradition.
    c) Training for change.
    d) Training for stagnation.

79. The conventional approach sees learning as:
    a) A process.
    b) A tool for creativity.
    c) A product.
    d) An open-ended method.

80. In a participatory approach, the role of a trainer is mainly of a:
    a) Dictator.
    b) Facilitator.
    c) Sole instructor.
    d) Passive observer.

81. Which of the following is NOT a participatory training method?
    a) Brainstorming.
    b) Lecture.
    c) Role Play.
    d) Group Discussion.

82. What does the participatory method emphasize regarding learners?
    a) Learners are not a rich source of information.
    b) Collective is not a powerful tool for learning.
    c) People must develop themselves.
    d) Acquired knowledge leads directly to action.

83. The participatory approach believes that:
    a) People are value neutral.
    b) People know everything.
    c) People cannot be developed.
    d) People need no change.

84. What is the role of a trainer in the participatory method?
    a) To decide the outcome.
    b) To impose values.
    c) To facilitate various learning experiences.
    d) To keep learners passive.

85. According to Lynton and Pareek (1996), which of the following is NOT one of the strategic issues to consider for effective training programmes?
    a) Setting goals.
    b) Choosing training location.
    c) Planning the specifications.
    d) Programming the resources.

86. In an effective training strategy, the role of a trainer expands to include:
    a) Only an instructor.
    b) Change agent and system consultant.
    c) External advisor.
    d) Auditor.

87. How should training be related to organizational action?
    a) They should be independent of each other.
    b) Training should always precede action.
    c) They should be closely linked.
    d) Only action should dictate training.

88. Who should take the lead in setting appropriate goals for training?
    a) The training system alone.
    b) The work organization.
    c) External consultants.
    d) The learners.

89. A failure in defining the goals of change with sufficient precision is the fault of:
    a) The trainers.
    b) The training system.
    c) The work organization.
    d) National policies.

90. The capability of an individual to learn is the ________ question regarding the usefulness of training.
    a) First.
    b) Second.
    c) Third.
    d) Fourth.

91. Planning training specifications primarily rests with:
    a) The work organization.
    b) The training system.
    c) Both the training system and the work organization.
    d) External consultants.

92. What is the core job of the training system?
    a) Setting organizational goals.
    b) Pinpointing changes required.
    c) Matching training methods to requirements.
    d) Deciding the number of trainees.

93. Which of the following services following participants' return from training might be carried out by the training system?
    a) Staff conferences.
    b) Introducing new technologies.
    c) Information dissemination and contact between former participants and training staff.
    d) Organizational restructuring.

94. What is the primary task of the training system?
    a) To educate participants on the importance of training.
    b) To use its current training resources advantageously.
    c) To provide facilities for training.
    d) To introduce a wide variety of training settings.

95. Development in the context of training strategy comprises which three phases?
    a) Freezing, moving, and refreezing.
    b) Planning, executing, and evaluating.
    c) Unfreezing, moving, and refreezing.
    d) Learning, application, and revision.

96. What is the significance of 'unfreezing' in the training process?
    a) To ensure participants have prior knowledge.
    b) To influence participants by questioning and disturbing their ingrained habits.
    c) To provide a relaxing environment for participants.
    d) To establish a foundation for new content.

97. What does the vertical axis represent?
    a) The sequence of training modules.
    b) The subject matter of the training.
    c) The primary use of the training received.
    d) The intensity of the training process.

98. Which training orientation focuses primarily on the practice of a particular skill?

a) Laboratory orientation.
b) Academic orientation.
c) Activity orientation.
d) Action orientation.

99. The organization-development orientation emphasizes:

a) The individual's personal growth.
b) Collaboration between the training institution and the work organization.
c) The practice of a particular skill.
d) Human relationships in the work environment.

100. A training strategy is:

a) A static blueprint that should be strictly adhered to.
b) Open to clarification, modification, and further development through experience.
c) Always focused on one specific training orientation.
d) Solely dependent on the resources available.

101. Which orientation uses methods like field training, simulation methods, and discussion of incidents and cases?

a) Academic orientation.
b) Laboratory orientation.
c) Person-development orientation.
d) Organization-development orientation.

102. Why is it important to choose the right training strategy?

a) Because training strategy doesn't need to be revised.
b) To ensure it meets the needs of the organizations and fits the training system's capabilities and vision.
c) To ensure all training units and systems are similar.
d) To make training more time-consuming.

103. Laboratory orientation is mainly concerned with:

a) Transmitting content.
b) Theoretical understanding.
c) Human relations and organizational behavior.
d) Specific job improvement.

104. What is the foremost characteristic of a good training?
   a) Engaging the best trainers
   b) Using audio-visual aids
   c) Following the training process
   d) Including variety of training methods

105. Which principle should be followed when selecting trainers for a training program?
   a) Choose according to convenience
   b) Go by familiarity
   c) Learn from the best
   d) Rely on affordability

106. How does inductive learning proceed?
   a) From general to specific
   b) Only through specific examples
   c) From specific to general
   d) Through random selection of examples

107. Which of the following techniques is NOT mentioned as a follow-up technique post-training?
   a) Back-at-work project
   b) On-the-job coaching
   c) Random feedback collection
   d) Video conferencing

108. What is a key advantage of using audio-visual (AV) aids in training?
   a) Saves money for the organization
   b) Stimulates multiple senses, enhancing learning
   c) Reduces the need for trainers
   d) Serves as a replacement for practical experience

109. Which statement best describes training follow-up?
   a) A trainer's job ends after the training session.
   b) Training is a process and not an event.
   c) Training should be forgotten quickly.
   d) Impact of training is always measured.

110. What percentage of training can be lost within six months without proper follow-up, as estimated?
   a) 25%
   b) 50%
   c) 75%
   d) 10%

111. What is the primary aim of a follow-up workshop post-training?

a) Provide a refreshment course

b) Assess the degree of training transfer

c) Introduce new topics

d) Offer additional resources

112. Why is selecting the right trainees crucial for a training program?

a) It makes training more affordable.

b) It ensures training remains aimless.

c) The right trainees help in promoting the training.

d) Wrong selection can render the training unfruitful.

113. Which of the following best defines training's inductive learning style?

a) Trainee-centered with active participation

b) Trainer-centered with minimal participation

c) Focused solely on lectures and seminars

d) Random exploration of topics without structure

114. What major shift did the IT revolution bring about in accessing knowledge?

a) From limited access to unlimited access

b) From knowledge available anytime to anytime restricted

c) From knowledge that was available at a certain time and place to knowledge accessible anytime and anywhere

d) From modern networking to traditional methods

115. Which form of online training requires both the instructor and learner to be online at the same time?

a) Asynchronous **b) Synchronous**

c) Both a and b d) None of the above

116. Which organization was established by the Ministry of Agriculture & Farmers Welfare in 1987?

a) NAARM **b) MANAGE**

c) IIPM d) ISTD

117. For which purpose are simulators primarily used?
    a) To promote products
    b) For financial predictions
    c) To imitate real-life processes for training
    d) For social media promotions

118. Which of the following is NOT a function of IIPM?
    a) Organizing short term executive programmes
    b) Analyzing rural development programs across states
    c) Offering post graduate diploma in agri-business & plantation management
    d) Conducting brainstorming workshops and seminars

119. The National Academy of Agricultural Research Management (NAARM) was primarily established to provide foundation training for:
    a) Students of agriculture
    b) Entrepreneurs in agribusiness
    c) New entrants of the agricultural research service (ars) of icar
    d) Agricultural extension workers

120. Which institution assists the Ministry of Rural Development and is recognized as one of the UN-ESCAP Centres of Excellence?
    a) ISTD
    b) EEI
    c) NIRD & PR
    d) IIPM

121. Which organization is affiliated to both the International Federation of Training and Development Organizations (IFTDO) and Asian Regional Training and Development Organizations (ARTDO)
    a) NAARM
    b) IIPM
    c) ISTD
    d) MANAGE

122. Smart classrooms utilize all of the following EXCEPT:
    a) Video data projector
    b) Augmented reality glasses
    c) Desktop computer system
    d) Mobile phones for social media

123. What is the primary mode through which ISTD conducts its Diploma in Training and Development?

a) Classroom-based learning
b) Online courses
c) Distance learning
d) Practical sessions

124. What is the origin of the word 'Lecture'?

a) Greek
b) English
c) French
d) Latin

125. Which training method focuses on the free flow of unrestrained ideas in a group setting?

a) Field method
b) Case study
c) Lecture
d) Brainstorming

126. The in-depth study of a selected individual or situation is known as:

a) Role play
b) Case study
c) Buzz group
d) Microlab

127. Which method offers a mix of education and entertainment by exposing learners to real-life experiences?

a) Lecture
b) Brainstorming
c) Field method
d) Business games

128. What is a significant limitation of the Lecture method?

a) Too interactive
b) Requires a lot of resources
c) Cannot handle voluminous information
d) Fosters passiveness

129. For which method is an experienced facilitator crucial due to its nature and group dynamics?

a) Field method
b) Case study
c) Brainstorming
d) Role play

130. Which of the following best describes the essence of the Field Method?

a) Learning by observing
b) Engaging in group discussions
c) Solving business problems
d) Analyzing past business decisions

131. The risk of researcher bias is most associated with which method?

a) Brainstorming
b) Case study
c) Lecture
d) Buzz groups

132. Which training method is the oldest and is primarily an oral presentation?

a) Brainstorming
b) Field method
c) Lecture
d) Role play

133. Which method requires careful planning due to potential expenses and time constraints?

a) Lecture
b) Brainstorming
c) Microlab
d) Field method

134. Group discussions are primarily aimed to assess:

a) Technical expertise
b) Teamwork and interpersonal communication
c) Intellectual capability
d) Memory retention

135. A potential limitation of group discussions is that:

a) All members always contribute equally
b) They are too short
c) Some members may not contribute as much as others
d) They are always efficient

136. The purpose of Sensitivity Training is to enhance:

a) Intellectual skills
b) Physical strength
c) Individual awareness of self and others
d) Memory retention

137. Buzz groups are designed for:

a) Long discussions
b) Solitary reflections
c) Quick solutions to an assigned problem
d) Team building exercises

138. The Microlab technique is mainly used:

a) At the end of a course

b) For long-duration courses

c) As an ice-breaking exercise at the beginning of a course

d) During breaks

139. The primary appeal of Role play in training is because:

a) It is easy to prepare

b) It engages multiple senses

c) It is short in duration

d) It is always accurate

140. Business games are increasingly transitioning to:

a) Books

b) Board games

c) Computer-based simulations

d) Face-to-face meetings

141. In the Fishbowl technique, the difference between a closed and open method is:

a) Number of experts

b) Presence of an audience

c) Empty chairs in the center circle

d) Duration of the discussion

142. The In-basket simulation technique primarily tests a candidate's:

a) Memory skills

b) Physical fitness

c) Adaptive thinking and problem-solving under pressure

d) Prior work experience

18

Incorporating Gender and Nutrition in Agri-Tech Extensions

1. According to the FAO report, which policy is NOT mentioned to promote gender equality in global food and agriculture systems?
   a) Ensure equal representation in politics
   b) Promote equal access to resources
   c) Eliminate outright discrimination under the law
   d) Ensure that women are equal participants in sustainable agricultural development discussions

2. Which statement best describes gender according to FAO?
   a) It is determined biologically
   b) It is related to how society is organized
   c) It is a result of sexual characteristics
   d) It is the physical differences between men and women

3. What does the term 'sex' refer to according to Robert Stoller?
   a) Behavior of individuals
   b) Physical differences between men and women
   c) Socially constructed differences
   d) Cultural practices of individuals

4. What does gender identity primarily relate to?
   a) Social construction of gender
   b) Behavior and cultural practices
   c) Existence as male or female
   d) Systematic, unfavorable treatment of individuals

5. What is gender discrimination?
   a) Network of structures in an organization
   b) Differences between men and women
   c) Gender differences and social relations
   d) Systematic, unfavorable treatment based on gender

6. Which consequence is NOT associated with gender stereotypes?
   a) Gender inequality
   b) Gender identity
   c) Gender-based violence
   d) Continuous reproduction of gender inequalities

7. What does gender analysis focus on?
   a) Gathering information on cultural practices
   b) The systematic gathering of gender differences and social relations
   c) Promoting equal access to resources
   d) Gender narratives in development discourse

8. Gender mainstreaming was first proposed at which conference?
   a) Fourth World Conference on Women in Beijing
   b) Third World Conference on Women in Nairobi
   c) United Nations General Assembly
   d) FAO Global Summit

9. The definition "women having the same opportunities in life as men" relates to:
   a) Gender equity
   b) Gender parity
   c) Gender equality
   d) Gender sensitivity

10. What does gender blindness mean?
   a) Recognizing the roles of women and men
   b) Failure to recognize roles based on gender in different contexts
   c) Gender narratives in development discourse
   d) Being sensitive to gender differences

11. Which term refers to the application of gender mainstreaming in the budgetary process?
   a) Gender planning
   b) Gender budgeting
   c) Gender auditing
   d) Gender division of labour

12. What is the focus of the Gender and Development approach?
   a) Inclusion of women in development
   b) Challenging existing gender roles and relations
   c) Economic and social efficiency
   d) Gender budgeting and planning

13. Gender parity in education means:
    a) Boys and girls have the same educational opportunities
    b) Boys are preferred over girls
    c) Girls are preferred over boys
    d) Girls and boys receive different levels of education

14. Which term relates to behavior that shows favoritism toward one gender?
    a) Gender blindness
    b) Gender bias
    c) Gender sensitivity
    d) Gender equity

15. The Women in Development approach became popular in which time period?
    a) Late 1970s and early 1980s
    b) Late 1980s and early 1990s
    c) Early 1970s
    d) Mid 1980s

16. Gender sensitivity differs from gender blindness in that it involves:
    a Failing to recognize gender roles
    b Being able to perceive gender differences and issues
    c) Not understanding social differences
    d) Ignoring gender differences in policies

17. The term 'gender' is used to refer to:
    a) Biological differences between men and women
    b) Cultural, socially constructed differences between sexes
    c) The systematic gathering of gender differences
    d) The roles and responsibilities in economic contexts

18. Gender policy seeks to ensure:
    a) Consistency of gender principles and accountability
    b) Gender stereotypes and consequences
    c) A gender-based assessment of budgets
    d) The inclusion of women in development

19. Which term involves the recognition of existing gender inequalities and formulation of policies to mitigate them?
    a) Gender auditing
    b) Gender planning
    c) Gender budgeting
    d) Gender mainstreaming

20. The systematic gathering and examination of information on gender differences is known as:

a) Gender division of labour
b) Gender planning
c) Gender awareness
d) Gender analysis

21. Gender narratives in development discourse can be identified as:

a) Women in Development approach and Gender and Development approach
b) Gender policy and gender planning
c) Gender auditing and gender budgeting
d) Gender equity and gender parity

22. Gender equity leads to:

a) Gender bias
b) Gender sensitivity
c) Gender equality
d) Gender blindness

23. The roles and activities deemed appropriate for women and men based on societal ideas are termed:

a) Gender division of labour
b) Gender mainstreaming
c) Gender parity
d) Gender auditing

24. The GAD approach came to the forefront in:

a) Late 1970s
b) Early 1980s
c) Late 1980s
d) Early 1990s

25. The United Nations defined gender mainstreaming as:

a) Process of assessing implications for women and men of any planned action
b The systematic gathering of gender differences
c) Gender-based assessment of budgets
d) Ensuring equitable sustainable human development

26. Which of the following focuses on inclusion of women in development?

a) Gender and Development approach
b) Women in Development approach
c) Gender mainstreaming
d) Gender planning

27. What is the primary difference between gender equality and gender equity?
    a) Equality is about equal representation, while equity is about fairness.
    b) They both mean the same.
    c) Equity leads to equality.
    d) Equality is about fairness, while equity is about equal representation.

28. What is Gender awareness?
    a) Recognizing gender roles
    b) Understanding socially determined differences between men and women
    c) Formulating policies to mitigate gender inequalities
    d) Challenging existing gender roles and relations

29. Gender management system (GMS) is:
    a) A process to eliminate gender bias
    b) A network of structures to mainstream gender in an organization
    c) The process of creating gender policies
    d) A method to plan gender roles

30. Gender stereotype consequences include all EXCEPT:
    a) Gender equality
    b) Continuous reproduction of gender inequalities
    c) Gender-based violence
    d) Gender inequality

31. When was the concept of gender mainstreaming first introduced?
    a) 1975
    b) 1980
    c) 1985
    d) 1990

32. Where was the United Nations Fourth World Conference on Women held, which established gender mainstreaming as a global strategy for gender equality?
    a) Nairobi
    b) New York
    c) Geneva
    d) Beijing

33. Which two dimensions need to be considered in gender mainstreaming?
    a) Gender sensitivity and gender responsibility
    b) Gender representation and gender responsive content
    c) Gender resources and gender relations
    d) Gender responsibility and gender representation

34. Which approach focuses on challenging the power relations and roles within society in gender mainstreaming?

    a) WID Approach
    b) GAD Approach
    c) Equity Approach
    d) Empowerment Approach

35. What is highlighted as the first essential step in the gender mainstreaming strategy by the Platform for Action (Beijing 1995)?

    a) Gender budgeting
    b) Gender analysis
    c) Gender representation
    d) Gender participation

36. What does gender mainstreaming not advocate for?

    a) Incorporating gender perspectives to make them very visible
    b) Focusing on both women and men
    c) Adding a women's component to existing programmes
    d) Giving attention to gender equality from the start of processes

37. What does a baseline gender analysis focus on?

    a) Assessing effects of a policy on men and women
    b) Assessing the situation at the start of an intervention regarding the balance between women and men concerning power and access to opportunities
    c) Introducing a gender perspective to the budgetary process
    d) Using gender-disaggregated data for decision making

38. What is the primary goal of a gender impact assessment?

    a) To allocate resources specific to women
    b) To assess a planned policy/intervention in terms of its effects on women, men, and gender equality
    c) To provide a positive public image for both genders
    d) To ensure gender-balanced participation in teams

39. Which method involves introducing a gender perspective at all budgetary process levels?

    a) Baseline gender analysis
    b) Gender impact assessment
    c) Gender budgeting
    d) Gender-sensitive communication

40. How can gender-sensitive communication benefit society?
    a) By allocating resources specific to women
    b) By avoiding perpetuating stereotypes and promoting a positive image of both genders
    c) By assessing the effects of a policy on men and women
    d) By ensuring gender-balanced participation in teams

41. Gender mainstreaming should be integrated into which of the following?
    a) Only projects
    b) Only programmes
    c) Only policies
    d) All policies, programmes, and projects

42. Which approach is ideal for understanding the training and extension needs of women through Gender Analysis?
    a) Progressive Approach
    b) Evolutionary Approach
    c) Participatory Approach
    d) Comprehensive Approach

43. What should gender-friendly technologies ideally do for women farmers?
    a) Increase the number of tasks they perform
    b) Reduce drudgery and prove profitable
    c) Only focus on profitability
    d) Simply replace traditional methods

44. What is the primary benefit of alternative ergonomically tested drudgery-reducing technologies for farm women?
    a) They increase the yield.
    b) They are cheaper.
    c) Women get technologically empowered with recognition of gender roles.
    d) They are easily available.

45. The strategy of posting female para-extension agriculturists in their own villages suggests the appointment of:
    a) Male supervisors
    b) Female supervisors and Subject matter specialists (SMSS) from R&D institutes
    c) Foreign specialists
    d) Male para-extension agriculturists

46. How can the stereotyped attitude of male agents towards gender roles be addressed?
    a) By sidelining them
    b) By promoting only female agents
    c) Through regular gender sensitization courses
    d) By reducing their pay

47. The Women's Empowerment in Agriculture Index (WEAI) measures women's roles in agriculture in all the following domains EXCEPT:
    a) Decision about agricultural production
    b) Leadership in the community
    c) Gender-based agricultural methods
    d) Access to and decision-making power over productive resources

48. What increases by 20% when the mother controls the household budget?
    a) Household income
    b) A child's survival chances
    c) Food security
    d) Women's empowerment

49. What role have women historically played in agriculture?
    a) Only consumers
    b) Both the source and custodians of traditional knowledge and skills
    c) Secondary roles in decision-making
    d) Only workers without decision-making power

50. For achieving long-term goals of gender equity and women's empowerment, the focus should be on:
    a) Only technological advancement
    b) Only agricultural development
    c) Strengthening the caring for women and adolescent girls
    d) Only policy reform

51. What is the central question of Gender Impact Assessment (GIA)?
    a) What are the negative consequences of a decision?
    b) How will the decision affect agricultural output?
    c) Does a law, policy or programme reduce, maintain or increase the gender inequalities between women and men?
    d) How many women are involved in agricultural production?

52. What is the final aim of the gender impact assessment?
    a) To increase the number of policies.
    b) To improve the design and the planning of the policy under consideration, in order to prevent a negative impact on gender equality.
    c) To provide more employment opportunities for women.
    d) To reduce the number of policies affecting men.

53. In a gender impact assessment, during which step do you analyze the situation of women and men in the field?
    a) Step 1: Definition of the policy purpose
    b) Step 2: Checking gender relevance
    c) Step 3: Gender-sensitive analysis
    d) Step 4: Weighing the gender impact

54. According to FAO 2010-2011, what percentage of the agricultural labor force in developing countries consists of women?
    a) 10-20%
    b) 43%
    c) 60-80%
    d) 90%

55. The Companies Act 2013 of India mandates companies with a certain net worth to allocate what percentage of their net profit from the last three years on CSR projects?
    a) 1%
    b) 2%
    c) 5%
    d) 10%

56. Which of the following is NOT a listed activity for CSR as per the Companies Act 2013 of India?
    a) Promoting gender equality
    b) Empowering women
    c) Enhancing agricultural produce
    d) Eradicating extreme hunger and poverty

57. Which mechanism is highlighted in the context of linking CSR with extension?
    a) Public-Private-Partnership in Agriculture
    b) Public-Private-Partnership in Extension
    c) Public-Private-Partnership in Health
    d) Public-Private-Partnership in Education

58. What is the primary purpose of gender sensitizing?
    a) To understand the differences between men and women.
    b) To change behavior and instill empathy regarding views on gender.
    c) To promote better health practices.
    d) To increase employment opportunities for women.

59. What does gender sensitization primarily aim to bring about?
    a) Reproductive health awareness.
    b) Economic growth.
    c) Equal opportunity, gender equity, and women empowerment.
    d) Political dominance for women.

60. For what purpose is the adoption of gender budgeting essential in gender sensitization?
    a) To increase the national GDP.
    b) To ensure women participation in governance at all levels.
    c) To provide more funds for male-centric projects.
    d) To increase foreign investments.

61. Which of the following is NOT highlighted as an area where gender sensitivity is required?
    a) Reproductive health.
    b) Stewardship of natural resources.
    c) Women's access to technology.
    d) Economic empowerment.

62. What is the main objective of gender sensitization training?
    a) To create job opportunities for women.
    b) To provide knowledge about political structures.
    c) To give insights into economic disparities.
    d) To develop awareness, knowledge, skill, and behavior in relation to gender.

63. Which of the following is NOT a goal of gender sensitization?
    a) Reviewing existing policies with a gender perspective.
    b) Formulating gender perspective guidelines.
    c) Increasing the salaries of women.
    d) Monitoring gender activities in all ministries.

64. Why should governance not ignore the current situation of women, as mentioned in the text?
   a) Because it's mentioned in international treaties.
   b) Due to the large percentages of women suffering poverty, poor health, and violence.
   c) Because of global pressure.
   d) As it affects the national economy directly.

65. What did the IFPRI study based on NFHS-4 (2015-16) data primarily highlight?
   a) The stunting of children in India.
   b) The malnutrition among pregnant women.
   c) Immunization rates in children.
   d) Maternal mortality rates.

66. Which programme was initiated by the Government of India in 1975 to reduce socio-economic and gender inequities?
   a) National Health Policy.
   b) Janani Suraksha Yojana.
   c) ICDS Programme.
   d) National Nutrition Mission.

67. Which of the following is NOT a component of the National Health Mission launched in 2013?
   a) The National Urban Health Mission.
   b) Human Resources for Health and Medical Education.
   c) ICDS Programme.
   d) Tertiary Care Programs.

68. What does the Pradhan Mantri Surakshit Matritva Abhiyan (PMSMA) launched in 2016 primarily focus on?
   a) Providing financial assistance to pregnant women.
   b) Encouraging women to have institutional deliveries.
   c) Improving the quality and coverage of antenatal care.
   d) Supplying free drugs to all pregnant women.

69. What is the primary aim of the Janani Shishu Suraksha Karyakram (JSSK)?
   a) To provide immunization to children below 6 years.
   b) To facilitate institutional deliveries and bear all associated expenses.
   c) To offer financial incentives to pregnant and lactating women.
   d) To provide primary health care to all.

70. What is the goal of the Swachh Bharat Mission?
    a) Improve maternal health.
    b) Construct toilets and change behaviors to make India Open Defecation Free.
    c) Improve infrastructure at the district level.
    d) Improve the quality of treatment in hospitals

71. The National Nutrition Mission (NNM) launched in 2017-18 is designed to:
    a) Focus solely on maternal nutrition.
    b) Map various schemes addressing malnutrition and act as a central nodal agency.
    c) Ensure all children receive primary education.
    d) Deal solely with micronutrient malnutrition.

72. According to MS Swaminathan's suggestions for NNM, which among the following is NOT listed as an interactive component integral to NNM?
    a) Overcoming under-nutrition through the Food Security Act.
    b) Increasing the production of rice and wheat.
    c) Overcoming micronutrient malnutrition through bio-fortified plants.
    d) Ensuring food quality through improved post-harvest management.

73. To tackle malnutrition in children and mothers effectively, what is suggested as necessary?
    a) Relying only on government-funded programs.
    b) Implementing health and nutrition programs effectively.
    c) Scaling down food fortification efforts.
    d) Avoiding public-private partnerships.

74. What does a gender budget imply?
    a) A separate budget exclusively for women.
    b) An attempt to assess government priorities and how they impact women and men.
    c) A budget that solely focuses on women's empowerment.
    d) A budget that emphasizes gender stereotypes.

75. Which terms describe initiatives that use gender as a lens to analyze budgets?
    a) Gender-responsive budgets and gender-insensitive budgets.
    b) Women's budgets and gender-sensitive budgets.
    c) Feminist budgets and men's budgets.
    d) Equality budgets and gender-neutral budgets.

76. A gender-responsive budget is one that:
    a) Is exclusive to women.
    b) Ignores societal gender patterns.
    c) Allocates money to reinforce societal gender patterns.
    d) Allocates money to change gender patterns and move towards a more gender-equal society.

77. When did the Ministry of Women and Child Development (MWCD) in India recognize gender budgeting as a tool for women's empowerment?
    a) 2001 **b) 2004**
    c) 2007 d) 2010

78. What purpose do gender budget cells serve?
    a) To allocate budgets exclusively for women.
    b) To coordinate gender budgeting initiatives intra- and inter-ministerially.
    c) To ensure an equal budget allocation for men and women.
    d) To oversee the implementation of gender policies at a local level.

79. What is the primary objective of gender analysis in agriculture?
    a) Exclusively increase women's participation.
    b) Improve overall project performance and promote equal opportunities.
    c) Focus only on economic outcomes.
    d) Challenge traditional agricultural practices.

80. Gender analysis in a socio-cultural context, especially in India, is subjective because:
    a) It focuses exclusively on women's roles.
    b) It does not consider societal influences.
    c) It examines how the role of men and women is constructed within various cultural and familial contexts.
    d) It only takes economic factors into account.

81. What are women's practical needs?

a) Needs related to legal rights and domestic violence.

b) Needs that revolve around day-to-day living such as housing and healthcare.

c) Needs that challenge their subordination.

d) Needs based exclusively on employment opportunities.

82. Which of the following best describes the steps of gender analysis as synthesized by the United Nations Development Programme (UNDP)?

a) Gender Equality + Representation + Budgeting = Gender Analysis.

b) Sex-Disaggregated Data + Analysis + A Gender Perspective = Gender Analysis.

c) Gender Budgeting + Equality + Perspective = Gender Analysis.

d) Gender Roles + Responsibilities + Equality = Gender Analysis.

83. Assessment of roles and responsibilities/division of labour involves considering:

a) Only formal employment roles of women and men.

b) Only the roles of boys and girls within the household.

c) Women and men's roles in relation to employment, community participation, and household roles.

d) The traditional roles of women in society.

84. What does technology encompasses?

a) Only electronic devices

b) Physical machinery

c) Social arrangements and processes along with equipment

d) Internet platforms

85. Which of the following is NOT a goal of integrating technology in agriculture for women?

a) Reducing work strain and drudgery

b) Ensuring timeliness in field operations

c) Amplifying aesthetic appeal of the fields

d) Enhancing the quality of work life of agricultural workers

86. Why might a drudgery-reducing technology have unintended consequences for poor women?

a) It might be too expensive.

b) It can potentially eliminate a vital source of income.

c) It might increase their workload.

d) It can expose them to harmful chemicals.

87. What is an important factor to consider when innovating technology for women in agriculture?

a) The technology should be complex to ensure efficiency.

b) It should focus solely on increasing income.

c) Improving upon existing skills and understanding the science behind processes.

d) The technology should always be digital.

88. Which of the following is NOT cited as a recommendation in the context of technology and women's lives?

a) Emphasizing on gender sensitization in research and technology.

b) Overlooking sanitation facilities for the sake of development.

c) Understanding the triple role of women during technology preparation.

d) Involving women at every stage of technology development, testing, and modification.

89. How can women leaders and members of local organizations act in the context of technology?

a) By opposing technological advancements

b) By acting as passive observers

c) By serving as active 'change agents' through various communication methods

d) By restricting technological access to certain groups

90. What is the role of traditional knowledge of women?

a) It is outdated and not useful.

b) It should be the primary base for innovating technology.

c) It is only related to folklore and legends.

d) It doesn't have any practical implications.

91. What is the outcome of technology on women's life?
    a) It hinders their ability to work efficiently.
    b) It opens pathways to entrepreneurship and improves various aspects of life.
    c) It has no significant impact.
    d) It creates unnecessary complications in their daily tasks.

92. Which aspect is crucial for the success of technological changes?
    a) Rapid implementation without feedback
    b) Ignoring community inputs
    c) Ensuring changes in attitudes and building up local capacity
    d) Sole reliance on international standards

93. The Digital India campaign places special emphasis on:
    a) Mobile phone access for all
    b) Digital financial transactions and cloud technologies
    c) Gender-neutral technology development
    d) Digital education only for children

94. What impedes rural women's access to business information and opportunities?
    a) Lack of interest in technology
    b) Higher prices of mobile phones for women
    c) Restriction from the community
    d) Lesser internet access and lower mobile phone ownership than men

95. Which initiative primarily focuses on digital technology for its functioning?
    a) Rashtriya Mahila Kosh
    b) One Stop Centres
    c) Ujjawala
    d) Dhanlakshmi scheme

96. Which of the following sectors is NOT considered a non-traditional skill sector for women as per the given passage?
    a) Mobile phone repair
    b) Masonry
    c) Pickle making
    d) Welding

97. Digital literacy can play a crucial role in:
    a) Restructuring government policies
    b) Strengthening Self-Help Groups (SHGs)
    c) Increasing women's workload
    d) Digitalizing urban areas only

98. Which mode has a transformational impact offering opportunities in made-to-order meals and handicrafts?
    a) Digital India campaign
    b) E-Kranti
    c) E-commerce
    d) National Portal of India

99. Which initiative by the Government of India in 2015 aims for a holistic development approach?
    a) Digital India campaign
    b) National Portal of India
    c) E-Kranti
    d) Ujjawala

100. The National Portal of India primarily serves as:
    a) A platform for women to communicate
    b) A mobile application for financial transactions
    c) A single window access to information and services provided by the Indian Government
    d) An e-commerce platform for businesses

101. Who traditionally are thought of as better communicators as per the passage?
    a) Men
    b) Women
    c) Both equally
    d) Not mentioned in the passage

102. According to the passage, digital technology can enable women to:
    a) Only access entertainment
    b) Only handle their financial records
    c) Form networks of business or mutual benefit socially and economically
    d) Replace traditional job roles

103. Who is primarily responsible for healthcare in India?
    a) Local communities
    b) Individual states and territories
    c) Private institutions
    d International organizations

104. According to the FAO, when is food security achieved?
   a) When the global population has access to food
   b) When there is an oversupply of agricultural products
   c) When people have access to nutritious food for an active life at all levels
   d) When a nation produces more than it consumes

105. What percentage of female main and marginal workers are agricultural laborers in India, as per the publication "Women and Men in India 2014"?
   a) 41.1%
   b) 24%
   c) 55%
   d) 35.5%

106. What is the sex ratio according to Census 2011?
   a) 933 females per 1000 males
   b) 918 females per 1000 males
   c) 940 females per 1000 males
   d) 927 females per 1000 males

107. What is the legal minimum age of marriage for girls in India?
   a) 16 years
   b) 20 years
   c) 18 years
   d) 15 years

108. Which of the following is a major cause of maternal death in India?
   a) Chronic fatigue
   b) Sepsis
   c) Infertility
   d) Chronic pelvic infection

109. How does maternal malnutrition primarily affect pregnancy?
   a) Causes hypertension in mothers
   b) Leads to poor weight gain and high prevalence of low birth weight
   c) Increases the risk of eclampsia
   d) Increases the chances of multiple pregnancies

110. Which program is NOT mentioned as targeting nutrition outcomes?
   a) Integrated Child Development Services (ICDS)
   b) National Food Safety Mission
   c) Janani Suraksha Yojana
   d) National Education Mission

111. What trend in Child Sex Ratio from 1991 to 2011 is seen as an indicator of gender bias in India?

a An increase from 945 to 927

b) A decrease from 945 to 918

c) A steady rate of 930 throughout the years

d) A significant increase from 910 to 945

112. Which is a challenge still faced by India despite significant economic gains over the past two decades?

a) Overpopulation

b) Maternal and child under-nutrition

c) Agricultural decline

d) Urban migration

113. What did the IFPRI study based on NFHS-4 (2015-16) data primarily highlight?

a) The stunting of children in India.

b) The malnutrition among pregnant women.

c) Immunization rates in children.

d) Maternal mortality rates.

114. What is the primary aim of the Janani Shishu Suraksha Karyakram (JSSK)?

a) To provide immunization to children below 6 years.

b) To facilitate institutional deliveries and bear all associated expenses.

c) To offer financial incentives to pregnant and lactating women.

d) To provide primary health care to all.

115 What is the goal of the Swachh Bharat Mission?

a) Improve maternal health.

b) Construct toilets and change behaviors to make India Open Defecation Free.

c) Improve infrastructure at the district level.

d) Improve the quality of treatment in hospitals.

116. Which initiative aims to ensure full immunization coverage of 90% children by 2020?
    a) National Disease Control Programs.
    b) Janani Shishu Suraksha Karyakram.
    c) Mission Indradhanush.
    d) Rashtriya Bal Swasthya Karyakram.

117. To tackle malnutrition in children and mothers effectively, what is suggested as necessary?
    a) Relying only on government-funded programs.
    b) Implementing health and nutrition programs effectively.
    c) Scaling down food fortification efforts.
    d) Avoiding public-private partnerships.

118. What is the primary purpose of gender sensitizing?
    a) To understand the differences between men and women.
    b) To change behavior and instill empathy regarding views on gender.
    c) To promote better health practices.
    d) To increase employment opportunities for women.

119. What does gender sensitization primarily aim to bring about?
    a) Reproductive health awareness.
    b) Economic growth.
    c) Equal opportunity, gender equity, and women empowerment.
    d) Political dominance for women.

120. For what purpose is the adoption of gender budgeting essential in gender sensitization?
    a) To increase the national GDP.
    b) To ensure women participation in governance at all levels.
    c) To provide more funds for male-centric projects.
    d) To increase foreign investments.

121. Which of the following is NOT highlighted as an area where gender sensitivity is required?
    a) Reproductive health.
    b) Stewardship of natural resources.
    c) Women's access to technology.
    d) Economic empowerment.

122. What is the main objective of gender sensitization training?
   a) To create job opportunities for women.
   b) To provide knowledge about political structures.
   c) To give insights into economic disparities.
   d) To develop awareness, knowledge, skill, and behavior in relation to gender.

123. Which of the following is NOT a goal of gender sensitization?
   a) Reviewing existing policies with a gender perspective.
   b) Formulating gender perspective guidelines.
   c) Increasing the salaries of women.
   d) Monitoring gender activities in all ministries.

124. Why should governance not ignore the current situation of women, as mentioned in the text?
   a) Because it's mentioned in international treaties.
   b) Due to the large percentages of women suffering poverty, poor health, and violence.
   c) Because of global pressure.
   d) As it affects the national economy directly.

125. What is the central question of Gender Impact Assessment (GIA)?
   a) What are the negative consequences of a decision?
   b) How will the decision affect agricultural output?
   c) Does a law, policy or programme reduce, maintain or increase the gender inequalities between women and men?
   d) How many women are involved in agricultural production?

126. What is the final aim of the gender impact assessment?
   a) To increase the number of policies.
   b) To improve the design and the planning of the policy under consideration, in order to prevent a negative impact on gender equality.
   c) To provide more employment opportunities for women.
   d) To reduce the number of policies affecting men.

127. In a gender impact assessment, during which step do you analyze the situation of women and men in the field?
   a) Step 1: Definition of the policy purpose
   b) Step 2: Checking gender relevance
   c) Step 3: Gender-sensitive analysis
   d) Step 4: Weighing the gender impact

128. According to FAO 2010-2011, what percentage of the agricultural labor force in developing countries consists of women?
   a) 10-20%
   b) 43%
   c) 60-80%
   d) 90%

129. The Companies Act 2013 of India mandates companies with a certain net worth to allocate what percentage of their net profit from the last three years on CSR projects?
   a) 1%
   b) 2%
   c) 5%
   d) 10%

130. Which of the following is NOT a listed activity for CSR as per the Companies Act 2013 of India?
   a) Promoting gender equality
   b) Empowering women
   c) Enhancing agricultural produce
   d) Eradicating extreme hunger and poverty

131. Which mechanism is highlighted in the context of linking CSR with extension?
   a) Public-Private-Partnership in Agriculture
   b) Public-Private-Partnership in Extension
   c) Public-Private-Partnership in Health
   d) Public-Private-Partnership in Education

132. Gender mainstreaming should be integrated into which of the following?
   a) Only projects
   b) Only programmes
   c) Only policies
   d) All policies, programmes, and projects

133. Which approach is ideal for understanding the training and extension needs of women through Gender Analysis?
   a) Progressive Approach
   b) Evolutionary Approach
   c) Participatory Approach
   d) Comprehensive Approach

134. What should gender-friendly technologies ideally do for women farmers?
   a) Increase the number of tasks they perform
   b) Reduce drudgery and prove profitable
   c) Only focus on profitability
   d) Simply replace traditional methods

135. What is the primary benefit of alternative ergonomically tested drudgery-reducing technologies for farm women?
    a) They increase the yield.
    b) They are cheaper.
    c) Women get technologically empowered with recognition of gender roles.
    d) They are easily available.

136. The strategy of posting female para-extension agriculturists in their own villages suggests the appointment of:
    a) Male supervisors
    b) Female supervisors and Subject matter specialists (SMSS) from R&D institutes
    c) Foreign specialists
    d) Male para-extension agriculturists

137. How can the stereotyped attitude of male agents towards gender roles be addressed?
    a) By sidelining them
    b) By promoting only female agents
    c) Through regular gender sensitization courses
    d) By reducing their pay

138. The Women's Empowerment in Agriculture Index (WEAI) measures women's roles in agriculture in all the following domains EXCEPT:
    a) Decision about agricultural production
    b) Leadership in the community
    c) Gender-based agricultural methods
    d) Access to and decision-making power over productive resources

139. What increases by 20% when the mother controls the household budget?
    a) Household income
    b) A child's survival chances
    c) Food security
    d) Women's empowerment

140. What role have women historically played in agriculture?
    a) Only consumers
    b) Both the source and custodians of traditional knowledge and skills
    c) Secondary roles in decision-making
    d) Only workers without decision-making power

141. For achieving long-term goals of gender equity and women's empowerment, the focus should be on:

   a) Only technological advancement

   b) Only agricultural development

   c) Strengthening the caring for women and adolescent girls

   d) Only policy reform

142. Who developed the Women's Empowerment Framework?

   a) P. Adhiguru

   b) Niketha. L

   c) Sara Hlupekile Longwe

   d) Letha Devi. G

143. According to the Women's Empowerment Framework, which level of equality relates to "Equal control in decision-making over factors of production"?

   a) Conscientisation

   b) Participation

   c) Welfare

   d) Control

144. What does a Neutral level of recognition for women's issues in a project signify?

   a) Project objectives are silent about women's issues.

   b) Project objectives recognize women's issues but remain neutral.

   c) Project objectives improve the position of women relative to men.

   d) Project objectives give women full control over the project.

145. Which plan recognized women's productive role and their contribution?

   a) Fifth Five Year Plan (1974-79)

   b) Sixth Five Year Plan (1980-85)

   c) Seventh Five Year Plan (1985-90)

   d) Eighth Five Year Plan (1992-97)

146. The 73rd constitutional amendment to the Panchayat Raj Act in 1993 specified what percentage of the posts of Sarpanch and Chairman to be occupied by women?

   a) 10%

   b) 25%

   c) 33%

   d) 50%

147. Which approach is promoted by UNIFEM to address the issue of resource allocation for women in all sectors?

a) Development Approach

b) Equality Approach

c) Gender and Development Approach

d) Gender Budgeting

148. What is the primary objective of the women's empowerment framework?

a) Achieve women's participation in administration.

b) Ensure equal distribution of resources.

c) Achieve women's empowerment by enabling equal control over factors of production and equal participation in the development process.

d) To increase women's welfare in society.

149. What does technology encompasses?

a) Only electronic devices

b) Physical machinery

c) Social arrangements and processes along with equipment

d) Internet platforms

150. Which of the following is NOT a goal of integrating technology in agriculture for women?

a) Reducing work strain and drudgery

b) Ensuring timeliness in field operations

c) Amplifying aesthetic appeal of the fields

d) Enhancing the quality of work life of agricultural workers

151. Why might a drudgery-reducing technology have unintended consequences for poor women?

a) It might be too expensive.

b) It can potentially eliminate a vital source of income.

c) It might increase their workload.

d) It can expose them to harmful chemicals.

152. What is an important factor to consider when innovating technology for women in agriculture?

a) The technology should be complex to ensure efficiency.

b) It should focus solely on increasing income.

c) Improving upon existing skills and understanding the science behind processes.

d) The technology should always be digital.

153. Which of the following is NOT cited as a recommendation in the context of technology and women's lives?

a) Emphasizing on gender sensitization in research and technology.

b) Overlooking sanitation facilities for the sake of development.

c) Understanding the triple role of women during technology preparation.

d) Involving women at every stage of technology development, testing, and modification.

154. How can women leaders and members of local organizations act in the context of technology?

a) By opposing technological advancements

b) By acting as passive observers

c) By serving as active 'change agents' through various communication methods

d) By restricting technological access to certain groups

155. What is the role of traditional knowledge of women?

a) It is outdated and not useful.

b) It should be the primary base for innovating technology.

c) It is only related to folklore and legends.

d) It doesn't have any practical implications.

156. What is the outcome of technology on women's life?

a) It hinders their ability to work efficiently.

b) It opens pathways to entrepreneurship and improves various aspects of life.

c) It has no significant impact.

d) It creates unnecessary complications in their daily tasks.

157. Which aspect is crucial for the success of technological changes?
   a) Rapid implementation without feedback
   b) Ignoring community inputs
   c) Ensuring changes in attitudes and building up local capacity
   d) Sole reliance on international standards

158. Which scheme provides training to poor and marginalized women aged 16 years and above in traditional trades to improve employability?
   a) MUDRA Bank
   b) DDU-GKY
   c) STEP
   d) Stand-Up India

159. What percentage of women and girls reinvest their earnings back into their families?
   a) 50-60%
   b) 20-30%
   c) 90%
   d) 75-85%

160. Which institution has a policy that aims to change the profile of rural credit and poverty alleviation in India?
   a) PRADAN
   b) NABARD
   c) RBI
   d) MUDRA Bank

161. The term microfinance (MF) refers to the provision of financial services to which of the following groups?
   a) Higher income groups
   b) Corporate businesses
   c) Lower income groups, disadvantaged women, and self-employed people
   d) International organizations

162. Which dimension of the Three-Dimensional Model of Women's Empowerment refers to an individual's personal beliefs and actions?
   a) Macro-level
   b) Meso-level
   c) Micro-level
   d) Meta-level

163. Under the 'Stand Up India' scheme, each bank branch provides loans to at least how many projects on an average for each category of entrepreneur?
   a) Five
   b) One
   c) Two
   d) Three

164. Which scheme was implemented by the Coir Board for the empowerment of rural women artisans in the coir sector?

a) Mahila Coir Yojana b) STEP

c) MUDRA Bank d) Stand-Up India

165. How is women's development primarily measured?

a) Number of children they have

b) Their participation in politics

c) Their participation in the workforce

d) Their household income

166. What percentage of women are in informal employment where they do not enjoy labor laws?

a) 50% b) 75%

c) 90% d) 95%

167. Which of the following is NOT typically an enterprise led by women in India?

a) Pickles production b) Agarbatti making

c) Electronics **d) Software development**

168. Which institution is an apex body for training and research in entrepreneurship?

a) IRDP b) NREP

c) NIESBUD d) FICCI

169. What is one major challenge faced by women entrepreneurs when procuring finances?

a) Women generally own a lot of properties

b) Banks favor women entrepreneurs

c) Men in the family are often unwilling to invest in ventures run by women

d) Women get loans easily from banks

170. What does the Census (2011) data reveal about the labor force participation rate of women in rural areas?

a) Increase from 33.3% to 40%

b) Decrease from 33.3% to 26.5%

c) Constant at 30%

d) Increase from 20% to 33.3%

171. For the growth of women entrepreneurs, what type of assistance is NOT mentioned?
    a) Financial assistance
    b) Achievement motivation training
    c) Assistance in choosing appropriate vacation spots
    d) Assistance in the choice of appropriate machinery

172. What is a significant problem for women entrepreneurs in food production and processing ventures?
    a) Overproduction of food items
    b) Too much financial support
    c) Difficulty in capturing the market and popularizing their products
    d) Easy access to modern technology

173. Which organization does NOT play a significant role in building and promoting women's entrepreneurship according to the passage?
    a) NAYE
    b) FICCI
    c) SIDO
    d) UNESCO

174. What should be the focus of programmes developing women entrepreneurs?
    a) Discouraging women from entering the workforce
    b) Addressing patriarchal social attitudes and discrimination against women
    c) Encouraging women to stick to traditional roles
    d) Reducing the number of training programs for women

175. What is the vision of the National Policy for Women, 2016?
    a) To promote women in leadership roles.
    b) To empower women economically.
    c) To create a society where women reach their full potential and influence social change.
    d) To address gender disparity in employment sectors.

176. Which among the following is NOT listed as a priority area in the National Policy for Women, 2016?
    a) Health and nutrition
    b) Violence against women
    c) Cultural awareness and heritage
    d) Environment and climate change

177. What does the National Policy for Women, 2016 mention about women's unpaid work?
   a) It should be reduced.
   b) It needs recognition and valuation.
   c) It is irrelevant to the economy.
   d) It is equivalent to men's unpaid work.

178. As per the Constitution of India, which article guarantees 'equality of opportunity' to women?
   a) Article 14
   b) Article 15(1)
   c) Article 16
   d) Article 39(d

179. During the 4th World Conference on Women in Beijing, 1995, what was NOT proposed as a qualitative indicator for women's empowerment in India's Draft Country Paper?
   a) Workloads
   b) Leisure time
   c) Political party affiliations
   d) Domestic violence

180. What percentage of India's population was classified as rural according to the 2011 Census?
   a) 50.23%
   b) 68.84%
   c) 72.15%
   d) 54.78%

181. What is a major barrier to women's education in India?
   a) Inadequate toilets and sanitary facilities.
   b) Compulsory vocational training.
   c) Mandatory participation in sports.
   d) Lack of digital infrastructure.

182. How does the level of women's education impact society?
   a) It has a direct implication on sports participation among children.
   b) It primarily boosts economic growth rates.
   c) It reduces political participation at the local level.
   d) It has a direct implication on nutrition and health indicators among children and maternal mortality rates

183. In which year was the National Mission for Empowerment of Women (NMEW) launched?
   a) 2005
   b) 2008
   c) 2010
   d) 2012

184. On what occasion was the NMEW launched?
   a) Republic Day of India
   b) Independence Day of India
   c) International Women's Day
   d) World Human Rights Day

185. What is the primary aim of the NMEW?
   a) To promote gender equality in politics.
   b) To strengthen the process of all-round development of women.
   c) To provide financial assistance to women-led businesses.
   d) To establish women's universities across India.

186. What does the name "Mission Poorna Shakti" imply?
   a) Complete financial autonomy for women.
   b) Holistic empowerment of women.
   c) Women's participation in sports.
   d) Women in leadership roles.

187. Which of the following strategies of NMEW focuses on skill development and vocational training for women?
   a) Inter-sectoral convergence of schemes.
   b) Strengthening of institutional framework.
   c) Focused research and gender audits.
   d) Investment in skill and entrepreneurship development, micro-credit, and SHG development.

188. What is one of the key strategies of NMEW related to local bodies?
   a) Provide direct funds to local bodies.
   b) Establish women-only local councils.
   c) Support to Panchayat Raj Institutions, Women's movements, and community representatives.
   d) Shift local governance responsibilities to state bodies.

189. What approach does NMEW take regarding media and communication?
   a) Avoidance of media
   b) 180-degree approach on selective media interaction
   c) 360-degree approach on media and communication for behavior change
   d) Engage only with women-led media houses

190. What is the primary purpose of Gender Analysis?
   a) To understand political associations
   b) To examine the relative status of men and women in a project
   c) To predict future gender trends
   d) To analyze historic gender-based movements

191. The Harvard Analytical Framework was developed by researchers at...?
   a) Harvard Business School
   b) Massachusetts Institute of Technology
   c) Harvard Institute of International Development
   d) University of Oxford

192. Which of the following is NOT a component of the Harvard Analytical Framework?
   a) The activity profile
   b) The social acceptance profile
   c) The access and control profile
   d) The project cycle analysis

193. What is the key principle upon which the Harvard Analytical Framework is based?
   a) Gender neutrality
   b) Gender-specific roles
   c) The efficiency approach
   d) Gender independence

194. Which of the following questions does the "activity profile" seek to answer?
   a) Who benefits from a given project?
   b) Who has control over resources?
   c) Who does what, when, and where?
   d) What are the factors influencing gender roles?

195. In the context of Gender Analysis, what does the 'Access and control profile' clarify?
   a) The hierarchy of men and women in a community
   b) Who has access to resources and who controls their use
   c) The daily routines of men and women
   d) The political power structures within a community

196. Why might data collection meetings for gender analysis be separated by gender?
   a) To get diverse opinions
   b) To ensure men and women are equally represented
   c) In case women do not feel comfortable speaking in mixed groups
   d) To validate the data collected

197. Which tool in the Harvard Analytical Framework helps to identify factors shaping gender differences?

a) The activity profile tool
b) Influencing factors tool
c) Access and control profile tool
d) Project cycle analysis

198. How can extension agents utilize findings from the Gender Analysis tools?

a) By solely focusing on market crops
b) By planning new extension activities tailored to men's needs only
c) By tailoring training sessions to women's needs
d) By completely changing the cultural dynamics of a community

199. Who developed the Gender Planning Framework?

a) Rani Parker
b) Naila Kabeer
c) Caroline Moser
d) Letha Devi

200. Which of the following is NOT one of the triple roles identified in the Moser framework?

a) Reproductive
b) Economic
c) Productive
d) Community management

201. The Moser framework aims to focus on:

a) Immediate gender requirements.
b) Practical gender needs.
c) Strategic gender needs.
d) Overall community needs.

202. Who developed the Gender Analysis Matrix?

a) Rani Parker
b) Naila Kabeer
c) Caroline Moser
d) Letha Devi

203. Which of the following is NOT a level of analysis in the GAM?

a) Men
b) Women
c) Teachers
d) Household

204. In the GAM, which aspect captures changes in access to resources and the extent of control over resources?

a) Labour
b) Time
c) Resources
d) Socio-cultural factors

205. Who played a leading role in originating the Social Relations Framework?

a) Rani Parker
b) Naila Kabeer
c) Caroline Moser
d) Letha Devi

206. The aims of the Social Relations Framework are all EXCEPT:

a) Analyse gender inequalities in distribution of resources.
b) Emphasize human well-being as the final goal of development.
c) Ensure gender balance in all communities.
d) Analyse relationships between people and resources.

207. In the context of development policies, which type of policy intends to transform existing gender relations?

a) Gender-Neutral
b) Gender-Specific
c) Gender-Redistributive
d) Gender-Blind

19

A Sociological Lens on Agricultural Extension

1. What is causing the deterioration of soil and water qualities in agriculture?
   a) Traditional money lenders
   b) Migration of male members
   c) Input intensive agriculture
   d) Marketing system by agents and traders

2. Who dominates the marketing system, causing farmers to sell perishable crops at a lower price?
   a) Farmers Producer Organizations (FPOs)
   b) Government agencies
   c) Traders and agents
   d) Small and marginal farmers

3. Due to the increasing challenges in agriculture, what is being formed to support farmers?
   a) Input intensive organizations
   b) Farmers Producer Organizations (FPOs)
   c) Traditional money lending systems
   d) Modern marketing systems

4 What is one chief obstacle to growth in rural India?
   a) Intra-caste marriage practice
   b) Lack of modern technology
   c) Caste system and ownership of land
   d) Rapid urbanization

5. How is the role of sociology in agricultural extension changing?
   a) Decreasing due to urbanization
   b) Increasing due to the emergence of farmers groups
   c) Staying the same
   d) Shifting towards urban planning

Bold Means Correct Answer

6. Which of the following is NOT a model of farmer groups?
   a) Food security group
   b) Commodity interest groups
   c) Farmers' friends
   d) Farmers interest groups

7. In developing countries, which sector employs the largest number of people?
   a) Service industry
   b) Information technology
   c) Agriculture
   d) Manufacturing

8. What is a society primarily defined by?
   a) Number of people
   b) Types of buildings
   c) Persistent social interaction
   d) Cultural festivals

9. In which type of society is information, services, and high technology most dominant?
   a) Hunter-gatherer
   b) Agrarian
   c) Industrial
   d) Post-industrial

10. What are groups characterized by impersonal and formal relationships called?
    a) Primary groups
    b) Secondary groups
    c) Informal groups
    d) Vertical groups

11. Which of the following best describes a belief?
    a) A formal declaration of truth
    b) An internal feeling that something is true
    c) A proven fact
    d) A societal rule

12. What do social norms represent?
    a) Official laws of the land
    b) Personal choices
    c) Informal understandings of how to behave in a group
    d) Formal contractual obligations

13. Which among the following is the weakest form of social norms?
    a) Mores
    b) Folkways
    c) Customs
    d) Folklores

14. Who was known to relate nature with agriculture through his couplets?

a) King Akbar
b) Khana
c) Ghag
d) None of the above

15. Which institution is undertaking the project of documenting indigenous farming methods in southern States?

a) Indian Agricultural Research Institute
b) Delhi University
c) Karnataka Folklore University
d) Bengaluru Central University

16. What is a value primarily concerned with?

a) A measure of truth
b) A measure of the worth or importance
c) A formal societal rule
d) A religious doctrine

17. What role do institutions play in relation to social structure?

a) They oppose the social structure
b) They become a part of the social structure
c) They are independent of the social structure
d) They redefine the social structure every decade

18. What is the primary functional unit of society?

a) Clan
b) Kin
c) Family
d) Community

19. Kinship primarily refers to:

a) Blood relations.
b) People from the same community.
c) People from the same geographical region.
d) Common interest groups.

20. What is the group that claims a common ancestry called?

a) Kinship
b) Family
c) Clan
d) Society

21. Social stratification is the ranking of individuals based on:
    a) Age
    b) Education
    c) Ability to make societal decisions
    d) Physical strength

22. In which system is vertical mobility difficult but not impossible?
    a) Caste system
    b) Class system
    c) Kinship
    d) Clan system

23. What comprises the basic elements of culture?
    a) Belief, Values, Norms, Expressive Symbols, Language
    b) History, Language, Art, Tradition
    c) Values, Art, History, Belief
    d) Language, Art, History, Norms

24. Cultural change often initiates from:
    a) Change in dressing style
    b) Change in beliefs
    c) Change in governance
    d) Change in economic status

25. Cultural relativism primarily assumes that:
    a) Some cultures are superior to others.
    b) All cultures have the same importance.
    c) All cultures are true against a context.
    d) Culture doesn't influence behavior.

26. What is the outcome of the cultural integration of two or more cultures?
    a) Cultural bias
    b) Cultural lag
    c) Acculturation
    d) Cultural diffusion

27. What is cultural lag?
    a) Adoption of new cultural practices
    b) Gap between material and non-material aspects during social change
    c) Process by which people learn about their own culture
    d) The effect of technological changes on society

28. Which of the following is NOT a form of social innovation?

a) Technology b) New beliefs

c) Social marketing d) Producer organization

29. When two or more people interact and develop unity, it is termed as:

a) Society **b) Group**

c) Clan d) Community

30. Which of the following is NOT a stage of group formation?

a) Forming **b) Arguing**

c) Norming d) Performing

31. Which type of group has more membership cohesiveness?

a) Primary groups b) Secondary groups

c) Reference groups d) Interest groups

32. A disagreement when one has to reject or select one's own relative is an example of:

a) Role conflict b) Conflict for position

c) Conflict of interest d) Internal conflict

33. Arbitration requires:

a) No prior agreement **b) A prior agreement**

c) Immediate court intervention d) A mediator

34. When individuals in a group act collectively without centralized direction, it is termed as:

a) Groupthink **b) Mob behaviour**

c) Community development d) Centralization

35. What does the formula B = f(P, E) represent in group dynamics?

a) Behavior is a function of position and extension.

b) Behavior is a function of personal characteristics and environmental factor.

c) Behavior is a function of problems and effects.

d) Behavior is a function of people and engagement.

36. How many stages are identified in the concept of transactional analysis?

a) 2 **b) 3**

c) 4 d) 5

37. In group behaviour, the desire for harmony or conformity in decisions is termed as:

a) Group shift
b) De-individuation
c) Groupthink
d) Conformity

38. Social change refers to:

a) A modification in the social order of a society
b) A change in the population of a society
c) The fashion trends of a society
d) The political regime of a society

39. Which type of change is gradual in nature?

a) Revolutionary
b) Evolutionary
c) Immediate
d) Unpredictable

40. What does "B" stand for in the group dynamics formula, B = f (P, E)?

a) Environment
b) Elicit Behavior
c) Personal characteristics
d) External factors

41. Which is NOT a stage of group formation?

a) Forming
b) Storming
c) Calculating
d) Norming

42. Which of the following best describes a primary group?

a) Groups formed for short term tasks
b) Role models for other groups
c) Groups with more membership cohesiveness lasting longer
d) Groups formed for specific projects

43. Conflict of interest arises when:

a) There's a power struggle
b) Two groups clash for a single interest
c) A person disagrees with oneself
d) There's a dispute about group roles

44. What is the primary difference between Arbitration and Conciliation?

a) Conciliation is a more formal process
b) Arbitration requires a prior agreement
c) Arbitration involves multiple arbitrators
d) Conciliation is done inside courts

45. Neighborhood is best described as:
 a) The entire city in which one lives
 b) A group that forms for a specific task
 c) The spatial unit in which face-to-face interactions occur
 d) A mob

46. Groupthink is:
 a) Individuals thinking on their own
 b) Desire for harmony or conformity in a group, potentially leading to poor decisions
 c) Shifting group decisions based on a leader's thought
 d) Analyzing transactions within a group

47. Which of the following stages in transactional analysis refers to the "Taught" concept of life?
 a) Adult
 b) Child
 c) Parent
 d) Adolescent

48. What do Sanctions primarily serve as?
 a) Technological innovations
 b) Mechanisms of social change
 c) Mechanisms of social control
 d) Mechanisms of group dynamics

49. Which of the following best describes "Group Shift"?
 a) A group moving to a new location
 b) A change in group dynamics over time
 c) The exaggerated position of individuals to adjust or dominate in a group
 d) Individuals losing their self-consciousness

50. Leadership is primarily about:
 a) Executing tasks
 b) Providing direction to a group to achieve goals
 c) Having the most knowledge
 d) Making decisions without consulting others

51. Which of the following is NOT a type of social conflict mentioned?
    a) Conflict involving social positions
    b) Conflict of interest
    c) Role conflict
    d) Conflict of technology

52. What kind of communities are classified on the basis of tribes, caste, and religions?
    a) Modern communities
    b) Transitional communities
    c) Worth-based communities
    d) Traditional communities

53. What does mob behavior refer to?
    a) The formation of community neighborhoods
    b) Individual behavior
    c) Individuals in a group acting collectively without centralized direction
    d) Leadership actions

54. Which of the following professionals may need to learn about government-imposed sanctions?
    a) Extension education professionals
    b) Agricultural workers
    c) Tech innovators
    d) Urban planners

55. Who among the following would be most responsible for organizing personal visits to farmers' fields?
    a) Extension advisors
    b) Extension communicators
    c) Extension leaders
    d) Extension field managers

56. According to the transactional analysis, our emotions:
    a) Have no influence on our behavior
    b) Only dictate a small part of our life
    c) Influence our behavior
    d) Are only relevant in the parent stage

57. De-individuation in group behavior refers to:
    a) Desire for harmony in a group
    b) Losing of self-consciousness of individual members
    c) A shift in individual positions to dominate
    d) Exaggerated groupthink

58. What is the concept of versatility in the context of a pluralistic society?
   a) Versatility refers to having many hobbies and interests.
   b) Versatility means being unyielding in one's opinions.
   c) Versatility involves adapting and responding flexibly in diverse situations.
   d) Versatility is about advocating for individual needs over community needs.

59. According to the text, what is the significance of "Image" in community versatility?
   a) Dressing formally is always the best choice for all situations.
   b) Dressing appropriately can help create a positive impression, regardless of the attire.
   c) Formal attire is the key to gaining trust in any situation.
   d) Casual attire is preferred in all professional settings.

60. Which of the following is NOT considered one of the four basic elements of an individual's Versatility, as mentioned in the text?
   a) Image
   b) Presentation
   c) Depth of competence and understanding
   d) Feedback

61. How does increasing community versatility impact vulnerability and vindictiveness?
   a) It increases vulnerability and intensifies vindictiveness.
   b) It eliminates vulnerability but has no effect on vindictiveness.
   c) It eliminates both vulnerability and vindictiveness.
   d) It empowers community members to overcome vindictiveness and eliminates vulnerability.

62. What does the term "feedback" imply in the context of community convergence?
   a) It refers to receiving constructive criticism only.
   b) It is a one-way process of communication from leaders to community members.
   c) It involves both sending and receiving verbal and non-verbal signals to enhance mutual understanding.
   d) It focuses solely on positive reinforcement.

63. Which of the following is NOT a type of Associative process?
    a) Cooperation
    b) Accommodation
    c) Conflict
    d) Assimilation and Acculturation

64. How do human beings meet their specialized needs?
    a) By isolating themselves
    b) By only depending on family
    c) By interacting and depending on specialized individuals
    d) By seeking out non-human resources

65. In Merton's Paradigm of deviant behaviour, which mode of adaptation is associated with the rejection of both the means and the goals?
    a) Conformity
    b) Innovation
    c) Ritualism
    d) Retreatism

66. What is the first dysfunction in Lencioni's theory?
    a) Lack of commitment
    b) Absence of trust
    c) Avoidance of accountability
    d) Fear of conflict

67. What does Differentiation refer to in the context of the Dissociative process?
    a) The contest among individuals to acquire limited resources
    b) The action or process of distinguishing two or more things or people
    c) An action that offends against a law, treaty, or other ruling
    d) The end of conflict

68. According to Lencioni's theory, what leads to the fear of conflict in a team?
    a) A lack of commitment
    b) Negligence to results
    c) Absence of trust
    d) Avoidance of accountability

69. What is Ritualism in Merton's theory?
    a) Rejection of both the means and the goals
    b) Attainment of societal goals in unexpected ways
    c) Acceptance of the means of the goals but rejection of the overall goal
    d) Attaining of societal goals by socially accepted means

70. In the Dissociative processes, what does Contravention imply?

a) A contest among individuals to acquire limited resources

b) Rejection of both the means and the goals

c) An action that offends against a law, treaty, or other ruling

d) The end of conflict

71. What aims to create a society free from religious bias and discrimination?

a) Meditation

b) Secularization

c) Pluralism

d) Monism

72. Which of the following is a result of meditation according to Neurotheology?

a) Rejection of societal norms

b) Enhanced memory

c) Sense of oneness with all

d) Improved motor skills

73. What defines a relatively stable method of interaction among members to reach long-term goals?

a) Social behavior

b) Social organization

c) Social norms

d) Social reform

74. Which of the following is a marriage relationship focused on providing security and prosperity for descendants of significant individuals in society?

a) Kinship

b) Religion

c) Clan

d) Occupation

75 Which of the following is NOT a type of social organization?

a) Kinship

b) Educational institutions

c) Occupation-based organizations

d) Economic policies

76. What is the primary objective of Extension Education?

a) To impart long-term academic courses

b) To provide targeted and short-focused education to disadvantaged communities

c) To ensure religious teachings are propagated

d) To promote entertainment and leisure activities

77. What does the term "human settlements" encompass?
   a) Only the physical structures where people live.
   b) The relationship between individuals and their pets.
   c) The totality of a human community, including social, material, and cultural elements.
   d) The natural landscapes untouched by human activity.

78. Which of the following settlement patterns refers to a clustered arrangement of dwellings?
   a) Linear settlement
   b) Dispersed settlement
   c) Nucleated settlement
   d) Fragmented settlement

79. What is the purpose of creating growth centers in rural areas?
   a) To encourage people to move away from villages and settle in cities.
   b) To provide opportunities for development, including services and facilities, to nearby villages.
   c) To centralize all economic activities within a single village.
   d) To create isolated areas with minimal human interaction.

80. What are "service villages" in the context of growth centers?
   a) Villages that offer services exclusively to urban areas.
   b) Villages that provide agricultural equipment to growth centers.
   c) Villages that demand specific services from growth centers.
   d) Villages that are self-sufficient and do not rely on external services.

81. Which settlement pattern involves dwellings being spread out over a large area?
   a) Linear settlement
   b) Dispersed settlement
   c) Nucleated settlement
   d) Fragmented settlement

82. Which of the following texts is written in Sanskrit but not by Brahmins?
   a) Upanishad
   b) Ramayana
   c) Rigveda
   d) Puranas

83. Which of the following factors made Sanskritization possible?
   a) Family traditions
   b) Spread of literacy
   c) Social hierarchies
   d) Ancient rituals

84. Parochialism can be applied when:
    a) Governments base decisions on universal values.
    b) A local area's government considers broader community interests.
    c) A local culture or area's government makes decisions based on solely local interests.
    d) Governments are influenced by external forces.

85. The phrase "Varudhaiva Kutumbakam" means:
    a) Universal truth
    b) The world is a playground
    c) All gods are one
    d) The world is one family

86. Universalization is the process of:
    a) Recognizing unique individual experiences
    b) Comparing oneself with others undergoing similar experiences and concluding everyone is similar
    c) Emphasizing one's own cultural values
    d) Upholding one's caste or religion above others

87. What role does the extension profession play in the universalization process?
    a) Suppressing local traditions
    b) Encouraging youths to focus only on modern values
    c) Initiating leadership development programmes in villages
    d) Limiting communication and mobility

88. The process resulting in a new type of integration due to sensitivity towards caste-based voting is described as:
    a) Sanskritization
    b) Parochialism
    c) Universalization
    d) Secularization

89 What is the gradual move of a social system to another referred to as?
    a) Progressive Revolution
    b) Social Change
    c) Collective Mobility
    d) Regressive Revolution

90. Which changes are slower: Structural changes in family, caste, clan, race, and religion or changes in habits like food and clothing?
    a) Structural changes in family, caste, clan, race, and religion
    b) Changes in habits like food and clothing
    c) Both are equally slow
    d) None of the above

91. Social innovations can be described as:
   a) Just technological changes
   b) Only changes in governance
   c) Policies, plans, strategies new to adoption units
   d) Only rural community changes

92. Agricultural extension in developing countries focuses on:
   a) Only technological changes
   b) Only social innovation
   c) Bringing technological changes and learning social innovation
   d) Typology studies

93. Which of the following is NOT a typology of social change?
   a) Regressive Revolution
   b) Social Dominance Theory
   c) System Justification Theory
   d) Natural Capital Theory

94. What is the motive behind the Social Identity Theory?
   a) For a community to remain dominant
   b) For a positive social identity
   c) For an individual's personal growth
   d) For technological advancements

95. What does the term "Amelioration" in the context of social change refer to?
   a) A form of creativity
   b) Bringing amendments and reforms in the system
   c) The exclusion of a group by a dominant group
   d) Collective mobility

96. What is the primary objective of the "Short term goal" in social change goals?
   a) For overall societal development
   b) For food and environmental security
   c) Facilitation of diffusion rate and generation of technical innovations among disadvantaged sections
   d) Only technological advancements

97. Which theory deals with cases where mostly the subordinate groups demand justice?
    a) Social Dominance Theory
    b) Social Value Efficacy
    c) System Justification Theory
    d) Social Identity Theory

98. What is the focus of social innovation?
    a) Solely on individuals
    b) Solely on organizations
    c) On the processes of generating ideas and solutions that create social value
    d) Only on technological solutions

99. What are institutions based on?
    a) Financial outcomes
    b) Stable relationships and accepted norms
    c) Profitable ventures
    d) External influences

100. Which of the following is NOT an example of peoples' institutions?
    a) Marriages
    b) Festivals
    c) Private companies
    d) Geographical proximity

101. What is the PPCP arrangement for development?
    a) Public Private Citizen Partnership
    b) Public People Community Partnership
    c) Public Private Community Partnership
    d) Public Personal Communal Partnership

102. What does a conscious person possess according to the community consciousness theory?
    a) Material wealth
    b) Knowledge of the future
    c) Awareness of why and how things are
    d) Access to higher education

103. According to the Barrett Model, what does the seventh (highest) level of community consciousness focus on?
    a) Economic Stability
    b) Social Stability
    c) Strategic Alliance
    d) National Sustainability

104. What is a major obstacle to economic growth and inclusive growth in communities?
   a) Modern technology
   b) Lack of education
   c) Systemic corruption
   d) International interference

105. In 2012, where did India rank in Transparency International's Corruption Perceptions Index?
   a) 176th
   b) 94th
   c) 1st
   d) 50th

106. Which initiative is NOT mentioned in the text as a method to restrict corruption?
   a) Right to Service (RTS)
   b) Digital Education
   c) Green Tribunal
   d) Direct Benefit Transfer (DBT)

107. The Barrett Model of community consciousness goes from what to what?
   a) Lower to Upper Level
   b) Internal to External
   c) Upper to Lower Level
   d) External to Internal

108. What does the term "poverty" in the passage mainly refer to?
   a) Lack of material possessions
   b) Lack of community events
   c) A society's susceptibility to corruption
   d) Absence of technology

109. How are rural settings primarily classified?
   a) On the basis of proximity to urban areas
   b) On the basis of livelihood dependent on natural resources
   c) On the basis of technological advancements
   d) On the basis of population density

110. Why do rural human resources often need assistance from government and private organizations?
   a) For personal gains
   b) For development due to low knowledge and profit margins in traditional production systems
   c) For urban migration
   d) To compete with foreign markets

111. Which of the following is NOT a barrier to social changes in India?
   a) Costly rituals
   b) Poor infrastructure
   c) Extension programmes
   d) Politics of poverty

112. What is considered the major stimulant of change in villages?
   a) Technological advancements
   b) Creation of job opportunities
   c) Increase in urban migration
   d) Reduction of traditional practices

113. What role do social institutions like caste and family size play in the context of this passage?
   a) They boost economic development
   b) They are irrelevant to poverty
   c) They play important roles in poverty
   d) They facilitate technological advancements

114. In the context of planning, how does the agrarian system of developed countries differ from that of developing countries?
   a) Developed countries have a tradition-based system, while developing countries have a science-based system
   b) Developed countries have a majority of their population in agriculture, while it's opposite for developing countries
   c) Developed countries have a modern science-based system, while developing countries are mostly traditional
   d) Developed and developing countries have similar agrarian systems

115. What does "contract farming" in the passage refer to?
   a) An evolving institutional arrangement integrating farm work and technology on different landholdings
   b) A method where only corporations are involved in farming
   c) Traditional farmers working without any contracts
   d) Outsourcing all farming activities to foreign countries

116. Extension education in developing countries demands:
   a) Only social innovations
   b) Only technical innovations
   c) Both social and technical innovations
   d) Neither social nor technical innovations

117. Who primarily conducts planning in India?
   a) Only sociologists
   b) Only community leaders
   c) Experts and people's representatives
   d) Only farmers

117. For an effective plan, the extension system should:
   a) Plan without community involvement
   b) Plan only for the community without their involvement
   c) Plan for the people, with the people to make it their plan
   d) Only focus on achieving targets without community expectations

118. Which of the following approaches involves extension experts, people's representatives, and subject matter specialists sharing their experiences considering farmers' needs?
   a) Radical
   b) Contingency
   c) Synoptic
   d) Transactive

119. A plan formulated for unexpected situations like climatic changes, floods, and earthquakes is called:
   a) Transactive
   b) Contingency
   c) Synoptic
   d) Incremental

120. Which approach emphasizes a gradual, flexible, and innovative strategy to achieve set targets within the extension system?
   a) Radical
   b) Incremental
   c) Advocacy
   d) Social engineering

121. The approach where the extension professional works as facilitators of social change through interpersonal dialogues with stakeholders and clientele is:
   a) Radical
   b) Advocacy
   c) Transactive
   d) Contingency

122. The approach that gives voice to the marginalized and underprivileged sections of the society is known as:
   a) Radical
   b) Advocacy
   c) Incremental
   d) Synoptic

123. When planning focuses on radical grassroots innovations and low-cost models for sustainable community-based programs, it can be termed as:

a) Incremental
b) Advocacy
c) Radical
d) Transactive

124. Which approach involves understanding and navigating the interests of various stakeholders such as peoples' representatives, private companies, and administration?

a) Managing of vested interests
b) Social engineering
c) Synoptic
d) Contingency

125. The creation of emotional attacks, possibly using social media, to achieve a particular outcome is termed as:

a) Transactive
b) Incremental
c) Social engineering
d) Advocacy

126. Which sociological tool involves organizing groups, developing facilitators groups as per the farmer's needs, and recognizing the achievers to double the farmers' income?

a) PRA tools
b) Social engineering tools
c) Participatory appraisal
d) All of the above

127. Who among the following might lobby with authorities to restrict technology transfer for small farms and create conflicts among farmers?

a) Small farmers
b) Agricultural extension professionals
c) Middlemen, moneylenders, and large farmers
d) Social media influencers

20

Incorporating Behavioural Science in Agricultural Extension

1. What does behavioural psychology focus on?

   a) Understanding genetic patterns.

   b) Investigating emotions and thoughts without observing actions.

   c) Studying and altering people's behaviours, including their actions, emotions, and thoughts.

   d) Analyzing the historical contexts of individuals.

2. In behavioural psychology, which of the following aspects of behaviour are deemed most valuable for investigation?

   a) Unobservable emotions.

   b) The historical context of the behaviour.

   c) Observable and measurable aspects.

   d) Subjective interpretations of behaviours.

3. According to behavioural psychology, what determines behaviour?

   a) Past experiences and memories.

   b) Outcomes, consequences, rewards, and punishments.

   c) Genetic makeup.

   d) Spiritual beliefs.

4. What should an extension professional primarily focus on according to behavioural psychology?

   a) Altering the learner's thinking patterns.

   b) Changing the learner's behaviour.

   c) Understanding the learner's past.

   d) Evaluating the learner's genetic makeup.

Bold Means Correct Answer

5. Which statement best describes behavioural psychology?
   a) It explores the unobservable depths of human consciousness.
   b) It is the study of the connection between our minds and behaviour, and conditions are created to bring desired changes in behaviour.
   c) It primarily relies on understanding an individual's genetics.
   d) It emphasizes the importance of the historical context of human actions.

6. How can educational psychology be best described in the context of extension education?
   a) It is the branch focused on diagnosing learning disorders.
   b) It addresses questions like, "Why do some people learn more than others" and "What can be done to improve that learning"?
   c) It primarily deals with the history of education.
   d) It investigates the spiritual aspects of learning.

7. Behavioural change in the field of agricultural extension is primarily applied to:
   a) Alter farmers' genetic predispositions.
   b) Modify farmers' behaviours towards better agricultural practices.
   c) Understand the historical context of farming.
   d) Focus only on the emotional well-being of farmers.

8. Which of the following is NOT a value that an extension psychologist should embody?
   a) Curiosity.
   b) Objectivity.
   c) Overconfidence.
   d) Critical thinking.

9. In the realm of psychology, why is human language considered challenging?
   a) It is too simple.
   b) It has numerous dialects.
   c) It is full of ambiguity.
   d) It is rarely used in psychology.

10. What is the significance of critical thinking for an extension psychologist?
    a) Evaluates only other people's work.
    b) Evaluates both their own work and others'.
    c) Believes in all findings without scrutiny.
    d) Ignores methodological flaws.

11. What step in the scientific method involves deciding which research method is the most suitable?
    a) Conceptualizing problems.
    b) Drawing conclusions.
    c) Analyzing data.
    d) Collecting data.

12. Why are follow-up studies often conducted in psychology?
    a) To gain additional funding.
    b) To eliminate loopholes in the original design and strengthen its findings.
    c) To prove other studies wrong.
    d) As a ritual in the scientific community.

13. Which value drives the problem conceptualization step in the scientific method of psychology?
    a) Overconfidence.
    b) Curiosity.
    c) Critical thinking.
    d) Subjectivity.

14. Psychology stands on a scientific foundation similar to which other fields?
    a) Only the physical sciences.
    b) Only the social sciences.
    c) Both social and physical sciences.
    d) Neither social nor physical sciences.

15. In extension psychology, critical thinking primarily aids in:
    a) Accepting all research findings.
    b) Identifying both strengths and weaknesses of findings.
    c) Believing in all anecdotal evidence.
    d) Ignoring contradictory evidence.

6. David Kolb's learning styles model, published in 1984, is based on:
    a) A four-stage cycle of learning
    b) Five distinct learning patterns
    c) A three-tier process of assimilation
    d) Two levels of cognitive understanding

17. In Kolb's experiential learning cycle, the stage where a learner applies the concept to see the results it produces is called:
    a) Concrete experience
    b) Reflective observation
    c) Abstract conceptualization
    d) Active experimentation

18. Which of the following best describes the term 'personality'?
    a) An individual's learning style
    b) The combination of characteristics that form a person's unique identity
    c) A person's outward appearance
    d) The knowledge an individual has acquired over time

19. Learned characteristics are acquired from:
    a) Genetics and heritage
    b) Physical attributes like eye color
    c) Institutions and surroundings
    d) None of the above

20. Which of the following is NOT a major personality trait as identified by psychologists?
    a) Flexibility
    b) Conscientiousness
    c) Agreeableness
    d) Extraversion

21. People who believe that their lives are controlled by external factors are termed as:
    a) Machiavellians
    b) Internals
    c) Externals
    d) Self-monitors

22. Machiavellianism is characterized by:
    a) High self-esteem and confidence
    b) Being practical and believing that ends justify means
    c) Taking high risks in decision-making
    d) Adapting behavior according to social situations

23. Individuals with what trait believe that they possess the necessary skills to succeed and thus take on more challenges?
    a) Locus of control
    b) Self-monitoring
    c) Self-esteem
    d) Risk-taking

24. Which personality attribute is the ability to adjust one's behavior based on external situations?
    a) Locus of control
    b) Machiavellianism
    c) Self-monitoring
    d) Self-esteem

25. Who among the following are more likely to perform well in structured, routine jobs?

    a) Internals
    b) Machiavellians
    c) Externals
    d) High self-esteem individuals

26. Which of the following is known as a primary emotion?

    a) Pride
    b) Rage
    c) Love
    d) Shame

27. Physiological theories of emotion suggest:

    a) Responses within the body are responsible for emotions.
    b) Thoughts and mental activity play a primary role in forming emotions.
    c) Activity within the brain leads to emotional responses.
    d) Emotions are learned through experiences.

28. Charles Darwin proposed which of the following theories of emotion?

    a) Schachter-Singer theory
    b) James-Lange theory
    c) Evolutionary theory
    d) Two-Factor theory

29. According to the James-Lange theory, emotions arise from:

    a) Cognitive assessment of a situation.
    b) Physical reactions to events.
    c) Brain activities and neural connections.
    d) Past experiences and memories.

30. The Schachter-Singer's Two-Factor theory emphasizes the role of:

    a) Physiological arousal and cognitive interpretation.
    b) Neural activities in the brain.
    c) Innate emotional responses.
    d) Learned emotional experiences.

31. What is a defense mechanism?

    a) A learned behavior to respond to situations.
    b) An unconscious mechanism to reduce anxiety from harmful stimuli.
    c) A conscious choice to avoid certain emotions.
    d) A physiological response to external threats.

32. If a person denies having a problem even when evidence suggests otherwise, they are using which defense mechanism?

a) Regression
b) Acting out
c) Denial
d) Projection

33. A child throwing a tantrum when they don't get their way is an example of:

a) Compartmentalization
b) Acting out
c) Projection
d) Reaction formation

34. Misattributing one's own undesired feelings or impulses onto another person refers to:

a) Dissociation
b) Reaction formation
c) Projection
d) Denial

35. Understanding the behavior of farmers and their learning patterns can assist in:

a) Cognitive emotional theories
b) Designing better agricultural tools
c) Improving farming techniques
d) Agriculture extension and transfer of technology

21

Key Agricultural Legislations in India

1. What was one of the main objectives of the land-reform policy in India

   a) Increase land mass for agricultural production.

   b) Eliminate all elements of exploitation within the agrarian system.

   c) Increase the power of Zamindars.

   d) Focus on urban land development.

2. Which among the following was NOT a category of land reform policy in India?

   a) Abolition of middlemen.

   b) Establishment of cooperative joint farming.

   c) Introduction of foreign crops.

   d) Tenancy regulation.

3. What percentage of landholdings are wholly owned and self-operated in the country today due to the measures implemented?

   a) 45% b) 68%

   c) 92% d) 77%

4. One of the deficiencies in tenancy reforms was:

   a) All tenants were given equal rights irrespective of the duration of tenancy.

   b) The right of resumption leading to land grabbing.

   c) All tenants were given ownership rights without any conditions.

   d) Fair rents were uniformly implemented across all states.

5. By when had all states passed the ceiling legislation?

   a) By 1975-76 **b) By 1961-62**

   c) By 1980-81 d) By 1950-51

Bold Means Correct Answer

6. In Uttar Pradesh, what is the ceiling on existing landholding?
   a) 40 acres
   b) 121/2 acres
   c) 75 acres
   d) 25 acres

7. The basis of application of ceiling in Madhya Pradesh and Maharashtra is on a:
   a) Per family basis.
   b) Per acre basis.
   c) Landholder basis.
   d) Crop type basis.

8. After the implementation of the Consolidation of Holdings Act, what percentage of cultivatable land had been consolidated by the beginning of the Seventh Five Year Plan?
   a) 45%
   b) 25%
   c) 33%
   d) 50%

9. What observation was made by the Food and Agricultural Organization (FAO) regarding the operation of the consolidation of holding act in Punjab and Uttar Pradesh?
   a) No significant change was observed.
   b) A significant reduction in the cost of cultivation was seen.
   c) There was a decrease in cropping intensity.
   d) The act was not implemented properly.

10. The transformation in Indian agriculture after independence was mainly facilitated by:
    a) Only technological advancements.
    b) Just the contributions of farmers.
    c) Legislative measures and policies.
    d) Introduction of new crops.

11. What does Agricultural law, or Ag Law, primarily deal with?
    a) Only with seed and water issues.
    b) Issues related to agricultural labor and marketing.
    c) Legal matters associated with farming rights and rural industries.
    d) All of the above.

12. With the implementation of modern technologies, which of the following issues are dealt with in the sphere of Agricultural law?
    a) Intellectual property.
    b) Trade and commerce related to agricultural products.
    c) Credit.
    d) All of the above.

13. What was one of the main goals after India's independence regarding its agrarian sector?
    a) To increase the land mass.
    b) To remove impediments to the progress of the agrarian sector.
    c) To solely rely on technological developments.
    d) To increase exports of agricultural products.

14. Which of the following has NOT been a factor in the transformation of Indian agriculture?
    a) The efforts of individual farmers.
    b) Introduction of foreign crops.
    c) Technological development.
    d) Legislative measures.

15. What was one of the main objectives of the land-reform policy in India
    a) Increase land mass for agricultural production.
    b) Eliminate all elements of exploitation within the agrarian system.
    c) Increase the power of Zamindars.
    d) Focus on urban land development.

16. Which among the following was NOT a category of land reform policy in India?
    a) Abolition of middlemen.
    b) Establishment of cooperative joint farming.
    c) Introduction of foreign crops.
    d) Tenancy regulation.

17. What percentage of landholdings are wholly owned and self-operated in the country today due to the measures implemented?
    a) 45% b) 68%
    c) 92% d) 77%

18. One of the deficiencies in tenancy reforms was:
    a) All tenants were given equal rights irrespective of the duration of tenancy.
    b) The right of resumption leading to land grabbing.
    c) All tenants were given ownership rights without any conditions.
    d) Fair rents were uniformly implemented across all states.

19. By when had all states passed the ceiling legislation?
   a) By 1975-76
   b) By 1961-62
   c) By 1980-81
   d) By 1950-51

20. The basis of application of ceiling in Madhya Pradesh and Maharashtra is on a:
   a) Per family basis.
   b) Per acre basis.
   c) Landholder basis.
   d) Crop type basis.

21. After the implementation of the Consolidation of Holdings Act, what percentage of cultivatable land had been consolidated by the beginning of the Seventh Five Year Plan?
   a) 45%
   b) 25%
   c) 33%
   d) 50%

22. What observation was made by the Food and Agricultural Organization (FAO) regarding the operation of the consolidation of holding act in Punjab and Uttar Pradesh?
   a) No significant change was observed.
   b) A significant reduction in the cost of cultivation was seen.
   c) There was a decrease in cropping intensity.
   d) The act was not implemented properly.

23. Why was fertilizer declared as an Essential Commodity?
   a) To increase its production.
   b) To regulate trade, price, quality, and distribution.
   c) To promote its export.
   d) To ensure adequate supply for industries.

24. Under which section was the Fertilizer Control Order (FCO) promulgated?
   a) Section 1 of Essential Commodities Act, 1947
   b) Section 3 of Essential Commodities Act, 1955
   c) Section 2 of Fertilizer Act, 1960
   d) Section 4 of Agriculture Act, 1975

25. What does the FCO mandate regarding the quality of fertilizers?
   a) Specification of all fertilizers.
   b) Optional registration of fertilizer manufacturers.
   c) Loose packing of fertilizers.
   d) Allowance of sale of non-standard fertilizers.

26. How many fertilizer quality control laboratories are there in the country?

a) 84
b) 64
c) 74
d) 54

27. Who has been primarily entrusted with the enforcement of the FCO?

a) Central Government
b) State Governments
c) Fertilizer Manufacturers
d) Private Organizations

28. Pest management integrates which approaches?

a) Control and Distribution
b) Prevention and Distribution
c) Control and Prevention
d) Export and Prevention

29. Under which act are pesticides regulated in India?

a) Pesticides Act, 1975
b) Insecticides Rules, 1971
c) Agriculture Act, 1980
d) Insecticides Act, 1968

30. Before being made available for sale or use, what must all insecticides undergo?

a) Pricing process
b) Registration process with the CIB & RC
c) Testing in international labs
d) Approval by State Governments

31. What is indicated on the label mandated by the Registration Certificate for pesticides?

a) Only the active ingredient
b) Only the caution sign and safety precautions
c) Recommended dosage and target pest(s)
d) All of the above

32. If a pesticide causes serious environmental and public health concerns, what can happen?

a) Its production can increase
b) It can be promoted for wider usage
c) It can be banned even after registration
d) It can be exported to other countries

33. The term "Restricted Use" for pesticides means:
    a) They are banned from registration.
    b) They can be used freely without any limitations.
    c) They can be used only for prescribed purposes by authorized personnel.
    d) They are available for household use only.

34. What does the CIB & RC do periodically?
    a) Increases the price of pesticides.
    b) Scrutinizes and reviews all pesticides and their usage.
    c) Registers all substances without scrutiny.
    d) Promotes non-registered pesticides.

35. How many central government laboratories are there for fertilizer quality control?
    a) 1
    b) 2
    c) 3
    d) 4

36. The FCO provides for the regulation of which of the following?
    a) Manufacture of food products
    b) Sale of electronic goods
    c) Manufacture of fertilizer mixtures
    d) Import of textiles

37. Which organization is mentioned in the context of obtaining the appropriate government license for restricted use pesticides?
    a) Indian Agriculture Association
    b) Indian Pest Control Association
    c) Indian Fertilizer Control Board
    d) Central Insecticides and Pesticides Board

38. An offense under the FCO is considered:
    a) Negligible
    b) Cognizable
    c) Non-punishable
    d) Minor

39. Which entity provides training facilities and technical guidance for the enforcement of the FCO?
    a) State Governments
    b) Fertilizer Manufacturers
    c) Central Government
    c) Private Organizations

40. A pesticide labeled for agricultural use should:
    a) Be used in any setting
    b) Not be used in a household
    c) Be used only for indoor plants
    d) Be diluted for household use

41. The FCO provides for the prohibition on the manufacture, import, and sale of:
    a) Standard fertilizers
    b) Non-standard/spurious/adulterated fertilizers
    c) Organic fertilizers
    d) Government-approved fertilizers

42. The professional pest manager should have:
    a) Only knowledge
    b) Only the latest products and equipment
    c) Knowledge, skills, latest products, and equipment
    d) Only skills

43. The Seeds Act was enacted in which year?
    a) 1960
    b) 1966
    c) 1970
    d) 1975

44. What is the main purpose of The Seeds Act?
    a) Promoting seed exports
    b) Regulating the quality of certain seeds for sale
    c) Establishing seed manufacturing plants
    d) Granting licenses to seed dealers

45. The Central Seed Committee advises which of the following?
    a) Seed Inspectors
    b) Central and State Governments
    c) Seed Certification Agencies
    d) Foreign Seed Certification Agencies

46. How long is the term for members of the Central Seed Committee?
    a) One year
    b) Two years
    c) Three years
    d) Four years

47. Which government body can establish a Central Seed Laboratory?
    a) State Government
    b) Central Government
    c) Central Seed Committee
    d) Certification Agency

48. The State Government can establish which of the following laboratories?
    a) Central Seed Laboratory
    b) State Seed Laboratory
    c) Private Seed Laboratory
    d) International Seed Laboratory

49. A certification agency is established by:
    a) The Central Government
    b) The Central Seed Committee
    c) The State Government or the Central Government in consultation with the State Government
    d) Seed Analysts

50. For how many days can an aggrieved person appeal a decision by a certification agency
    a) 15 days
    b) 30 days
    c) 45 days
    d) 60 days

51. Who is considered a public servant under the Act?
    a) Seed Analyst
    b) Central Seed Committee member
    c) Seed Inspector
    d) Certification agency member

52. Which of the following is NOT a power of the seed inspector?
    a) Taking samples of any notified seed
    b) Sending samples for analysis
    c) Deciding the germination rate for seeds
    d) Searching any place where they believe an offence under this Act has occurred

53. How many representative samples does a seed inspector need to take?
    a) One
    b) Two
    c) Three
    d) Four

54. Whose report supersedes the report given by the Seed Analyst?
   a) Seed Inspector
   b) Central Seed Laboratory
   c) Certification Agency
   d) Central Seed Committee

55. Which of the following is NOT allowed for the export or import of seeds of notified kinds or varieties?
   a) The seed must meet minimum germination standards
   b) The seed must come from a recognized foreign certification agency
   c) The container must bear the correct particulars
   d) The seed must be sold within 30 days

56 The maximum penalty for a person convicted for the first offence under the Act is:
   a) Imprisonment for 6 months
   b) Fine of 1000 rupees
   c) Fine of 500 rupees
   d) Both a and b

57. If a company commits an offence under the Act, who can be held responsible?
   a) Only the company
   b) Only the director of the company
   c) Both the company and the person in charge at the time of the offence
   d) Only the employees of the company

58. The certification agency can revoke a certificate if it has been obtained by:
   a) Overpaying for it
   b) Fraud or misrepresentation
   c) Using foreign varieties
   d) Excessive advertising

59 For what purpose can the Central Government make rules under the Act?
   a) To regulate the appointment of seed inspectors
   b) To determine the functions of the Central Seed Committee
   c) To regulate the export of seeds
   d) All of the above

60. Who appoints a seed analyst under the Act?
   a) Central Seed Laboratory
   b) Central Government
   c) State Government
   d) Central Seed Committee

61. The appeal against the decision of a seed analyst lies to:
   a) Central Seed Laboratory
   b) Certification Agency
   c) Central Seed Committee
   d) State Seed Laboratory

62. Which seeds are primarily covered under The Seeds Act?
   a) All kinds of seeds
   b) Only notified kinds or varieties of seeds
   c) Only those used for planting purposes
   d) Seeds used for consumption

63. What protection is offered under the Act for actions taken in good faith?
   a) No legal proceedings shall lie against any person.
   b) Only a suit can be filed against the officer.
   c) No suit, prosecution, or other legal proceedings shall lie against the Government or any officer.
   d) A complaint can be made to the Central Seed Committee.

64. Who has the power to give directions to any State Government for the execution of the provisions of the Act?
   a) State Seed Laboratory
   b) Central Seed Committee
   c) State Government
   d) Central Government

65. Which seeds are exempted under this Act?
   a) All seeds of notified kind or variety.
   b) Seeds grown and sold by a person on his own premises for sowing or planting.
   c) Seeds used for consumption.
   d) All kinds of seeds.

66. Which Act regulates the Agricultural Produce Marketing in India?
   a) Agricultural Marketing Act
   b) Seeds Act
   c) Agricultural Produce Marketing (Regulation) Act
   d) Food Safety and Standards Act

67. What is the purpose of the APMC Act?
   a) To promote foreign trade.
   b) To ensure quality of seeds.
   c) To protect the farmers from exploitation by middlemen.
   d) To monitor and regulate fertilizer use.

68. The Protection of Plant Varieties and Farmers' Rights Act, 2001 is designed to:

   a) Only protect the rights of farmers.

   b) Only encourage the development of new varieties of plants.

   c) Recognize and protect the rights of farmers and encourage the development of new plant varieties.

   d) Establish a seed bank for rare plant varieties.

69. Who appoints the Registrar-General of Plant Varieties?

   a) Central Government
   b) State Government
   c) The Authority
   d) The Central Seed Committee

70. What is the duty of the Protection of Plant Varieties and Farmers' Rights Authority?

   a) To encourage only the development of new varieties of plants.

   b) To ensure high-quality seeds to the farmers.

   c) To maintain the Plant Varieties Registry.

   d) All of the above.

71. Where is the National Register of Plant Varieties kept?

   a) Local office of the Registry
   b) Agricultural department
   c) Head office of the Registry
   d) Ministry of Agriculture

72. What is essential for a new variety to be registered under the Act?

   a) Distinctiveness and novelty
   b) Uniformity and stability
   c) All of the above
   d) None of the above

73. How long before the date of filing can the propagating material of a new variety be sold in India?

   a) Six years
   b) Four years
   c) Two years
   d) One year

74. Who can make an application for registration?

   a) Breeder of the variety

   b) Farmer

   c) Publicly funded agricultural institution

   d) All of the above

75. A new variety shall NOT be registered if its denomination is:
   a) Different from other varieties
   b) Likely to hurt religious sentiments
   c) Capable of identifying the variety
   d) Comprised of diverse elements

76. Who receives the application for an essentially derived variety?
   a) The breeder
   b) The registrar
   c) The Authority
   d) The National Gene Bank

77. What is issued to the applicant once a variety (other than an essentially derived variety) is registered?
   a) Certificate of novelty
   b) Certificate of origin
   c) Certificate of registration
   d) Certificate of deposit

78. How often does the Authority publish the list of registered varieties?
   a) Annually
   b) Bi-annually
   c) At intervals they see fit
   d) Monthly

79. Who can submit claims for benefit sharing of a registered variety?
   a) Only the breeder
   b) Any person or organization
   c) Only farmers
   d) Only governmental organizations

80. Where should the breeder deposit seeds or propagating material of a registered variety?
   a) Local agricultural office
   b) National Gene Bank
   c) State agricultural department
   d) Breeder's own bank

81. An extant variety needs to meet which criteria for registration?
   a) Novelty
   b) Uniformity and stability
   c) Distinctiveness
   d) Both b and c

82. Which section of the Emblems and Names (Prevention of Improper Use) Act, 1950, prohibits the use of certain denominations?
   a) Section 1
   b) Section 2
   c) Section 3
   d) Section 4

83. Which variety is considered novel outside India for trees or vines if not sold earlier than:

a) Six years b) Four years

c) Three years d) One year

84. A variety is homogeneous if:

a) It varies widely in its characteristics

b) It is uniform in its essential characteristics

c) It changes characteristics after propagation

d) None of the above

85. The Registrar can accept an application:

a) Only after public consultation

b) Absolutely or with conditions

c) Only after a trial period

d) After approval from the central government

86. The opposition to registration can be raised:

a) Within six months of advertisement

b) Within three months of advertisement

c) Anytime after advertisement

d) Only before advertisement

87. An essentially derived variety is tested to determine if it:

a) Has better quality than the original

b) Is derived from the initial variety

c) Has a longer shelf life

d) Is similar to existing varieties

88. If registration isn't completed within 12 months due to the applicant's fault, the application:

a) Is put on hold indefinitely b) Is immediately rejected

c) Is treated as abandoned d) Gets an automatic extension

89. The funds from benefit sharing are deposited in:

a) The Central Bank b) The Breeder's Bank

c) The National Gene Fund d) The State Bank

90. A variety is distinct if:
    a) It cannot be differentiated from other varieties
    b) It has a similar name to another variety
    c) It is distinguishable by at least one essential characteristic from commonly known varieties
    d) It has better quality than other varieties

91. What does a certificate of registration for a variety confer as per SS 1?
    a) Right to produce the variety only.
    b) Right to market the variety only.
    c) Right to use the variety in any fashion.
    d) Exclusive right to produce, sell, market, distribute, import, or export the variety.

92. When can an agent or licensee register his title according to SS 4?
    a) After payment of prescribed fees and providing proof of title.
    b) By just making an application.
    c) After getting permission from the breeder.
    d) After selling a certain amount of the variety.

93. What is the conclusive proof of entitlement according to SS 5?
    a) The application form.
    b) The receipt of payment.
    c) Certificate of registration.
    d) Verbal confirmation from the registrar.

94. Who has the right to institute proceedings for infringement under SS 6?
    a) Breeder only.
    b) Licensee only after breeder refuses to take action.
    c) Any person with knowledge of the infringement.
    d) Registrar only.

95. Who is entitled for recognition and reward from the Gene Fund as per Farmers' rights?
    a) A farmer who has bred a new variety.
    b) A farmer engaged in conservation of genetic resources of land races.
    c) A farmer who uses a registered variety.
    d) All farmers by default.

96. Who can stake a claim on behalf of a village or local community as per Rights of Communities SS 1?

a) Only the village head.

b) Governmental organizations.

c) Any person or group or any governmental or non-governmental organisation.

d) The breeder of a variety.

97. Where is the compensation granted under sub-section (3) of Rights of Communities deposited?

a) National Treasury.

b) Bank Account of the claimant.

c) Gene Fund.

d) The Authority's Fund.

98. For what can the Gene Fund be applied according to its provisions?

a) Only for benefit sharing under sub-section (5) of section 26.

b) Expenditure for supporting the conservation and sustainable use of genetic resources.

c) Only the compensation payable under sub-section (3) of section 41.

d) Expenditures of the schemes unrelated to genetic resources.

99. When does the National Biodiversity Authority come into effect?

a) With immediate effect

b) From the date mentioned in the official gazette by the Central Government

c) After 6 months from the announcement

d) None of the above

100. Where is the head office of the National Biodiversity Authority located?

a) Delhi

b) Mumbai

c) Kolkata

d) Chennai

101. Who appoints the Chairperson of the National Biodiversity Authority?

a) The President of India

b) State Government

c) Central Government

d) Ministry of Environment and Forests

102. How many ex officio members representing the Ministry dealing with Environment and Forests are appointed by the Central Government?

a) One
b) Two
c) Three
d) Four

103. Which among the following is NOT one of the ministries represented by ex officio members in the National Biodiversity Authority?

a) Ocean Development
b) Biotechnology
c) Tourism and Culture
d) Agriculture and Cooperation

104. Who is the Chief Executive of the National Biodiversity Authority?

a) Director General of Forests
b) Chairperson
c) Any ex officio member
d) None of the above

105. In the absence of the Chairperson, who presides over the meetings of the National Biodiversity Authority?

a) Director General of Forests
b) Any ex officio member chosen by the members present
c) A designated vice-chairperson
d) None of the above

106. Under which section is it the duty of the National Biodiversity Authority to regulate activities and issue guidelines for access to biological resources?

a) Section 3
b) Section 10
c) Section 18.1
d) Section 20

107. Who has the power to oppose the grant of intellectual property rights on any biological resource obtained from India in another country?

a) Central Government
b) State Government
c) National Biodiversity Authority
d) Ministry of Environment and Forests

108 Who should apply to the National Biodiversity Authority if they want to obtain a biological resource occurring in India for research?

a) Any person in India
b) Only academic researchers
c) Persons referred to in sub-section (2) of section 3
d) Only international researchers

109. What does the National Biodiversity Authority do after receiving an application under sub-section (7) or sub-section (2)?

a) Immediately approve the application

b) Conduct an inquiry and consult an expert committee if necessary

c) Directly reject the application

d) Send the application for international review

110. Under which section is the approval for transferring any biological resource given?

a) Section 18

b) Section 19

c) Section 20

d) Section 21

111. The term of office and conditions of service of the Chairperson and other members of the National Biodiversity Authority are determined by?

a) Chairperson

b) State Government

c) Central Government

d) Supreme Court of India

112. Where can the National Biodiversity Authority establish its offices other than its head office?

a) Only in state capitals

b) Anywhere in India with the previous approval of the Central Government

c) Only in Tier-1 cities

d) Only in cities with a population of more than 2 million

113. Who has the deciding vote in the event of a tie during National Biodiversity Authority meetings?

a) The eldest member

b) The junior-most member

c) Chairperson or, in his absence, the person presiding

d) It is decided by a coin toss

114. What is the role of the National Biodiversity Authority regarding intellectual property rights outside India?

a) They grant the rights

b) They advise on the rights

c) They oppose the grant of such rights

d) They have no role

115. How many non-official members are appointed in the National Biodiversity Authority?

a) Three **b) Five**

c) Seven d) Ten

116. To which entity should a person apply if they want to transfer any biological resource or related knowledge?

a) Ministry of Environment and Forests

b) State Biodiversity Board

c) National Biodiversity Authority

d) Ministry of Science and Technology

117. Who should disclose their interest or concern in a matter to be decided at a National Biodiversity Authority meeting?

a) Only the Chairperson

b) The person presiding over the meeting

c) Every member directly or indirectly concerned or interested

d) External experts

118. What does the National Biodiversity Authority do after granting approval under section 19 or section 20?

a) Sends a private notification to the applicant

b) Gives public notice of the approval

c) Holds a press conference

d) Sends a report to the Central Government

119. The National Biodiversity Authority, when granting approvals under section 19 or 20, ensures:

a) Maximum monetary gains.

b) Equitable sharing of benefits from accessed biological resources.

c) Sole ownership of intellectual property rights.

d) Prioritization of foreign technologies.

120. Which of the following is NOT a method of benefit sharing as determined by the National Biodiversity Authority?

a) Transfer of technology.

b) Organizing eco-tourism initiatives.

c) Joint ownership of intellectual property rights.

d) Location of production in areas beneficial for the claimers.

121. If money is ordered by way of benefit sharing, where might the National Biodiversity Authority direct it to be deposited?
   a) In a private bank.
   b) In the National Biodiversity Fund.
   c) Directly to the Central Government.
   d) In an international fund for biodiversity.

122. Who establishes the State Biodiversity Board?
   a) The National Biodiversity Authority.
   b) The Central Government.
   c) The Local bodies.
   d) The State Government.

123. Who exercises the powers and performs the functions of a State Biodiversity Board for a Union territory?
   a) The Central Government.
   b) The State Biodiversity Board of the neighboring state.
   c) The National Biodiversity Authority.
   d) The Union territory's local governance.

124. What is the function of the State Biodiversity Board?
   a) To solely grant ownership of resources.
   b) To regulate commercial utilization of biological resources by foreigners.
   c) To advise the State Government on matters like conservation of biodiversity.
   d) To facilitate foreign investments.

125. Before undertaking any activity referred to in section 7, who should provide prior intimation to the State Biodiversity Board?
   a) Any citizen of a foreign country.
   b) Only government officials.
   c) Any citizen of India or a registered body in India.
   d) International environmental organizations.

126. Which section's provisions apply to a State Biodiversity Board with certain modifications?
   a) Sections 1 to 8.
   b) Sections 9 to 17.
   c) Sections 18 to 25.
   d) Sections 26 to 34.

127. Who appoints the Chairperson of the State Biodiversity Board?
   a) The Central Government.
   b) The National Biodiversity Authority.
   c) The State Government.
   d) Local bodies.

128. What is the maximum number of ex officio members to be appointed by the State Government to the State Biodiversity Board?
   a) Three
   b) Five
   c) Seven
   d) Ten

129. In which city was the General Agreement on Tariffs and Trade (GATT) established in 1947?
   a) Paris
   b) New York
   c) Geneva
   d) Brussels

130. Agriculture was first included in GATT negotiations during which round?
   a) Tokyo Round
   b) Uruguay Round
   c) Doha Round
   d) Kennedy Round

131. Which of the following is NOT an objective of the Agreement on Agriculture (AOA)?
   a) Market access restrictions
   b) Domestic support policies
   c) Export subsidies
   d) Import licensing procedures

132. Market access restrictions typically take the form of all EXCEPT:
   a) Tariffs
   b) Import quotas
   c) Direct payments
   d) Variable levies

133. Domestic support policies that raise the domestic market price above the world market price, achieved through government intervention are called:
   a) Deficiency payments
   b) Input subsidies
   c) Market price support
   d) Export support

134. Which of the following does not fall under domestic support policies?
   a) Direct payments to farmers
   b) Input subsidies
   c) Export subsidies
   d) Government purchase of farm production

135. Export subsidies are used to:
   a) Support domestic production
   b) Encourage imports
   c) Dispose of surpluses on the world market
   d) Enhance internal consumption

136. Which document provides specific quantitative commitments on a country by country and commodity by commodity basis post-Uruguay Round negotiations on agriculture?
   a) The AoA
   b) The Country Schedules
   c) The Modalities
   d) The GATT Principles

137. The process during which members could question and seek changes in the Country Schedules is termed as:
   a) Ratification process
   b) Verification process
   c) Adjustment process
   d) Notification process

138. Tariffication in the context of the Agreement and the Country Schedules refers to:
   a) The application of new tariffs
   b) The reduction of existing tariffs
   c) The conversion of NTBs to trade into tariff equivalents
   d) The removal of all tariffs

139. What is the primary aim of Market Access Commitments?
   a) Encourage development of agriculture
   b) Ensure existing export markets are maintained
   c) Reduce tariffs
   d) Prioritize domestic markets

140. The base period for maintaining the current levels of access for imports is:
   a) 1984-86
   b) 1988-90
   c) 1986-88
   d) 1990-92

141. For developed countries, the minimum access should rise to what percentage by the year 2000?
   a) 2%
   b) 4%
   c) 5%
   d) 6%

142. What is the main goal of Domestic Support Commitments?
   a) Enhance domestic production
   b) Limit trade distortions caused by domestic agricultural support policies
   c) Increase exports
   d) Prioritize food safety

143. What is the Aggregate Measure of Support (AMS)?
   a) Quantifying all domestic support
   b) Reducing trade tariffs
   c) Encouraging exports
   d) Categorizing WTO members

144. Policies with a substantial impact on the flow of trade are classified in the:
   a) Green box
   b) Amber box
   c) Blue box
   d) Development box

145. Policies that are not deemed to have a major effect on production and trade are placed in the:
   a) Green box
   b) Amber box
   c) Blue box
   d) Development box

146. Which box contains policies that are somewhere in between green and amber boxes?
   a) Green box
   b) Amber box
   c) Blue box
   d) Development box

147. What does the 'Green box' primarily consist of?
   a) Trade-distorting policies
   b) Non-trade distorting policies
   c) Policies affecting only developing countries
   d) Policies from the post-Uruguay Round

148. The most notable 'blue-box' policies are associated with:
   a) African Union's Agriculture Policy
   b) EU's Common Agricultural Policy
   c) ASEAN's Farming Principles
   d) SAARC's Green Revolution

149. How many WTO members committed to reduce their trade-distorting domestic supports in the Amber Box?
   a) 20
   b) 25
   c) 30
   d) 34

150. The Development Box was proposed by:
   a) EU
   b) USA
   c) Like-Minded Group of developing countries
   d) African Union

151. Subsidies that are non-trade distorting are organized under which color box?
   a) Green
   b) Blue
   c) Amber
   d) Red

152. What agreement sets constraints related to food safety and animal and plant health?
   a) Agreement on Development
   b) Agreement on the Application of Sanitary and Phytosanitary Measures (SPS)
   c) Food and Health Agreement
   d) Agricultural and Livestock Agreement

153. Risks to animal life or health can come from:
   a) Only diseases
   b) Only contaminants
   c) Both diseases and contaminants
   d) None of the above

154. Which organization is associated with food safety as per the SPS Agreement?
   a) The International Office of Epizootics
   b) The Secretariat of the International Plant Protection Convention
   c) The Codex Alimentarius Commission
   d) United Nations Food and Agriculture Organization

155. The central goal of agricultural law should be:
   a) Ensuring profitability for farmers
   b) Sustainable production and delivery of healthy food
   c) Increasing export potential
   d) Focusing only on domestic needs

156. How many countries had larger subsidies than the de minimis levels at the beginning of the post-Uruguay Round reform period?

a) 15
b) 20
c) 30
d) 35

157. Members without Amber Box commitments have to keep within what percentage of the value of production for developing countries?

a) 5%
b) 10%
c) 15%
d) 20%

158. Who sets the international standards, guidelines, and recommendations for plant health?

a) Codex Alimentarius Commission
b) International Office of Epizootics
c) Secretariat of the International Plant Protection Convention
d) World Health Organization

22

IPR, Agri-Tech Management and Commercialization

1. Innovation can be described as the process of:

   a) Creating new music genres.

   b) Introducing new products and services to the market.

   c) Generating new ideas without implementation.

   d) Only manufacturing new products.

2. What role does a system of intellectual property rights play in innovation?

   a) Makes innovation more challenging.

   b) Encourages potential imitators.

   c) Protects investments of innovative companies against potential imitators.

   d) Has no significant role.

3. The spectacular growth in agricultural production is closely linked with:

   a) Fashion industry. b) Digital marketing.

   c) Information technology. d) Tourism.

4. To achieve sustainable agriculture, it is crucial to:

   a) Increase the number of farms.

   b) Empower farmers with the latest technical knowledge.

   c) Focus only on large farms.

   d) Discourage information technology in agriculture.

5. What is lacking in the current relationship between research institutions, universities, industries, and farmers?

   a) Proper management. b) Sufficient funds.

   c) A full-fledged partnership. d) Interest in agriculture.

Bold Means Correct Answer

6. One of the issues with the current extension system for farmers is:
   a) It provides quick information.
   b) It is very efficient.
   c) It is focused only on large farmers.
   d) It consumes more time and money.

7. What is essential for farmers concerning agriculture commodities?
   a) Knowledge about manufacturing.
   b) Quick and latest information on marketing trends.
   c) Information about the history of farming.
   d) Details about urban developments.

8. The current approach at the national level aims to:
   a) Focus only on industrialization.
   b) Build agriculture as a primary livelihood source.
   c) Limit the use of technology in agriculture.
   d) Prioritize non-agricultural professions.

9. SETU under NITI Aayog aims to:
   a) Only focus on urban development.
   b) Support start-up businesses and self-employment activities.
   c) Limit the use of technology in industries.
   d) Discourage agricultural initiatives.

10. What is a significant concern that requires more innovations in agriculture?
    a) Entertainment options for farmers.
    b) Energy crisis and declining water resources.
    c) Implementation of old farming techniques.
    d) Focusing only on cash crops.

11. Which was the first legislation in India relating to patents?
    a) Act IX of 1857
    b) Act XV of 1859
    c) **Act VI of 1856**
    d) The patterns and Designs protection Act of 1872

12. The Act VI of 1856 was repealed because:
    a) **It had been enacted without the approval of the British crown.**
    b) It did not encourage new inventions.
    c) It was found to be not effective.
    d) It clashed with the Act of 1859.

13. The Act of 1872 was amended in 1883 to protect:
    a) All kinds of inventions.
    b) Only machine-related inventions.
    c) **Novelty of the invention disclosed in the Exhibition of India.**
    d) Agricultural inventions.

14. The Indian Patent and Designs Act of which year replaced all previous Acts?
    a) 1920 b) 1883
    c) 1911 d) 1872

15. After independence, who was appointed to review the patent law in India in 1949?
    a) Justice N. Rajagopala Ayyangar
    b) **Justice (Dr) Bakshi Tek Chand**
    c) Justice P. N. Bhagwati
    d) Justice K. N. Singh

16. In which year was the Patents Act, 1970, passed?
    a) 1965 b) 1967
    c) **1970** d) 1972

17. Which Act remained in force for about 24 years without any change?
    a) Patent Act, 1965
    b) Patent Act, 1911
    c) **Patent Act, 1970**
    d) Patent (Amendment) Act, 2002

18. The second amendment to the 1970 Act was made in:
    a) 1975 b) 1980
    c) 1995 d) **2002**

19. The third amendment to the Patent Act 1970 was introduced in which year?
    a) 2002
    b) 2003
    c) **2005**
    d) 2010

20. The Act of 1859 was consolidated to provide protection related to:
    a) Patents and designs.
    b) **Designs.**
    c) Novelty inventions.
    d) Exhibition disclosures.

21. Under which section of the patent Act, 1970 is the Central Government empowered to make Rules for implementing the Act and regulating patent administration?
    a) Section 140
    b) **Section 159**
    c) Section 132
    d) Section 110

22. When were the patent Rules, 1972 first brought into force?
    a) 1.1.1970
    b) 20.5.2003
    c) **20.4.1972**
    d) 11.5.2001

23. When did the last amendment to the patent (Amendment) rules become effective?
    a) 1.1.1999
    b) 30.12.2014
    c) 20.5.2003
    d) **1.12.2017**

24. Under which Act is the registration and protection of industrial designs in India administered?
    a) Designs Act, 1911
    b) Designs Act, 1999
    c) **Designs Act, 2000**
    d) Designs Act, 2001

25. The Trade Marks Registry in India was established in which year?
    a) **1940**
    b) 1999
    c) 2000
    d) 1970

26. Which of the following is not a dimension used to assess the strength of a patent regime?
    a) Length of the patent term
    b) **Depth of the patent application**
    c) Breadth of the patent
    d) Height of the invention step

27. What is the main function of the Trade Marks Registry in India?

a) To provide legal counsel for inventors

b) To register trademarks which qualify for registration

c) To assist in drafting patent applications

d) To mediate patent disputes

28. A majority of patents are allowed to expire before their statutory maximum lifetime because:

a) Their holders find the renewal fees too low

b) The patents become technologically obsolete

c) Their holders consider the renewal fees too high compared to the value of the patent

d) The patents are often invalidated by new inventions

29. When was the IP and TM scheme launched by ICAR?

a) 2000 b) 2004

c) 2006 **d) 2008**

30. ICAR institutionalized a decentralized three-tier IP management mechanism from:

a) 1st January 2004 b) 15th August 2005

c) 2nd October 2006 d) 5th March 2007

31. What is the aim of NAIF Component I (Innovation Fund)?

a) To promote creativity and innovations in ICAR institution

b) To provide financial assistance for farming

c) To boost agricultural exports

d) To promote organic farming in ICAR institutions

32. What does Component II (Incubation Fund) primarily focus on?

a) Promotion of biodiversity in agriculture

b) Establishing agri-business incubator centers and supporting potential entrepreneurs

c) Implementing new agricultural policies

d) Conducting agricultural surveys and research

33. What does the Intellectual property and Technology Management Unit (IP and TM) in ICAR oversee?

    a) Matters related to intellectual properties and technology transfer/ commercialization

    b) Matters related to agricultural machinery and tools

    c) Matters related to seeds and fertilizers

    d) Matters related to international collaborations

34. What does technology transfer refer to?

    a) Process of transferring technology from its origination to a wider distribution

    b) Process of creating new technologies

    c) Process of exporting technology products

    d) Process of reviewing and updating existing technology

35. What does commercialization involve?

    a) Turning an invention or creation into a commercially viable product, service, or process

    b) Creating marketing campaigns for a new product

    c) Setting prices for agricultural products

    d) Analyzing customer feedback for product development

36. Which of the following does the MoU include clauses about?

    a) Technology transfer fee and annual payment of royalty

    b) Employment conditions in the agricultural sector

    c) Agricultural export regulations

    d) Safety protocols for farmworkers

37. Who were the primary sources of technology innovation, demonstration, and transfer in the field of agriculture till the mid-80s in developing countries like India?

    a) Publicly funded R&D institutions

    b) Private companies

    c) International agricultural organizations

    d) Smallholder farmers

38. What did the earlier approach of providing sample kits to producers and demonstrating technology often undermine?

    a) The contributions of publicly funded R&D towards improving technologies and enhancing agricultural productivity

    b) The financial gains of private seed companies

    c) The environmental conservation efforts in agriculture

    d) The efforts of international collaborations in the agricultural sector.

39. Which of the following best describes the process of commercialization?

    a) Turning a concept into a tangible item

    b) Conducting research on an invention

    c) Turning an invention into a commercially viable product or service

    d) Registering a patent for an invention

40. Public research organizations (PROS) usually:

    a) Have the resources and appetite to commercialize their own inventions

    b) Need no commercial partners

    c) Focus solely on domestic markets

    d) Do not always wish or have the resources to commercialize their own inventions

41. For the commercialization of biotechnology innovation, sales revenues:

    a) Provide significant funds in the short term

    b) Are the only source of funds

    c) Are unlikely to provide a significant source of funds in the short term

    d) Are not needed for successful commercialization

42. Which of the following is NOT a condition necessary for obtaining a commercial return from IP?

    a) The ability to create customers

    b) The existence of a competitor

    c) An entity controlling the sale of the resulting products

    d) The existence of a customer

43. Which of the following is a legal vehicle for commercializing IP?

    a) Renting the IP

    b) Licensing the IP rights

    c) Sharing the IP

    d) Borrowing the IP

44. An advantage of assigning IP compared to licensing is:
   a) Opportunity to partake in additional profits if the invention becomes valuable
   b) Regular royalty payments from the licensee
   c) Simplified negotiations involving only two parties
   d) The burden of ensuring the licensee is exploiting the invention properly

45. A disadvantage of assigning IP is:
   a) Risk that the assigned patent may never be properly exploited
   b) Continuous involvement in the commercialization process
   c) Regular income in the form of royalties
   d) Short term immediate rewards

46. Joint ownership of IP holds the disadvantage that:
   a) A joint owner cannot use the patent without the other's consent
   b) Joint owners always share profits equally
   c) A joint owner may sell its interest to any other party without agreement from other owners
   d) All joint owners need to be consulted for every decision

47. What does a license allow patent owners to do?
   a) Share inventions with an unlimited number of entities.
   b) Share inventions in a controlled manner and to receive royalties.
   c) Transfer full ownership of the patent to another entity.
   d) Terminate their patent rights.

48. Who retains the ownership of the IP when it is licensed?
   a) Licensee
   b) The government
   c) Licensor
   d) Both licensee and licensor

49. An exclusive license is best described as:
   a) Granting multiple entities the right to use the intellectual property.
   b) Permitting only the licensee to exploit the invention, excluding even the owner.
   c) Allowing both the owner and the licensee to exploit the intellectual property.
   d) Giving everyone, including the public, the right to use the intellectual property.

50. Which type of license allows both the licensor and multiple licensees to exploit the IP?

a) Sole license **b) Non-exclusive license**

c) Exclusive license d) Shared license

51. One of the advantages of licensing from the licensor's point of view is:

a) Full transfer of IP risks to the licensee.

b) A source of revenue helping to develop new products.

c) The licensee gaining full ownership of the intellectual property.

d) Avoiding the need to monitor the licensee's performance.

52. A potential drawback of granting an exclusive license is:

a) The patent owner can grant further licenses to others.

b) The patent owner retains full rights to promote or sell the invention.

c) The licensee might not effectively promote or sell the invention.

d) The licensee can easily transfer their rights back to the licensor.

53. What can be a disadvantage of a non-exclusive license from the patent owner's perspective?

a) Only one entity can use the licensed property.

b) The patent owner would typically be responsible for commencing an infringement action against a third party.

c) The licensor will have to pay higher royalty rates.

d) The licensor cannot grant any other licenses.

54. Which licensing type requires a licensor to pay the most attention to monitor the licensee's performance?

a) Non-exclusive license

b) Sole license

c) Exclusive license

d) Both exclusive and non-exclusive licenses

55. What is typically included in the basis of negotiation for the grant of a license?

a) Licensing duration and region

b) License initiation fees and running royalties

c) Patent expiry date

d) Number of users allowed under the license

56. What factors determine specific payment amounts and royalty rates for licensing?

    a) Strength of protection and market of the invention

    b) Number of previous licensees

    c) Duration of the licensing agreement

    d) Availability of competing licenses

57. Why is IPR enforcement crucial for successful commercialization?

    a) It helps in attracting more licensees

    b) It protects against competitors creating similar products

    c) It increases the lifespan of the patent

    d) It reduces the licensing fees

58. Which of the following is a limitation of technology transfer among Agricultural IP?

    a) Increased focus on patentable technologies

    b) Trend of secrecy among the scientific community

    c) Assigning value to intellectual efforts by scientists

    d) Public research organizations always benefiting from global opportunities

59. How is the income generated from the utilization of IP assets typically used?

    a) It is solely distributed among the scientist innovators

    b) It is fully kept as core fund for IP-related activities

    c) A portion is distributed to scientist innovators, while some is reserved for IP activities

    d) It is used for advertising the invention

60. What has the growing interest in research led to in the context of technology transfer among Agricultural IP?

    a) Diminishing focus on patentable technologies

    b) Shift towards trait specificity and patentable technology generation

    c) An emphasis on non-commercializable technologies

    d) A decline in the value assigned to intellectual efforts by scientists

61. Why are some public research organizations unable to capitalize on global business opportunities?
    a) Because of high licensing fees
    b) Due to institutional bottlenecks such as NBA clearance requirements
    c) Lack of international interest in their innovations
    d) Inability to enforce IPR globally

62. Which positive outcome of technology commercialization is mentioned in the passage?
    a) Increased reliance on public sector for technology adoption
    b) The scope for scientist innovators to become entrepreneurs
    c) A consistent growth in licensing fees
    d) More transparent sharing of knowledge among the scientific community

63. Intellectual Property Right (IPR) protection in research institutes and universities globally is viewed as a tool to:
    a) Enhance creativity and innovation.
    b) Limit scientific research to a few institutions.
    c) Reduce technology transfer rates.
    d) Focus only on local market needs.

64. What is a primary aim of global technology transfer policies?
    a) Limiting the development of new technologies.
    b) Transforming scientific discoveries into industrial applications.
    c) Establishing singular global governance for all research institutions.
    d) Promoting sole ownership of technologies by individual inventors.

65. Which statement is true regarding policy emulation for economic development?
    a) Every policy that works for one country will surely work for another.
    b) Only high-income countries should adopt policies from others.
    c) What works for one country might not necessarily work for another.
    d) All countries must adopt identical policies for development.

66. The Bayh-Dole act in 1980 influenced:
    a) Decrease in technology transfer from universities in the USA.
    b) Global harmonization of IPR policies.
    c) A reduction in the number of tech startups.
    d) A surge in R&D budget allocation globally.

67. What significant change did US universities exhibit between 1991 and 1993?
   a) A decline in gross royalties from licenses.
   b) A reduction in technology transfer offices.
   c) A substantial increase in gross royalties from licenses.
   d) A halt in R&D activities.

68. The Technology Transfer and Commercialization process involves:
   a) Allowing any individual or company to use a technology without any agreement.
   b) Licensing technology to private entities under specific terms and conditions.
   c) Permitting licensees to change the original technology without constraints.
   d) Universities and research organizations relinquishing all IPR over a technology when licensed.

69. What are Technology Transfer Offices (TTOs)?
   a) Independent research entities exploring new technological domains.
   b) Entities focused only on patenting technologies.
   c) Bodies that handle operational and legal aspects of technology transfer.
   d) Organizations responsible only for the commercialization of technologies.

70. Which country's technology transfer policies from the 1980s and early 1990s are deemed significant?
   a) Brazil
   b) Chile
   c) China
   d) US

71. Which of the following countries has modified their legislature on IP rights management for industrial and agriculture-related goods primarily in line with the TRIPS agreement and the WTO?
   a) Brazil
   b) India
   c) Chile
   d) All of the above

72. The Indian Council of Agricultural Research (ICAR) is an autonomous body under which Ministry?
   a) Ministry of Science and Technology
   b) Ministry of Commerce
   c) Ministry of Agriculture and Cooperation
   d) Ministry of Industry

73. Who adopted the IP policy in 2006 in India?
   a) DST in the Ministry of S&T
   b) ICAR
   c) Protection of Plant Varieties and Farmers' Rights Act
   d) NRDC

74. Which of the following is NOT true about China's technology innovation policy?
   a) Law for the Promotion of Transformation of Scientific and Technological Achievements was in 1996.
   b) The details for managing IPRS were through China Bayh-1 dole system 2010.
   c) China has the China Bayh-2 dole system.
   d) Industrial Technology Research Institute (ITRI) is associated with China's IP policies.

75. In which country does the Industrial property law decide that IP belongs to the University, but employees get a share in the benefits?
   a) India
   b) Chile
   c) Brazil
   d) China

76. What was Brazil's significant step in 1997 regarding IP and technology transfer?
   a) Enactment of the 'law on industrial property no. 9.279
   b) Joining the WTO
   c) Formation of the Brazilian Agricultural Research Corporation (EMBRAPA)
   d) Adoption of the Innovation Law

77. Which country established a separate organization to coordinate domestic institutions for the benefit of technology transfers from outside the country?
   a) Brazil
   b) Chile
   c) China
   d) India

78. What is the key incentive for technology transfer from a commercial perspective?
   a) Policy of distribution of benefits from commercialization
   b) Establishment of more TTOs
   c) Acquiring more patents
   d) Scaling up research and development efforts

79. Which Indian entity has established a 'corporate face' to promote technology transfers in a centralized manner?

a) NRDC

b) DST in the Ministry of S&T

c) Agrinnovate India Limited (AgIn)

d) Ministry of Agriculture & Farmers Welfare

80. What is the fundamental precursor for a country to adopt technology transfer and commercialization as cited in the literature?

a) Introduction of a technology innovation and promotion policy

b) Setting up of multiple TTOs

c) Partnership with private industries

d) Investment in R&D

81. Which institution is responsible for the horticultural research in Bengaluru?

a) Indian Institute of Agricultural Research

b) Bengaluru Institute of Horticulture

c) Indian Institute of Horticultural Research

d) International Institute of Horticultural Research

82. When was the technology transfer and commercialization office set up at IIHR?

a) 2006 b) 2007

c) 2008-09 d) 2010

83. What is NOT one of the five major theme areas under which IIHR has licensed its technologies?

a) Seed and Planting material

b) Biotechnological products

c) Engineering tools and machinery designs

d) Weather prediction tools

84. What is the range of the "royalty component" that licensees are required to pay based on the type of technologies?

a) 1-3% **b) 2-5%**

c) 3-6% d) 5-7%

85. Over the past seven years, approximately how much income has IIHR generated from its IP assets?

a) 5.50 crores **b) 6.22 crores**

c) 7.35 crores d) 8.00 crores

86. Which among the following is NOT a lesson learned or limitation experienced by IIHR?

a) An increasing trend of secrecy among scientists

b) Shift towards distinct trait specificity in research

c) Every licensed technology being a huge success

d) A drive towards technology generation and commercialization

87. What is the primary goal of ICAR as mentioned in the passage?

a) To increase the revenue from technology transfer

b) To mitigate famines and ensure food security

c) To expand the urban areas and improve infrastructure

d) To establish international collaborations for research

88. Which revolution was NOT mentioned as a contribution of ICAR in the passage?

a) Green revolution b) Pink revolution

c) Diamond revolution d) Golden revolution

89. What will be the future challenge for ICAR and the National Agricultural Research and Education System, as per the passage?

a) To ensure adequate food supply

b) To provide optimal nutrients based on an individual's genetic profile

c) To combat climate change

d) To collaborate with international research institutions

90. Who are the primary beneficiaries of ICAR's research results as mentioned in the passage?

a) Large corporations

b) Foreign countries

c) Farmers and common people of India

d) Wealthy individuals